AF477324

MEYER
SCHAPIRO
ABROAD

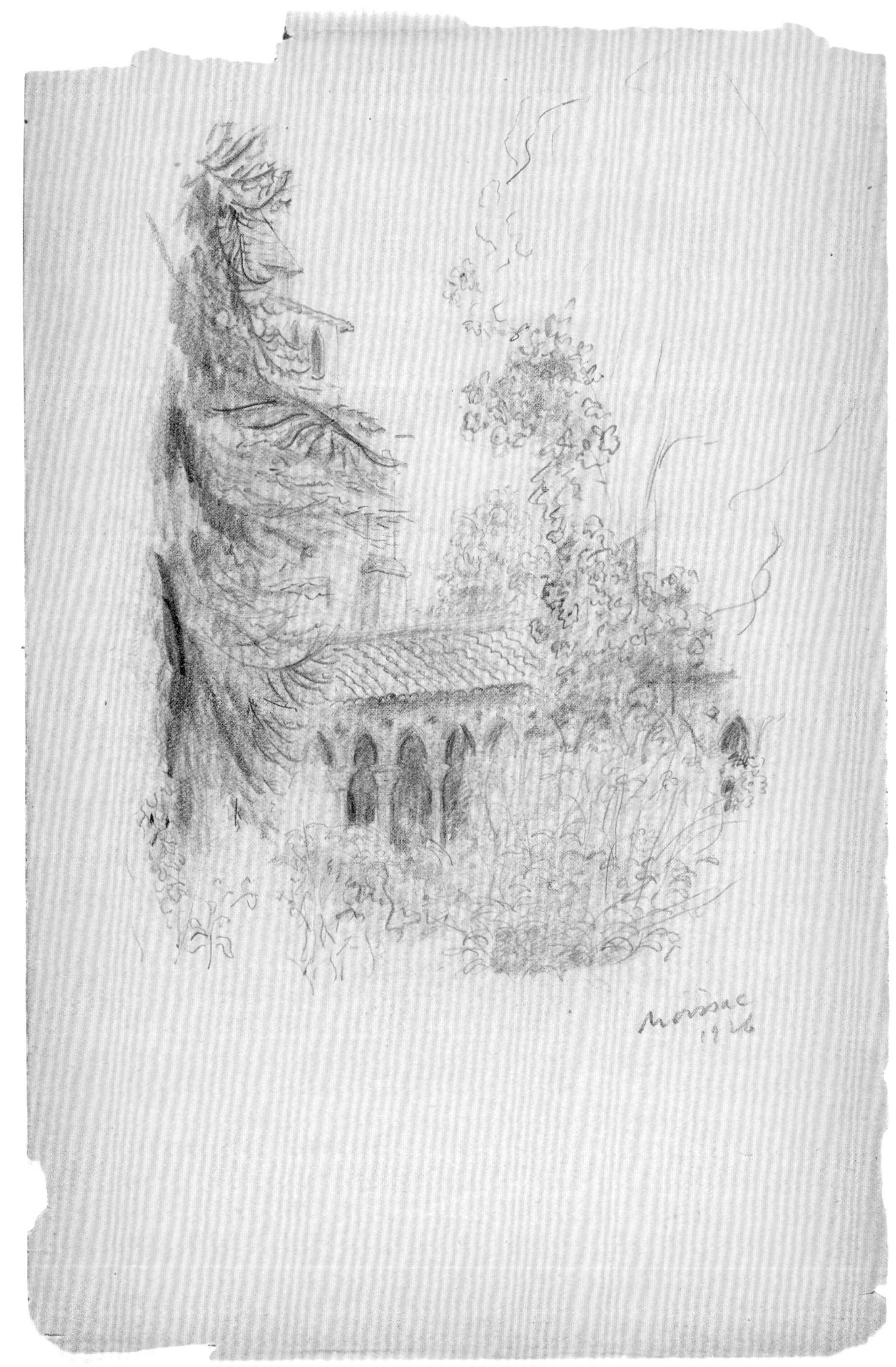

MEYER SCHAPIRO ABROAD

Letters to Lillian and Travel Notebooks

Edited by Daniel Esterman

PUBLISHED BY THE GETTY RESEARCH INSTITUTE

Meyer Schapiro Abroad: Letters to Lillian and Travel Notebooks
David Rosand, *Editorial Consultant*
Michele Ciaccio and Lauren Edson, *Manuscript Editors*

Hubert Damisch's essay "These Are All about Me" was translated by John Goodman

Published by the Getty Research Institute, Los Angeles
Getty Publications
Gregory M. Britton, *Publisher*
1200 Getty Center Drive, Suite 500
Los Angeles, California 90049-1682
www.getty.edu

13 12 11 10 09 5 4 3 2 1

Front cover: Passport of Meyer Schapiro (detail), 1926. Courtesy Miriam Schapiro Grosof
Frontispiece: Meyer Schapiro, Sketch of Abbaye de Saint-Pierre, Moissac, 1926
Back cover: Meyer Schapiro, Sketch of Cathédrale de Notre-Dame, Moulins, 1926

Library of Congress Cataloging-in-Publication Data
Schapiro, Meyer, 1904-1996.
Meyer Schapiro abroad : letters to Lillian and travel notebooks / edited by Daniel Esterman.
p. cm.
Includes bibliographical references and index.
ISBN 978-0-89236-893-8 (hardcover)
1. Schapiro, Meyer, 1904-1996—Correspondence. 2. Schapiro, Lillian Milgram—Correspondence. 3. Art historians—United States—Correspondence. 4. Schapiro, Meyer, 1904-1996—Notebooks, sketchbooks, etc. 5. Schapiro, Meyer, 1904-1996—Travel. I. Esterman, Daniel. II. Title.
N7483.S292A4 2009
709.2—dc22
[B]

2008012832

CONTENTS

FOREWORD

The published writings of Meyer Schapiro, as a contribution to the history of art and of human cultural endeavor, would suffice for far more than one distinguished career. But those readers who have found profound inspiration in his texts have invariably been left wishing that he had written at even greater length. For all the precision and resonance of his prose, he seems, as his own career progressed, to have despaired of his written words' ability to carry beyond a relatively indifferent coterie of fellow scholars: increasingly, he sought to convey the intelligence of visual form to audiences for whom art had been largely a matter of casual delectation or illustration to history. To initiate such a public required the skills of performance, of verbal persuasion and exciting improvisation, which he possessed in abundance. Though his steady output of exacting scholarly articles and notes continued, he thus came to divert a large portion of his intellect and intensity into the spoken word.

A seeming army of New Yorkers witnessed Schapiro's public lectures and the classes he taught at Columbia University, speaking in unison of their mesmerizing quality, of his ability to perform before their eyes the process of visual discovery and recognition of meaning in even the most abstract or marginal form. But such influence within a local sphere (however grand that locality might have been) could come only at the expense of his insights and ideas being disseminated through the channels of publication—though any such shortcoming is surely as much that of the art history profession, which largely failed to act on the challenge laid down in his early work and thereby hid its importance from the wider world of humanistic learning. As a result, we are left with a longing (no weaker word will do) for a larger lasting record of that mind at work.

These letters to his future wife, the late Dr. Lillian Milgram, arrive to fill that desire in the most fresh and unexpected way. In place of the consummate public performer, we find in these remarkable small essays that same mind in the process of discovering its vocation in an intimate exchange. Certain passages speak for the whole with an eloquence difficult to imagine in a young man writing late into the evenings after exhausting days of research. He reflects at more than one point on the painstaking attention to detail—poring over intricate manuscript illuminations and peering upward at obscured architectural ornament—that seemed to indenture his consciousness to the most grotesque pedantry, as in this passage from 21 July 1927:

> I detect a peculiar length of the ears in one figure, a deformed uncial M (ɱ) in a border inscription, & relate A to B to C to D. & do not regard the works in themselves—as art until the bell rings & I am about to leave. I am professionalized, dear, sweet Lillian: I am a monster of measurements, plans, transverse sections, squinches, arabesques & orthostatic courses.

While the persistence of such monsters of the scholarly profession has bedeviled the discipline and, for many years, obscured Schapiro's innovations, he in no way exempts himself from the same impulses. Yet the difference between his own vision and the blinkered outlook of the mainstream emerges as he rehearses, in this same letter, the objections to his labors on the part of his idealistic political peers: "what is the value of such a point?" he hears them saying, "what light does it shed on our future? what new happiness does it bring to the great mass of suffering mankind?" He imagines himself replying:

> you stand too close to the truth to see the whole of it: & the little you can see from your place[] is so tiny, so insignificant that you must question its value & the labor devoted to its discovery. But at a distance of 1 kilometre (the scientific distance) or better 2, or 3 kilometres—you will see 1000 details form a perfect pattern in which will rejoice your eyes—& which will lift man from a brutish ignorance to a sublime mastery of his own life—((& of nature)—no distinction)[.] It is only from the complete probity of such details that the whole derives its force.

Schapiro was to make good many times over on that high-flown youthful ambition, and it drove him over the extraordinary year documented in these letters to register, record, and assimilate every scrap of primary information that came his way. The rich record of his drawings, sampled in the present volume, does more than attest to a time when photography was unwieldy and unreliable; few scholars have left behind any comparable body of work. The rare talent and energy he invested in his graphic notations manifest his totalizing absorption of everything he observed, touched, and measured.

From France to Spain, Italy, and Greece, with a leap to Egypt, Palestine, Transjordan, Syria, Lebanon, and Turkey, he refused to rely on received knowledge for any detail of his research. Facile theories of cultural diffusion from the Near East would require a journey to see for himself (where relatives were on the ground to help). But the remarkable outcome of this adventure was less a fascination with the exotic than it was a recognition of the strange and elusive character of the cultural record back where he began his inquiry—an insight that mitigates the suggestion of hubris in the quotation above. On his return in August 1927 to Toulouse in southwest France, the regional focus of his research, he acknowledges deep disappointment with his initial, optimistic efforts: "To-day I re-examined St. Sernin, my old notes in hand. They are very primitive & insufficient... I swim only in the darkness: & mistake flashes for fixed stars. I often disturb the water with my flapping. When I dive there is a great splashing, which subsides quickly; my mouth is always full of water—"

His feeling of drowning in a flood of information arises, however, out of an ultimate conception of culture as a complex distributed intelligence beyond the reach of individual introspective consciousness, including his own. And his thinking anticipates the outlook of advanced information science in our own day. "[W]e may abstract," he reflects to Lillian on 14 August 1927, "from all the works—qualities, habits of mind & hand, ideas & call them, the mind of the culture—give it thought processes, feelings, animate it completely on the pattern of a single man: remembering always that this huge mind which contains & does all things, is not the model of the little ones & may be strange to most of them."

— THOMAS CROW

ACKNOWLEDGMENTS

Lillian Milgram Schapiro lived a long time, from 1902 to 2006, but regrettably not long enough to see the publication of this book. Without her it would never have been published.

This project was encouraged by colleagues and friends of the Schapiros, especially David Rosand, Thomas Crow, and Hubert and Teri Damisch. I thank Miriam Schapiro Grosof and the Rare Book and Manuscript Library of Columbia University for allowing me unfettered access to the letters and travel notebooks. Because I value his judgment, I am grateful to R. O. Blechman. His admiration of the notebook drawings many years ago gave me further confidence to bring them to the light of day. It is difficult to imagine completing this book without the constant support of Linda Seidel. She has listened to my ideas, discussed them with me, and inspired me for decades.

At the Getty Research Institute, Gail Feigenbaum was a strong advocate for the project, while Julia Bloomfield's determination and understanding gave stability to a long and shifting process. The photography of the notebook pages and letters was superbly executed by John Kiffe of Visual Media Services. The manuscript has benefited from the meticulous attention of Michele Ciaccio, Lauren Edson, and Jonlin Wung. My thanks also go to Amita Molloy for her high standards of press production and Jim Drobka for his thoughtful design.

Finally, I am indebted to my wife Vicki Rosenwald, who brought clarity to my writing. Everyone who worked on this project honors Lillian and Meyer Schapiro. I hope that we continue to be inspired by and learn from them.

— DANIEL ESTERMAN

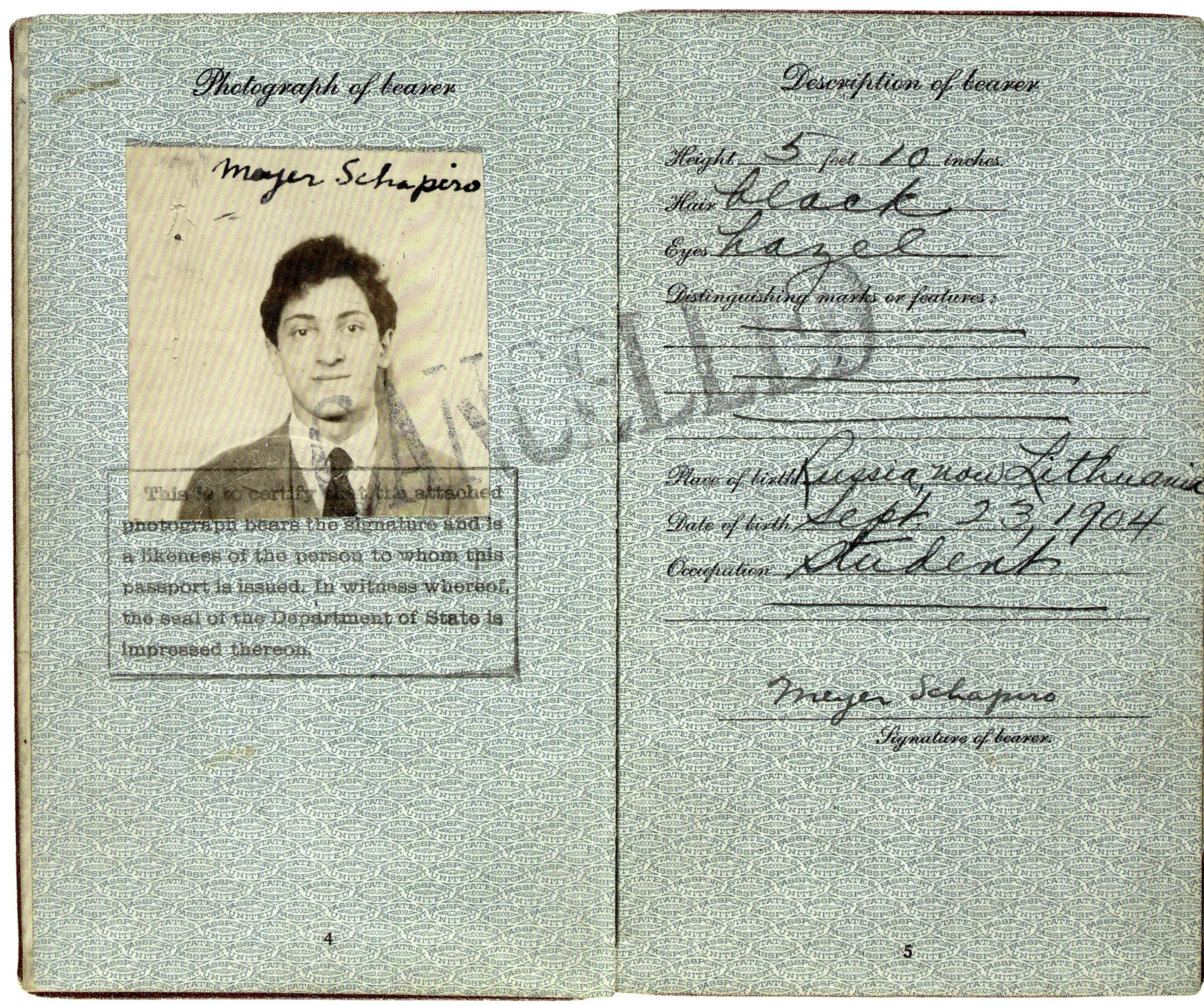
Photograph of bearer

Meyer Schapiro

This is to certify that the attached photograph bears the signature and is a likeness of the person to whom this passport is issued. In witness whereof, the seal of the Department of State is impressed thereon.

CANCELLED

4

Description of bearer

Height 5 feet 10 inches

Hair black

Eyes hazel

Distinguishing marks or features:

Place of birth Russia now Lithuania

Date of birth Sept 23 1904

Occupation Student

Meyer Schapiro

Signature of bearer.

5

Passport of Meyer Schapiro, 1926

Introduction

Daniel Esterman

In July 1926, Meyer Schapiro began a fifteen-month journey, funded by a grant from the Carnegie Corporation, to Europe and the Near East to research his doctoral thesis on the Romanesque sculpture of the abbey of Moissac in southwest France. He was not yet twenty-two. Lillian Milgram, whom he would marry in June 1928 after his return from Europe the previous October, was in her last year at New York University's medical school. The most complete records of this formative journey are the letters Schapiro wrote to her and the travel notebooks he filled with drawings of the buildings and the objects he studied.[1]

Schapiro carried on a continuous conversation with Lillian in his mind: "all thru the day I stop to talk to you."[2] He put those thoughts on paper in love letters, written mostly late at night. They are full of humor and joy, of discovery and commitment, and also of difficulties and doubts. Many deal with both general and specific problems that would occupy Schapiro for the rest of his life. They illuminate his confrontation with a particular moment in history and his first real encounter with ancient art and architecture in their original settings. This encounter and the feelings it engendered are summarized in his first note from France:

> The 3 days seem enormous.... I foresaw nothing of these days. Even the architecture is new, beside the few bare details we had learned at school. To walk in and out of a cathedral, to follow the vaulting from below & to trace its ribs, supports, & buttressing from all sides, to climb the towers & pass thru the triforium openings & galleries & to discover the adjustment of parts everywhere, and the variation from bay to bay, & column to column, & to see the whole in space with such liberty of movement that I seem to learn at each step,—is an awful sentence to finish, dear—but these things quite fill me & I easily lose myself in amazement & then fall into reverie which descends to melancholy historical retrospection & I awaken to a beautiful tolling in the lantern which tells me to draw & take notes & give up dreaming.[3]

Upon returning to Paris after a tour of the provinces, he writes:

> I have concluded a happy voyage in which I have seen wonders, and learned gaily & with passion. My mind feels differently & thinks in other ways about matters that had occupied me long before; but it has happened unconsciously, as if I have acquired a new craft—And it is a craft—for the greater part of the journey's experience was in learning by touching, seeing & moving about objects—school now seems strangely passive or another habit with other ends.[4]

Reactions like these permeate the letters and culminate in his first view of Moissac: "The portal & cloister of Moissac are better than what can be said of

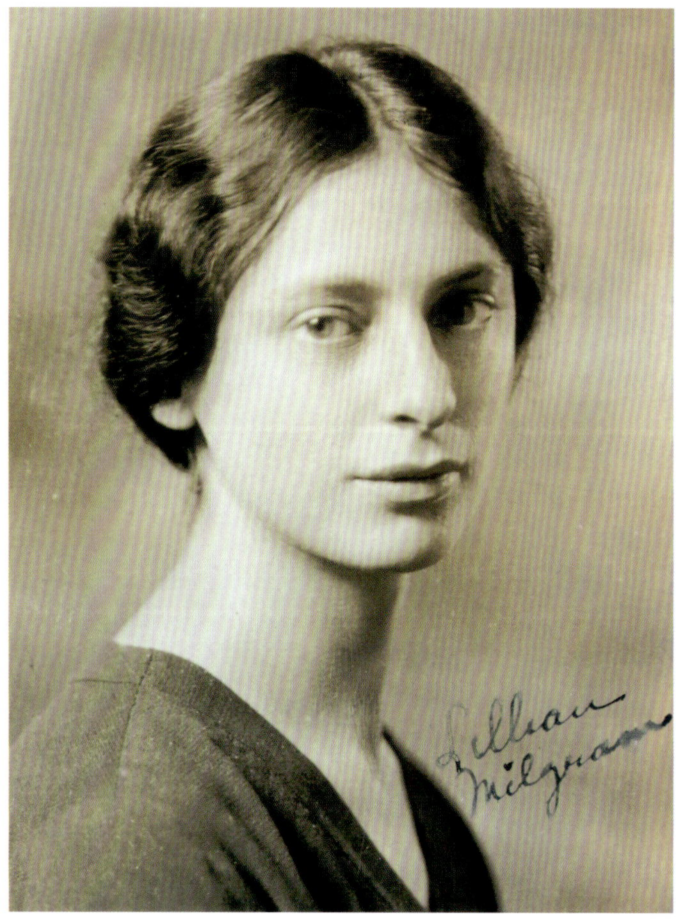

Lillian Milgram, 1928

them. . . . To be with them is to be happy indeed. And to study their details is to live in perpetual discovery and pride."[5] Almost eighty years after the arrival of this letter, Lillian said upon hearing the passage read aloud, "You'd think that an art student was the luckiest man in the world." She consented to have Schapiro's letters to her published because she "felt that the letters could somehow turn a young student to delight in beauty."

Some letters, such as those from Luxor, Tel Aviv, Barcelona, and León, are complete, constructed compositions. The same is true of many of the notebook pages in which Schapiro's delight and passion are reflected in quick and skillful drawings set in well-composed pages. (This ability to extemporaneously create art appears later in his wonderful lectures, seemingly delivered from a few notes.) The eighty drawings in this book are a selection from the many hundreds of pages of drawings Schapiro made during his travels. Almost all are devoted to his studies, with only an occasional tourist view or hint of sentiment.[6]

Made while he was seated and working on a flat, stable surface, Schapiro's meticulous sketches from the Bibliothèque nationale are approximately the same scale and medium as the illuminated manuscripts he was studying. The fine quality and detail of his drawings reflect those conditions. However, while examining sculpture and architecture in situ, Schapiro drew standing up, hunched over his notebook. His skill improved rapidly as he drew every day. In fact, Schapiro drew more during this trip than he ever would again, and many of these drawings are among his best. At the earliest stage of his career, the artist, the writer, and the scholar are merged: "a hand teaching the eye to see."[7]

Schapiro started taking drawing classes around the age of twelve at local art schools in Brooklyn, New York, and continued into his college years. It is clear from anecdotes and memories collected later by Lillian that he wanted to be an artist until some time in his later college years, when he gave up that path with regret. He considered becoming an architect, and it is evident from many of the sketches collected here that he studied architectural drawing.[8] Asked once why he had become an art historian, he answered, "I knew I could be great at it," implying what he said in a later interview: "I thought it would be wonderful if I could be a real artist, but I didn't have the confidence....I didn't think I could make something so wonderful as the paintings I admired."[9] During his years as an art student, Schapiro had learned to study an object by drawing it, and in his courses he advised everyone, artist or not, to do the same. This technique, illustrated here in his travel notebooks, is fundamental to the way he looked at, understood, and described works of art. As an artist, it led him to search for and to understand the artist's way of working—the foundation of all his writings.

Notes

1. Other accounts include Schapiro's many letters to his younger brother, Jakey, and the photographs referred to in the letters and notebooks. The photographs were meant for study purposes, and the surviving prints are generally of poor quality. As Schapiro notes in his letter of 4 September 1926, it was often quicker for him to draw than to set up his cumbersome camera. The photographs and the notebooks, along with all of Schapiro's scholarly work, are held at the Columbia University Rare Book and Manuscript Library.

2. See the letter dated 18 August 1926 in this volume.

3. See the letter dated 12 July 1926 in this volume.

4. See the letter dated 21 November 1926 in this volume.

5. See the letter dated 4 November 1926 in this volume.

6. But see Linda Seidel, "'Shalom Yehudin!' Meyer Schapiro's Early Years in Art History," *Journal of Medieval and Early Modern Studies* 27 (1997): 559–94; from the one notebook from the Near East available to her, Seidel analyzes the range and complexity of Schapiro's notes. This article also reproduces several drawings from the notebooks. Other drawings from notebooks from 1926, 1927, and 1931 are reproduced in Meyer Schapiro, *Meyer Schapiro: His Painting, Drawing, and Sculpture,* ed. Lillian Milgram Schapiro and Daniel Esterman (New York: H. N. Abrams, 2000), 79–93, 117–22.

7. Seidel, "'Shalom Yehudin!'" (note 6), 566.

8. Schapiro, *Meyer Schapiro* (note 6), 19.

9. Helen Epstein, "A Passion to Know and Make Known," *ARTnews* 82, no. 5 (1983): 71. This interview of Schapiro appeared in two parts; see *ARTnews* 82, no. 5 (1983): 60–85; and *ARTnews* 82, no. 6 (1983): 84–95.

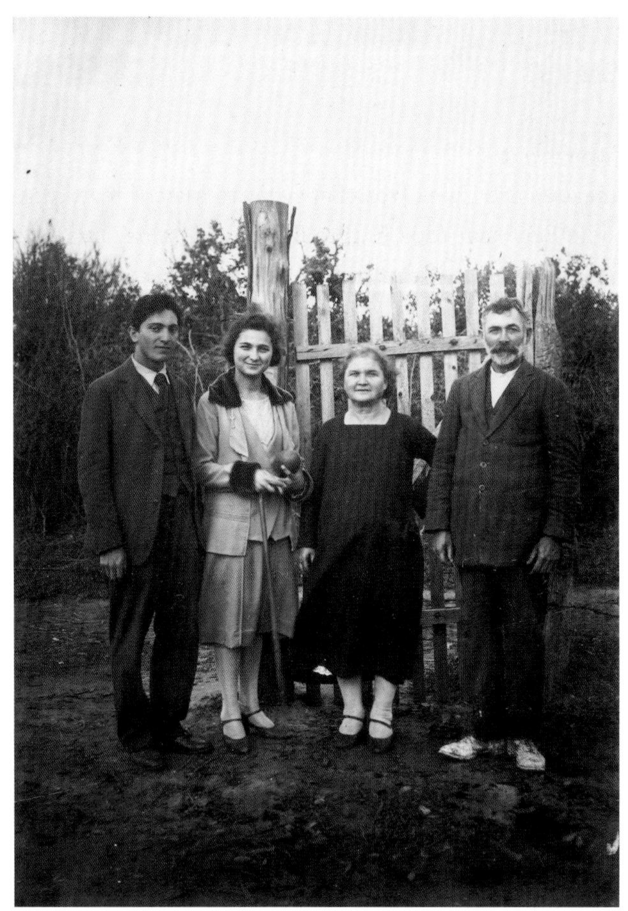

Meyer Schapiro with his relatives, Rachel Lifschitz and Mr. and Mrs. Lifschitz, Petach Tikvah, Palestine, 8–10 March 1927

"These Are All about Me"

Hubert Damisch

Translated by John Goodman

In early July of 1926, a young American student named Meyer Schapiro embarked alone from New York for Europe; he would remain there for more than a year. His first stop was France, where he would spend most of his time, alternating Parisian sojourns with study trips to some of the great religious complexes of Romanesque art. Then, from February to May of 1927, came an extended foray to the Middle East that took him to Egypt, Palestine, and—on the first leg, by way of Italy—as far as Constantinople, as well as, on the return trip, to Greece and back to Italy. The circle was closed in the summer of 1927, after three weeks in Paris, by a trip to Spain and southern France that culminated in a return to Moissac, not far from Toulouse, where the adventure came to an end. Overall, the journey was analogous to the Grand Tours of continental Europe that, from the sixteenth to the nineteenth century, after the ban against travel in Catholic territory was lifted, were an obligatory rite of passage for wealthy young male aristocrats from Britain. But there were significant differences. The author of the letters written during the trip was born in Lithuania, early in the century, into a Jewish family that soon immigrated to the United States. He completed his studies in New York, first in the public school system and then at Columbia University, which would remain his professional home for the whole of his career. His only means of support was a grant from the Carnegie Corporation for the completion of his art-historical education and for travel abroad, enabling him to experience the works he was studying firsthand. In his case, then, the possibility of making such a trip had nothing to do with class-based privileges and protocols but was due solely to his own merits: a point not to be taken for granted in this period, when anti-Semitism, more or less openly avowed, was still pervasive in American higher education.

In fact, after being refused admission to Princeton University—where Ernest DeWald, a specialist in medieval illuminated manuscripts, was on the faculty—Schapiro, a brilliant student, had the good fortune to see DeWald hired by Columbia. In what amounted to another stroke of luck for Schapiro, DeWald had the foresight to suggest that Schapiro write his master's thesis on the sculpture of the portal and cloister of the abbey church at Moissac and, what's more, obtained a prestigious two-year research grant for him that he could use however he liked. Schapiro undertook the project without unduly privileging the relation he had been cultivating, since early youth, with a young medical student some two years his senior named Lillian Milgram. She had almost completed her studies, so a lengthy separation was unavoidable, but she got the better of the deal insofar as the resulting correspondence with Lillian—who was to remain his lifelong companion—occasioned an exercise in writing whose quality and ambition are immediately apparent, and to which the "other" would have been constantly associated in the person of the recipient of these letters, distance playing a determining role. For both parties kept to a decorous tone that, of necessity and by mutual agreement, was integral to the results.

The exercise was less analogous to a chapter from a bildungsroman than to scouting, in something like the cinematographic sense: scouting out locations; scouting out objects—there were many—that called for attention; scouting out people, whether the resulting encounters pertained to the task at hand, were serendipitous, or perhaps reconnected with a far-off familial past, and, one thing leading to another, established points of reference for the individual whose first-person writing here is a kind of self-recognition through his own nascent voice. But young as he was, the author of these letters was not just the apprentice medievalist, who through observation and reading was beginning to demarcate the field within which he intended to maneuver under the more general title "art historian"; he was also a "subject," in the sense Schapiro used the word after having met with the formidable personage and great scholar Salomon Reinach ("Reinach is more officially himself than Enlart;[1] speaks ex-cathedra, with a sense of personal responsibility as if, in him the whole subject spoke"; 28 August 1926). But this subject had none of the pomposity and self-importance often characteristic of such interlocutors. And it is not the least of the attractions of this correspondence—now available to us thanks to the generosity of Lillian Milgram and the affection and diligence of her nephew, Daniel Esterman, who together made this edition possible—that it prompts us to reflect on this point.

For that is indeed the crux of these letters: the becoming of a *subject,* in all senses of the term, and in all the depth of a relationship of love, with all the effects that must have been generated by the couple's separation. At every moment, distance obliged the author of these letters to question what he should reveal of himself, even regarding the choice of sites and monuments that he hoped to see again with the object of his affection beside him. In terms of writing, his task amounted to finding the right speech position. The pole, the fixed point, that Lillian Milgram constituted for Schapiro throughout his life—to the extent that, upon her retirement, she devoted herself completely to the organization of his archives and manuscripts and the publication of many unpublished texts, finally authorizing the edition of these letters shortly before her death in 2006, at the age of 104—provided a safe harbor that can only have been beneficial to him.

If we set aside the migratory adventure that ended with his family's settling in New York in 1906, the young man had crossed the Atlantic for the first time three years earlier—at age nineteen—on a ship bound for Rotterdam and Hamburg on which he had found employment as a dishwasher, a trip augmented by a brief escapade without papers in Berlin. In his first letter to Lillian, he notes a striking difference between this initial voyage, in which he apparently wanted to reconnect (traveling in the opposite direction) with the trial of immigration, and the second crossing, which was altogether more comfortable. The experience, under squalid conditions (he was quartered close to the machine room), of an ocean that seemed monstrous was followed by another, quite delightful and even sublime, that made the sea seem much less vast, if still large enough, absent any fixed reference points, to baffle comprehension. The tone was set from the start with a remark that, as we shall see, is not unrelated to the definition of a field, in the epistemological sense of the term, even as there began, with this crossing, "a regular pattern of observation, of interest, of objects, of reading, eating & sleeping" (12 July 1926): a list to which we should add the drawings that filled notebook after notebook. But this pattern changed when, after a two-week detour through Nantes and a few other places such as Angers and Chartres, he arrived in Paris. For other occupations, encounters, and pleasures awaited him there, beginning with evenings on the boulevards and in the neighboring cafés, with, as an added attraction, an apprenticeship in the *flânerie* that would soon receive its Baudelairean letters of nobility from Walter Benjamin; and, by way of intermission, the first train trips, which provided this man, who never traveled without a book in hand or pocket, with a long-standing metaphor of Western culture: that of the "window" through which something in the world offers itself to view or to be read ("There is little to read from the window after the first few minutes.... So I read from a book"; to which, after the signature, he added this postscript: "What a great part of my life is summed up and rationalized in these last two sentences"; 27 July 1926). As might be expected, the image proved trickier than it seemed. Finding himself at the end of the trip, between Madrid and Segovia, in a seat with views of both sides of the tracks, Schapiro despaired at having to turn from one to the other, a unified prospect being impossible ("the angle is unpleasant, & the full extent of the desired object is not seen"; 4 August 1927).

The letters written to Lillian during these first trips and the more far-ranging expeditions to follow, as well as during the more or less extended sojourns in Paris (largely devoted to preparing for the trips and drawing conclusions from them), are extremely various. If they take on the appearance of a travel diary, they do so in a discontinuous way and at the cost of lacunae that correspond, as is usual in such cases, to moments of particular intensity that vary widely in tone, from quite lively to extremely reflective: descriptions, stories of encounters, etc., the correspondent scarcely having had the time to write them up. There's a bit of everything here, but especially anecdotes: portraits quickly but crisply sketched, such as that of Salomon Reinach or, on a completely different register but just as passionately drawn, that of Pierre-Jules Momméja, the old local scholar who agreed to share his knowledge about Moissac;[2] accounts of visits and conversations both erudite and worldly; and, of course, many observations and insights about medieval art and the different ways of dealing with it, and about specific monuments (his thoughts about Conques, spread over seven postcards, marking in this regard a decisive moment). Not to mention the more intimate pages, which invite the reader to come a bit closer to what, in the end, is the heart of the matter.

The importance of this trip in the formation of the historian of medieval art that Schapiro would become emerges clearly from what Thomas Crow and Michael Camille have had to say about his manner of writing.[3] The Grand Tour analogy would suggest that, in order to reclaim the artistic legacy in question and assure its reproduction, he conform to the prevailing model of a medievalist as someone committed to the preparation of exhaustive inventories of monuments of a given period, region, or school and of repertories of all kinds, publications that offered a rich harvest but that gave short shrift to thinking. Schapiro must have grasped the limitations of such undertakings early on, even when they were as ambitious and brilliantly conceived as Arthur Kingsley Porter's ten-volume survey of sculpture along the pilgrimage roads to Santiago de Compostela, published three years earlier.[4] In this regard, too, the tone is set from the start, or very nearly so. Scarcely having disembarked at Cherbourg—the only major monuments he had yet visited were the cathedral at Coutances and Mont-Saint-Michel—the inexperienced traveler avowed frankly that, to his astonishment, everything seemed new to him, even the architecture, save for some insignificant details absorbed during his graduate studies, to such a point that, while trying to describe an experience for which nothing in his training had prepared him, he got lost in one of those interminable sentences for which, much later, he would take me to task in my own writing:

> To walk in and out of a cathedral, to follow the vaulting from below & to trace its ribs, supports, and buttressing from all sides, to climb the towers & pass thru the triforium openings & galleries & to discover the adjustment of parts everywhere, and the variation from bay to bay, & column to column, & to see the whole in space with such liberty of movement that I seem to learn at each step,—is an awful sentence to finish, dear—but these things quite fill me & I easily lose myself in amazement & then fall into reverie which descends to melancholy historical retrospection & I awaken to a beautiful tolling in the lantern which tells me to draw & take notes & give up dreaming.

And with no more ado, the young visitor concludes in the most abrupt way: "I observe most efficiently & with least distraction in the ugliest buildings" (12 July 1926).

"An awful sentence," but one that says a great deal about something best described not as Schapiro's method but as his approach: his way of clearing a path through works of art and of breaking down their specific economies insofar as these could be translated into the terms of their construction, of the ordering of their parts, and of variations, even transformations, that seem to call for structural analysis, unless the emphasis placed on the dynamic, even motivating, double aspect of the observation—both ambulatory and graphic, the movement of the drawing hand being substituted for the ambulation of the body—was not meant precisely to reveal the full indebtedness of the object when grasped as a totality, in its spatial disposition ("to see the whole in space"), to a generative approach more than to a structural one. (Another "awful sentence," one that I fear the translator might feel obliged to break up, as is the tendency in American publishing, at the risk of shortchanging some of the thinking at work in it, and even the very thing that the writing means to grasp. I like it that Schapiro himself had such an experience at the start of his project, even if he later kept to a kind of writing better suited to his own thinking.)

The same fault, the same difficulty holding to concise formulations, recurs at the end of the trip, when, spurred by his discovery of Spain, and of how different its art could be ("here the remains are richer, more imposing—almost stuffily furnished with imagination"; 20 July 1927), he became gripped by doubt. A long and remarkable letter in dialogue form, written in Barcelona on 21 July 1927, served as a pretext for him to ask whether minutely detailed readings of medieval manuscripts make any sense, given that such readings interest only the specialists who earn their living from them: "I am professionalized, dear, sweet Lillian: I am a monster of measurements, plans, transverse sections, squinches, arabesques & orthostatic courses—What will I say to you when I return?" And he goes on to wonder whether his wearing himself out by splitting hairs in this way doesn't mean that he's lost all sense of proportion, all sense of his "noble Jewish tradition": "what light does it shed on our future? what new happiness does it bring to the great mass of suffering mankind?" Early the next morning, he had found the answer to his question, which he had been turning over in his mind: "why do we despise 'hair-splitting[']? The word itself should inspire us—as the very summit of dexterity & detachment. What can one do with a split hair? what future life is there in it? But the process of its 'becoming' is wonderful—a spectacle, only the elect can assist at, & a feat that demands the subtlety of every touch & the most ingenious attentiveness to immeasurable parts." The Talmudic humor of this answer is consistent with the evocation of his "noble Jewish tradition," while the emphasis on "the process of its 'becoming,'" in addition to echoing what was said above about the becoming of the subject named Meyer Schapiro, corresponds to one of the most striking of the many qualities that would make Schapiro's analyses of medieval art so remarkable, something that he seems to have intuited from the start: the ability, when assessing Romanesque sculpture as well as architecture and illumination, to recognize the most salient formal traits and elements in the becoming of a style, and in the sometimes startlingly abrupt transition from one style to another.

The shift from Romanesque to Gothic in the first half of the twelfth century unfolded with just such abruptness, and not without the object of study having raised the stakes of structural analysis through its very dynamism, when, within a single building, "the actual process of change" was made visible, in the clearest possible way, by changes introduced from one bay to the next. In Le Mans, "the lower nave of the cathedral was of the 11th c[entury], the upper parts and the vaulting of early and middle 12th, the choir of the 13th, and several chapels of the 14th" (27 July 1926).

But in rigorously synchronic terms, nothing would equal the competition between two styles revealed in the admirable study of the sculpture of Santo Domingo de Silos, in which the dialectical exchanges between manuscript illumination, sculpture, and architecture were complicated by an extremely subtle interaction between the Mozarabic and Romanesque styles—to such an extent that Schapiro could begin to form some idea of what, in the previously cited letter of 21 July 1927, he called "the Silos 'situation,'" solely on the basis of having seen some miniatures and the depiction of a relief copied into one of them, before recognizing that *the process of its becoming* was a constitutive dimension of "formal structure" as understood by him in his dissertation on Moissac. As if the very notion of structure could be fully grasped only by becoming alert to the mode of historicity specific to art and its works. To quote Schapiro himself: "Some day the hair-splitters will come into their own. As Mortimer Adler[5] has hoped—when philosophy abandons its moral or dogmatic ends—only dialectic will remain" (22 July 1927).

So much the better for dialectic, especially if it enables an understanding of how the minutest attention to detail should go hand in hand with constant reference to the work as a whole. There could be no finer illustration of this than the way the notes and drawings in the young Schapiro's travel notebooks mutually clarify one another. But there is a necessary caveat, one about which the author pointedly warned his readers through the person of his dulcinea: he understood the significance of these analyses to be a function of their relation to aesthetic experience, narrowly construed. Visiting Auxerre, he found the cathedral so "ravishingly beautiful" that he was spurred to write: "I feel silly to have to talk about it and futile to make drawings. But I do both; my notes & sketches will fill a hundred sides in 2 more days" (4 September 1926).

Certainly, he was more comfortable studying buildings whose ugliness was not conducive to dreaming, in line with what he says at the end of the dreadful sentence discussed above. But he nonetheless thought—and so argued in a controversial article—that the "aesthetic attitude" was extant and active in the Romanesque period, and was even a necessary prerequisite for any approach to artistic production that could come to proper terms with it.[6] That these terms might have a meaning that transcends differences of time and place is nowhere more apparent than in these letters, which still make scant mention of modern art, almost to the point that we must significantly revise our understanding of Schapiro as a modernist unafraid of looking at works of art from the past with the eyes that were his own. If this entailed "anachronism," and it certainly did, it was a function of his eyes having been preeminently drawn to and shaped by works of art from the past that had been made to induce ravishment, if not reverie, and were thereby conducive to what Schapiro characterized as a kind of "historical retrospection" tinged with melancholy. Doubtless the moment would come when dreams gave way to critical description pursued along the paths of writing and drawing. But for him there was no such thing as a worthwhile work of art that failed to instantly impress as precisely what it was, whether the resulting effect seemed to him a bit too peremptory—Michelangelo's fate ("I came to like Michaelangelo"; "I tremble before his work: & I tremble instantly for it imposes itself so quickly"; 23 May 1927)—or just marvelous in its dexterity—Velásquez's case. To say nothing of El Greco, whose work tempted Schapiro to shout for joy in Toledo.

Also in Toledo, Schapiro made a point of visiting the two old synagogues transformed into Christian churches, one of which, El Transito, is famous for its sculpted plaster decoration in Andalusian style, below which, like a frieze, runs a relief inscription in large Hebrew letters. It occasioned the following observation: "What a pride could be *ours*—if we knew these things as our culture & felt within us the continuity not merely of the inscriptions, but of the rich fascinating ornament in which these Hebrew characters are set—But they are Moorish work (rather Persian) & we have not the capacity to recreate them: nor do we possess even a descendant of these forms or their idea" (my emphasis; 4 August 1927).

Although this can be seen as the expression of a sense of belonging to a lost culture, that is not sufficient justification for using Schapiro's earlier allusion to the "noble Jewish tradition" as grounds for aggressively looking for reasons that might have led him, like so many other art historians of Jewish ancestry, to focus on forms of art that are completely alien to the Hebraic tradition, and that often directly violate the prohibition against representation. But it may be precisely their Jewish background that, without its being said, explains the force and penetration of these art historians' analyses. The very possibility makes Schapiro's letters relaying his discovery of the "Jewish question" in Paris, as well as those written in Palestine after a reunion with part of his extended family, seem all the more interesting: some of them (especially the long letter of 28 August 1926) because they give some idea of just how big a gap there could be, in the years following World War I and preceding the rise of Hitler, between two forms of "Jewish consciousness";[7] and others because they testify to the importance of the parental bond as imprinted, even after the diaspora, in the name of the father.

Judging from the account of his visit to Salomon Reinach, a kind of French Aby Warburg, it seems that, during the group interview with the master of the house in which Schapiro took part, Reinach made no allusion whatsoever to Judaism. The archaeologist, whose publications on the history of religions did not escape Freud (who cites them several times in *Totem und Tabu,* 1913), was a master of Hebraic studies; he was also the grand Jewish bourgeois who, with his two brothers, Théodore and Joseph, was among the earliest defenders of Captain Dreyfus. But the vice president of the Alliance Israélite Universelle was preoccupied by something else that day, the interview having taken place just after Reinach had spent two days supervising excavations at Glozel (in the department of Allier, not in northern France, as Schapiro wrote), where a group of artifacts thought to date from the Neolithic era had just been discovered—artifacts that were to become the focus of heated controversy. Among them were a series of small clay tablets covered with inscribed characters that seemed to document the existence of a form of writing close to the Phoenician alphabet, characters that moreover were found close to an incised drawing of a reindeer similar to Paleolithic depictions in caves in Périgord. The discovery would have been momentous if it had undermined the generally accepted view that writing originated in the Middle East, that is, if Reinach's concerns—according to Schapiro, he exclaimed, "If these are genuine, then we are lost"[8]—had not finally proved groundless.

Having gained admittance to the residence and the immense library of this formidable personage, Schapiro met with a group of young German Jews there whom he later came to regard as friends; he was still quite unprepared for some of the things they said: "I was surprised to hear so much discussion of Judaism, especially by these people. It is not really, of religion; or politics, but of race as an introspective revelation, as a spiritual solvent, taken merely as a thought.... these men, to escape association with a detestable culture, from which they have suffered—prefer to be Jews than Germans, and invoke doubtful biological notions to sustain them" (28 August 1926).

Although he had just arrived in Paris, the young American was not fooled by any of this. And he did more than anticipate the thesis later advanced by Hannah Arendt, namely that the so-called Jewish question existed only in the German-speaking portion of central Europe, during a period extending from the birth of Zionism to the rise of Nazism.[9] Schapiro did not neglect to note the unstable mixture of admiration and hatred in his new friends' comments about Germany: "They are very proud of German science & arts, idolize particular Germans & despise the race." But the paradox did not end there: not satisfied with understanding their difference in profoundly biological terms, these angry young people had internalized the loathsome image of the Jew enforced by racist ideology, to the point of preferring assimilation to Zionism in the hope that this would gradually lead to the elimination of traits that the prevailing scientific authorities held to be "Jewish"—some having gone so far as to speed up the process by having their noses altered to attain an acceptable curvature, "the figure 6 nostrility."

The time would come when, to echo Arendt once more, the "Jewish question" would be swept away, so to speak, by the catastrophe that struck the European Jews, and thus forgotten. But at the time of Schapiro's first Grand Tour of Europe, the problem of Jewish identity was formulated very differently in the United States, where the dominant social metaphor was that of a melting pot in which the most diverse ethnic groups supposedly merged. Everything suggests that Schapiro had no strong convictions about the matter. And as for Zionism, although he was sympathetic to the idea, it was not his affair ("I had no objections, but could not resolve sympathy into action"; 18 March 1927). When, due to pressure from the mounting crisis and the rise of Nazism, the time came for him to take a political stance, he would join the ranks of many of his friends, both Jewish and non-Jewish, under the banner of Marxism. This was consistent with the model that would seal the tragic fate of Walter Benjamin: the same Benjamin whom Schapiro would meet in Paris, in 1939, in an attempt to persuade him to seek asylum in the United States,[10] and who constantly alternated between two scenarios, on the one hand brandishing his Marxist convictions to fend off Gershom Scholem's periodic invitations to join the Zionist enterprise in Palestine, and on the other hand arguing his attachment to the Jewish cause to avoid a total commitment to communism as understood by Bertolt Brecht, with whom he had an unshakable friendship.

On the other side of the Atlantic, the debate did not initially take such an extreme form, and there is no foreshadowing of it in the young Schapiro's letters. It is only after the arrival in successive waves of the many intellectuals, writers, and artists in exile who were to revolutionize the New York scene; the exposure of the project to annihilate the Jews of Europe; the creation of the state of Israel; and the first skirmishes of the cold war that we find him caught up again in the contradictions of the time. But from the moment of his first visit to Palestine, Schapiro was aware of the existence of a family tie that, in his view, affected his destiny only insofar as it undercut the notion of there being any contradiction between a successful art-historical career ("I am professionalized, dear, sweet Lillian") and the critical activity, the rigorous thinking that would make him one of the great American intellectuals of the century.

The letter written in Jerusalem on 13 March 1927 after his visit to Petach Tikvah, where some of his relatives were thought to reside, resists summary. But the true meaning of this encounter for all involved is captured by these three lines: "When I announced myself as the son of my father, the cousin of at least one of these ladies, I created only worse confusion, for his name was unknown to them. It seems that it was not Nathan Meiny but Nahum Menahem; I agreed, & it was all love between us." Despite being already deeply committed to the work of thought, the son of immigrants was delighted to learn that a dedication to study and reflection had been a part of his familial heritage, beginning with the maternal grandfather whose name he bore. He was much amused by the ruckus coming from a rabbinical school like the one where his father had spent several years before he began to study European literature and the sciences ("recalling the traditional wisdom, receptivity & erudition of these students, I wondered if perpetual clamor was not as ideal for study as complete silence"). Nonetheless, and despite his inclination to test the boundaries on all sides and in every direction, the field that he was beginning to shape could not help but expand as his studies progressed. In this process, anthropology—as taught at Columbia since 1899 by the great Franz Boas, whose seminars Schapiro had attended with Lillian—doubtless played a more determining role, on the symbolic level, than what he had managed to absorb from his art history professors, to say nothing of the "noble Jewish tradition." When the moment of his success arrived, Schapiro was especially keen on the commission for the article "Style" from Boas's best student, Alfred Kroeber, for a new edition of his anthropology textbook.[11] But the anthropological thematic continued to echo, as is evidenced retrospectively by the appearance in one of the earliest letters to Lillian from France of a motif that would return, years later and on the other side of the Atlantic, in the structuralist saga—fifteen years before the day in 1941 when Claude Lévi-Strauss, in a bookshop on Broadway, came across a complete collection of the *Report of the Bureau of American Indians*.[12] On the third day of his French sojourn, Schapiro discovered, on sale for a few cents in a secondhand bookstore in Nantes, the *Handbook of American Indian Languages* (1911) by Boas, as well as a complete series of the *Bulletin of the Bureau of Ethnology*.

"Everything interests me": in a letter from Milan (6 June 1927), Schapiro reports having overheard this remark (an unwitting quote from Paul Valéry) uttered by a seven-year-old boy, in response to his mother's trying to divert his attention, in a museum, from objects that she judged to be of little interest. But there are different ways of being interested in things, as in people. And as early as January 1927, Schapiro could write from Paris:

> A whole half-year gone! I have hardly moved: but I feel as if space is different & the whole world more accessible. Once distance was so forbidding that I circumscribed my studies to avoid travel—now I touch nothing which does not suggest some trip, & my summers are filled for twenty years—What shall I choose?—No sooner did I read Contenau than I was resolved to study Semitic philology when I returned to NY, but why not Iranian or Chinese—why not more palaeography or prehistories? These are all about me—neighbors whom I salute every day.

"These are all about me": Semitic philology, but also—why not?—Chinese writing, whose survival was perhaps open to question, on the same grounds and for the same reasons as the reviviscence of Hebrew. And since we are dealing with an exchange of letters between two people in love, why not procreation and lubricity, which Schapiro treats humorously—under the guise of the church fathers—in the balance of the same letter? All these things were of concern to him, they were all related to him, they all might have something to teach him, they were all points of reference that, at least potentially, might help him to situate himself in the field that was opening before him. From the crossing of an immeasurably expansive sea with which it begins to the vision with which it ends, this set of letters, once read in full, has all the attractions of an artfully paced and composed narrative: the story of a quest that draws to a close and comes to an end, during the return to Moissac, with a kind of epiphany, one centered on the monument that was his authorized object of research and of which Schapiro now says he saw nothing during his first visit to the place, the church having been obscured by rain:

> Last night, I saw the abbey church for the first time by starlight & the few street illuminations—There was such richness of sky, the piled forms of the tower & porch & buttresses, in a most powerful impressive light & dark seemed the great heavens, & the numerous stars, the world that depended on them. I saw the portal for the very first time, I thought—since I recognized no figures or sacred imagery—but only the finely serried lines & masses—another architecture. Last night was the building's true destiny: & all the days I have beheld it, & worried in it, imperfect accidents of a strange world—How could I leave it? I could not turn back to see it a last time—The train was a half hour late; there were almost no regrets—I wished I could stay another day, & not night: to check up a few details & renew controversies—(22 September 1927)

Here the quest draws to a close. But not without, in the best Talmudic tradition, a taste for controversy and hairsplitting having contended with the lyricism of a cosmic abstraction, until that moment in the (re)search when, finally, the subject becomes fully integrated.

—LE SKEUL, BELLE-ÎLE-EN-MER, JULY 2007

Notes

1. Salomon Reinach (1858–1932) was an archaeologist and historian of religions. Born into a family of German Jewish bankers, he directed the Musée des antiquités nationales at Saint-Germain-en-Laye and founded the art history program at the École du Louvre. The author of a substantial body of work, he also served as vice president of the Alliance Israélite Universelle.

Camille Enlart (1861–1927) was a curator at the Musée de sculpture comparée au Trocadéro and author of a large *Manuel d'archéologie française depuis les temps mérovingiens jusqu'à la Renaissance,* 3 vols. (Paris: A. Picard, 1902–16). He extended an especially cordial welcome to the young Schapiro, who then used his name as an "open sesame" during his trip, before learning of his death when he returned from the Middle East (see letter dated 13 June 1927).

2. Schapiro, however, did not include a portrait of the art historian and collector Bernard Berenson—whom he met in May 1927 during a visit to Florence—in a letter to Lillian. Instead, this encounter is described by Schapiro in a letter to his younger brother, Jakey (21 May 1927):

> At 4 I visited Berenson, an historian of art—born in Vilna, & brought up in Boston—Harvard, etc. He has become very rich—by dealing in art objects—has written many fine books—& made a truly beautiful collection of his own—of exquisite taste—of all arts—Chinese, Greek, Italian, Indian, Romanesque, etc—The villa is grandly located and is itself, splendidly furnished. His library is the finest I have seen. When he learned that I was a student of Prof. Dewald he became furious & spent a whole hour denouncing Dewald for some dishonesty: Dewald had rehashed an article of Berenson's, added a detail: & called it his own—but he quieted down—& led me thru his place, & talked with me for several hours—Flies annoyed him very much—he killed all he saw & begged me to help him—Then I returned from Settignano to Florence at sun-down to write this letter (& eat this bad meal—which is nothing)—Affectionately, Meyer.

The next day Berenson wrote to Arthur Kingsley Porter of these events. Berenson's letters to Porter, including the one reproduced below, are stored among the Arthur Kingsley Porter Papers in the Harvard University Archives (HUG 1706.185). Schapiro's correspondence with Porter is stored in the Porter papers (HUG 1706.102) as well. For some discussion of this letter, see also Linda Seidel in *Schapiro, Romanesque Architectural Sculpture: The Charles Eliot Norton Lectures* (Chicago: Univ. of Chicago Press, 2006), xli n. 1. Berenson's letter has been reproduced here without correction.

> Dearest Kingsley,
> Yesterday a very handsome youth named M Shapiro sent up his card on which was written Columbia Univ. Mary went down to inspect him and after quite a while brought him up. I asked him at once under whom he had learned and when he answered "de Wald" I had a horrid outburst whereof I am thoroughly ashamed. However when I recovered and inquired further it turned out that he had been sent by Creswell whom he had seen at Cairo and R [*Rudolf Riefstahl*] that whom he had seen at Constanople. R by the way is settling down in that capital to start a school for Oriental studies.
>
> As for the youth, he is the recipient of a Carnegie scholarship. He has it for three years two of which he must spend at Columbia under a Prof. Murray (who is he???) and ONE year all abroad. So this youngster has been dashing through the whole de Wald-Cook-Smith-Morey-Strzygovski universe and has found it good. This Schapiro is 22 yrs old. He has painted sculpted architected. He is acquainted with the entire personnel of the arts and the antiquities. He has devoted years and years to coptic and as many again to the local schools of Ajurbajan. Decades has he spent in Spain and South France and for the remotest corners of Byzantium and Cappadocia art he has explored and delved and assimilated and incorporated.
>
> I put him to task. I showed him my jade libation cup and my little bronze

candlestick and he praised them and interpreted them and discoursed about them as smartly as Solomon did about the hysop that grows in the wall. In the South of France he came across Hamann whom he found passionately photogr St-Gilles in endless details and other monuments. He himself has discovered a cache of illum mss at the B.N. which belonged to Moissac in the 11th and 12th cent but threw no light on the evolution of sculpture in that abbey.

Two days later Schapiro wrote to Lillian (23 May 1927), describing another wonderful day in Florence without mentioning this incident. In 1931, he again visited Berenson at his villa, I Tatti.

3. Thomas Crow, *The Intelligence of Art* (Chapel Hill: Univ. of North Carolina Press, 1999), 6–23; Michael Camille, "'How New York Stole the Idea of Romanesque Art': Medieval, Modern and Postmodern in Meyer Schapiro," *Oxford Art Journal* 17, no. 1 (1994): 65–75.

4. Arthur Kingsley Porter, *Romanesque Sculpture of the Pilgrimage Roads,* 10 vols. (Boston: Marshall Jones, 1923).

5. Mortimer Adler (1902–2001), an American philosopher whom Schapiro must have met during their contemporaneous student years at Columbia University, where this adept of Aristotle and John Stuart Mill took part in the famous Honors program (forerunner of the present Core Curriculum), after which he went on to establish the Great Books Foundation in Chicago with Robert Hutchins.

6. Meyer Schapiro, "On the Aesthetic Attitude in Romanesque Art" (1947), reprinted in Meyer Schapiro, *Romanesque Art* (New York: George Braziller, 1977), 1–27.

7. Apart from discussions of Germanophobic comments heard in Paris, and of the threat that Germany represented in the eyes of his German Jewish interlocutors, the letters to Lillian avoid political questions. Although Schapiro mentions Mussolini in his letters from Italy, he limits himself to objective comments about public works and other projects that might have some bearing on his own activity.

8. Reinach himself, after an initial moment of doubt, took an active role in the controversy, denouncing what he called the "oriental mirage" and bringing up again, as he did in Schapiro's presence, the question of *fakery:* a possibility all too familiar to him, seeing as in 1896 he had advised the Louvre to acquire the tiara of Saitapherne, later revealed to be a fake. See Salomon Reinach, *Éphémérides de Glozel,* 2 vols. (Paris: Kra, 1928–30), which includes an appendix on the history of the tiara.

9. See Hannah Arendt, *Men in Dark Times* (New York: Harcourt, Brace, 1968), 207–49.

10. For an account of this meeting, see the interview of Schapiro conducted by James Thompson and Susan Raines, "A Vermont Visit with Meyer Schapiro (August 1991)," *Oxford Art Journal* 17, no. 1 (1994): 7–8.

11. Meyer Schapiro, "Style," in Alfred L. Kroeber, ed., *Anthropology Today: An Encyclopedic Inventory* (Chicago: Univ. of Chicago Press, 1953), 287–312; reprinted (with revisions) in Meyer Schapiro, *Theory and Philosophy of Art: Style, Artist, and Society* (New York: George Braziller, 1994), 51–102.

12. See Claude Lévi-Strauss, "The Art of the Northwest Coast at the American Museum of Natural History," *Gazette des beaux-arts,* 6th ser., 24 (1943): 175–82.

Letters to Lillian, 1926-1927

Letters to Lillian, 1926-1927

Note on the Letters

Following the publication of *Meyer Schapiro: His Paintings, Drawing, and Sculpture* (2000), Lillian, at the age of ninety-eight and unable to rest if another project concerning Meyer could be under way, asked me what more I would like to do. Intrigued by his travel notebooks, I had already begun researching them with an eye to publishing the drawings of Moissac. However, I was confronted with hundreds of pages of drawings and notes, most out of order and undated. I asked Lillian if other sources existed that might help me date the notebook pages. She said, "You know there are letters from those years in boxes in the closet in Meyer's study." I recognized the boxes, handmade by my grandfather. They were the same ones that my mother and my aunt, Lillian's sisters, kept in their closets.

Inside, tied up with a pink ribbon, were Meyer's letters to Lillian. Her letters to him, saved and carried through all of his travels, were there as well, tied with a string. Lillian's were diffident masterpieces of brevity, written in a careful hand on paper with matching envelopes; Meyer's were written on whatever paper he had at hand.

In the transcriptions of these letters, little attempt has been made to regularize Schapiro's syntax or punctuation. Emendations essential to the reader's understanding have been placed in square brackets, with empty brackets indicating a deletion, usually involving punctuation. Editorial comments appear in italic in square brackets, noting, for example, where drawings appeared in the letters.

The letters are now in the possession of Miriam Schapiro Grosof, the Schapiros' daughter.

Cunard R.M.S. *Andania*, 8 July 1926

Dearest Lillian,

We arrive in Cherbourg to-morrow evening (Friday). The voyage has been so pleasant that no one minds the slowness of the boat. The first 2 days we had warm weather, calm sea, & the most spectacular sunsets lasting for hours—Later the water roughened, but it was never so stormy as to cause sea-sickness—For a few days there was alternate drizzling and sunshine accompanied by strong winds, as three years ago in Rotterdam. This weather was exciting; few of the people stayed indoors: we marched round and round the deck, stood out in the rain, and even swam in the open air pool that had been improvised on deck with canvas sides and rope. Since Tuesday it has been perfect seashore weather—Nothing would be more delightful than to stop the ship, lower the row boats and play about in the water for a few hours before dinner. The illusion would then be almost complete, for the deck is a boardwalk filled with sunburnt men, women and children, dressed for the beach,—leaning on the rails, or drinking, eating, smoking—or playing games at little tables,—and there is the same music we hear at Brighton and Coney Island with an occasional refined intermezzo. And there are many in city dress who look as if they have just come out of the subway, and are unbuttoning their jackets or wiping their brows. The ocean looks much smaller now than 3 years ago—it is more like the water near a bathing resort, a deeper blue, more restless, perhaps—The boat is so safe, so terrain, so completely domesticated and civilized that the ocean, as a threat, dwindles in this fine weather, and becomes a seascape background. The vastness is not observable. Our sense of its space we derive indirectly from its time.—the calendar. The horizon is at most 12 miles away—Every day we pass at least one boat, so we are not utterly alone. There is even a daily paper which prints baseball scores, stock quotations, some politics and a scandal—Three years ago we worked for hours with a sort of mechanical urgency meal after meal, day after day—And when we fell asleep it was near the bottom of the boat in a dark room, where we heard the great engines buzzing and pounding away without end—so that the few hours we could spare on the narrow triangular deck roped off for us on the very bow, were tired ones and very limited, and ended abruptly in renewed labor—We saw the ocean as monstrous and more beautiful engines (which we do not work) beating forever against our ship sides and rolling on and returning,—a more fearful urgency than our own—It was the largest example of our own life on the boat, our only surcease from it, and yet the great obstacle to freedom—As long as we moved thru it, the machinery about us maintained this deafening rhythmical agitation, and we ourselves rushed madly with food and dishes and silver and pails of dirty water. But once passed, the engines stopped, and our own work was over.

"three years ago in Rotterdam." Schapiro went to Europe in summer 1923.

To-day, however, I am more comfortable than I have ever been on land. I have no responsibilities. I am all leisure, all choice. My only compulsion is to appear in time for meals which are much too elaborate—There are people about me who change their clothes three times a day—If I am a student, there is a library with good books, if I am athletic, there is a variety of games and swimming, if I wish to be gay there is dancing, music, masquerades, vaudeville & liquor—And if [I] simply wish to rest, there are luxurious couches within, and clever deck chairs without, which can be transformed into beds, half-beds, chairs with footstools, davenports, rocking-chairs, thrones, swivels, etc. When I reach land, this comfort ends—

Under such conditions, and especially with so favorable weather, we are independent of the ocean, having our own closed universe—When the sun went down last night, it was like a burning penny which lay down on its belly on the water [*in margin:* ?!?!], showed a flickering rim, beneath its vague foreshortened face and disappeared—And just because the sky was all its own, and there were no small houses or roads or hills to serve as unit scale, or give suggestion of unseen space beyond, the sun was curiously near, and unimpressive. We might have stretched a hand over the railing and taken it from the water's surface, for a watch fob. Associated with small pleasures, gayety, and precise comforts, nature about us can hardly be a sublime phenomenon or imaginatively inspiring. But an elderly Catholic Swiss, (whose patron saint is the ulcered paralytic Alfonso Liguori, the father of equiprobabilistic theology,) returning from the Eucharistic Congress, found the ocean, "merveilleux, merveilleux!" It showed the hand of God, he said, and defied ultimate scientific explanation, tho completely rational in structure. It humbled our senses, in that it presented to them, of its thousands of miles, only a short space at a given time. Its abundance of animal life, so different from land forms, attested to the ubiquity of God's creative powers and the unfailing variety of a supreme genius. The contemplation of these works gave him "la douceur interieure," and from that alone he perceived how perfect they were, and how godly.

Saint Alfonso Liguori (1696–1787). Italian noble turned priest and spiritual writer.

He was so sweet and saintly in conversation that almost always I found some way to agree with him. He spoke only French and German, and, with him, my understanding and use of the languages improved rapidly. He told me that he had managed 1, 2, 3, and 4 large insurance companies and finally organized one of his own; that he was self made, self-educated and relied upon experience, rather than books. He had built himself a house upon the highest point in his home town, and there he lived a bachelor, with his old sisters, worshipping "la lumière" which was so uncommon in American buildings. He had a great contempt for women, which he expressed with Jesuitical astuteness by conceding her a higher sensibility and profounder feelings, due to physical inferiority—but reason was man's birthright; yet each has a place, etc—When he lost at chess he became disgusted and said that he had little patience and could not think long but moved from "feeling." He did not approve of my reading a novel, because novels appealed to the sensibility, and were fantastic rather than real. His talk ranged from the most charming, enthusiastic (literally) Catholic platitude to less consecrated stupidities of narrow-minded business people—I gradually tired; I was irritated by his insistence on my age, inexperience and purely academic education, whenever there was a slight disagreement. And today, our theological sessions have become formal "bon jour" and "bon soir"—

I had very good fortune with my sleeping quarters. Of the 4 berths in the cabin only 2 were occupied, and since we were on the upper deck we received air from the portholes, and were not stifled like the poor people below. The other man is a professor in the University of Montana, & head of the economics department. He looks exactly like Bairnsfather's "Ole Bill," whenever I look at him he seems to be on the point of some joke which I never hear. Or he begins to scratch his head. He never shuts drawers, trunks, valises, or doors, that he has opened; but his shirt and trousers are carefully buttoned—There must be about a dozen professors on board, and at least 300 school-teachers in the cabin class alone. The remainder are for the most part students, wealthy wives, husbands, and a rare man traveling alone. I have become acquainted with few of the passengers, beside the people at my table & my room mate and the Swiss. At first I was busy with a Spanish grammar, and then I read a volume of Thomas Mann's *Buddenbrooks,* which is a great novel, and Barrès' *Un homme libre,* and the *Letters* of Ninon de l'Enclos—I wish I had more time to write to you of them, dear; for the one had the greatest dignity and seriousness together with a classical style, and the other was provokingly complicated by ideas, by sincere introspection and current shallowness—and the last was a great surprise, for Ninon appears very brilliant, and in some of the letters, as fine as Fontenelle & Voltaire in ideas and style.

"head of the economics department." J. H. Underwood was chairman of the Economics Department at the University of Montana from 1925 to 1926.

"Ole Bill." Cartoon character of World War I British Tommy created by Bruce Bairnsfather (1887–1959).

Thomas Mann (1875–1955). German novelist and social critic.

Maurice Barrès (1862–1923). French author of *Un homme libre* (1889).

Ninon de l'Enclos (1620–1705). French courtesan and author whose memoirs were published as *Correspondance authentique de Ninon de Lenclos* (Paris: E. Dentu, 1886).

Bernard Le Bovier, sieur de Fontenelle (1657–1757). French writer, a favorite of Schapiro's.

Voltaire (1694–1778). French writer and philosopher.

Joseph Milgram (1900–1989). Lillian's older brother; a doctor and Schapiro's friend from childhood.

Before I forget,—will you tell Joe that both the smallpox & typhoid "took," but neither inconvenienced me. I had an amusing time with the ship's doctor, who prepared me & himself for the injection as if for a major operation and then bent the needle as it entered the muscle, and cursed it for an English needle—and made apologies for British medical schools, as if there were a suspicion of incompetence—and mentioned the names of some of the great doctors his school, "Edinborough/urgh," had produced—and finally he told me that in 48 hours the injection would take effect & that I would pass thru a short period, in which, if I were to be stricken by typhoid, I might possibly die—"the opsonic index, you know"—

At the time you receive this I will be in Paris, where I will stay for a week, & leave for Languedoc by way of Burgundy. I do not know yet what large city will lie on the route, so that until I have found out, I will receive my mail from the American Express Co. in Paris—

Will you give my regards to your mother and the family, dear—and to Natalie, if you see her. She sent me very beautiful flowers—

Natalie Jaros (1902–?). Friend of Meyer and Lillian's from Barnard College.

Meyer.

Northern France, 12 July 1926

Dear Lillian,

I landed at Cherbourg on July 10 at 6 in the morning & since then I have been to Coutances to Mont-St.-Michel, to Dol, Rennes & Redon—The 3 days seem enormous. I have seen so much in this time & have moved so rapidly that even the ocean trip seems far away. What a contrast with the voyage—where all was the same about me for 10 days. But the vacation continues—and amid all the change I already detect a regular pattern of observation, of interest, of objects, of reading, eating & sleeping.

I foresaw nothing of these days. Even the architecture is new, beside the few bare details we had learned at school. To walk in and out of a cathedral, to follow the vaulting from below & to trace its ribs, supports, & buttressing from all sides, to climb the towers & pass thru the triforium openings & galleries & to discover the adjustment of parts everywhere, and the variation from bay to bay, & column to column, & to see the whole in space with such liberty of movement that I seem to learn at each step,—is an awful sentence to finish, dear—but these things quite fill me & I easily lose myself in amazement & then fall into reverie which descends to melancholy historical retrospection & I awaken to a beautiful tolling in the lantern which tells me to draw & take notes & give up dreaming: I observe most efficiently & with least distraction in the ugliest buildings.

Meyer

Nantes, 19 July 1926

Dear Lillian:

The fun continues. I came to Nantes for one day but I have stayed five & will not leave for two more: The city was depressingly shabby and hot when I entered; the train passed for miles along dirty water, with dilapidation on each side: But since then I have seen so many good things and enjoyed such amiable company, and books and buildings that I walk by the same river and find it dull but not horrible. By chance I met the director of the Musée Dobrée, an old abbé, who kept me for hours and showed me everything personally and gave me access after hours and on the five days the museum is closed. When he learned that I was interested in Romanesque sculpture, he took me to an old chateau on the grounds, where were preserved beautiful carvings of the period, fragments from the now destroyed Romanesque cathedral of Nantes, sculptures that have never been published or edited, & which reveal details, monsters and folk motifs from Scandinavian mythology. He went thru early mediaeval manuscripts & illuminations with me page by page—and verified ideas and parallels, carrying me from case to case in the rooms below [*in margin: drawing of one man carrying another man between the cases*], from Romanesque to Merovingian to Gallo-Roman to proto-historic La Tene & Hallstatt. The Dobrée Museum is rich in prehistoric material, remarkably so for a provincial city—Artifacts are arranged in careful typological series—swords, hatchets, celts, and fibulas; & there is a whole room devoted to the comparison of prehistoric forms with modern primitives; & rooms in which are traced evolutions of characteristic stone & metal types in various parts of Europe—The Museum is arranged like a book with the most obvious transitions and is more readable than any manual. After 5 days it is still new to me and I will surely return to it in the late autumn. It is also rich in paintings and mediaeval textiles and metalwork and enamel, and has beautiful incunabula & block books and woodcuts and engravings & early etchings. And it abounds in local material pertaining to Brittany & the Lower Loire country,—furniture, pottery, costumes, and architectural drawings. There are 2 rooms filled with 18th & 19th c. Chinese art in imitation of Western models, and Western Chinoiseries

"an old abbé." Georges Durville (1853–1943).

La Tène. Archaeological site on Lac de Neuchâtel in Switzerland, dated to about 450–150 B.C. **Hallstatt.** Village southeast of Salzburg, dated to about 1200–500 B.C.

copied from the East or originated as Eastern. Do you remember the portrait of the Chinese girl with a very refined face and enormous finger-nails that we saw beside the doorway at Yamanaka's on Fifth Avenue[] (on Monday June 28, about 8.00 PM[])[.] Well its counterpart, perhaps a work by the same man, is here (on Monday July 19, all hours, Rue Jean V)[.] It is the same girl, the same nails & color, the same conception—This is the more sensational aspect of Nantes, dear, or perhaps of New York.

Yamanaka's. Importer of Asian art, opened by Sadohiro Yamanaka (1866–1936) in New York.

Nantes has a fine chateau of the 15th c. that belonged to the Dukes of Brittany, and a cathedral of the same period whose unrestored parts are rapidly crumbling inside & outside. There are many other churches, mainly 19th c. versions of the Gothic after Viollet-le-Duc and two or three 18th c. pseudo-classic monstrosities. The private dwellings are architecturally more interesting; and well preserved for their 200 years. The modern buildings show the common decadence, like the modern industrial arts exhibited at the chateau—These were wretched things, spiritless for all their originality, and quite artless—In one part of the chateau are textiles, clothing, pottery, furniture and decoration by living craftsmen & art shops and in another, similar things fashioned in the neighborhood in the past 250 or 300 years. And how the latter, which have been supposed barren years, produced beautiful things with the most limited means, & how they contrast with the cheap ingenuity of this other exhibit of a modern business—for each article has a card and a statement of copyright & the punishment of all who dare to borrow these terrible designs. In the same buildings is a collection of N. Colin, the inventor of the canned food, (sardines, in fact) pertaining to his industry,—the literature of canning, its first advertisements, engravings of the 1st establishments, their workers, their boats and voyages, specimens of the first cans, derisive cartoons and speculations, crockery, metal work, old prints, and antiquities of Salorges, where Colin first housed his enterprise—Well this museum has high art beside the modern decorative exhibit—It seems that the decline in applied decoration in the great centers, courts and schools has been going on since the High Renaissance period, but that in the provinces good design has flourished almost everywhere until recently, & still exists in places where handicrafts are neither subdivided nor unduly academized, and among individuals who work independently outside any overbearing tradition. The modern exhibit was full of archaistic affectations, especially where figures were employed; & where the motifs were geometrical or foliate, the designer's incapacity was all the more obvious—The children in school produce better decoration but grow up to buy these things. The decay in taste may simply be the limitation of choice & the fixing of such preferences by indispensable familiarity; just as at Mont-St.-Michel, the most wonderful architectural conceptions are surrounded by ugly little shops which sell knickknacks to the tourists who are their only customers.

Eugène Emmanuele Viollet-le-Duc (1814–79). French architect known for restorations of the Cathédrale Notre-Dame de Paris and of Carcassonne.

Joseph Colin. Frenchman who invented canned sardines in 1824.

Dear Sweetheart, Lillian,

Meyer

Angers, 21 July 1926 [postcard]

Angers is less than ½ as large as Nantes, but has even more Romanesque & pre Romanesque architecture & sculpture—Carolingian illuminated Mss—The finest collection of Mediaeval tapestries in France—12th c glass intact—chateaux—great library, beautiful 16th c. houses—early Gothic cathedral—cloisters, Romanesque tower—ptgs, good museum—the Loire river—bookshops, & only 80,000 people—but they cannot repeat—the recent buildings & arts are faint echoes or loud imitations.

Meyer

Paris, 27 July 1926

Dearest Lillian:

From Nantes, I rode to Angers where I spent two very happy days. There was so much to see that I had to limit myself,—with the idea of a future return. I found five Romanesque buildings, and a beautiful Gothic church of the 12th c; and much fine sculpture, weaving and illumination. If I was seven days at Nantes, Angers surely deserved two weeks. And there was the whole countryside about me, dotted with monuments I could not visit. I could easily devote a profitable summer to this small region.

At the library I studied manuscripts of the 9th and 10th c. in which I found the source of the motifs carved upon the later buildings of the town. It was very exciting for me; I had never handled original material in such abundance and with such freedom: At the Morgan Library, the mediaeval books were of scattered groups, & fewer in number; while Miss Greene stood by and turned the pages.

Belle Da Costa Greene (1883–1950). Director of the Pierpont Morgan Library in New York City.

I was amazed to find so many Romanesque remains in a small city and in a Northwestern city, removed from the creative centers. They were all new to me; they showed exceptional forms which our courses at school had passed by, but which were mechanically interesting, important for later development, and in themselves beautiful. The cathedral is an early Gothic structure, with only one aisle and a peculiar domical vaulting in ribbed bays—I was permitted to climb between the vault tops and the roof and examine the masonry—It was a great joy to find in one place a whole series of buildings showing successive changes for 150 years and yet with certain unmodified characters thruout which set them apart and united them as a group.

And in the next city, Le Mans, there were contemporary churches which I had studied at school, but had known in the most general and verbal manner—And there, too, as at Angers, I could see the actual process of change, often within the same building, from bay to bay. The lower nave of the cathedral was of the 11th c, the upper parts and the vaulting of early and middle 12th, the choir of the 13th, and several chapels of the 14th. There was another church with 10th c parts of great magnificence—and still another, whose construction allied it with the earlier portions of the cathedral. At the library I came upon manuscripts of the 9th to 12th c. but fewer than at Angers. The stained glass of the cathedral includes the oldest surviving panels in France; they follow the manuscript illumination style, and are much finer to me than the 13th c glass in the same building. At Chartres, too, I saw 12th and 13th c glass side by side, but in greater, more imposing quantity—

It is hard to pass thru this country & fail to note with what rapidity the Romanesque arts developed, flowered out and produced Gothic. Everywhere the most beautiful monuments abound, and with unmistakable signs of their origin and direction. This rapidly evolving productiveness in all the arts, the great energy of the builders, and the transmission of the newer ideas over large areas from North France to Spain to Italy or even Syria in little time, remind one of the history of the modern sciences. Between 1100 & 1150 there was a great burst of originality and experimentation in architecture and the other arts, which, tho ultimately based on the preceding 400 years, achieved a disproportionate effect and determined the forms for several hundred years to follow. The 12th c. now looms larger than ever, but Porter[,] who has been studying its origins for the past 4 years, recently wrote that it is the 11th which was most productive—

At Chartres I saw Houvet's photographs of the Portail Royal of which I once spoke to you but forgot to show you at Avery. I thought you would like them, and had the bound volume sent to you—together with two transparent prints of a window panel, which reenforce each other's color and begin to approximate the original.

I do not know if you have received 2 other books that I had mailed to you from Nantes—monographs on Maillol and Daumier. At Nantes I found a Bookshop with a remarkable collection on all subjects and I bought over 40 volumes for very little. I am having them bound at Nantes, & sent to me in the winter. I also bought bound books, some of them English and American publications. Imagine, dear, I picked up Boas' *Handbook of American Indian Languages* in Nantes for less than 15 cents! and a whole series of Bulletins of the Bureau of Ethnology. I see a great deal of medical and biological literature, especially on the physics and mechanics of the body, in which the French take great interest; but I do not know if there are any particular works which you would like to read—Tell me of any and I will surely send them. I meet them on every street, and they are practically for nothing. I have read some popular works by living French physiologists & biologists in the Payot series, which is like the Home University Library, but with a wider range & greater detail; and in the Scientific Library edited by Le Bon. Riding in trains has given me more leisure than I had at home. There is little to read from the window after the first few minutes,—the landscape is so uniform, and the trains so swift in passing the exceptional. So I read from a book—

Meyer.

P.S. What a great part of my life is summed up & rationalized in these last two sentences in fresher ink

Arthur Kingsley Porter (1897–1933). Professor at Harvard University whose richly illustrated *Romanesque Sculpture of the Pilgrimage Roads* (1923) was very important for Schapiro. By 1927, Schapiro was corresponding with Porter.
Étienne Houvet (1867?–1949). French historian and photographer.
Portail Royal. West portal of the Cathédrale Notre-Dame de Chartres.
Avery. Avery Architectural and Fine Arts Library, Columbia University.

Franz Boas (1858–1942). German-born pioneer of modern anthropology and professor at Columbia University; Schapiro took introductory anthropology with Boas the fall term of 1921.

Paris, 2 August 1926

Dear Lillian:

I am spending several weeks in Paris; I was told at the Office of the Minister of Public Instruction that it would take at least 15 days before my permit to study & photograph would be ready. This is a lucky delay; there is so much to do here, & I am forced from my pre-arranged plan, because I was forced to give up the first. With so much time I can work more comfortably & vary my studies — I have not yet been to the Louvre or the Luxembourg or seen the interior of Notre Dame: & I have put off visiting the Trocadero & Guimet (Oriental) Museums for a whole week: But there is so much time that I can wait until I have finished at the library & attended to lots of petty business & calls & consuls, before I return to my first plan.

Pelliot introduced me at the Sorbonne Library where I received stack privileges. It is a wonderful collection, much much larger than Avery & the Metropolitan together & very comfortable — But it is open only from 2–6 PM & closed for the summer on July 31. I saw Pelliot's own library of Oriental Languages, Literature, Anthropology, Arts & Sciences which filled 3 large rooms & is so rich & near completeness that he has hardly ever to leave his house except to lecture or conduct excavations.

Now I use the Bibliotheque Nationale. An old Jesuit, Père Munier, whom I met at the Sorbonne Library, sits opposite me & will not let me fill out a slip or do a thing myself; he asks what I wish & gets the books for me, shaking hands with every clerk, attendant & official on the way. This charming old man hates Mâle & Diehl & Strzygowski — & is delighted if one only listens to him. When I showed interest he invited me as his personal guest to an international archaeol. congress to be held at Dijon or Lyon next year & at which he will read a paper —

I have found several old friends in Paris & made some new ones — Kip's brother is here with his wife & baby. I met Ernest Gross with whom I took a small suite of rooms — & a cousin of his — an Austrian doctor studying Roentgenology in Paris — & Kinne, who taught me French, 5 years ago, & several students from Columbia — & a Viennese who had taught in the college in Kovno near where I was born, & who curiously, knew Hammer, one of the graduate students at Columbia; now teaching at Hunter — the man whose shoes, Teddy told us, creaked badly — But such connections are inevitable; even in the North Pole I shall find Eskimos who have met N.Y. anthropologists whose cousins know friends of mine.

Ernest's cousin is very interesting — we go out together at night — he has been here a good while & is acquainted with the city. We speak only German. To-morrow I shall go to the clinic with him. He promises to show me some interesting cases & Roentgen diagnoses — We visited Montmartre & the Paris slums — most wretched hangouts, designed for tourists with second rate entertainment, bad music — over expensive food — & all the obvious depravities crudely displayed — The boulevards are beautiful, much finer than in New York — & the streets are made easier, more inviting for idleness by the open cafés & restaurants — the bookshops, parkways & squares — But what foolishness at the end! I do not know if this is Paris in its cosmopolitan quarter — at least we are told that there are two million foreign-

Paul Pelliot (1878–1945). Prominent French Sinologist and professor of Central Asian archaeology at the Collège de France; Schapiro attended his courses at Columbia University and the Collège de France and received a letter of introduction from him dated 25 July 1926.

"Pelliot introduced me." Schapiro was introduced to André Joubin (1868–?), director of the library, and Paul Léon (1874–1962), head of the Service des monuments historiques.

"Sorbonne Library." Bibliothèque littéraire Jacques Doucet.

Adrien Munier (1869–1928). Jesuit father.

Émile Mâle (1862–1954). French medievalist and historian of Gothic art.

Charles Diehl (1859–1944). French archaeologist and professor of Byzantine history at the Sorbonne.

Josef Strzygowski (1862–1941). Austrian professor of art history at the Universität Wien.

Clifton "Kip" Fadiman (1902–99). Friend from Columbia College; his brother Edwin spent time with Schapiro in Paris.

Ernest Gross. American friend, or perhaps a distant relation.

Willard Austin Kinne (1892–?). Scholar of theater who graduated from Columbia University.

"where I was born." Schapiro was born in Shavli (Šiauliai), Lithuania.

Teddy. Nickname of Katherine Milgram (1908–72), Lillian's youngest sister, who attended Hunter College.

ers in the city & that in the summer good Parisians go to the country—The city is freer than New York in many ways. Every day placards appear denouncing the gov't or particular economic or political groups—in the most violent language—criticism is quite free. The gov't even goes so far as to post public replies begging its critics to relent a while & cooperate in so critical a time—There are fewer crimes reported in the papers than in NY—private morality is hardly a public concern & what would be flagrant indecency at home is normal here—But a good, or bad, part of it is concentrated in the tourist resorts & is more or less a business run by Frenchmen rather than a home industry—The city has adapted itself to the perpetual holiday ground it has become & there are amusements & vices for all nationalities: There is an unbelievable number of diseased people in the streets & public places—mainly where crowds of foreigners are found—There are whole sections of the city that are slices of Coney Island and the foreign parts of New York with the added disgrace of the most unattractive & yet most insistent public prostitution—And nearby are the boulevards & museums & cathedral so that tours of Paris move readily from one to the other—all good sights—

There is no place where one can study as cheaply as in Paris. It costs only 7 dollars a week to live here in comfort, & books & fees are equally inexpensive—And there are so many books, shops, schools, collections, clinics, courses—libraries—one could wish to remain here forever—but for the social distractions & the common contagious idleness—

with love, dear

Meyer.

Paris, 12 August 1926

Dearest Lillian:

You send me the only news I have had from home: Jakey has not written, not even for bolognas, which I would gladly send him. How dear of you to give me three letters in as many days. I feel rich and well connected in a downright smug way—An Australian lady I met in a garden told me that I was soon to hear bad news from home: How did she know? Why, she had studied mathematics and had learned that all things "give off energy," and that some bodies were attuned to receive it. She could tell more by reading my hand but the lines in my face were sufficiently clear. I would pardon her rudeness; she could not help but convey an insight so swiftly attained—and she must presume to say even more: I confessed that I had received word that my father was ill. She smiled modestly and accepted this confirmation with a fine objectivity. I was to suffer a great deal, but thru my own fault; I was unhappily sensitive, referring society, events, people, to my own feelings, and fluctuating with them. Yet this sensitivity was to be my salvation: I would grow by it, learning from suffering. My especial talent was for sculpture which she earnestly recommended I pursue if I had not yet done so. If I was already engaged in the path, let there be no distractions.

Jacob "Jakey" Schapiro (1912–40). Schapiro's younger brother.

Her little boy having heard that I studied about Egypt asked me how dates and priority were determined. He was intrigued by the astronomical method, but

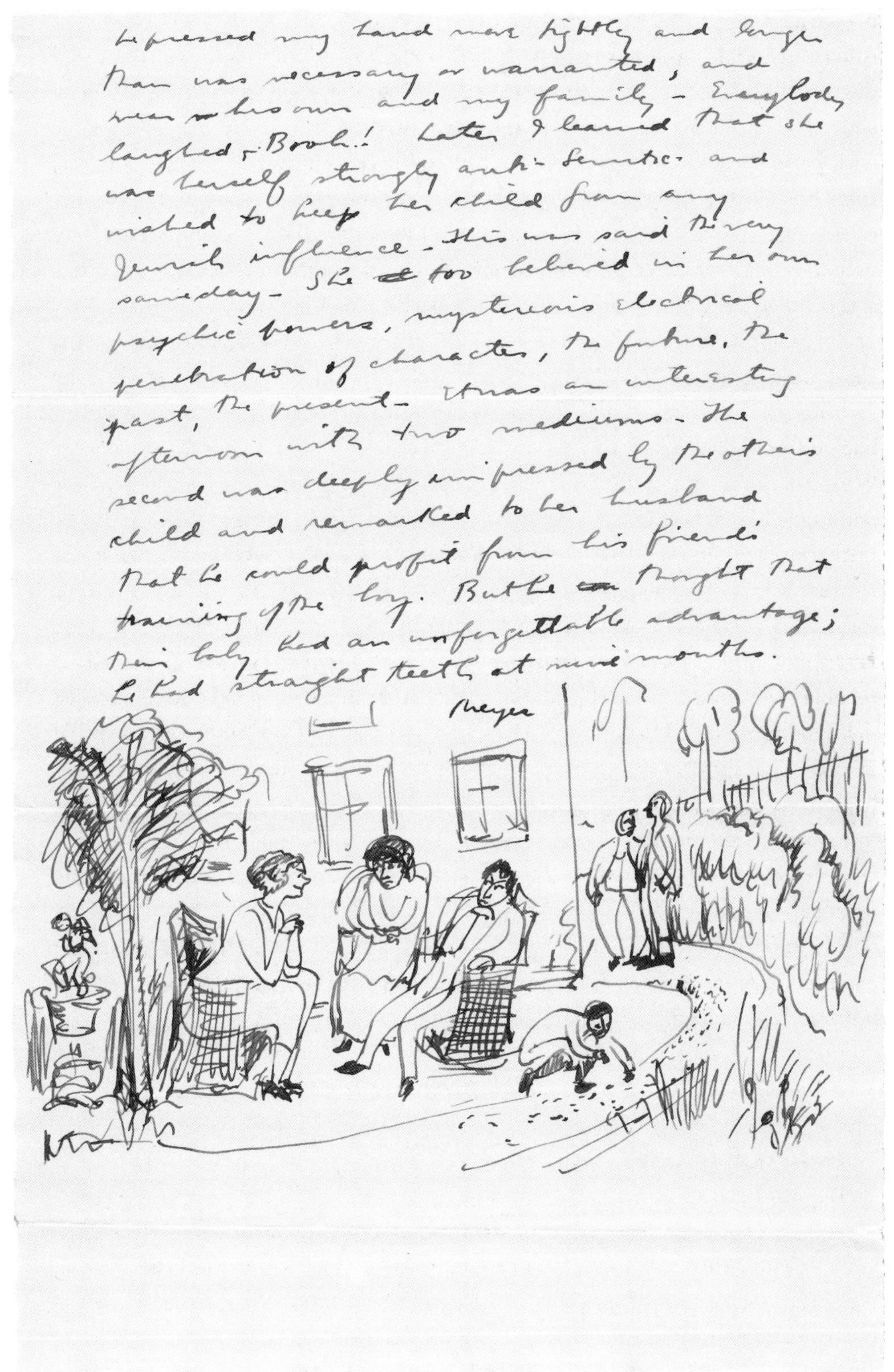

he pressed my hand more tightly and longer
than was necessary or warranted, and
near his own and my family - Everybody
laughed, Booh! Later I learned that she
was herself strongly anti-Semitic and
wished to keep her child from any
Jewish influence - this was said the very
sameday - She too believed in her own
psychic powers, mysterious electrical
penetration of character, the future, the
past, the present - It was an interesting
afternoon with two mediums - The
second was deeply impressed by the other's
child and remarked to her husband
that he could profit from his friend's
training of the boy. But he thought that
their baby had an unforgettable advantage;
he had straight teeth at nine months.

Fig. 1. Schapiro with the ladies and the little boy, Paris, 12 August 1926

preferred geology, with reservations. He described parallels in artifacts of the American Indians and Egyptians with great clarity and told me of pieces he had dug up in Long Island and of his geological collection.—For a 10 year old boy he showed a marvelous memory of shapes, and intelligence. He was frail, a pallid boy with very crooked teeth; unlike his rich healthy parents. His father was telling their hostess that he was troubled by the boy's religious education, the conflict of two teachings and the boy's scepticism. She replied that her own parents were orthodox Jews, that she herself was not religious, but that her baby was to receive a thoro Jewish training and know the greatness of his tradition & the beauty of his religion. When he had left with his wife and son, she thanked me, saying that knowing me as she did, she had feared that I would laugh outright while my fortune was being told, and that nothing had made her happier than the story I had concocted on the spot about my father's illness—I assured her it was true—What admirable politeness in me! What a comical lady that was with whom she had made agreement all afternoon. The Australian had come on business to her husband. It was an unexpected, troublesome visit. She warned her husband not to trust him; he was a sharp scoundrel and an Anti-Semite. He had obtained his fortune of $2,500,000 by marrying this woman. But the family protested in his favor, having had business dealings with him and having found him eminently reliable. Well, she concluded, I cannot trust him; in saying good bye he pressed my hand more tightly and longer than was necessary or warranted, and near his own and my family—Everybody laughed,—Booh! Later I learned that she was herself strongly anti-Semitic—and wished to keep her child from any Jewish influence—This was said the very same day—She too believed in her own psychic powers, mysterious electrical penetration of character, the future, the past, the present—It was an interesting afternoon with two mediums—The second was deeply impressed by the other's child and remarked to her husband that he could profit from his friend's training of the boy. But he thought that their baby had an unforgettable advantage; he had straight teeth at nine months.

Meyer

[*Drawing of Schapiro with the ladies and the little boy (fig. 1)*]

Paris, 18 August 1926

Dearest Lillian:

It is so good of you to write me as often as you do. I have had a letter from you every day this week—just as I am about to leave Paris—I wish I could write, too, but I can not easily establish myself in the position—I am pursued by the recurrent thought of letters as responsibilities when I can write nothing. And yet all thru the day I stop to talk to you; I find so many things which I must tell you, vain ideas over which I chuckle for a while, and indignation or joy of a moment in which I find myself memorably eloquent in a purely day dream discourse. There are too many distractions which I resent only in theoretical anticipation, that break up my plans at every step, make me happy and leave me tired. Then I can not write. Every recollection is crossed by a little weariness, and I recall in passage or when retiring. I seem to be rushing up and down a boat which is moving slowly—and which all this agitation only retards—What charming days I have spent, how little I have done—I have used three weeks finding out what at home would have taken three days.

My real annoyance, dear, comes from having discovered after many days in the library that all I wanted was in another place, and that my permit to photograph had not reached me because I gave the wrong address—Can such wrath be in celestial minds, souls, breasts, spirits, etc? No, darling,—and if you were with me I should be much happier—

Meyer.

Paris, 28 August 1926

Dear Lillian:

I read in the preface of a book written shortly after the war: "If you wish to reward me for my labors, hold the Germans forever in hate." The work is in 5 vols. & practically an encyclopedia, and without the many German contributions to the study could never have had its present richness & interest. Later I had occasion to meet the author, Camille Enlart, & was very much surprised—This man who preceded scientific studies with hymns of hate, & unjustly singled out trivial details to condemn the solid labors of hard working Germans, was so mild, gentle, courteous, innocent & humble that one could never have connected him with his wicked writings. He was a bearded child in a nursery of books. He blushed violently at any reference to his own writings & seemed embarrassed by questions—I asked him about some buildings he had listed; he could not tell me; there were at least 20,000 he had mentioned, & it was several years ago. He could not locate references in his own works: had forgotten most things or knew only the most general facts about them—felt shaky on many problems & scratched his head a great deal & thought of some other people who could tell me, offered me the use of photographs he had collected, (over 100,000) & his library in the Trocadero—said a few words in English, which he speaks perfectly, & stopped with a smile, to see how I took them: Then he led me thru the Museum of Casts, & showed me the most familiar objects, making commonplaces, & apologizing all the time for more in his books & his ignorance of these objects: I remembered how Prof. Westermann, who has done much less than Enlart (& perhaps is therefore in a greater hurry) used to take out his watch when questioned, & say—I have eight minutes: Papyrology burns holes in the trousers: & run off. But it happened that Westermann gave me more information personally, & good suggestions whenever I did disturb him: & once he offered me an article of his own in reply to a question; & signed it with his compliments, unasked, & rushed me out. But I have three volumes of Enlart's *Manuel,* which tho very dull in style, and tastelessly compiled, deriving its form from similar works of the last century, & written mechanically, like an inventory, is however, so rich in facts, & details of every sort—on history, architecture, sculpture, ornament, archaeology, costume, taste, religion, geography, sociology, that one can discover new things from it alone, by rearrangement

Camille Enlart (1862–1927). French historian of French and Gothic architecture and director of Musée de sculpture comparée du Trocadéro.

William L. Westermann (1873–1954). Professor of history at Columbia University, who had assembled Columbia's papyrology collection.

Enlart's *Manuel.* Camille Enlart, *Manuel d'archéologie française depuis les temps mérovingiens jusqu'à la renaissance,* 3 vols. (Paris: A. Picard, 1902–16).

& selection—Then I have the use of the library & photographs, which is a great convenience—& even greater pleasure, for the library is beautifully situated—quiet, large, cool—& I am there all alone, with access to the stacks; & M. Enlart in the next room; & in the same building are casts of most of the important carvings from the earliest times & a large museum of Ethnology.

A friend took me to Reinach's home last Sunday—Many people came & went while we were there, Americans, English, French, Russian, & others whom I glimpsed for a moment—Reinach was quite different from Enlart. He works at home in a magnificent library, covering a larger number of fields, and in a great house, furnished like an 18th c. palace, with butlers & servants, elaborate rooms, & decorations, & a garden, fenced with iron—Reinach is more officially himself than Enlart; speaks ex-cathedra, with a sense of personal responsibility as if, in him the whole subject spoke: He was very interesting, talked well on many things, clarified quickly, & drew us all into discussion: He laid before us the reports of some recent discoveries of a Neolithic culture in North France at Clozel, which show a paleolithic Perigord style of animal art (an incised reindeer), pottery with advanced profiles but of crude manufacture, votive harpoons, practically useless, glass ware, figure sculpture, face-urns resembling Hissarlik, & strangest of all, an alphabet of 90 characters, a whole series of inscribed tablets, resembling Phoenician & Greek forms, but quite different from hieratic—There was no metal, some polished stone, & bricks. Reinach said: If these are genuine, then we are lost: several of the company called them rank forgeries, malicious concoctions: But Reinach gave an account of the history of several forgeries, & supposed falsities that proved true & indicated various possibilities, the relation to present knowledge of the present details, the possible prototypes, & so on—in a very efficient manner. Then an old gentleman showed a picture by a follower of Leonardo on which he wanted Reinach's opinion—Reinach showed me a recent report of excavations in the South West Black Sea country in Turkey, of neolithic mounds, relating to the work I had done with Young on Aegean prehistory, that I had not seen. There was an Englishman who discussed American Universities & museums & who knew more about them than I had ever heard at home, but said, at last, to indicate what a barbaric place the U.S. was that Columbia U. perhaps the largest in the world, had had no course in Italian Painting until 1926! [*in margin:* I must write Prof. Murray at once; what a scandal!] He has 40,000 catalogues of auctions, & museums & private collections of works of art—which Reinach called the largest personal library he knew & easily, the worst—This man was highly cultivated, spoke every visitor's language with ease, was at home in several fields in archaeology, history, art, annoyed us by his manner, which is the traditionally American one—& finally made us laugh, as if he were illustrating Bergson's theory, by the mechanical turn of his gestures, assurances, & information—I asked him his name just as he was about to leave & he spelled it out, for it was an Italian name & easily mistaken.

Reinach's wife, a Russian Jewess, was very charming—She was happy that there were young people in the house, for a change; she served us tea and insisted on stuffing us with chocolate afterwards—Then she saw [us] looking at books &

Salomon Reinach (1858–1932). French archaeologist, art historian, and epigrapher.

"Clozel." Schapiro likely misheard Clozel instead of Glozel, a hamlet in central France where over three thousand artifacts were discovered between 1924 and 1930. The finds initiated a series of heated debates. **Hissarlik.** Deserted settlement in Turkey believed to be the site of Troy in Homer's *Iliad.*

Clarence H. Young (1866–1957). Professor of Greek archaeology at Columbia University. Schapiro took his course "Fine Arts 149: Introduction to Greek Art & Archeology" in winter 1924.
S. Butler Murray Jr. (1888–?). Art historian who founded the Department of Fine Arts at Columbia University in 1921. Schapiro took many courses with Murray, who also served as Schapiro's thesis adviser.

Henri Bergson (1859–1941). French philosopher who denounced Jacques Loeb's ideas as dangerous. **Jacques Loeb** (1859–1924). German-born American Jewish biologist who saw Henri Bergson as a mystic and charlatan.

Ludwig Lewisohn (1882–1955). German-born American Zionist writer, prominent during the 1920s.

Karl Mendel. Austrian cousin of Ernest Gross.

offered to take us into the cellar, where there are countless others, but we found enough in the library to content us,—& almost all were inscribed "en homage" by the author. In these stacks I bumped into an old lawyer who is also an orientalist, & a friend of the family & we got to talking about the Jews in France, turned to Bergson—Loeb, Germany & the decay of Europe—We sat in the garden for a while, where a French mathematician joined us: his side interests were tennis & archaeology. About Europe every intelligent man I have spoken to is depressed—This is the end of the world; all culture, & goodness are dying from external economic & political troubles. Science keeps on producing in a blind, mechanical way things intrinsically beautiful but unavailing: there is still a little art, decadent, however—; the hegemony passes to America—There is such certainty about this in the few I have heard, that it is impossible to question,—to demand reasons: why—look around—There is also a feeling of helplessness before America, & sometimes of rage, which I find in most of the newspapers. The German boys tell me that in a few years, Germany will wipe out France completely; Th. Mendl, who was brought up in Vienna & Berlin, but is now a Czecho-Slovak (the most enlightened republic in the world—it has no wars & has legalized abortion) thinks that the French were too kind to Germany in the Versailles Treaty, acted unwisely in not crippling her completely, since all treaties are in self-interest. How he hates Germany, & how do the others, who find her a terrible menace & describe a German psychology, unchangeably proud, malicious, megalomaniac. And always they point to their own experience—thirty years as students, doctors, teachers—; disclaiming the effects upon themselves, since they are Jews, & Jews are ineradicably Jews. They are very proud of German science & arts, idolize particular Germans & despise the race. In separating themselves in the name of a profound biological Judaism, they talk of a mystical difference—of an unexplainable understanding with each other, that is not intellectual—exactly like Ludwig Lewisohn:—but which is at once felt. And truly we are very often together—except for one Roumanian doctor, who is so fanatically Zionistic & reminiscent of local persecutions, that his company is difficult—Yet these Jewish men are so very different from some of the Jewish boys at school, that I wonder if they would recognize each other. I told Karl that many of them were thoroly different from their own fellows in other parts of N.Y. & resembled gentiles more than Jews. But his family had lived for generations in a little Bohemian village—he had met no other Jews till he entered the University, yet he felt his race in every act & could not help but acknowledge himself—Still, he is very obviously Jewish in the traditional physical marks, in fact, uncomfortably so; & I was told by his cousin that as a boy he was worried for years, lest his nose grow longer. I met the mother—who is blue-eyed, & hardly like the son, except for the mouth & head shape (bullet shaped like Bavarians & north Alpine peoples)—Karl's cousin, Ernest, would never be taken for a Jew—especially since an operation on his nose has combined with his blond features to make him look like a Dutchman with American manners. Karl then notes something deeply Jewish in the bottom of his own soul, which rises, surmounts his German culture & reveals his Judaism; when it is his face, an exception in his family, (Ernest tells me) that is "obviously Jewish," & all his manners, language, habits, interests, unmistakably German.

But of Gruenberg no one can say the same thing. If anything, he resembles a tall Japanese; his skin is yellow, his dark eyes slant, he has straight, black hair & fine long fingers. He is extremely polite, deferent, smooth spoken, unengaged, slightly melancholy—so that one can still say, he is oriental, hence he betrays his race—If Karl's nose is curved & has the figure 6 nostrility, [(]that investigation is still afraid to define as exclusively Semitic), Gruenberg's is concave & spitzig—yet he too feels that way down, and in the middle and on top of his soul, he is a Jew; he says that he finds German friends more amiable, he lives more easily with them; but he understands Jews better & they understand him, whereas with Germans such rapprochements are impossible—Ernest & I admire him very much—he has the most exquisite manner, and is very good to us—Perhaps he will come to America in a year or two, as Karl will—Like true German students, they study the language in preparation, inform themselves in advance, know a great deal about N.Y.—the streets, subways, people, amusements—and have very decided notions about American life—

Gruenberg. Perhaps identified elsewhere as Greenberg, a Viennese who had taught school in Kovno.

I was surprised to hear so much discussion of Judaism, especially by these people. It is not really, of religion; or politics, but of race as an introspective revelation, as a spiritual solvent, taken merely as a thought—I used to read similar ideas in the *Menorah Journal,* where they were bound up with Zionism & personal Journalism—Here, these men, to escape association with a detestable culture, from which they have suffered—prefer to be Jews than Germans, and invoke doubtful biological notions to sustain them. They tell me that they are not at all so bad as they seem, that there is to-day in Germany, among the intellectual Jews, a cult of the Eastern Jew—the Russian, Galician, Roumanian Jew whom they had once despised—because that Jew lived in a ghetto & survived intact, with a more genuine race consciousness. "We must be real Jews to enter the Kingdom of Heaven"—But my friends deplore such extremes & avoid nationalism—preferring gradual assimilation to Zionism, as a solution. The heredity which reproduces these inexpugnable traits can diminish them by crossing—Tho Karl forgets how his nose re-emerged after generations, & with what barbarians one must cross. He denies that head form is alterable without crossing unless thru embryological complication; & mistrusts Boas' & Levi's figures as bad medicine—

Menorah Journal. Jewish monthly started in 1923.

I hear occasional stories of German anti-Semitism, but they are not different from American, and by themselves would not produce the ideas of Karl & his friends. But the Roumanian tales are horrible ones. They obsess this Roumanian Jew; he devotes hours to the subject,—& is further embittered by his own appearance, which is small & ungainly—His feelings about Zionism are so strong that he writes down objections that have encountered him and replies to them in syllogistic form to demonstrate the logic of his position—

Dear Lillian, I am writing in the park behind the Trocadero; it is warm & delightfully sunny between the small trees—or rather it was, since it will be dark soon. I have sat here so long without knowing it. I have spent such a happy day,

I should run home to you now and sit with you all evening, dear. Once the train came out of the subway on the L in-to a street that was so like Brooklyn; I thought I was soon to get off and change for the trolley to Brownsville—But in a moment we were on a bridge & crossing the Seine, a narrow river with low bridges & lined with small houses at this point—so different from the East River—which makes angles in all dimensions, up & down and across and far below—no flat picture—The bridges here seem designed for pedestrians: in N.Y. the footpaths are a grudging concession, one should take a trolley over: The Riverside has fine parkways for miles, schools, bathing houses, bookshops, public buildings, yet seems domestic beside ours. But how much more exciting was the ride over Brooklyn Bridge especially in the early evenings of winter when all the big buildings were illuminated one above the other, & the bridge rose higher as we reached the water and led us into the very heart of the city over roof tops and between many streets. There is nothing parallel here; but other scenes which we are lacking, & as fine—The island in the Seine on which Notre Dame is built is lovely at night—Once very late Ernest and I came upon the open square before the cathedral very suddenly, & we seemed to view the buildings for the first time, and were so amazed we thought of staying all night; until the shock passed; we heard voices, people crossed, and we tried to laugh away such nonsense. Tho we left soon we walked along the quais for another hour, & each felt very happy to be alone, and we felt as if alone, tho together, and agreed how much better it was to travel alone on such nights—like the hermits who sang together the praise of solitude—But this space was not solitary,—rather; full in a quiet way—a solitude, civilized & without walls, & provoking no introspection—Besides such sweetness, the National Library is a noisy house of deformed people, not well up on German books since 1914—But to-day I enjoyed working there—I felt like a happy Russian; what a nice ear the next man had, how I should like to be bald in the corners of the brow, what an excellent fellow was this author, I thought, when not reading; the first time in a month, I ate in the library restaurant—then walked half the way to the Trocadero which is several miles off—The attendant would not let me drag the folios of photos from the shelves; he said they were too heavy & the ladder was weak: to keep him from working I had to ask him for things on the lower shelves which I could take myself—He wrote letters while I was studying. Later he showed me in de Lasteyrie's book on Romanesque architecture an acknowledgement to the Trocadero Staff "without which this book . . . etc.["] "C'est moi" he said, and remarked that it was an excellent book, & a pity de Lasteyrie died as soon (He was 65)—He brought me some things I had not asked for & which were no use to me, out of good will—thinking that another work by an author I was reading might be interesting, however remote the subject. Before I left, Enlart came into the hall & spoke to me, & curiously he brought up de Lasteyrie—Think of what a beautiful place to work in—there are 8 large folding windows opening on a garden with the Seine and the city below—The room is very long and over 20 feet high—It is not a formal library with seats and desks, but has one large table in the center running lengthwise and joined to another; & a few chairs. The place is quite empty, the

Brownsville. Jewish neighborhood in Brooklyn where Lillian and Meyer had lived.

East River. Tidal strait between Manhattan and Long Island.

"de Lasteyrie's book." Robert de Lasteyrie, *L'architecture réligieuse en France à l'époque romane* (Paris: A. Picard, 1912).

walls seem far away — It is right that such a room should close at 5, for by artificial light it loses everything; there is no exterior; the windows are meaningless, & the soft shadows disappear.

So I sit in the small park outside, happy that I can write to you. I have forgotten the sun which drew me here, and the trees of which I made some sketches — Forget what I have written darling; let me write my love, which troubles and rejoices me more than these things —

Meyer.

Auxerre, 4 September 1926

Dear Lillian:

This is the third day on the road and a happy change from Paris, which was pleasant enough, but no place to work in at the time. Ernest left for England the day before, and Karl was planning to return home for a while because he could do nothing at the clinic, with the professors away and things in the hands of such slow schrecklich sorglos assistants. In Vienna he treated 70 patients before noon, here less than a dozen; and the amount of surgery he performed in a day was appalling. He was a little sick himself now.

schrecklich sorglos. German for "terribly careless."

The last few days in Paris were very happy ones and I neglected work almost completely. I saw five moving pictures. Charley Chaplin twice, Harold Lloyd, Cambodian dancers, etc. and met many friends with whom I spent much time. I learned that Stanley Hart was in town, but I called too late. He had left Europe after 4 days fearing that return passage could not be obtained later — Flores and his wife I came upon in the Louvre, and while standing with them on a street corner, I met friend after friend from home as if by appointment. The days were beautiful and the nights bad for sleeping. A meal lasted for more than 2 hours — I walked to the museums & libraries, rather than use the subways or buses, and I never reached them, or too late — My impression is of loitering day after day, hours by the book stalls, cafés, movies, parks, & in little rooms. Looking for Stanley, I met George Antheil, a musician, who has been here for many years — He played beautiful mediaeval Arab music on the phonograph & showed me moving pictures in his own room — some he had taken himself in Carthage & Tunis, & some by Charley Chaplin, which I had seen the night before with Karl & Ernest — I was to the Louvre & the National Library, but not for more than a hour or two at one time. The preparatory exertions left me quite weary or restless. I was tired by sundown, but when night came, it was better to stay awake in the streets for many hours.

Charles Stanley Hart. Instructor in the Fine Arts Department at Columbia University from 1924 to 1925.

George Antheil (1900-1959). American concert pianist and composer.

Now it is quite different — I was at Sens for two days — I rushed about in a most unsystematic way from early morning till dark; there was so much that any fragmentary study was rich in detail and absorbing. The cathedral, besides being an architectural masterpiece, has beautiful glass of the 12th, 13th, & 15th centuries, intact, and the best Gothic sculpture — of the 12th as well as 13th. Then there is the treasure of the Cathedral, with early ivories, and a collection of Persian, Coptic, Byzantine and Sicilian silks of the earliest times that I could not go thru in five hours—There were beautiful parish churches of the Romanesque period in the city—a great Synodal Palace and the Archbishop[']s House—and two museums. In the Archaeological Museum I had a chance to study a large group of Gallo-Roman, prehistoric, Celtic arts and crafts from one region, over a very long period of time.

I was delayed coming to Auxerre this morning because of bad trains—When I arrived I learned that the Library which has Romanesque manuscripts was closed for the month; but the adjoining local museum had good things—I foolishly spent the afternoon there on details I could find all over the country & in the Paris collections, and had less time for the Cathedral, Palace and smaller churches, which are unique and imposing monuments. This architecture is ravishingly beautiful; I feel silly to have to talk about it and futile to make drawings. But I do both; my notes & sketches will fill a hundred sides in 2 more days: already my writing is short hand—alas that the night should be so soon; and these joys so fragmentary. I look forward to the smaller Burgundian towns, where I shall find only one building that I can study all day & draw, dissect and measure completely. How I jump, in & out, up & down & gather striking pieces or the most general observations. Auxerre has marvelous Gothic sculpture in equally fine architectural frames, but so much of it that one glances here, there and off to another part of the building—There were figures—purely 5th century Greek in this 13th c building (pardon the inaccuracy; it is this bit of wall only—the whole varies from 12th to 16th) to which the weathering had added a beautiful rough vibrant surface—I saw similar carvings at Sens; but these were even finer. I drew some of them—I did not have the patience to set up tripod & camera & focus, etc.—& I recalled photos in Mâle, Roussel and the other books that I have home.

Jules Roussel (1865–?). French historian of medieval sculpture.

From every visit I select for the future—for this, to-day, is so incomplete and so enjoyable. We shall see these things together, dear; and new ones with them—For the past three days, I left for my room at sundown, reached the hotel in the dark, near the railway, and had a late supper, with neat relish (not the dish) as if I had worked all day, and truly, I carried a pack on my back as I sat down—the tripod & box that I rarely use—It was good to work, eat, and sleep, with the sun. The day, then, is happily long and I am not anxious for its end as a means of rest. Drawing from a tower I felt a new wind & I saw that it was growing dark. This alarmed me; but when it was all dark I could do no more and I was glad walking home. I look thru the papers and I see that I remember not even half of what I saw or did.

Meyer.

Nevers, 14 September 1926

Dearest Lillian:

This last week I was to Vézelay, Aval[l]on, Dijon, Tournus, Autun and Nevers. Vézelay now seems very remote, tho I stayed there two days and enjoyed its church and high setting more than any till the time—I cannot begin to speak of how beautiful was its colored Romanesque nave and how rhythmically powerful and subtle the hundred carved capitals and the great portal. I knew then that the Romanesque surpassed the Gothic, that the latter was a mechanical development rather than an intrinsic perfecting; and that just as the Renaissance sculptors of the early time were more naturalistic Gothics, the latter were less imaginative, more tool preoccupied and skillful craft-ridden Romanesque outgrowths—Yet they all worked beautifully, and this country is full of their finest works—

I have had different things in each place & I am happily surprised every day. I was in Dijon 3 days, found the library with its Cistercian manuscripts closed, but there were interesting if plain buildings, and a 10th c crypt—elaborately built, and still unchanged. I met some people, bought about 60 books that I could not find in Paris, and worked in the Museum with the Gallo Roman & prehistoric objects.

Tournus has an 11th c church, which I photographed in detail, & studied all day, but could not finish—In Autun, I found the library closed, but I gained admission privately, meeting the Keeper thru the Abbé Terret, a local Emile Mâle, who has written several volumes on Cluniac art & Iconography. He, Terret, received me in his water-closet, spoke a great deal of money-matters, and complained of the speed with which Porter and Mâle write and deceive themselves and others. He showed me Mss. of 30 years work, still unpublished, and on the most absorbing problems.

Victor Terret (1856–1935). French abbot who published several books on the Cathédrale de Saint-Lazare at Autun.

He led me to the Librarian; who was cross-eyed, and very kind and humble. Terret cannot read English or German, and this man translates for him the essential works—I was in the library a long time, and tho this is M. Gillot's vacation; he stayed with me from morning till 7 in the evening, while I copied every ornament, initial and miniature in the Gundohinus Gospels, an 8th century book, that is well known but has never been published or analyzed. I do not know if I will carry the study further now; but I have all the material, notes, descriptions, & drawings; & they fit in very nicely with what I have already studied in oriental christian and Hellenistic—Gillot insisted on my reasons for every observation I made, & copied them down, along with references to the literature on each point. There was another man in the library, paleographizing the Sacramentary of Autun—an American; & it turned out to be Prof Rand of Harvard, to whom I had a letter of introduction from his friend Strittmatter, but whom I had not called on in Cambridge, and had forgotten completely—

André Gillot. French librarian at Autun.

Gundohinus Gospels. MS Lat. 3, Bibliothèque municipale, Autun.

Sacramentary of Autun. MS Lat. 19 bis, Bibliothèque municipale, Autun.
Edward Rand (1871–1945). American classicist and Latin paleographer.
E. Anselm Strittmatter. American liturgical historian.

When I had done with the Ms. I had to leave in a few hours & there were two museums to visit, but already past closing time. I came to one, and found a man there, who seemed of some influence, for he arranged that I stay as long as I wish; and he conducted me personally to the other, a mile off, and opened it for me. Then I learned that he was a friend of the librarian who had told him that I had come 3000 miles to study in their little town—which is rare and remarkable.

But in the Municipal Museum of Nevers, I was told that I could not take a note without a letter from the mayor or the Conservator, who was elsewhere—In the church of St. Etienne, an all Romanesque building from East to West & top to bottom (Vézelay & Autun have only the naves Romanesque, the east ends, all things undesirable & imperfect) the sacristan let me climb all over, even during services, and for the 1st time in weeks, I finished a transverse section in detail and completed all the elevations, profiles and plans.—This was a beautiful church, dear how I leaped and scribbled in it:

Meyer.

Rodez, 24 September 1926

Dear Lillian:

I am now making long jumps to reach Toulouse, traveling three, four and five hours at a time—It is hopeless to attempt a complete study of any region, however small, in one summer; and to add to it a general knowledge of the country for two or three hundred miles around was a crazy idea. So I am going to Toulouse (with a stop at Albi) where I will consult the Statistique Monumentale and the Archives and draw up a less aimless and more essential list—But what fun it has been apart from the trains, belly-aches, weariness, and closed monuments—I spent a month in Paris, preparing, reading, planning, and I foresaw almost nothing but my own excitement—Now I should retrace my way and study more carefully, for the earlier notes & drawings pass over too many details I suspect for the first time—As I grow more observant and suspicious I need more time and I break up my plans and come to see less, with the consolation of quality > quantity, etc. and the "long run"—

Louis Bréhier (1868–1951). French professor of the history of antiquity and the Middle Ages at Université Clermont-Ferrand.

I was three days at Clermont-Ferrand, I called on Bréhier but he was on his vacation. There was no catalogue of the Museum which has fine prehistoric, Gallo-Roman and mediaeval works, and I had to catalogue the objects myself and draw them. I never finished—I was happy to spend three hours walking the volcanic cones outside the city—I found a 7 vol. set of Fontenelle's works, incomplete, (2 vols of his poetry are missing), in the 18th c. binding, for sixty cents,—and many beautiful prints of the 17th century. The 11th century church, Notre Dame du Port, I studied in great detail, but could not finish the upper part of the transverse section since there was no access to the aisle galleries which have curious half barrel vaults of quarter circle section abutting the nave vault. At Issoire, thirty miles away I found a slightly later building which was almost an exact copy—In the four hours of the morning I was happily done, since there were only the differences to note and the ornament to copy—My valise and camera outfit were at the hotel, when I rushed to catch a train to Brioude, an hour's ride off—I reached this town before two o'clock and thought to work all afternoon and return to Issoire in the evening. But St Julien at Brioude was so complicated and reconstructed and part laid over part, that I missed the last train which left at 8:15. There were no autos or buses—no roundabout trains, and I had to sleep over—at 4 in the morning I rode back to Issoire and paid for the unslept-in-bed and left at 6 for Brioude again where I had to change on the way to Rodez.—How I know that road—It was my birthday as I learned twice in filling out my Police Blank at the two hotels—At Brioude the first three hotels were full and I had to walk towards the town to find a place. The early morning walk to the station was in the dark with howling dogs and the alarms of trains moving away and whistling good bye to me again—

The ride to Rodez was the finest I have had so far—over mountains, viaducts, barren rocks, cliff edges, and heights overlooking half the world—It was difficult to read—Villages sprang up out of grass between stone like their own walls, remote from each other in these unattainable heights. At one station the empty car filled with peasants, strong handsome far spitting red faces who argued about socialism for a half hour but in a language I could only catch in big words—one of them would turn to me and ask me if it was not true what he had said of the prrroprrrietaires—In the old days he rolled his own cigarettes he said, but I do not know what time and capitalism have done to this right of self-respecting virility—Part of the way an idiot boy[] in military uniform sat opposite reading a catholic manual of spiritual welfare, over which he fell asleep, dribbling at the mouth, finally dropping the book, awakening and reading once more. He kept smiling like your doctor's patient, of whom I read again on the trip—

At Paray-le-Monial, a little boy with a paralyzed arm[] followed me in the church while I worked, and told me he was half-witted, tapping his head several times, and begged money for a candle—There were also half-witted nuns and religious folk about and a museum called the Hiéron dedicated to the Eucharist and the Social Reign of Jesus—in which paleolithic implements labeled with the conventional Solutrean, Acheulian, etc. were given recent dates and explained in Biblical terms; and Egyptian and Gallo Roman figures labeled as forerunners of the Virgin & fulfillments of ancient prophecies—Most wonderful of all as a piece of inspired anthropology was a culture area map of the geographical distribution of miracles of the 1st—to 4th class, since there are Miracles, miracles, miracles, and—miracles, the latter being petty victories won by prayer and, the 1st, prodigies sanctified by a papal recognition. The 2nd and 3rd, degrees of popular celebrity or supernatural efficacy—The map is an interesting document, but there were no photos of it to be found at the time—The church, a beautiful piece of Romanesque architecture has its interior defaced by banners, pennants, statues and all [*illegible*] dedicated to the Sacred Heart of Jesus who is never less attractive than in this modern sloppy cult for whom he wears his heart radiant on the breast bone in a hundred icons—The town is given over to this cult of Sacre Coeur; hotels, streets, stores, thrive on the pilgrims—wax works and post-cards, shrines to Marie Alacoque the local founder—I was sold a pamphlet to aid the conversion of the remaining Jews who with their concealed financial trickery sap morals, religion, motherhood, patriotism, etc. and yet can be saved—

Saint Marie Marguerite Alacoque (1647–90). French nun at the convent in Paray-le-Monial who promoted Catholic devotion to the sacred heart in its modern form.

I visited Cluny, beautifully situated in country more domestic and cheerful than Rodez, if less grand. We must spend a summer in this part of Burgundy, dear—This is land I shall surely revisit—and also the present mountains, the Causses plateaux and villages about Rodez, Marvejols and Severac.

Meyer.

Forgive me, for not writing so long. It was difficult.

seven postcards. These postcards are in an almost cinematic sequence: the first postcard shows the exterior of the Abbaye de Sainte-Foy from the east with town buildings in the foreground and on the right, and in the background the surrounding hills and valleys; the second shows the west façade partially hidden by town buildings; the third is of the tympanum; the fourth is of the interior, down the nave to the apse; the fifth shows the north side of the nave and half the organ against the west wall; the sixth shows the gold reliquary of Pepin from the treasury; the seventh shows the reliquary statue of Sainte Foy, also from the treasury.

Conques, 26 September 1926 [seven postcards]

1 Here is where I live the next few days—I sleep in a farm, and I work in the church and in the remnants of the ancient cloister, which to-day is a museum. From the road one cannot see the church for the hills, and from above, the village for the church. It is so picturesquely massed that no one view begins to tell the tale; and of course there is no proper scale, with mountains and village houses—The

2 façade, alas, is cut off in part by the houses, and the upper towers seen are modern restorations, but how fine a piece remains, what swell buttressing & surface divisions. The photo gives no just idea of the relief of the wall strips, the arcades, the portal—and measurements won't do—nor a longitudinal section. And there is also the color which is suggested by the picture, the variety of stone and mortar, in surface, tint, size, grain, and moulding—Parts were once painted, especially the interior carvings, in blues and reds, but

3 the colors have disappeared almost entirely. On the portal tympanum they are still strong, and not at all more gruesome in hell than in heaven—Pity I have no details of this sculpture which has everything any tradition has had; the[]r[e] are heads of classic smoothness and regularity, archaic draperies, details of African abstraction and the most barbaric folk fancies in the Hell Torment; and with it all an architectural composition of as complicated groups as are found in the Renaissance. But apart from its beauty, it offers the most at-

Alfred D. F. Hamlin (1855–1926). Professor of architecture at Columbia University. Schapiro took his yearlong history of medieval architecture course from 1924 to 1925.

4 tractive problems in comparative religion, in theology, history, archaeology, folk-lore, esthetics, and geometrical design. These are not its only distinctions—It leads to a fine interior, to what Hamlin called a "nave not as lofty as Amiens but perhaps better disciplined," or would have called, since he never mentioned this church, but others like it in Toulouse, and Santiago and Bari. This picture does not show clearly the triforium gallery elevation which duplicates the rhythm of the lower nave arcade at twice the velocity and half the size; nor the carvings of the

5 capitals, the fine foliage, fantastic heraldic monsters borrowed from the east, and the local iconographies. I am photographing most of them, some from the top of the organ case, others from the gallery parapets, and similar dizzy places, than from which there is no better to see space—architectures. But tell me, dear, don't you like the building from these few cards? and the country about it is as remarkable, not as hard and barren as in the first photo, for there are real forests and groves in the mountain hollows—And within the treasure in this treasure there is another treasure

prunkhaft glanzend unfesselnd. German for "splendid gleaming captivating."

6 this time of gold and precious stone, mediaeval jewelry and metalwork, cloisonné enamel, reliquaries with inlaid cabochons and intaglios, filigree patterns and beaten gold figures prunkhaft glanzend unfesselnd[?]—and they contain the

Foreskin of Our Lord Jesus Christ ("Relique de la Circoncision," the Catalogue says), the blood which flowed from his side, the bread he consecrated at the last supper, the balm with which his body was perfumed, relics of the cloth with which he wiped the feet of the apostles, the food he gave them after his resurrection (["]coprolites"?),

7 of the seven breads, the hair of the Blessed Virgin, of his tomb, of his seamless tunic, a great trick in those days, of the column to which he was bound; the knucklebones of St John Baptist, the bones and hairs of Mary Magdalene, St. Stephen, the Apostles, including the teeth of St. James, the handkerchief of Peter, the bones of Daniel and the three Hebrew Children, and the head of Habbacuc, the thumb, right foot and one finger of Peter, and a miscellaneous collection of minor sacred anatomy from no less than fifty different saints. The body of Sainte Foy is, needless to say, in her church at Conques. Hence such splendors in a village of less than a thousand—

Love, Meyer.

Toulouse, 4 October 1926

Dearest Lillian:

I do less and less as I reach south. I feel I shall soon become "overwhelmingly idle"—But this is no tropical disease as was foretold to me—It has become colder, windier, more rainy. I have spent two afternoons reading, and the hours in the churches and museums were more sight-seeing than study. I must laugh to think how much more archaeologically invigorating was Conques—In a large city there is no end to aimlessness. The square I live in is a grand Q & D; and only the absence of friends limits my time in the open all night sidewalk coffee-houses. It is good to read in my room till late and drink a while and return. Since Conques I feel a degradation of energy not only in myself but in everything about me—There we used candles at night and saw nothing but stars from the window; we were hemmed by mountains. Conversation was loud and rixious, with powerful dogs in the company. The old woman sewed designs by stitching on a quilt cover; the forms were remarkably like those on upper Mongolian nomad work of two thousand years ago. She worked by an oil lamp whose light she made smaller and smaller—My bill was rendered on a slate and incorrectly added in my favor—I remained a third day, but did not complete my work at the church—The curé was very good to me and offered to photograph details if I should have need of them. Together we removed the heavy reliquary of the bones of Ste Foy herself from the presbytery altar so that I could copy the old oriental silks in which they had been wrapped for a thousand years. I did not dare to ask to have them unwrapped and detached; there were eight pieces, each in the other's way—

"Q & D." "Quick and Dirty," nickname of a snack shop on Amsterdam Avenue that Schapiro and his friends frequented.

The last night I was so possessed by you I could not sleep until very late—There is a sweet weariness which when quietly enclosed and alone in mountains now dark remembers you. I am homeless without your hands. I have a routine in which to dissolve the distractions of constructed beauty—Such nights I have been only with you—I lay my head in a hundred ways and cannot find you—your touch is so slight and tender I am disheartened by the distance—I hear between trees our two o'clock wind, when we smiled and shook the chill gliding, with a small caress. I confound the garden in one long night but distinguish many postings when we kissed in hilarious haste on an uncertain doorstep,—your jolly body with mine. You were never more prodigal, darling Lillian: and I was happy to tell how late it was. Could we spend silent hours, sitting straight, consulting darkness now—Sometimes we sat an afternoon together; once, a morning in a happy disordered house which might have belonged to us.

Meyer

to his Lillian, sweetheart and beloved—and good angel

Toulouse, 6 October 1926

Dear Lillian:

Raymond Rey (1890–1958). French professor of the history of medieval art.

I called on Prof Rey of the University of Toulouse. Enlart had told me of him as a young man who could help me. He is already grey haired, almost 40; as Enlart had said, very keen and learned—He teaches Human Geography and mediaeval architecture, and combines the two in his works which are real anthropology, and not only according to himself—"fondemental"—He has made a very fine study of French pendentives and shown how the remarkable parallels in Armenian and Perigord Romanesque architecture are convergences from a common source under similar geological conditions, rather than a borrowing—He disengaged the empirical methods used in solving problems of statics involved in adapting domes to square plans and showed how they were developed step by step rather than obtained from elsewhere in a finished condition. When I told him of my studies he gave me a long list of sites I had not known—and photographs, and an old book (of his own) now out-of-print in one of them—He is working in the same field. He told me to spend three years in the Pyrenees, learning the language, customs, geology, flora and fauna, if I wished to handle the subject properly. He has collected rich material on the persistence of Roman culture in this most backward and isolated region, "long after it died out in Auvergne and Burgundy"; but I think it is because he has not attended to these two, since Terret has a similar book (unpublished) on Burgundy, and Bréhier the same thesis for Auvergne—We had a pleasant afternoon and forgot dinner—His eagerness, rapidity, and pure mechanical knowledge were charming—He could speak of the importance of his discovery as if he were the speaker and proud of it, but as if these incidentals were simply further contributions to knowledge as dispassionate as the others.

Émile Cartailhac (1845–1921). French professor of prehistoric archaeology at Toulouse.
Jean-Baptiste Noulet (1802–90). French scientist who proved the existence of the human fossil.
Édouard Lartet (1801–71). French vertebrate paleontologist and stratigrapher whose studies of prehistoric sites yielded evidence of the contemporaneous existence of man and certain extinct mammals in Aurignac.

The Museum of Natural History has a beautiful collection of French prehistory. No wonder with members like Cartailhac, Noulet & Lartet. Toulouse is in the very paleolithic region these men explored, and reaped well. It is strange to read labels written thirty years ago—; some still preserve a faint anti-theological odor—and some recount circus marvels now poo-poohed by children—After the restrictions of other museums it was a joy to read a printed notice that the museum would be glad to facilitate note-taking and drawing from its collections. In Sens, Moulins,

Cluny, I had to see the Mayor; and in other places the Conservator, who was usually away—One must pay the city of Toulouse 20 francs for permission to photograph a fig in the Museum of Art, unless one is authorized by the Minister of Public Instruction in Paris in which case credentials must be shown to the Director of the School of Arts and an appointment made for the limited time in which the photography is to be celebrated—How lucky I am to have this permit since I have over sixty figures to photograph! And such figures! I could die for them—

Meyer.

Toulouse, 15 October 1926 [postcard of a reliquary bust captioned "XIIIe Musée St. Raymond, cuivre doré et cabochons"]

and what an impossible wouble[?]-U for a what! It should be seen upside down & from [*illegible due to postmark*]

What a grand buste reliquaire for a bone; he is perfection in every detail, not a line or plane wrong—supreme homeliness of face neck and shoulders with such beautiful result—like African wood carving—try him upside down from close by and away for detail—such surface should be touched as well as seen—there are nice asymmetries of modeling as well as line; & the profile is as subtly round and angular—

Love, Meyer.

"wouble-U." At the start of his note, Schapiro made a decorated initial *W* for the first letter of "What a grand buste reliquaire." He must have realized later that what he had drawn looked more like an *M* than a *W*. He then added, in pencil, the first two lines about how the *M* should be read upside down.

Toulouse, 15 October 1926

Dear Lillian:

When I read that "there is such a thing as malpractice by omission" I trembled for myself before reading further. What have I not forgotten of those I love!

The last few days I have had sad news of my friends. You have said little of yourself all this time, dear. Are you well, darling? I shall be so happy to be with you again.

Meyer.

Toulouse, 23 October 1926

Dear Lillian:

In a few days I will leave Toulouse for the Pyrenees & then return to Paris—The three weeks in the city have been very pleasant; I learned new things but I hardly did all that I intended—and I shall have to come back next summer to fill large gaps in my plans. Now it becomes too dark & rainy for work—it is difficult to photograph, & church interiors show almost no details. For two weeks it was midsummer here—& I was not sorry to prolong my visit—I met the president of the Soc. Archéol. du Midi abbé Auriol, who gave me the keys to the society library, which is now closed, this still being the vacation period—it was delightful to study, alone in this fine Renaissance palace, with four rooms of books & photos—& the greatest freedom—There were hundreds of volumes of journals of departmental scientific & historical societies—which we have not at home, & which in Paris I can use only after much formality and only one by one.—The material was

Achille Auriol (1865–1937). French abbot and president of the Société archéologique du Midi de la France from 1921 to 1937.

distracting, for the articles I sought were between others, seemingly more interesting & more important, and in an afternoon I read of architecture, prehistory, folk-lore, the teaching of medicine in the 16th century, provencal literature, ancient law, and mediaeval chronometry—Such idle reading I had not practiced for years—These articles are mainly publications of documents by native archivists—or of new finds in digging; sometimes, a general work. Years ago when travel was difficult & libraries small, pharmacists, notaries, school teachers, priests & business-men in small villages in Aveyron, in Gascony, even in the Pyrenees, published serious studies that are still very valuable—The Aveyron papers were full of geological notes each month, eighty & ninety years ago—& the southern societies printed the first scientific prehistoric studies—The Gascon journals are especially rich in philology & folk-lore, the Languedoc in Romance literature & prehistory, the Provence in classical archaeology—all of them print cartularies of churches, inscriptions, charters, legal processes, & investigations of the native problems in biology & agriculture—There are over a hundred such journals in France. When Reinach heard that there was a new magazine in America devoted to mediaeval history & literature he was disgusted, because he thought that publication should be consolidated to facilitate research.

Most of these articles are not by professors & are without any scientific pretension—Those published from Bordeaux or Toulouse or university towns are different—more scholarly—many notes, discussions, photos & citations. Besides these there are larger regional societies—of the South, the Pyrenees, the West, the North, the Center of France,—and they too publish quarterly journals & yearbooks of Congresses: and above them are national societies, & finally the annual Bibliographical Repertoire of the whole hierarchy of wisdom & research—When I saw all these books of the past 100 years so neatly stacked before me, I thought, above my depression, that I could spend the winter in Toulouse, & read—But there is no comparative material—very little outside France—

So I shall stay in Paris & have the museums as well—I must postpone the Spanish trip to the summer, & hasten thru Languedoc & the Pyrenees in November.—

I was glad you wrote me of Natalie—but it was bad news, & yet from Natalie, not unusual—I sent her a post-card—it was many months ago—from Nantes—I wonder if I misaddressed it—since I wrote to her c/o of the Amalgamated, Union Square West. Do you know if she reads French, dear?

with love, Meyer

Toulouse, 25 October 1926

Dearest Lillian,

This is a delightful report of Dr. Barrish & Mr. Grady: the clean-cut American drug addict with medical interests. He says he walks once in a while! The surprise ending in medical literature—but with a question.

After all!

Peptic ulcer [*drawing of two puzzled men*]

His platform:

more Pool Parlors for American

womanhood — [*drawing of a person speaking and a crowd below*]

[*drawing of man lying in an elevator cab*]

Thomas Grady lies down on his job

Your dialogue, dear, gives me a ~~thousand~~ a hundred (rather), images — I wonder if you eat regularly, yourself — & how are your father & mother — I am so happy to hear from you — I cannot tell you in words or pictures. After a sunny morning it began to rain & has drizzled all afternoon — I was with the Abbé Auriol for a few hours: he showed me his family album for generations — What beautiful photographs they are: photography has had its primitives like painting & sculpture — His sister, seventy years old, sat beside him and knew of everything he discussed, including mediaeval iconography. I saw her, as a baby and a child and a young girl — very beautiful — and always with her brother who has changed in the same way — He wrote on his card an introduction to a friend in Paris, and added[:] "I have just read your first volume — which gives me unspeakable joy" (did I recall this from what I wrote above of your letter? or did I write of yours, recalling this?) His rooms are crowded with furniture & knicknacks & pictures and books, some classic & some utterly tasteless: — he has six chairs heavily upholstered arranged in a circle but one chair I could not sit in; I do not know why — perhaps it is the bishop's or cardinal's — I could mention nothing that did not excite him to arise & totter across the room for books or pictures — In the meantime his old sister, in black, and with eyes deep like the shadows in a skull, smoothed his seat for his return, & piled cushions upon it. He called [on] me in my room one morning & seeing nothing but bed and table and chair, remarked — You live like a monk. — which pleased him greatly — But, darling, let me tell you, I have been twice to the movies, smoke ten cigarettes every other day, drink cognac with black coffee, read Stendhal and Sorel, buy books & pictures & even rarer objects, and have grown powerful black whiskers to diminish the effect of my hair which falls to my shoulders. All this is surely not monasticism. But I would be the last to undeceive this good man, who has been so gracious — Your

Stendhal (1783–1842). French writer.

George Sorel (1847–1922). French writer, a favorite of Schapiro's friend Whittaker Chambers, who was corresponding with Schapiro about Sorel at this time.

Meyer —

[*Drawing of Auriol and his aged sister*]

Dear, I am sending some books that I have bought in Toulouse & in them I am enclosing several engravings. If any of them are held up at the customs you may be put to some trouble; — they are not subject to duty, since the English books are more than 70 years old & are second hand.

[*Next page: drawing of a man examining another on a stage before an audience; below, an angel with a scroll descends toward a crowd*]

ANGELUS DOMINI DICENS

ECCE HELLUO MORPHINAE

ET MENDAX ULCERUM

DISSIMULANS CAVETE

MEDICULI!

Voix sceptique:
Mais d'abord, un examen gastrique, les anges se trompent souvent.

Montauban, 27 October 1926

Dearest Lillian:

You know why your letter was returned; it had waited more than 15 days for my arrival in Toulouse—To-day it sounds like an allegory;—of you & me—"If she knows a man's voice then reality compels the typist to adjust the Dictaphone to her memory of it."..."the careless operator takes the sounds as transmitted by her machine's chance adjustment." But you, darling, are a paragon of discreet & scrupulous attention—If you can make allegories, you can also receive them. So many things happen in a day, so many in a week in which one writes, that surely a selection is not aimless, however impulsive. You wrote me that the time passes swiftly; for me, too, darling Lillian—

Meyer.

Moissac, 4 November 1926

Dearest Lillian

I have been here a week, which is hardly more than a beginning, but I must leave to-morrow—The cloister is beautiful to sit in and regard for a while; study is impossible with such rain & storm as we have now—After a few minutes I run around the galleries to warm myself—By 4:30 it is dark; before 9 in the morning it is too damp and misty—Such days are best spent indoors. Yesterday I walked to a village in the neighborhood where there is an old church, older than Moissac—A peasant, on the way, said it was built in 1000—The walk itself was fine, for one rain had ended, leaving the country magically fresh and cool—while I worked in the building another storm darkened the church. Two days before it had been hung with black banners, white crossed, to commemorate the dead—These had not been removed—I did not dare unhook them. The church is so small, it has no sacristan or suisse to attend to it, and the curé was not at home. An old lady helped me pull them down. I photographed three parts, but I learned to-day that only one plate was sufficiently exposed to produce a clear print—I have complete drawings and some measurements which will do till next summer, when there will be light in this dark country. I was happy in these discomforts for I discovered remarkable things. Later the rain stopped & I worked outside in the cemetery. The few exterior details were as interesting. The building had last been studied fifty years ago; no drawings or photos had been published—I was told of it by an old archaeologist at Moissac, Comméja with whom I have spent my evenings. He gave me books, journals, and enormous information—I have the most pleasant hours with him. Once, another old man was there, who could hardly stand up, when he learned that I was interested in Moissac, he told me of many things to see in the region—He has collected material for more than fifty years which he will give in manuscript to the town—Momméja spoke of their duty to me! of the decay of intellectual activity in the Tarn & Garonne, the flight to the cities; his loneliness

"village in the neighborhood." Probably Pommevic, fourteen kilometers west of Moissac. Schapiro later wrote to Arthur Kingsley Porter that he had walked to Pommevic on 1 November 1926.

Pierre-Jules Momméja (1854–1928). French folklorist of the region who was highly respected by Schapiro. **"another old man."** Joseph Dugué, the keeper of the cloister of the Abbaye de Saint-Pierre. Schapiro's notes on conversations with Momméja about Dugué's excavations as well as notes regarding the tour Dugué gave Schapiro through the cloister can be found in Schapiro's papers at Columbia University, file I, 1.

at 75; his own late maturity, for he understood little before 50; & the difficulties of work at his age—But tho ill, his mind is vigorous & he remembers very well.

The portal & cloister of Moissac are better than what can be said of them. How glad I am DeWald thought of assigning them to me, two years ago at this very season. To be with them is to be happy indeed. And to study their details is to live in perpetual discovery and pride—When it grows dark, there is no one in France with whom one can better discuss these things than Momméja—who has studied them since 1870—and with great care—Only the bad weather interrupts my work; I think it will be better to return in the summer—With love, darling—

Ernest T. DeWald (1891–1968). Assistant professor at Columbia University from 1923 to 1925; in 1924, he assigned the topic of Schapiro's master's thesis: "The Sculpture of Moissac."

Meyer.

Moissac, 5 November 1926 [postcard]

It was so fine to-day, I stayed in Moissac—& how pleasant it was to work here—Momméja was as good as ever: he had found an old out of print book that we have not in NY. & he gave it to me, with other things of his own. He will write to me what he had not thought of during our conversations—These are more than I can remember—

Love, Meyer.

Poitiers, 14 November 1926

Dearest Lillian:

When I left Moissac, I thought to visit several towns in the region. At Agen it rained miserably, and the second morning it was so bad that I took a train to Périgueux, 120 miles north, & on the road to Paris—In a few hours the sun appeared, & I was sorry to have skipped Monsempron, Duravel, Cahors, Souillac & Brive in such fine weather. When it began to rain again I was really delighted, for my change of plan was justified—I struggled with these reassurances for two hours. Every few miles weather changed. But the trip was thru beautiful country, past the prehistoric grottoes, thru the Dordogne valley, thru Les Eyzies, which I once thought I would surely visit—there was much architecture & geography to observe on the way; details disappeared as rapidly as they were discovered but returned so often that they were not entirely lost.

I stopped a day at Périgueux, Limoges and Angoulême—hardly enough for one building and each of these has many, & museums besides. In Périgueux & Angoulême the mediaeval churches are domed and on pendentives, & give the cities a characteristic oriental horizon. But they have been so completely restored in their interiors, and so coldly and academically, that they resemble certain banks in New York—more than their prototypes: Only one, St. Etienne in Périgueux[,] has preserved its original structure; and Angoulême has its ancient façade which is all sculpture and ornament. The feeling for space & for surface in this region is entirely different from anything I have seen before; & when I reached Poitiers I saw still another type, unlike the South & Ile-de-France, but much like that in Anjou from which I had proceeded—At Limoges it rained & rained: I passed a tailor and furrier's shop owned by "Monsieur Bégeleisen"; in the museum was an

"Monsieur Bégeleisen." *Bügeleisen* is German for "flatiron." Schapiro is amused by the appropriateness of the name and perhaps understands it as Jewish.

enormous collection of glazed ware from all the world, but very little of the mediaeval enamel which I had hoped to find—The towers of Limoges churches are marvelously staged and arcaded; the interiors less interesting, tho one small church was sufficiently eccentric and complicated to keep me happy for several hours.

Poitiers is the ideal city for the end of this journey—I am fortunate to have come to it after the others & not before—It is so rich in Merovingian, Carolingian, Romanesque, etc. churches, sculpture, artifacts, painting, metals, manuscripts that one can resume a whole history of this one town—& also a prehistory. What buildings & in what fine preservation! I am here six days & have only begun. When we revisit France together, we will head for Poitiers—also for my purposes, since I am leaving it half unseen ("it," not "me"). Archaeologically, there are problems here for generations; and artistically, joys forever.

With my love, dearest Lillian & how I do wish to see you; these long evenings I cannot escape loneliness by reading—

Meyer

Paris, 21 November 1926

Dearest Lillian:

You send me the very first news I have had of my mother; the one time she has written she said nothing of herself: & I have learned nothing from Jakey. (His last letter was quite gay but not without a certain virile disgust without which he would be without himself[.]) The tea, lemon & crabapple jelly are so clear, darling; they are the germs of home-sickness, when you place them between yourself, your mother, and mine—

What did Eloway & Blatteis say of the mass in her lower abdomen near the scar? I hope, since they subordinate it to her serious trouble, that it is not serious. She has always returned from the country marvelously improved & fretted herself into her old condition in a few weeks. With her children away, she becomes melancholy very soon. But Jakey writes that Morris will return shortly; & for my mother such an event is a renaissance; the whole house changes and she is a hundred times as vigorous. The moment he leaves, I ought to return, & these delightful shocks never end—

Morris Schapiro (1903–96). Schapiro's older brother.

You say, she looked at you when she spoke of me! why she always looked at me when she spoke of you—in fact she would speak of you to look at me—

Nov 22

I was interrupted, dear, & this is another day with another letter from you—I assure you I am well, have neither the heart-disease nor the constipation nor the leprosy you studied recently. Like everybody else, you say, you have passed your state-boards; but nothing I am sure became you so well as the "passing" of them.

Rey came from Toulouse to-day to lecture at the Louvre; & we spent the evening & afternoon together. His lecture was fine: he was comical to my friends & myself—He spoke on the architecture of Toulouse, began in a slow deliberate manner with impeccable enunciation, discussing mechanical problems very precisely, but soon he had to explain first causes, became more & more excited, lapsed into southern accent, emotion, rapidity, gesticulation; until the projecting machine failed to work & he had to stammer his way back to clarity. After supper we were to have coffee—He did not like the first few cafés we passed, because they were not "serious"—He chose one which was frequented by southerners who played cards, but where exceptionally fine coffee was served—

The Sorbonne does not open until Dec. 3—what a wonderful schedule it posts in the streets; I do not know what to choose: it may be that I shall only attend occasional lectures. The science courses are especially attractive: Perrin & Becquerel & Brunhes are listed—There are no general subject-matters as at home but single problems considered for several months, different each year. Now I am working with the manuscripts in the library which closes at 4 PM since one dares not install lights in the manuscript room; it has the most precious objects in the world—When I asked for the Godescalc Evangeliary the attendant was very angry as if I were Oliver Twist—really scandalized—why did I want it? was I not satisfied with the facsimiles? They are incomplete, reproducing only a dozen pages. I will have to wait a few days until the Administrateur, Omont, signs my request—When the attendant learned that I was a Carnegie Fellow, he said "Why don't they give us some money?"—a good question that Shapely asked at home once. In the afternoon there are no seats for study in the Bibliotheque Nationale, the building is shabby & too small, the service very poor—no books given after 3 PM, etc, etc.

The manuscripts are fascinating to study,—even the less precious ones—I came upon a catalogue written in the 12th c. of the library of the abbaye of Cluny—It should be published with every mediaeval history; it tells us what was read or known at this time in a remarkably clear way; the list is astonishing, it is a real inventory of intellectual culture—Most of the books have disappeared with the religious wars & the Revolution & I am studying the miniatures of those that survive: I have found clear Byzantine & Greek types, Irish initials, a few Germanic details, & the presence of an actual oriental worker—perhaps a Syrian,—beside the local traditions. But these manuscripts are little things beside the Godescalc about which I am excited in anticipation—I learned at Toulouse, where I had observed many oriental details of architecture & ornament, that the Basilica of St. Sernin had possessed a richly illuminated Evangeliary, given to it by Charlemagne and that it was now in Paris. I was surprised in Paris to read that this St. Sernin Ms. was the Godescalc, written in 781/2: for we had studied it with Dewald & read Strzygowski's proofs of the Syrian origins of its miniature style, but had never noted its long history in Toulouse—Since it is believed to-day that monumental sculpture first appeared in Western Europe in Toulouse, and under the influences of manuscript art and oriental objects, this Evangeliary, the only illuminated one preserved from early mediaeval Toulouse, should be of capital interest—It may be that its figures & ornaments have nothing to do with Toulouse Romanesque sculpture, which should delight some students, & be as interesting as any confirmation. This "orientalistic" scholarship is still a vague business—At Poitiers a drunken man engaged me in conversation while I was drawing & taking notes of

Jean Perrin (1870–1942). French physicist and recipient of the Nobel Prize in Physics in 1926.
Jean Becquerel (1878–1953). French physicist and one of the first in France to teach quantum theory and Einstein's theory of relativity.
Jean Brunhes (1869–1930). French geographer who pioneered the study of human geography in France.
Godescalc Evangeliary. Paris, Bibliothèque nationale de France, MS n.a.l. 1203.
Henri A. Omont (1857–1940). French paleographer, medievalist, and keeper of manuscripts at the Bibliothèque nationale de France. When Schapiro asked why it was so difficult to see the manuscripts, Omont said that they were "saving the manuscripts for posterity." Schapiro told Omont, "Consider me the posterity for which you are saving them." Omont laughed and agreed.
John Shapley (ca. 1890–1978). Art historian who taught at New York University and headed a project for the Carnegie Corporation.

the Romanesque façade of Notre-Dame-la-Grande—He told me that all the birds, beasts, scrolls & monstrous combinations in the spandrels came from the East—How do you know? He answered—how do you know? When I told him I didn't, he said he learned it at school—Evidently one taught these ideas at least 30 years ago—but he was even more precise[;] he mentioned the crusades & added that another church in Poitiers built before the crusade had none of these motifs. This was an equal exaggeration but quite familiar. I read an article written about 1835 which said that after a period of darkest, artless barbarism it was the Orient which supplied fresh motifs & formed Western arts—But the "Orient" is 3 times the size of Europe & is not divided from it; perhaps it will be possible some day to trace these changes more precisely.

In the meantime—I have concluded a happy voyage in which I have seen wonders, and learned gaily & with passion. My mind feels differently & thinks in other ways about matters that had occupied me long before; but it has happened unconsciously, as if I have acquired a new craft—And it is a craft—for the greater part of the journey's experience was in learning by touching, seeing & moving about objects—school now seems strangely passive or another habit with other ends. I love architecture all the more. May we make this same journey many times together, sweetheart—

Meyer.

Paris, 2 December 1926

Dear Lillian:

You must not call me "wise," because I once seemed weary of trifles—I might simply have been weary. I prefer your own sweet evenness of temper, which it gives me joy to reflect upon & recapture, if only in thought.

Lars Olof Jonathan Söderblom (1866–1931). Archbishop of Upsala in the Church of Sweden and recipient of the Nobel Peace Prize in 1930.

Robert Lowie (1883–1957). Austrian-born American anthropologist whose fieldwork was on Native Americans and who taught at the University of California, Berkeley.

To-night I heard a beautiful man, Bishop Söderbloom of Upsala, talk on the French in Sweden & the Swedes in France. But really he spoke of himself—of his student days at the Sorbonne & of his teachers—He has written fine books on comparative religion (Lowie discusses them, you remember) & theology. Sometimes he became very dramatic in elocution, like stereotyped orators; but with such beautiful tone that the audience applauded in the midst of the speech, & he stopped to drink water—He seemed to give himself cues,—which was delightful to watch—he was so honest with his audience & his ideas—And when, after much hoarse patriotic trembling, Jeanne d'Arc, etc, he described how noble were his Paris professors[,] how generous this foreign university to one poor eager Swede, the chairman concluded by a speech equally stirring, of his own visit to Upsala & the kindness of Sweden to a poor foreign philologist—What especially excited Söderbloom were certain coincidences of his own life & the past history of the intercourse of France & Sweden. His cathedral was the first Gothic church in Sweden & was built by French architects & workmen in the manner of Notre Dame de Paris where he had so often studied; the 1st bishop of Upsala was ordained in Sens, which he visited recently; he stood before the very altar: And more astonishing to him—the sacramentary used in that, for him so memorable occasion[,] has been in Stockholm the last hundred years. It was bought in Paris by a Swedish princess—While a student in Paris, he felt it a sacred duty to his country to seek its souvenirs in France—& he hunted in mediaeval cartularies for names of Swedish students: he found many engraved on the walls of an old church, St Julien-des-Pauvres—He recalled in piety that if the first Scandinavians in France came as robbers, the 1st French came as noble Christian missionaries. (Et me voila un evêque!—he might have said) Since then it has been a contact only of the spirit—The chairman felt that the celebrated atheism of the Sorbonne owed some apology to so learned & gracious an archbishop & so liberal a student of comparative religion; & he pointed out that altho the Faculty of Theology has been abolished, never have religion & theology been more seriously pursued as scientific subjects; & he listed the new courses, which the ancient faculty never dreamed of—

I am still with the manuscripts which will never end—Omont told me of a vast collection—of Coptic & Ethiopian books—when I have finished the Cluniac mss, I will turn to them—In the meantime I am neglecting the museums (the Cernuschi[] of the Far East is 10,000 distractions) & the architecture—except on Sundays when the library is closed—What items for future trips I store up now—But I will be glad to return home & hop with you the live long day: with love, dear Lillian,

Meyer.

Paris, 10 December 1926

Dearsest Lillian:

It is good to hear what you say of Jakey. It was already in the air several weeks ago: he wrote me that he was not displeased with himself & enjoyed the company of Sam Rosenberg & Haggin—School no longer bothered him—but not because he managed his studies—He had won the good will of his "lady" teachers! He commented with a charmingly complacent asperity on the "educational system—" & its "so-called liberalism"—

Bernard Haggin (1900–1987). American writer and music critic who corresponded with Schapiro through the 1930s.

Marty tells me that Jakey wishes to write—that Kip, like a father, or better—an uncle, asks the real father, Marty[,] to dissuade Jakey, for Kip knows the business, its trials, pains, & disillusionment! But Marty would rather have him play football—& like himself, write in leisure moments.

Martin "Marty" Raphael. Friend of Schapiro's from Columbia University.

If your ills are only experimental, dear, & escape even your mother—I am very happy—But you would only speak of such & no others, & I can only hope—There has been a great fog over Paris these last 2 days, & one can see nothing—

Meyer.

Paris, 15 December 1926

Dearest Lillian:

The study of the Cluny manuscripts is so much more than I had thought that it requires a routine—a daily session from 9 to 4 in one place for several weeks—And I have found about 40 Mss. from Moissac which are still unedited, and over

65 from Limoges—all bearing upon Romanesque problems—I do not think I will have any time for any Coptic or Byzantine Mss.

Occasionally I find amusing marginal comments in an 11th or 12th c hand—"by no means not beautiful" or "thus the deep Cyprianus," and at the end of one book a novel theory of inspiration—

"Perdito dente compulsus sum versum componere.
Potridus engive[?] deus nostrae cecidit ecce.
Prandens multa tulit pransus et ipse perit"

Richard Hamann (1879–1961). German professor of art history at the Philipps-Universität Marburg who corresponded and exchanged photographs with Schapiro from 1927 into the 1930s.

Paul Deschamps (1888–1974). French historian of Romanesque sculpture.

Karl Hermann Usener (1905–?). German historian of medieval art.

"Clemen & Goldschmidt." Paul Clemen, *Kunstschutz im Kriege…*, 2 vols. (Leipzig: E. A. Seemann, 1919), and Adolph Goldschmidt, *Die Elfenbeinskulpturen*, vols. 1 and 2, *Aus der Zeit der karolingischen und sächsischen Kaiser* (Berlin: B. Cassirer, 1914–26).

Camille Jullian (1859–1933). French historian and philologist.

I met a German student from Marburg, who is preparing a work on the Romanesque of the Low Countries—His professor, Richard Hamann, (whose fine photographs of the Olympia sculptures, at the German Book Exhibit, you may remember) made a journey thru France with 4 students, & 5 specially constructed cameras, & photographed over 3,000 details of Mediaeval architecture & sculpture, for the Kunstgeschichtl. Seminar of Marburg. This is more than the French have ever done in their own country & Deschamps grew pale when he heard of it; I trembled for my own inefficiency—Usener showed me very beautiful prints of Belgian architecture made in 1915 during the German occupation. A group of professors had invaded the libraries & buildings & classified & studied everything—Shortly after the war, Clemen & Goldschmidt published 2 large volumes on Belgian monuments, & I am assured that these are a very small fraction of what was actually done—I have interesting talks with this student; I know nothing of his subject, he has very confused recollections of "mine" from Prof. Hamann—In spite of all the detailed studies, & methodical investigations, & the contempt for "theoretische" works, his reasons for any solution are usually "feeling,["] "Stil,"—something looks earlier, or later, related or unrelated—with nothing more precise—It is clear that the same man can be absolutely scientific in details, in gathering materials, etc—& crown his labors with "intuitions" or spiritualistic conjectures, sometimes with great success. But it is not only the German who does this; to-day I heard Camille Jullian, who writes beautifully on Gallo-Roman archaeology, history, language, etc—lecture on Gallo-Roman industry—But instead of the facts which he has unearthed after years of research—he gave, in a trembling voice & with the contrasts of a sick prophet, a highly imaginative account of the dignity of the life of the Gaulois, the beauty of their reverent gestures, their ideal home environment, the artistic perfection of their implements, arising from perfect & undisguised utility,—& he concluded with an attack on bobbed hair & short skirts & the wicked Americans, the modern Romans, who despoil the French.—the modern Greeks—There were more than 200 present; I seemed to be the only one under 50—The applause was terrible to hear—it was frequent; for he often mentioned the greatness of France & the Church—

At one point, an asymptotic digression, trying to demonstrate how the contact of the Church made all things divine, he read with wonderful impressive feeling the verses of the Chanson de Roland which describe how Roland tried to break Durendal, his sword, & how it resisted the stone & flew to heaven—Who did not weep? The applause was the longest — I did not think Jullian had such a wicked face, from his fine books — Momméja told me that he is a victim of his gifts of presentation — that confronted by a public & his own voice, the more austere investigations of his solitude take wings — I was often warned against him — sometimes by people who knew nothing of his subject, but had overheard criticisms — This is always annoying —

How are you, dear—after this long speech—& academico-theologico-archaeologico tractatus—? Mine are lonely pleasures—Ten times during the day I think that I will tell you this or that — for which writing is no substitute. Writing demands some continuity & whereas we sat for a long time together & occasionally spoke (or I made a speech — an amorous quantum theory) — I have heard twice from Jakey since my last letter: He often writes beautifully — suspecting nothing — His first letters seem from a different person — He says "Hell" occasionally, — but he has found other ways of being forceful, & inelegantly virile — He likes many things —

with love, darling,

Meyer.

Paris, 23 December 1926

Dearest Lillian —

It is so good of you to wish me many happy voyages: I could wish them myself — & especially one, home, to you at this moment — what I wrote you was the excitement of a first trip; I must demand new things of each succeeding, or interest will stale, & the duplication of the inevitable troubles will be the clearest fact & a great annoyance — Once, dear, you wrote me "promise you will revisit the things that delighted you." To-day such fulfillment seems remote, except where dictated by the work. I cannot travel for the pleasure, but what pleasure follows, in what I call "work" — even among arid details.

I finished the Cluny Mss — & now I am working with those from Moissac — which are much richer, & more important — tho even less known — I am afraid that I will not finish the study — since there are so many other things to be done — To day I left Paris for the St Germain-en-Laye museum, which has materials for a year's work — wonderful prehistoric collections, & rooms of primitive cultures for comparison, and Celtic, Gallo-Roman & Folk-Wandering remains. The museum is almost as large as the Metropolitan & more crowded with objects — Here is something to which I will often return — The town itself & the country about it are charming — small, domestic, with many rivers & bits of wood — You remember how troubled I was over the reports of Paris winter weather — It hardly rains or snows — the days are clear & windy as in late autumn at home when we walked so much — & returned to drink tea, our noses quite red & happy —

with love, darling Lillian

Meyer.

Paris, 30 December 1926

Dear Lillian:

You wrote me of your professor who recommended personal suffering to students—to make them better physicians—and of Mrs. Geltman & Betty. I once heard your aunt say that she herself wished to study medicine—Recently I heard another mother say the same thing, & regret her advanced years—At least her child would be a doctor. She had a profound admiration for the man who delivered her baby, and went into great detail to describe his charms, kindness, intelligence, superiority, reputation, etc—She despised women who were fussy or cowards in illness, who screamed excessively in labor, who demanded constant attention and sentimentalized suffering—I learned that hers was a Caesarian baby. She recounted all her operations to expose her courage.

"Mrs. Geltman & Betty." Lillian's aunt and cousin, respectively.

I find that among the news of South American society in Paris in the *Paris Herald,* operations are frequently mentioned as social notes. Perhaps there are no competent physicians at home, & one travels to Europe—A few years ago such details were common in NY. & were caricatured in the comic papers as parvenu ostentation—The earnest talk I heard of operations was almost unreal—as if I were listening to an unbroken series of quotations—

You surely need no illness, dear, to be sympathetic—Here, illness had become a source of pride, and ordinary sympathy overlaid by contempt—

Meyer.

I must tell you, dear, about the work. The manuscripts from Moissac are so rich & fruitful, that I jump with every new volume. It is all brand new to me. In addition, I am studying a new problem. Prof. Rand wrote me from Tours that he had discovered a distinct break in the system of confronting and ruling pages in the Carolingian period which could be used to determine the chronology of various undated Mss—I spoke to Omont of it: & he showed me an old discussion of it 40 years ago, by an American—the first and last essay on the subject; he was delighted that the matter was being restudied—But in the last dozen Mss I have handled I have found still another system—but with many complicated exceptions, that are interesting to analyze—In Greek Mss. there is believed to be an almost unvarying method of quaternions, hair side always facing hair; and flesh side flesh. Rand has found an HFHF (instead of HFFH) Latin group after 850 AD. In Moissac the leaves are HFFH, the old style, but with the ruling, leaf by leaf, instead of 2 at a time, or with one broad leaf folded and ruled—But this is a side issue: the ornament, miniatures & palaeography occupy most of my time. I showed drawings of them to my German friend who is all excited, since the Moissac Mss are neither catalogued nor published—& bear upon his studies—he is going to photograph them with Prof. Hamann.——

"HFHF." Abbreviation for hair, flesh, hair, flesh. Schapiro's examination of this problem can be seen in his notes on MS Lat. 1822 (Paris, Bibliothèque nationale de France); see notebook transcription no. 36, in this volume.

with my love,

Meyer—

Paris, 3 January 1927

Dear Lillian:

Will you send me a list of the books which have arrived. Five packages were sent to NY: you mentioned only three. Perhaps by this time the other two have arrived, & this trouble needless. Since I leave France in less than a month, I wish to be sure of the delivery. Later, communication with the dealer will be more difficult.

What a gruesome story of the pregnant woman & the not-up-to-the-minute-on-his-pathology-surgeon! It is wonderful that she can be mis-judged, abandoned, reopened, & cut so easily—You do not say if she survived all this guess work & manipulation—When I was a child I heard gossip about ladies who lived with sponges in their bellies, that careless nurses or doctors had overlooked: & the outcome was a lawsuit for damages. I read in Augustine that God is a divine lake in which floats a great sponge, the world, which swells with divinity—

With love,

Meyer.

Paris, 10 January 1927

Dearest Lillian:

I am not so far away when I read your letter about Christmas which is already remote. Why Elsa has a friend in Japan who calculates for replies, & your Dr. Cherin (there was a Dr. Chubb who writes on Lord Byron) delays opening packages till Christmas. And now it is the middle of January, or has been, since really, it is the end of the month & I will read your reply in February somewhere in Italy. A whole half-year gone! I have hardly moved: but I feel as if space is different & the whole world more accessible. Once distance was so forbidding that I circumscribed my studies to avoid travel—now I touch nothing which does not suggest some trip, & my summers are filled for twenty years—What shall I choose?—No sooner did I read Contenau than I was resolved to study Semitic philology when I returned to NY, but why not Iranian or Chinese—why not more palaeography or prehistories? These are all about me—neighbors whom I salute every day—I draw up lists of things still to be done in Paris in the remaining two weeks—I am disturbed, as if pursued & sure to be overtaken; I compromise hour after hour—omit this & that—postpone perhaps forever—Do you remember, dear, you told me to revisit everything I loved—I think I have said this before—you can see me scratch my head, & refuse to follow the thought—

Edwin W. Chubb (1865–1959). *Stories of Authors, British and American* (New York: Sturgis & Walton, 1910).

Georges B. Contenau (1877–1964). French curator of ancient oriental art at the Louvre who led and published on excavations in the Near East.

I still see Deschamps & Enlart & Omont, but more of German friends whom I have met in the library—Prof. Hamann (I mentioned him in the summer without naming him), teaches at Marburg—travels much in France, photographing everything—He is here with wife, son & daughter, who look like healthy peasants beside him, with fat red cheeks & slow talk—There are other students of his in Paris—each different from the other, so that one could hardly give the Germans a name on the basis of their behavior—one is astonishingly "American"—sports, pep—slapstick, chewing-gum—etc—[] a Ph.D. in "Kulturgeschichte" (which interests him in obscene Folk-lore & art to explain Zeit-geist & Volkstreben). He tells me he is a boy-scout & crazy about America, which he will soon visit—But some are high-minded Kantian philosophers—who nevertheless will play with a baby in a restaurant——

Your account of the birth of the baby was lovely, darling—How nicely the preparations ended in the little head—I forgot how gruesome & terrible is the whole process, in the conclusion—You mention only the danger, the precaution, & the successful outcome, whereas ordinarily I can think of birth only in terms of the shrieking & agony. I have heard in great fear about me since I was a little child; and my own body, similarly wracked, with so many people walking the streets full grown, and some already in decay, birth seems a remote thing & a small event, once in every lifetime & no woman is regarded, in memory of such experience, in any new light, & judgment is sooner determined by a pimple or a gesture than by regard for an experience, whose analogue in suffering or importance would elicit the most profound respect & curiosity for all time. Perhaps in nature it is like breathing or eating and an indifferent matter, so necessary, mechanical, fixed, as to be capable of little development or variety. You know the saying about "the powerful faculty of forgetting which renders women true forces of nature," said, I am sure, a good distance away from a hospital to gild a perplexing fact—Even women will pull each other's hair, & between periods of pregnancy identify the whole dignity of human beings with particular manners or possessions. It is a little strange that the Church Fathers who taught that marriage was justified only for procreation, that desire is a wicked excess, should have regarded women as unclean beasts—I read it only today in Gregory the Great & Halitgarius—The latter says that desire comes from what is left in the belly, since the genital organs lie directly beneath it (which can be cited as a mediaeval anticipation of modern studies of protozoan reproduction). Then he should not blame women as agents-provocateurs of the devil—But, says Jerome, lubricity is the way of adolescence, and Augustine—it is a rare youth who has not committed enormities—And so on, ad inf.—

At the same time I received your letter & one from a friend at home who is despondent & wishes to die—& from another that he will soon make 20,000 dollars a year, & has no illusions (I guess)—Jakey seemed unhappy in his last letter, which reached me more than 2 weeks ago—and after such a long period (2 months) of cheerful correspondence! It is good of you to speak to him about medicine; tho it is hardly likely that he will undertake anything which demands so violent a break with his habits & so much work—at the present time—He wrote me once that he didn't like something because it was archaeology. I think he can easily be excited by it, yet I do not know if it would be at all wise.—I wish we could travel together for some short time—I will always encourage him to cross the ocean, to learn languages, to move alone among new people & objects. At this distance I love him more than ever & I am eager for any word from him. Sometimes I must hurt him by unkind or thoughtless writing—I can never guess in what mood I will reach him—

His letters have improved enormously—in the beginning they were confused, & pathetically rambling & desperate. And now when he has to express the same feelings, his insistence takes on form, he talks to his own self and to me, and unconsciously attains an elegance, which is not at all ornamental—Once he entered into a long dialectic on happiness that was a delight to read, and was unpleasant to think upon—I am sure he is growing; it appears in every sentence, with crudity & all—I can only hope that I will find him with some eagerness for life; he is so quickly depressed, & without resource for recovery.

With my love, darling,

Meyer.

Paris, 17 January 1927

Dearest Lillian:

I have just written to Jakey—in reply to a long letter of his—as long as all the others put together, & even more cheerless. But it began so happily, with news of his reading, & his admiration for Romain Rolland—quel homme! quelles ideés! & soon he remembered school, home, future—etc—& became despondent—

Romain Rolland (1866–1944). French novelist, dramatist, and essayist.

His hand is so uneven that the words seem to betray some confusion & instability—But he addressed the envelope in another style, with letters regular—as if written on ruled lines—And he wrapped the letter in 2 envelopes, each addressed to me with only the outer stamped—Touching precaution—He appeals to me for advice which he anticipates, & begs me not to give him—The act of writing—itself—depresses him—so he can say nothing without confronting me with questions. And since I see him only in his letters—& since he will write usually when sad or troubled or become so in writing—I form a dark picture of his mind—

He has met Natalie & likes her very much—; he wrote me he would like to dine with her—I am ashamed to have neglected writing to her, dear—Surely—this week—

With love,

Meyer

Vienne, 26 January 1927

Dear Lillian:

My friend was anxious to make this journey, because when I returned 2 months ago, I gave such scandalously lurid reports of the provinces—Now after 5 days, he is quite weary—We have had long train rides, poor meals & hotels, unexpected expense, rain, snow & slush, closed museums—& worst of all things—we have missed trains twice—

"My friend." Herman Wechsler (1904–76) accompanied Schapiro to Egypt; he is mentioned by Edward Rand in a letter introducing Schapiro to George A. Reisner (1867–1942).

We were very glad to leave Paris—not that we disliked it—I would gladly have remained & continued to work there as before—& my friend loves the city—for it is quite comfortable, exciting & free—But once we had decided to go, there were such tremendous details of moving & closing up—really, like a business—or a registrar's office at the beginning or end of school—that they alone made the trip essential—if only as a conclusion to our troubles—We left on our predicted day—

On the way to the station I had letters from you & Jakey, darling—You spoke of cool windy days & the meridians between us. I was too confused to calculate the hours—; but since I sprawled for 5 hours in an empty train, I dared not think that I, too, was fighting—It was dark and wet, the windows could not forever be wiped with the fingers to reveal a moment's landscape—& we accepted our cabins, playfully recounted the possibilities of travel, read a little Italian to teach each other—(what color is this book? It is not red, it is black—The pencil is long & thin, & etc) observed the few others in the train—and even slept—In Dijon we saw snow cover the ground—the 1st time this winter—My friend was a little sick—

The next day I spent in the library with Cistercian Mss and some books from St Bénigne of Dijon—I used Deschamp's name as a means of introduction to Oursel, the librarian. I was given whatever I wished, overwhelmed with favors, personal attention—& even given reprints of Oursel's articles—But so many hours were spent in talk with Oursel, that I had little chance to see all I wished & I promised myself to return. The Mss. were magnificent works: my friend was ravished by them—they were the first he had ever handled & he thought the day happily spent—

Charles Oursel (1876?–1967). French director of the Bibliothèque municipale de Dijon from 1904 to 1959.

Then our train was held up miles away—we waited 3 hours in the cold station, & in despair returned to the hotel—The next morning—on the way to Lyon we stopped at Beaune to see Roger van der Weyden's retable of the *Last Judgment* & the 15th century hospital of Rollin—A wicked old man refused us admission until 3 PM—& our train was to leave at 2:40. We met a French boy who told us of fine Gothic houses & led us to them—we missed our train—There was no other till 8 in the evening—we could return to the hospital & see the picture—& other beautiful things—that repaid us for the delay—But the days were miserably wet—And it was hard to oppose beauty & understanding to discomfort—For me the rides were happy since I read for the first time books by Rainer Rilke, and Marcel Schwob—& I dozed into pleasant dreams when I did not read & lived in a melancholy haze.—

Nicolas Rolin (1376–1462). French chancellor of Burgundy for whom *The Last Judgment* was painted. *The Last Judgment* was created for the altar of a chapel adjoining the principal hospital ward of the Hôtel-Dieu in Beaune.

Rainer Maria Rilke (1875–1926). German-language poet.
Marcel Schwob (1867–1905). French writer.

The morning in Lyon was so like N.Y.—we remarked it together—& were continually felicitating each other on this resemblance—The obscurity of certain grey streets, with trolley cars, small stores, & odors,—& then the rivers sides—the long island, like Manhattan between two streams, and palisades with stepped buildings on one shore—and the play of dotted prismatic houses with broken silhouettes—these were very much like NY—The church of St Martin d'Ainay was delightful—It grew so cold as I studied its exterior—that I gave up & worked within—There the darkness was a difficulty—the spring of the vaulting uncertain—pilaster cap ornament, at best a conjecture—& so on, till at noon, after what seemed an endless baptism of some atheistic baby who bawled & bawled, the church was closed till 2;—There was a later cathedral of the 13th & 14th c. & a 15th c. church which the Age of Reason had further disfigured with some classic pretensions—The toes of a bronze St. Peter shone beyond the dull figure from the polish of pious kissing—It was interesting to regard in these 3 buildings constructed in a period of over 400 years in 3 different styles—with different ornament & equilibrium, how the same plan and conception of interior spacing persisted.

At the Lyon library we studied more Mss—& were as graciously received, in an office—that was more a salon than a work room. We hardly studied—there was little time for systematic notation & analysis—we ran rapidly thru a half dozen volumes—wrote a bit—& admired the beautiful—

To-day we visited the textile museum built by the Chamber of Commerce of the town—Nothing could honor a Chamber of Commerce more than this collection—Everywhere I select in thought some few objects or sites that we will surely visit together, dear—How you will love this place & the silks & damasks, brocades, velvets, tapestries & rugs—The richness & no. of specimens made study impossible—we walked from Coptic to Persian to Byzantine to Sicilian to Venetian & so on & overlooked much & contented ourselves with a few pieces of each—Such fantastic cloth—for rooms we saw only the perfection of cultures & styles—Their uses were hard to conceive—when they were so satisfying, so complete here on the walls—

In the afternoon, we learned that the Museums of Painting & Sculpture & Ethnography & Archaeology were closed for the day—which was irritating—& which made my friend very melancholy—

Here we are in Vienne—tomorrow afternoon in Valence, then Orange & Avignon & the warm Mediterranean coast where we hope to lie in the sun—To-day in Lyon we sat for 2 hours in the sun—but we could not imagine it spring—We moved our places & turned our heads to remain in the sun—

with love, darling Lillian,

Meyer—

Avignon, 28 January 1927

Dear, dear, Lillian:

How all things have changed since I last wrote you—If there were nothing but the sunlight we would be happy—In each town, for several days, we calculated southward, and wondered how far off was the sea, how soon we would approach warm weather—In Dijon, snow, Beaune, slush—Lyon, clear and very cold and damp—In Vienne, a little brighter, in Orange: at last, some warmth, hill tops and sunshine—

But to-day at Avignon we entered the promised land—we are 2 hours from the coast (which matters little—), under the bluest sky, which hardly changes, always clear & cloudless—There is a river, ramparts, castles, churches, palaces & frescoes—Roman antiquities—& other objects to occupy me—It was so lovely on the palace terrace, beside the church of domes, (Our Lady of the Domes, it is called), gardens about, river and bridge below, and more distant castles, on the opposite, rising banks—that we lay for hours, sat and mused—my friend read *The Life of Jesus* (Renan)—& did little work—Yet surely the place is more interesting than the comfort & the sentiment—which we could not easily shake off—We agreed Avignon was to be our next vacation—our ideal convalescence from all miseries—

Ernest Renan (1823–92). French philosopher, historian, scholar of religion, and author of the controversial *La vie de Jesus* (1863).

And this is January, N.Y.'s latitude—a little way from Paris—

We had been so depressed by the bad days so far south as Vienne, that to lighten the shock of impending disappointments we thought—it is winter, and everywhere in France—and even in Marseilles & Nice—this will continue—what a gracious surprise! I planned to stay another day—for there was much to be done as well as enjoyed in Avignon—a whole museum of the choicest classical and early mediaeval objects—pre-Visigothic horseshoe arches—complete series (in time) of inscriptions—sculpture, glassware & pottery, & a sufficient no. of specimens of single ornaments to trace things with simplicity—And the Palace of the Popes—which we hardly saw—or seeing, could only admire—and ah! & oh!, and use as an elevated platform for panoramic thrills—the palace is too fine & complicated as architecture to be understood in an hour indoors—And I do not mention, the churches of the town—and the old houses & Manuscripts—Girard, the museum director permits me to photo what I please—with no fees—or restrictions (Enlart's name is the pass-word)[.]

Joseph Girard (1881–1962). French curator of the Bibliothèque et musée Calvet.

But I am going on to Arles instead—with the idea that in June or July I will return, & work more systematically.

The same at Vienne—a town dirty, but rich—& picturesque in rivers & mounting house-clusters—I enter an old church, now a museum—& I see architect[ural] forms that are astonishing,—that recall a 1000 things—& suggest more—& before I can begin to draw—details spring up—bits of sculpture & old Roman pieces.—& the distraction is so complete—that I must give 2 or 3 days to the place—But I must leave it promising to return—It is so, that travelling, I leave behind a secondary trail of temporarily abandoned clues which I must surely pick up,—or make an indifferent face and regret—

In Orange, we had a foretaste of Avignon—sitting on the hillside above the theater & climbing the rocks, to photo the town, the circles of seats and stage—It was market day, the whole town looked mean, crowded & noisy—but where songs were peddled—it was very gay—The theater was too isolated from its surroundings to impress its sentiment or its power in construction on the whole town—But in Avignon—the palace & church & gardens were of one piece with the geography & the city walls—the whole region was glorified—A single chamber in the palace has such a superiority of shape—even of thoughtfulness—over the whole modern growth—that soon one relapses into "the good old days" & there are tears for things, etc—The elegance is in places fantastic, the wardrobe has choice pagan frescoes to amuse popes who call this "a Babylonian captivity"—the courtyards are great gardens, seen from a loggia which is a chapel porch—all varieties of vaulting—barreled and ribbed, fan, squinches, elliptical domes, and penetrations, are nicely displayed—To suffuse light, & make fine shadows—the windows are splayed with enormous concave jambs—There are tombs to celebrate the masters—some decorated portals, but otherwise there is little carved ornament—only paintings—frescoes, and tapestries, and I suppose great ceremony & the costumes of those who entered—But all this is a small part of what is seen or felt—It is good to be here—Renan's play "L'eau de Jouvence" ("Fountain of Youth") is set in Avignon—& John Stuart Mill came here to die—Your sweetheart,

Meyer.

John Stuart Mill (1806–73). English philosopher, economist, and exponent of utilitarianism.

Pisa, 2 February 1927

Dearest Lillian:

I have changed my plan & am leaving for Egypt in a few days. I will embark at Naples, Feb. 7, on the Katori Maru—I could take this same boat at Marseilles on the 5th—but Marseilles is unpleasant to wait in, and the archaeological excitements of the surrounding country (Nîmes, St. Gilles, Vaison) do not move my friend—So we are rushing thru Genoa, Pisa, Florence, Rome & Naples, riding a good deal in trains, our eyes jumping from books to landscape when we emerge from the tunnels along the sea. What we have seen of Genoa & Pisa is so wonderful that I regret to move on, & my earlier allotment of time to Italy, France, Spain, etc now seems very bad—

I began earlier this evening to write about the last few days of travel,—of Arles, Marseilles, Nice, Ventimiglia & our day in Italy—but I was dissatisfied, & imagined all these things with us, dear, rather than between. I attended a mass for the dead in the cathedral of San Lorenzo in Genoa,—distracted by my curiosity—for I had attended the same service many times in Toulouse, until the triforium could be opened for me—And there was this difference between them—that in Genoa the procession was very long & more solemn & was led by long gowned boys who were either angelic and in terrible fear or little black imbeciles with dainty candles—Behind were older boys some already tonsured—some with a peculiar adolescent greasiness, shamefaced and hairy, followed by the canons, whose candles were immense—When the procession ended, to occupy the sanctuary, & the sacred vestments were assumed with the barest rite, the mass began as in Toulouse, in Autun, in Moissac and Paris and I left the hall. In Toulouse I had entered long before and as I worked in the galleries among the capitals, I could see the choir cleared by the men, & the funeral furniture erected from separate pieces marked & painted for certain architectural illusions—In Toulouse the friends sat, & rose from time to time—but in Genoa—they seemed so overcome by some sense of spectacle that they stood in disorder watching the procession—& then gathered before the choir, still standing—The procession was a spectacle—what notion could one form but of senility & impotence from such expression & such choice of celebrants—There were old canons whose noses almost touched the ground, and others whose candles shook; before one man who seemed self-satisfied as well as stupid, women knelt & beggars put on very pious airs—Later I reentered the church, but the service was still on, & in a dark corner I began to make notes of the structure, the vaults, the arcading and ornament. In the north aisle & chapels are wonderful mediaeval tombs of Genoa prelates & nobility; their heads are carved in marble—such fine sturdy heads, even when malicious, that the whole church & the city are plausible as their creations. But I must go into the streets to find these men again. An usher told me "it is mass & one must not draw or write."—and I left the interior—the last time—

In St Sernin at Toulouse the service was mainly in the nave, which is a long gloomy vault on powerful arcades—Here the nave is empty during the mass; The office is sung in the apse, the crowd watches in the transept—And all this is curiously bound up with the architecture itself, for the nave, the beautiful portion of the church, is of the 14th century, in the belated Romanesque style of the region, a simple structure, very light, incompetently balanced (tie rods were added later); while the East End of the church is of the late Renaissance, a gaudy expensive business, strange to its neighbor—You should see the exterior of this building, dear—full of jewels of stone work—& itself made of exquisite walls—only this late afternoon at Pisa I saw pieces as fine—with a similar lightness & elegance of parts—There is no understanding of solid masses like that of the French builders—but always beautiful walls, arcades, colored marbles and "endless" (technical term here!) ornament—And at Pisa, a rare setting, with plain grassy grounds for several blocks about, and four such buildings, each different in plan, grouped in happy silhouettes.

I return to them to-morrow morning, to look more closely (the Leaning Tower is quite simple to explain; I am amazed by the awful fuss Goodyear made over it) to see the interiors & the details. There is also a Museum of painting & sculpture & the old Campo Santo with frescoes of the Plague & the Last Judgment—Then Florence—where I shall try to find Rand, who wrote me at Marseilles, but left no address—

William Henry Goodyear (1846–1923). American archae-ologist and architectural historian who decried those who believed that the Pisa campanile would soon collapse.

Tell me how are you, darling Lillian—The time flies for me—

With love,

Meyer.

Rome, 5 February 1927

Lillian, dear:

You are kind to send me Allen's address & should have no scruples about my desire for this information. I wrote to my father for an address in Palestine—but received no reply. Since then Deschamps has told me of several friends in Jerusalem, Beyrouth, Damascus, etc and Enlart, of others. In Paris, I learned from an American, Prof. Radin of California[] (brother of a Radin I knew from the anthropology seminars at Columbia) that there were many synagogues of the Hellenistic period in Galilee that were little known; & when I mentioned to him the expeditions of Kitchener & Conder & the work of the Palestine Exploration Society & the German Palestine-Verein he assured me that even these hard-working gentlemen have neglected the Galilean synagogues. And since years ago I had read various theories of early Christian architecture that tried to parallel the recent results of comparative mythology in relating Christian architecture to individual cult constructions & liturgy, I thought it would be a fine idea to study Galilean synagogues—And I wrote home to my father for addresses of natives who could give me practical geographical & travel information, & perhaps even more: But these are hardly necessary now—Galilean synagogues remain an interesting problem, but they are neither as wonderful nor as unknown as Radin supposed. I found a large literature on the subject in German and French—including a 2 vol. resumé of the whole matter by Watzinger and Kohl, and a monograph by Orfali—At any rate it will excite Jews to know of a distinctive architecture & orna-

Mordecai Allen. Former resident of Jerusalem whom Schapiro's brother Jakey recommended as a source of information.

Max Radin (1880–1950). Polish-born professor of law at the University of California, Berkeley, who had previously taught at Columbia University; brother of Paul Radin (1883–1959), an anthropologist at Columbia University.

"Kitchener & Conder." Horatio H. Kitchener, first Earl of Kitchener (1850–1916), and Claude Reignier Conder (1848–1910) were British officers in the Corps of Royal Engineers; they had published notes on their expeditions in *The Survey of Western Palestine* (1881, 1884).

"Watzinger and Kohl." Carl Watzinger and Heinrich Kohl, *Antike Synagogen in Galilaea* (Leipzig: J. C. Hinrichs'sche, 1916).

Gaudentius Orfali (1889–1926?). Franciscan who examined and restored parts of the synagogue at Capernaum.

ment of their (?) race in Hellenistic & early Christian times. I hope to see some of these buildings, & if time allows, the Jewish painted catacomb of Palmyra—but I will hardly be able to study them in detail.

Allen's address is only a few blocks from where I lived—perhaps I will meet him next summer—or, better, in Jerusalem, as we say on Passover. When I began to day-dream, quite shamelessly about Galilean synagogues (lovely name) I met Zionists everywhere—where I never sought them—great numbers of them, of all nations—all ready with news from Galilee, the latest harvest of Palestine, the bad season, England's perfidy,—and all good Jews must stand together.

At Florence I met Rand again thru the kindness of my landlady who inquired at the police for his registration. I had only his mailing address. How he & his wife love Florence—; they would stay here forever; but she also loves the French Gothic—Since they have so much time they see very little each day in the museums, but have come to know the city & certain individual pieces very well. We talked about many things—always with the shadow of trivial laughter hanging over us—about Florence & Paris and Dante and mystics & some professors. It was said that the use of "sense" as a verb was freshman English, & condemned the style of Prof M. The talk was clearly of its surrounding, and after a pleasant meal, in a foreign city, of people who would soon part, it was quite proper, even delightful in its relaxation of the normal proprieties between strangers. The evil in my mind was that under no other circumstances could it be different—that always it would assume the character of these conditions & accept no debate, novelty (unless renounced by some adroit inconsequence) or criticism—Then Mrs. Rand went to sleep, & Rand and I retired to argue about "ruling & confrontation in quaternions"—& I was very happy to bring him notes of a Carolingian Ms. at Lyon which he had overlooked & which caused him to reserve some statements—& he told me of still further complications—details to observe that I had never observed and he gave me the address of a friend who had been working on the Gellone Sacramentary & who would help me with the Gundohinus & others. And after some very funny remarks, he went to bed.

Gellone Sacramentary. Paris, Bibliothèque nationale de France, MS Lat. 12048.

How I rushed about Florence that afternoon & the following morning—to see almost everything—if only to glimpse what I desired—I knew that I would return & stay then a whole week—but I moved as if this were my only day here. I found the aimlessness of such rapid observation, & its vagueness,—a trouble, and to-day at Rome, I saw very little, but learned the roads & topography for my next visit—I saw Masaccio, Giotto, Arnolfo and Brunelleschi at their very best and was repaid for everything, and tied, in hopes, to this city (Florence)[.]

To-day at Rome I met Westermann (at the American School) who on learning that I was to visit Egypt—wrote out for me, with a graciousness & benevolence unknown in him as Columbia papyrologist, a list of pensions in Egypt—routes & towns & names of good people. The academy itself is so attractive—in a fine villa on the hilltop of S. Pancrazio—with tennis courts—library & gardens—& few people—that I regretted not having gone there last year—(but only for a moment, dear—until I proved how much better is my present fortune, contingent on my remain[ing] last year in America & my visit to France)[.] There were several students in the lounge—all handsome & well satisfied loafers—I remembered the works of artists who had come to the School with prizes; & it was simple to see how 3 years in this spot, in complete ease, among kind academicians, wealthy visitors, Roman traditions & a garden existence—they could only be confirmed in an art of "mural decoration" with classic symbols, affected archaism, & the utmost finish of surface. Hermann, who was with me, was excited by the thought that he could live here, as a Fellow, & began to consider serious study which he had long abandoned—

With love, dear—

Meyer.

Cairo, 12 February 1927

Dear Lillian:

We were delayed almost a day crossing to Port Saïd—We had hardly left Naples when a bad storm arose that put us all to bed & made half the voyage very gloomy. One man died—Some were very seriously ill. We were assured that this is the one week of the year when the Mediterranean is so violent—Beyond Greece, the sun reappeared, we came out once more upon the decks, & thought to recover in the remaining stretch to Egypt. But the storm was renewed, and even more violently than at first—yet it hardly troubled us this second time, and for 2 days while the boat rocked & pitched between sliding water that was surely to overwhelm us, we were playful & easy, & slept well.

We had none of the sunshine & calm that we had so enjoyed in the small intervals of the coast at Marseilles, Nice & Genoa. Some of the passengers felt wickedly cheated, & swore never to travel on this hateful sea or on a Japanese boat again. But what of the man, John Long, who was sent on this voyage by Harley Street specialists to cure him by its restfulness, and died at midnight during the great storm? and a friend of his family, a French lady, who must wait in Port Saïd & arrange for the transportation of the body and return with it alone to the widow & six children, her own rare voyage cut so darkly.

The last night I heard this man, a wealthy journalist, describe his troubles to two young Egyptian doctors—His friend brought out diagnoses, reports & letters from Paris & London—The talk was in English & Arabic; for, years before, the journalist had worked in Egypt, which he was to visit on a vacation.

The news of his death hardly stirred passengers confined by their own nausea, dizziness, & vomiting (not me, dear; besides the others, I was disgustingly comfortable, bedridden by the difficulty of standing up, and a slight headache.) Some did not leave their cabins till we reached Port Saïd. One French lady had this sad story: She had been called from Bagdad that her husband, an English engineer, had fallen & fractured his skull. She was to ride by train from Egypt to Syria, and then for 3 days by auto across the desert to Bagdad. She did not know if her husband was alive—Soon after she suffered from the storm; she thought it was good for her—At Kantara, she changed trains, to Palestine—alone, & very much harassed by the natives whom she could not understand or fight off.

The two Egyptian doctors became good friends of mine, & I will see more of them here—They made at least part of the voyage pleasant for me. And when I have left Egypt far behind, their sayings & doings will always make me happy in recollection. One, Dr. Latif, who had just completed his studies in Munich, was carried off at Port Saïd by his family, & we have not seen him since. What a circle they formed around him! When they heard him actually speak German they beamed upon each other & embraced for joy—On the boat he was very playful & child-like, mimicked what amused him, & was so fascinated by "magic" (sleight-of-hand) that nothing could interrupt his curiosity: he asked again & again that the coin be produced & lost, & then with merry gestures he exhibited how clumsily he could do the same tricks—He was a very serious man, however, & neither drank nor smoke[d]—& practiced fasting—He did not fast merely from medical conviction, but because he thought that the practice of voluntary sacrifice accorded with moral perfection, that it accustomed us to more serious deprivations, & acknowledged the poverty of mankind—This deeply moved a German rabbi present. But Dr. Latif's mood could not sustain the weight of such profundity & the learned applause of the rabbi who commended his "oriental wisdom," and he jested about the whole matter, saying that his four days of fast on the boat, partly occasioned by the storm & prolonged by conviction beyond the period of his own illness would be counted by him towards the 30 days of obligatory Mohammedan fast (Ramadana)—The two joined in mutual praise of German universities & Kultur, & they became quite serious—They showed me with what difficulties their Ph.D's & M.D's are earned, how superior to American or English—& they inventoried the great academic names. Later, the Egyptian parodied the whole discussion & his own university manners—but he also gave me a copy of his doctoral thesis—on the causes of sterility in woman—which is simply a brief review of the literature of the subject with some recent statistics that had been collected by his professor rather than by himself—His own was a paragraph on the rôle of superstitions, magic, etc curing Egyptian women of their ideas of conception & sterility.

His friend, Wassif, had studied in London, & thought little of German schools—We occupied the same cabin, and in the 2 days when we lay in bed, he told me many things about Egypt, the agricultural & Coptic country of his origin, education, manners, & politics, and of his schooling at London and travels on the continent—He himself shone beautifully among these facts; I like him very much. He is much slower spoken than Latif, seems less intelligent, but I think he has a better mind; observing much more rapidly & accurately.

Since he knew the language he offered to accompany us to Cairo & deal with the natives for us—As soon as the ship entered Port Saïd many small boats swarmed about us & shrieked names of hotels & offers to carry baggage & ourselves to shore—We were asked outrageous prices—Natives came on the decks, begging for money, some offering to change piastres for pounds, some juggling, some hunting for bits of luggage, some with hotel badges & the most persistent entreaties—

9.

pieces – Natives came on the decks, begging for money, some offering to change piastres for pounds, some juggling, some hunting for bits of luggage, some with hotel badges & the most persistent entreaties. We were rowed to shore by handsome Arabs in blue jerseys with whom Wassaf had contracted. The ship was being hastily coaled, & with the flat coal boats joined as a ~~bridge~~ pier on either side and the black red men mounting with their baskets up ladders on the sides, was a very fine sight to us, moving to the shore.

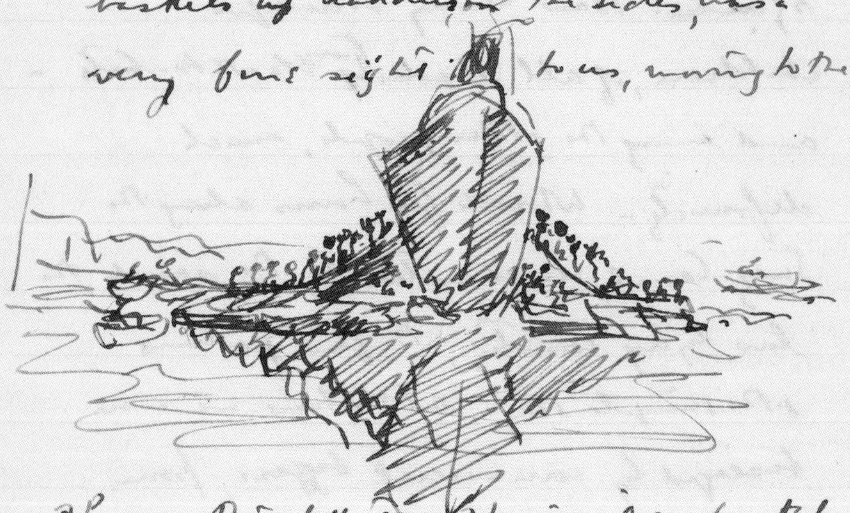

This is nothing like it & the background is infinitely blacker & more imminent:

9

Fig. 2. The ship at Port Saïd, Cairo, 12 February 1927

We were rowed to shore by handsome Arabs in blue jerseys with whom Wassif had contracted. The ship was being hastily coaled, & with the flat coal boats joined as a pier on either side and the blackened men mounting with their baskets up ladders on the sides, was a very fine sight to us, moving to the shore. [*drawing of the above-described scene (fig. 2)*] This is nothing like it—The original is infinitely blacker & more imminent:

On shore we paid 75 cents apiece as a "quarantine" fee. Then I learned that some of the money I had received in change on board was false. A great crowd of natives followed us from quarantine to customs house to the station thru muddy streets in rain, a distance of almost a mile, trying to win some piece of baggage from the porters Wassif had found. And when we reached the station these last bickered & fought with him, & finally compromised—Each of us (4) paid 25 piastres ($1.25). In the train we met others who not speaking Arabic had paid two or three times as much & had suffered from the "animals,"—nervous shock, fright, & disgust. The little we saw of Port Saïd between landing & our train was very much like the poorer parts of Coney Island & the summer bathing slums of Rockaway—Signs are in English & French—on frame houses with superposed wooden balconies which would have seemed little different had bathing suits been hung from them to dry. Few streets were paved: newer constructions were rising everywhere amid easy-going squalor. I saw many beautiful children, of all shades from black to white—and among the older people, much deformity—We rode for hours along the Suez Canal, enchanted by the sand, the low lying country, the few palms & the simple sky. At stations we were besieged by commercial beggars, from whom we bought bread, eggs, chocolate & enormous (thick-skinned) oranges—Sudanese Negroes alighted & mixed freely with the Arabs—Wassif told us what he could remember about these people & their relations with the natives—They are much finer in appearance than our N.Y. blacks. They intermarry with the white Egyptians, & the children belong to the race of the father—tho the distinction means very little—only religion limits mixture—so that white Christians will sooner marry black Christians than white Mohammedans. Wassif was amazed by stories he had heard of American treatment of negroes & he recounted them earnestly to me & asked if each was true—He thought the Scandinavians (Danes) the finest Europeans he had met—He spent a few weeks in Denmark which delighted him more than any land.

Rockaway. Beach on the Atlantic coast of Queens where small bungalows could be rented during the summer.

The French lady, en route to Bagdad[,] was with us for an hour; very much broken. There was a copy of *Sourire,* an indecent French journal, in the compartment, which revolted her—Before she left, she told us of a beautiful seaside home near Sable[s] d'Olonne, where any of us could stay for 20 francs a day (80 cents) complete pension, & live happily, riding horses thru the nearby woods & bathing on empty beaches. She gave us a photo of her friend who owned it—tending pigs—& a card of introduction.

We came into Cairo at 10:30 PM—& the disembarkment of Port Saïd was repeated, only with more fury. By this time gestures appeared so mechanical that we could predict & laugh at the whole business—A hotel agent named a price—

When we arrived at the hotel he raised it 5 piastres—It was called "Royal Hotel"—Once it had been an elegant building; its central court was still charming—but now the rooms had become like the street itself, backward & poor. Even when we removed our baggage this morning, natives followed us, and one hotel servant, unfaithful to the Greek, Caspris, who employed him, told us of a pension—French, clean & very reasonable. It was above the Italian Società Leonardo da Vinci e Dante Alighieri for the application of Art to Industry and under Yung Sun & Cie. It was a gloomy place—large & bare—The Italian lady had us wait till a blind man in pajamas, with a face much like Nat Cantor's (Tomasello), came to bargain with us—He asked three times as much as the Arab had told us—When we left the Arab ran after, begging money.

We found an excellent Jewish Kosher Hotel, with pension; and much to amuse us. I will tell you of it another time, dear.

Our first hours were not all bargaining. Wassif stopped at a pharmacist friend who was delighted to see him after 7 years and ordered a fine native breakfast for the three of us, and offered us his help as long as we are in Cairo. On learning that I wished to visit Mosques & Coptic churches he gave me addresses & names & even called on the phone to inquire about some details—Later in the afternoon, on the trolley in Boulaq, natives offered me beans to eat, & were jolly about my ignorance of Arabic. Near the museum I was accosted by an Egyptian, with a false scarab & a genuine Ptolemaic statuette—I could have the latter for 5 piastres—; a hundred yards beyond, it was 4, then 3, and finally, since he needed cigarettes, 1 piastre—It was too heavy & ugly to drag about the near East,—impossibly expensive to ship—& I had already refused.

I walked with Herman along the Nile for three hours till we were well out of Cairo. I have seen no landscape as placid, no shore-line so gently inhabited as this one. As we walked North we could see the great rocks behind the city and the mosques built near them so close in substance and color as to estrange them from the more artificial dwellings by the water. We saw beautiful slender horses, cavalcades with lances cross the bridge—numerous curved masts and distant minarets in one picture—Besides the poor town & beggary we had first known as Egypt this was another country—Along the way we met another people—well fed Egyptians in Western clothes, and handsome schoolboys—and poorer folk with trades. It was on the way home—it was dark & difficult to find the way by foot—that we ate beans in the trolley—We traversed Old Cairo,—more miserable than the worst of the New—to our hotel, where,—supper & the most hilarious international intellectualism,—two Jewish families, one American, the other Palestinian, debating, if eggs are alive, if the roundness of the earth is an undisputed scientific fact or just a theory, the astrologer Einstein, if God is our Father, why can't we be gayer & more personal with him, as with our own respected progenitors, the lynching of American negroes (but Americans are no angels, yet it happens only once in 15 years, & that's nothing)—and so on.

With love, blessings, kisses, and my whole heart to you, darling—

Meyer.

Cairo, 17 February 1927

Dear Lillian:

Why did you ask me, Jan. 28, if I were well? You had just described a "euphoric" (eutocia?) mother Charleston — I was in Avignon then & quite happy — I shook off an annoying cold that had followed me from Lyon. At Marseilles it returned. It finally disappeared in Nice — I have heard it sworn that love has a special telepathy & nothing is more swiftly felt than sickness. If you thought to write the evening of the 27th, then you perceived quickly — But our longitudes differ; perhaps I stirred uneasily in my sleep.

Always when you ask me, if I am well, darling, I wonder if you yourself are not ill or unhappy — you say so little of yourself, & you speak so much of sickness.

Be well, dear, & may I return soon to be with you.

I really wish to stay here a long time — but a time which will pass swiftly. When I count backwards I am delighted that seven months are gone. I am troubled to fill wisely those that remain — And when I see the end, I enrich it with you and dream endlessly:

Meyer.

Luxor, 25 February 1927

Dearest Lillian:

If I had begun gestating a baby when I left — it would be very sad if I had to bear it in Egypt & raise it here — unless I were extremely rich — Most likely it would die soon — if it lived, it would drink dirty Nile water, next to its mother who is washing clothes; and flies would creep upon its face, resting especially on the eyes, which are beautiful but sore, and often gruesomely infected — and its food and shelter & clothing likewise be poor & squalid — But it would live in the finest river land I have seen — the sky always blue — the days warm, or hot and dry, and the mud walled houses, without roofs, no discomfort at all.

In Cairo, its fate would be even more horrible, — in a large slum — It seems wonderful that any survive among the poor — when I gestate babies, dear, I shall return at once to New York —

Meyer.

Aswan, 28 February 1927

Darling Lillian:

First I say I will write to you, dear. I reread your letters, and I am delighted by a few words, even if an anecdote that is less than I wish from you or a sentiment too strange or timid — The assurance of your love, that concludes, enlivens me, & I wish more and more to write, and to rub your cheeks and hold your head in ecstasy, as in our little corner.

But when I have written "Darling Lillian" I am stopped by my own ignorance, — for, what can I say of myself, of Egypt, that approaches the beginning, or my intention: I begin with joy: and my habit is exposition or narrative, — other matters.

This is not the first time it happens so. I have begun many letters, where your name was not the formality to precede a letter, but the letter itself. And I wonder with what formality, with what story to conclude this letter, which is "Dear Lillian," and I wonder a long time, tearing up sentence after sentence, until wearied I resign and go to bed—Later I will be overtaken by a subject—to which I will prefix your name, and the letter so long agitated will be done.

In the one, I dream before writing, and cannot fit at once to this dreaming, the last days and the actual experience that I would recount—In the other I begin with the daily matters, with things seen & heard that excite me to relate them, and I have no sooner finished than I find that they are too coarse or remote, for the emotion with which I conclude a letter to you—Only if I am so thoughtless, so happy in one or the other that I can forget consequence or effect, I write untroubled, and talk of anything without criticism.

And this moment there is an enormous world to tell you, dear, which I would commence at once—did not a tired boy look anxiously to me to leave the only lighted room in this desert camp, that he might finish his own work, & go to sleep—I will write you soon. I send you my love, darling, and my gratitude for your goodness to me, always—

Meyer.

Tel Aviv, 7 March 1927

Dearest Lillian:

Here I am from the oldest to the newest. I made the same trip as our ancestors from Mitzraim, by way of Kantara, Sinai, Gaza, Askalon and Jaffa, but in one night, in which it was too dark to see the desert. In the early morning I passed over a flat country, part desert & part reclaimed, & saw Jewish farmers. There were Arabs, who from life with them, had learned Yiddish. At Tel Aviv the sun was suddenly so bright the whole town was blessed & no street seemed commonplace. There was nothing that was not very recent. The little houses, plastered white, each different from its neighbor, are in the "New Architecture" designs, of a poor simplicity, excused by the cleanliness, the order, & the happy people who live in them. I was charmed to hear Hebrew everywhere. I was always addressed in it, even when taken for a manifest foreigner. I watched a game of soccer football, in which the boys called to each other in Bible language. Once I heard "goal!" My father, years ago, would tell me that Hebrew could never be a living tongue, tho he & I conversed in it, because as the celebrated Darwin had observed, extinguished forms are not to be revived and is not language an organism, with growth & history? And he tried to show me how its primitive 3 consonantal system was inflexible, a hindrance to free word building, and that its vocabulary, formed in a state of culture, so different from our own, could hardly describe this new world, or express modern concepts, without doing violence to its own character. But here Hebrew is not spoken as by us, as children, in our Hebrew school, in a fluent, severe, unmodulated tone, for a few hours, & then abandoned for English. But I hear it shrieked & sworn with & used in all public-business & at the dinner table. The radical labor journal is written in Hebrew. At its office I heard the daily busi-

Mitzraim. Hebrew for "Egypt."

ness conducted in the language without strain or effect of a special manner for a special occasion—like Latin or Hebrew liturgy.

In Cairo I met a Palestinian Jew who had been educated in Italy, received a Doctorate in Philosophy & had returned to his country for Zionist work. He showed me a translation into Hebrew of Windelband's *History of Philosophy,* of Kant, and others: & he himself was engaged in translating Italian classics into Hebrew—He thought the language especially rich in philosophic terminology—; it had been cultivated by mediaeval philosophers who knew the classic & scholastic speculations—The technological & scientific schools in Palestine also employ Hebrew—

Wilhelm Windelband (1848–1915). German philosopher of the Baden School.

Immanuel Kant (1724–1804). German philosopher and influential late Enlightment thinker.

This man, Chaim Wardi, was very beautiful and a noble person. I was sorry to leave him for Luxor, but in Florence or Turin we shall meet again. He is fair, Northern in appearance; he would hardly appear a Jew; but nothing seems so important to him as his Judaism, which he is anxious to develop, enrich, & extend to others. We had been together at the hotel four days before we exchanged a word—His wife, having left the table, we began to talk. (Dear Lillian; do not suppose anything). He asked me what I thought of certain Cairo mosques. He had seen only the ugliest & most pretentious & was overwhelmed by their sublimity. This he described in language that showed a study of the philosophies of art and history. He was especially interested in learning of past Jewish arts, & hoped that in Palestine a distinctive style of architecture derived from some great past[] might be developed. We discussed Palmyra, Gammart, Santa Maria la Bianca, the Jewish Psalters, and the local, exile character of Jewish creations. He had been brought up to believe that there is a strict identity between the moral life of a people & the beauty of its arts, & his admiration of Croce confirmed this earlier idea. But he did not limit style to the works of man, but also to his gestures and habits. It is so that he judged that we are in full decadence, since there is no style in art or manners; he found America much to blame—In the beginning of our talk he was a passionate Zionist, committed to active schemes: now, he was very melancholy, & talked of the need for retreat from a life which daily grew more vulgar & ignoble. His whole notion of "style" in life, which alone gave life dignity, was rooted in imaginative pictures of past aristocracies. At the same time he was animated by his respect for great traditions to give his life to a people entirely remote from him in "style." But they could create their own together. Of America he had the strangest notions, he was amazed to learn that Croce has been read in America, that there are courses in philosophy, that there are other interests besides business, that American philosophers consider technology as significant as art, that some Jews have no active interest in their racial past, that some do not object to complete assimilation: and that among these last two groups are well educated folk: All this he found surprising. He simplified all America as = $, blind industry, which was destroying European culture, by the excessive demands of its competition. I had heard similar ideas from others. They are common editorial comment. Here they were a momentary weakness—; a distant dragon was blamed for local devastation; & tho never seen, every impiety was attributed to it, & all its features described as monstrous. I am faced so often by such accusations,

Chaim Wardi (1901–75). Educator and editor.

"Palmyra, Gammart, Santa Maria la Bianca." Sites of early Jewish art: Palmyra is northeast of Damascus; Gammart is in Tunisia on the coast north of Tunis; Santa María la Blanca is a converted synagogue in Toledo, Spain.

Benedetto Croce (1866–1952). Italian critic, idealist philosopher, and politician.

that in discussing America, I talk as in self-defense, & say much of it that is partial. A year ago it would never have occurred to me to point out American virtues; I laughed at such propaganda in others—Here it happens often. Wardi, before we parted, gave me addresses of his friends in Palestine—I saw one to-day, the editor of "Davar" the labor journal.—He lives in one room, alone, on the roof, of a new building, surrounded by books whose titles & appearance & variety show a fine individual mind. He is cross-eyed; humble looking, of very simple manner. His seriousness won me instantly & I was embarrassed to remain & encroach on his time. He asked me of my plans, of American schools, Zionism, students, radicalism, & arts. He too was surprised that Croce was known in Columbia, that there are poor workingmen in N.Y.; that music is much cultivated, etc.; but unlike Wardi, there were no presumptions to make wickedness or lack of art a cause for retirement in despair. This man seemed too much absorbed in his own object to brood over foreign evils; or invoke single causes to explain them. I was awed to read the titles of his books, most of them unbound, and observe the breadth of culture of this poor man in a small colony of Near Eastern Jews. His grey hair, his sadly crossed eyes, the black collarless shirt of Russian students, and the chamber on the roof, almost in the sky, made the books more precious to me as part of him. He told me to visit an exhibit of paintings on Herzl Street; and in parting wrote for me a letter to an archaeologist friend in Jerusalem.

"the editor of 'Davar.'" Berl Katznelson (1887–1944), who was a Russian leader of the Zionist Labor movement, educator, and writer.

This exhibit I might have seen in Paris: it presented scenes of Palestine in the modernistic naïve manner, with clumsy figures, clear colors, & monocular panorama. There were humorous affectations: the artist's portrait with a lamb, a scene in a barber shop, in which the man, while shaved, offers a slice of watermelon to an ass in the doorway: Sometimes there were bold patternings of flowers and robes, without shadows; winding roads & hills with regular fall & rise, the sky always the same blue graded, and cut by little stylized clouds. In another room were two portraits by this artist made twelve years ago, which I could never have guessed as his—They were common academic pieces, with no imagination, or idea of form. There was no bridge between these and the others. It seemed that the artist had not by long effort developed towards his recent style, but that the latter was uncovered, fresh and complete. It bore no traces of the other; it was unspoiled by the earlier habits of hand. Even tho it was not great work, suffering a little from monotony of detail & color, from lack of rich color, and from a type of line which was either too ornamental in its regularity, or too much broken by little masses to attain powerful rhythms,—despite all this—the archaism was fresh and genuinely simple—a real achievement after the earlier style. How I regretted that I did not paint more in recent years. This man's work, besides its charm, was a victory. There are hundreds who have tried to do as much—having turned from the common ways—and have produced false things. I saw the painter: he appeared a simple, homely man, with a great head of black hair, like my friend Greenberg.—

Of art, you would like more the reliefs (painted) of the tombs of Ti and Ptahotep, of the Old Kingdom, at Saqqârah. I spent a happy day at Memphis and Saqqârah,—before I left Egypt; among these magnificent walls on which moves

unspoiled by the earlier habits of hand. Even tho it was not
great work, suffering a little from monotony of detail & color,
from lack of rich color, and from a type of line which was either
too ornamental in its regularity, or too much broken by little
masses to attain powerful rhythms, — despite all this —
the archaism was fresh and genuinely simple — a real
achievement after the earlier style. (How I regretted that I
did not paint more in recent years.) This man's work,
tenderest charm, was a victory. There are hundreds who
have tried to do as much, having turned from the common
ways, — and have produced false things. I saw the painter:
he appeared a simple, homely woman, with a great head of
black hair, like my friend Greenberg.

Of art, you would like most the ~~tomb~~ reliefs (painted)
of the tombs of Ti and Ptahotep, of the Old Kingdom, at
Saqqarah. I spent a happy day at Memphis and Saqqarah, —
before I left Egypt, among these magnificent walls on which
moves the whole Egyptian world. The carving is stupendous;
the life represented as attractive as its rendering and form:
a boat with men is a system of harmonies; a group of birds;
an elaborate ornament made of scientific observation; & the
human beings and beasts, — the servants, the acrobats, the
farmers, fishermen and scribes, the animals fighting and
mating, the hippopotami in the marsh. These are an impulse
to run with them in great joy — The Metropolitan Museum
library has photos of all of them. You will surely love them,
darling. Nothing later was as fine, — in Egypt, few things
elsewhere. — Such works repay the most exacting pedantry,
and costly expeditions — I should instantly take up Egyptology;
but first I must finish Coptic, which, from what little I saw
in last month, is more than I had dreamed — with long
embraces, rousing cheers for you, darling, whose thought keeps
me happy now & forever (but there are exceptions; melancholy moments)
I will soon need a flock of fine pistols — Your Meyer & Meyer, Meyer, Meyer.

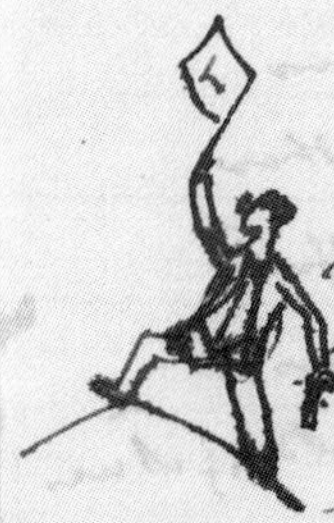

Fig. 3. Man on mountaintop waving a flag and holding a pistol, Tel Aviv, 7 March 1927

the whole Egyptian world. The carving is pluperfect: the life represented as attractive as its rendering and form: A boat with men is a system of harmonies; a group of birds, an elaborate ornament made of scientific observation; & the human beings and beasts,—the servants, the acrobats, the farmers, fishermen and scribes, the animals fighting and mating, the hippopotami in the marsh—these are an impulse to run with them in great joy—The Metropolitan Museum Library has photos of all of them. You will surely love them, darling. Nothing later was as fine—in Egypt—few things, elsewhere—Such works repay the most exacting pedantry, and costly expeditions—I should instantly take up Egyptology; but first I must finish Coptic, which, from what little I saw in the last month, is more than I had dreamed—with love, embraces, rousing cheers for you, darling, whose thought keeps me happy now & forever (but there are exceptions, melancholy moments)[.] I will soon wave a flag & fire pistols—[*in margin: drawing of man on mountaintop waving a flag and holding a pistol (fig. 3)*]

Your Meyer, Meyer, Meyer, Meyer.

Jerusalem, 13 March 1927

Dearest Lillian:

I was three days with my relatives at Petach Tikvah—These were fine people who would not let me go & had no scruples about keeping me several months: They were astonished that I had come this distance only to leave in a few days. I was even more astonished by their interest in one whom they had never seen before, & whose father,—my only tie with the family—was only a boyhood recollection. Later I saw how unusual was the visit: my existence was unknown; a letter I had written did not arrive: & my father's correspondence had lapsed many years ago. I thought I had strayed into the wrong house when I came upon three women washing clothes in the "garden." I saw a cow, a donkey and an orange grove beside them. When I announced myself as the son of my father, the cousin of at least one of these ladies, I created only worse confusion, for his name was unknown to them. It seems that it was not Nathan Meiny but Nahum Menahem; I agreed, & it was all love between us. My cousin could not contain herself for joy and asked me a hundred questions; and remarked on that marvelous resemblance to the boyhood image of my father, which my maternal relations have always given to my maternal grandfather, whose blessed name I bear—

You can imagine how troubled I was when the present name of my father was unrecognized—in this remote village,—how happy when my relevance to the spot was assured. But my cousin was full of a great hope—for when I seemed a stranger, she was sure I was a relative, and asked me to enter and reveal a relation she could not doubt. She felt thirty five years younger to see a son of Nahum Menahem with whom she was brought up as a sister in the same house. It made me older to hear her recitals of family history, which my parents had never told me. For all her fifty five years she was delightfully young and fresh—not a grey hair—and very active. She knew many languages—English, French, German, Russian, Hebrew and Arabic,—and while keeping house and farm, read a great deal. She told me of her father, my grand-uncle, who was a chemist, philologist and exegetical writer, and showed me his note-books in Hebrew and German, great piles of paper in beautiful hand. She spoke of another grand-uncle who was a celebrated Kovno doctor & of my great grandfather, whose Talmudic reputation would give me a welcome entrance in any Yeshivah. I visited one Yeshivah in the town, but the loud studying of the hairy scholars and their thumb demonstrations kept me from entering—All read aloud at the same time from different books—I watched them thru the window; & recalling the traditional wisdom, receptivity & erudition of these students, I wondered if perpetual clamor was not as ideal for study as complete silence—My father spent many years in such a school, until he turned from it to private studies of Western science and literature. His father & grandfather, too, had been Yeshivah students—But in all times there were dissenters, who usually became doctors and emigrated to larger cities—I was glad to learn these details of my family's past. Sometimes I felt them to be very intimate—to concern me especially, and constitute my own life—The account of my father's childhood—and Yeshiva morality—helped to clear for me much of what he does to-day. Even though the story of the scientific and scholarly members of the family was an abstraction of some events and said little of character or determining circumstance; the fact of rebellion and distinction was good to hear. I felt a little of that family glory which had seemed to me so vain in others.

My cousin has a daughter of 19 who after completing gymnasium with high honors, has languished at home, forbidden (or prevented) by her parents to complete her favorite studies—mathematics, music, etc—in a University—It is not a financial problem, I was told—since in Florence there is no tuition fee for foreigners, and living is 20 to 25 dollars a month—but a moral and social one difficult to clarify—The mother thinks four years a long period, in which absorption with intellectual matters may unfit for marriage or domesticity—There is also the fear to trust the girl such a long distance from home—among strangers. So she has stayed at home the last two years, her time divided between house-work and books—growing melancholy—One son studies engineering in Paris, another assists his father in the groves—

I had thought to stay only one day, as if the family were another Palestinian monument—a piece of family archaeology—meriting inspection and a greeting—Apart from the limits of my program, I could not stay more than three days; but I desire much to return at intervals, to see my cousins many times, rather than to spend a long period with them.

This is my third day in Jerusalem—as full for me as any of the voyage. I will have great difficulties in seeing even the more important remains in a week,—tho the city is as small as Brownsville. It is wonderfully set on a platform separated by deep valleys from the Judean hills. Yesterday, I was to the Dome of the Rock, and to the Church of the Holy Sepulchre, whose façade was designed and ornamented by the very men whose works I have studied in Languedoc and Provence—Today at the museum, I saw the Galilee Skull, and pottery series thru the Bronze and Iron Ages; in the afternoon, I walked the Mount of Olives to Gethsemane and

Galilee Skull. Found in 1925 in a cave in upper Galilee, a fragment thought to be first Neanderthal skull found in Asia.

the Virgin's Tomb, the Tombs of Absalom and David, the old Jewish cemeteries, the ancient and modern walls, and returned at sundown thru the Dung-Gate into the vaulted streets of the city—The surrounding hills are a romance of roads, churches, tombs, and villages of stone, superposed—

"Next year in New York." The close of the Passover seder is "Next year in Jerusalem."

Be well, darling—Here, I say, "Next year in New York"

Meyer.

Amman, Transjordania, 18 March 1927

Dearest Lillian:

Amman was to be a halting place on my way to Jerash, but I must remain here till after-tomorrow when there is a train to Deràa. This morning I set out for Jerash: the auto promised for 9 was not ready at 10; and at 12 it led me in another direction to keep me on the road until more passengers could be found: At 1 it was too late: since Jerash is 2 hours off; work impossible after 5[:]30 & a return auto uncertain the morning after—The Arab did not wish to give me the money I had paid: Finally he handed me counterfeit money: which he would not correct without much argument. There was similar difficulty at Jerusalem, riding to Amman. But what a beautiful journey! We rode five hours until sundown—in the mountains till the Dead Sea and then along the Jordan from Jericho to Es-Salt. A tire was punctured with a great explosion: The Arabs located Mecca & prayed. All this time we did not speak. At Shuri I saw a strange form of tomb in the fields and I jumped out to draw & take notes. Then I was asked questions which I could not understand—The chauffeur translated into French: The Arabs taught me the words for sky, sun, numbers, domestic articles, & objects we passed. To-day in the market at Amman I was greeted by one of them, who shook my hand & introduced me to his friends.

All morning I was kept at the garage; except for snatches of 15 or 20 minutes when I walked thru the town until the car was to leave. One Arab spoke German. There were handsome Circassian boys in the streets—with blue eyes and intent expressions—I was angry to be occupied with transportation & helpless to enforce my wishes. I could think of nothing long without impatience: If I observed a distant theatre or mountain; I had soon to leave it—for an appointment that was vain. At 1 I gave up Jerash, I climbed the mountain above Amman to the citadel which commands a grand view of the valley and town. The hotel owner's son joined me, & with the greatest kindness & amusement held the other end of the tape-measure & squatted on the vaults, delighted. I photoed him with several details—Nuns came with school children, and watched for a half-hour—Later there were two old Arabs who remembered the form of the dome which had fallen in recent years, and identified among the debris, some of its fragments—I made conjectural designs of its spring & drum until they identified the one they had known. They said Jerash was more interesting, far richer: How sad I was! I asked of Mshatta. They recalled the Germans (Strzygowski) who had carried away its façade in 1904: & described its ornament; comparing it with some pieces in the Roman theatre in Amman.

Mshatta. A famous desert castle from the early Islamic period, located on the edge of the desert in Jordan, southwest of Amman.

We were in an old Arab(?) palace, of which I had heard much but never seen pictures. Each detail, cross plan, vaults, horseshoe arcades, ornament, suggested wonderful complexities, making me ambitious—Nearby were Roman and later Arabic remains—ruins of a gigantic temple, and mounds covering barrel vaults and columns. On the mountain slopes long black herds of goats moved between the caverns; there were smaller files above between the scattered stones—A dog ran from us—At one end we looked down upon the city & saw how well the Romans & Arabs had chosen: Along the stream at the very base of the valley were other monuments, better preserved—a theatre. The surrounding houses were built of the ancient stones.

To-night the boy at the hotel spoke of the cities he had known. He loved Constantinople best; of Damascus, Jerusalem, Beyrouth, Cairo, Alexandria, Marseilles, Paris—Paris he thought very "chic"—N.Y, by report, wonderful—Three years ago Amman was barbarous; no European clothes were seen in it—now it is a big city (c. 15,000 people) with a theatre, cinema, autos, and three hotels. The most beautiful land was Tripolitania: there he had learned Italian; & heard the purest Arabic as in the old books—His hobby was carbon enlargement of photos. He had left his camera with a friend in Damascus to record the bombardment, & the street warfare of French & natives. He begged me to draw his head—in profile, since one eye is a blind discolored mess; then he turned the other way, & asked for a picture of the ugly side—Later I showed him how omelettes are made. This pleased him. He prepared Turkish coffee for me & served me with elaborate attention. To-morrow he will accompany me once more to the citadel and palace to finish our work. A Druse boy waits at the hotel in his stead.

I sigh over Jerash, & find Baalbek which I shall visit from Damascus & Reyak no substitute, but a separate thing—I met the director of antiquities of Jerash at Jerusalem. His name is Horsfield. We spent an afternoon at the British School—He asked me if I was related to Shapiro the famous forger of antiquities—of manuscripts, so near perfection, that not palaeography or matter, but philology caused their rejection, and then by British Museum experts: In despair he committed suicide—His daughter—Miriam Harry, is now famous as a novelist in France. I remembered that Mrs. Reinach had asked me if I were related to her father, & everyone laughed. Horsfield was very gay, became more and more handsome, until he appeared entirely misplaced as a digger—He had found a certain celebrated Assyriologist very intelligent in latrine service at excavations—Field work has little glamour; in fact it is difficult to find people for expeditions; he could give me several places at the moment. He mentioned one campaign as an "awful season": there were "females["] present. His friend Fitzgerald, acting Director of the school in Garstang's absence—also said "females." These were the males, and very male, like type pictures of Englishmen, Arnold's hunting Philistines: beautiful vigorous faces. They go to church, but not when some disagreeable preacher attends. I became uneasy soon; for a whole afternoon could be spent in indolent talk; they showed no desire to leave: this was a vacation. Later I visited the library of the Dominicans, where a fine monk in cream and brown led

George Horsfield. Archaeologist who was excavating at Jerash in 1925.
"Shapiro the famous forger." Moses Shapira (1830–84), a Jerusalem antiquities dealer and purveyor of fake biblical artifacts.
Miriam Harry. Pseudonym of Myriam Perrault-Shapira (1875–1958).

G. M. Fitzgerald (1883–?). Assistant director of the British School of Archaeology in Jerusalem in 1927.
John Garstang (1876–1956). British professor of the methods and practice of archaeology at Liverpool University.
Matthew Arnold (1822–88). English Victorian poet and social critic.

"Watzinger and Wultzinger." Karl Wulzinger (1886–?), German scholar and coauthor, with Carl Watzinger (1877–1948), of *Damaskus: Die islamische Stadt* (Berlin: W. de Gruyter, 1924).

me thru quiet chambers—I read Watzinger and Wultzinger (who are called the Tweedledee & Tweedledum of Oriental Studies) & finished to find the room locked & no one about—Thru a side window I hailed a monk, & was released—But I could well have remained; the library was so gently illumined and appetizingly stocked, and I all alone—

The whole week at Jerusalem was eventful and rich in sights. At the Pension I met a Jewish philologist who, alone, kept his hat at meals, & blessed regularly. He spoke to me of the necessity for Jewish studies, Palestinian studies of local Jewish arts, the anti-Semitic tendency in archaeology, of the buried treasures in the soil, of the very early period of the tombs to the East of the city & their Jewish character: There were the daughters of the owner, who were strongly communist & so passionate for music that often during meals, there were sudden abortive fragments from Beethoven & Brahms—sung or beaten. I heard much denunciation of America: It was said that American schools were bad—because the last American visitors, a Rabbi & college (Hebrew Union) graduate could not distinguish between "real value" & "price"—that culture was lacking: Another American—(Russian Jewess) homely & with a loud voice, unmarried & middle aged, only confirmed the opinion. The lady of the house earnestly exhorted me to become an active Zionist—I had no objections, but could not resolve sympathy into action. My insufficient Hebrew only inflamed her; I was a strayed lamb. One evening I ate elsewhere with a friend—I was minutely questioned about this meal; and I had to balance my answers in a tragicomical spirit, for the poignancy of the inquest soon became alarming beside my indifference. Her last words were to remember Zion: her first had been justifications of an exorbitant price which was finally reduced by a third—She remarked well that, besides those of the Jews, the sufferings of the Arabs were negligible, since as a race they were spiritually strong, "children of Nature" who rarely washed, while the Jews were introspective cowards. This she drew from herself—this drew her to Zionism—

Leo Ary Mayer (1895–1959). Historian of Islamic art and architecture.

Keppel A. Creswell (1879–1974). English historian of Islamic architecture, who was associated with the University of Cairo.

I met a Dr. Mayer, an official of the Dep't of Antiquities, a friend of Creswell & Shapley and student of Strzygowski's, who outlined part of my route for me, & gave me much good information. He showed me his excavation of the third wall of Jerusalem by moonlight. At great expense of labor—after weeks of digging it was proved that the third wall, long disputed, was north of the existing Muslim wall, & not coincident with it. This has caused great excitement in the city. It is depressing to regard the holes, little mounds and rocks for 500 metres. Such knowledge seems a mad luxury: Perhaps Dr. Mayer's officious manner made the whole undertaking so small. He has a friend, a professor of Bio-chemistry, who is also an archaeologist and has written a book on "Palestinerisische Klein Kunst" which has a larger interest than this third wall. He is a charming man: He will visit New York in June: I will write to Oscar Budansky; I am sure they will be good friends—

"He has a friend." Adolf Reifenberg (1899–1953), author of *Palästinensische Kleinkunst* (Berlin: R. C. Schmidt, 1927).

Oscar Bodansky (1901–77). Russian-born biochemist and physician; Schapiro's neighbor and friend.

With love, darling—

Meyer.

Damascus, 25 March 1927

Dearest Lillian:

I wrote last from the Hotel Engeltera, Amman: now from the Hotel Darel el Farah, Sandjakdar, Damascus,—but between these, was the German Hospice of the "Weltgeistlichen" at Tabgha, on Lake Tiberius, Galilee—where Father Täpper & 24 Swedes kept me company.

German Hospice. A hospice established by the German Catholic Palestine Society; south of the spring 'Ain et-T,bigha, according to Karl Baedecker, *Palestine and Syria, with Routes through Mesopotamia and Babylonia and the Island of Cyprus: Handbook for Travellers* (Leipzig: K. Baedecker, 1912), a book that Schapiro carried.

These last few days have been mainly in trains & autos; I am alarmed by mounting expenses, insufficient travel, & the confused itinerary. But since always the trouble yields some interest & not merely interest, but experience that afterwards seems an indispensable destiny, always good to recall, I excuse myself readily & return to new calculations—

The evening before I left Amman I met at the hotel a Jew, who told me of the great struggles of Zionism & the necessity of defeating its present leaders, who were indifferent if not hurtful to the movement. He had a red beard, & suffered from a severe head-ache—which confined him to bed—He would not eat Arabic food, which was not Kosher. Together, we walked thru the town, & having bought cheese, dates, fruit, bread & eggs, we made a meal in our room. He prayed several times. The next morning, he suffered from indigestion.—On the way to the train, he told me how much he suffered to see the maladministration of Zionist funds, especially since he was a member of one of its committees—& he urged me to fight for the cause—At the station he was refused a ticket to Deràa (Syria) and Damascus, since he lacked a Transjordan visa. I too was refused the ticket, but I was changing at Deràa for Samakh and needed no visa, & finally obtained a ticket—an officer accompanied me to Deràa, to see that I was honest—But my friend's papers were in bad order—He could not explain his roundabout way of reaching Damascus from Jerusalem; & his foolish statement of an intention to visit Beyrouth,—a port in Syria—when his family was in Haifa, a port in Palestine,—excited the officials to telegraph to Jerusalem. Several days later, returning to Deràa I met the Circassian detective who had kept my passport from Amman to Deràa; he told me that the man was a bankrupt who had sought to escape from Palestine by way of Syria—On this trip I met other detectives. They were my company almost two whole days. One, a Turkish aviator, in French service, rode with me from Samakh to Damascus, led me to a hotel, & took me the same evening to the movies—He entered, of course, without paying: & every few moments, the management & visitors saluted him like a high person. We saw ancient American pictures—two serials of adventure, one Yukon-Alaska-gold-outlaw-film: the other—Texas-Mexico-cowboy-barroom buried treasure-secret document-film—One fought every few yards of the picture—one fought & fought—while the Arab audience read the Arab translations interspersed between the French—in a great murmur—Colored post-card views appeared at the end of each reel. We were served tea & cigarettes—The boy poured the remaining water on the floor when a glass was returned—My friend explained everything in the pictures—He said he learned from them much that was useful to his profession—He often disguised himself—in fact: he had 3 different hats—1) a cap for railroad work:

2) a national tarboush (red fez) for Damascus wear: and 3) a hat—that transformed him completely, deceiving his only brother-in-law—In a few years I will meet him in NY, which he intends to reach by way of Canada—

On the way to Damascus he was a delightful companion—for he remained by my side for half-hour stretches, absented himself—introduced me to Arabs, & acted as our interpreter. He knew Constantinople well, admired it above all cities—called it "chic" & "civilized"—civilized, since almost everyone spoke French. His Arab friends excited me enormously—for when they learned I was a student, they proceeded to tell me of strange monuments & unknown cities in the desert & beyond the Jebel Druse—I wrote down names & resolved to return to this region: And even more wonderful—I learned that with proper credentials, I could apply to the military commandant at Damascus, & obtain from him a Bedouin, who would guide me, (likewise in Bedouin dress) thruout the farther country. To-day this is impossible, since the land is disturbed by wars—but when these end, I can go—This is a great hope—From the train I noted many mounds, apparently tells or human deposits, with indications of ancient settlements—(walls & pottery fragments[]) & in Amman there were hillocks whose topography was architectural in character: covering vaults & bases, & corresponding to fragments above soil.—Of the disturbances I saw very little: only the remains of them—ruined houses & barricades in Damascus—many negro & French soldiers—shell holes in walls & vaults—& the reports of the people—But at Deràa I saw the Druse prisoners. Two were fighting each other. They pulled hair, bit & struck, until separated by officers & severely whipped—Then they returned bleeding to their work mending the roads.—

"disturbed by wars." From 1925 until mid-1927, the French Mandate of Syria was faced with a Druse-led revolt.

I have seen many quarries in the last month—& men cutting stone. The labor is still primitive; the men squatting & working with simple tools—so that only a few small prisms are smoothed in a day: When I view them from above in a deep quarry, between rocks that are a prison & a promise of endless toil, the whole creation of monumental architecture, which for us to-day, best symbolizes the success or power of past cultures, seems a sacrifice & no simple pleasure. If in a half hour a small block is trimmed, then an ancient temple with great ashlar, hundreds of columns, paving, roofing, lintels & walls, was a proposition to annoy & enslave men as well as to delight them. For it was hardly necessary—only a small number were artists & carved mouldings or ornament; a brutal task preceded—A farmer, at least, follows the whole life of his crop & his labors are successive—In Egypt the phases of the Nile gave the agricultural people several months of leisure, which the kings enlisted for the quarries. It may be that much of the progress in tools & crafts came from just such monumental ambitions: & that in a thousand years the sweat and agony of one class will return to bless it, and the pride of the other suffer from the diffusion of the knowledge or power it had encouraged. There are scholars who privately detest monumental stone arts—consider human representations foolish (one called mediaeval church façades, "stone cockroaches with haloes creeping on portals.") & prefer handicrafts with abstract or foliate & animal ornament—But there is little reasoning on these matters, & it is not clear whether the preference is moral or aesthetic—or the usual reasoning about one in terms of the other—

To-day in front of the Ommayad Mosque, an American boy asked me to speak for him. We were pleased to learn we were both from NY, excited that we came from Brooklyn; but when we found out that we lived in Flatbush, in Midwood—in Ave I & Ave U—a few blocks from each other: we threw up our hats & fell upon each other's necks for joy. We have been together all day. We ate in the Jewish Orphan Asylum in the Ghetto—where only Arabic & Hebrew are spoken; & later walked thru the city's bazaars, workshops & suburbs—

He told me of his 8 months in Palestine—He lived a while with the Chalutzim, communist colonists, and labored in the fields—His report of their life and character is very stirring and I regretted not having spent time with them. In the past month what I have seen and heard of Zionist activity wins me more and more to it—It is much richer than I had fancied it: nobler than its own arguments, & not to be judged by the "waterflies" who write about it. It is not Tel Aviv—a business enterprise—or Jerusalem, an old sentiment—or any large Jewish city that attracts me, but the language, soil, & free life in poor, small communities—Here Zionism is hardly a religious, or nationalistic (political) matter—The bare common living, hard work, & simplicity—the great ideal & the freedom, seem a cure for a whole race—All I have seen and heard may be much exaggerated: but the idea formed from it is of a great & noble effort, no matter what the individual mainsprings, or the official program. In the meantime the country lives thru a hard time, waiting upon America, its industries confused by the gap between old plans, recent structures, & present resources—& its leaders fighting with each other. I could pray for it: & wish myself nearer to its whole life—

with love, darling—

Meyer.

Beyrouth, 30 March 1927

Dearest Lillian:

I come from Baalbek, of which, two years ago at this very time, I gave a seminar report. Therefore I returned to see details formerly discussed: in my preoccupation with them I saw little of the rest, which is enormous. In this work which is impressive by its size, its masonry and the elaborate planning of large architectural groups, I remained the greater time with the small ornament—This is concentrated in the upper parts of the buildings—on cornices & ceilings, which are very high; but earthquakes have (almost "fortunately") reduced them, & they can be studied on the ground: I saw a variety of motifs & a technique which I had never thought of [*as dating to*] this early time; the beginnings of Mohammedan & much Romanesque ornament are suggested in the 2nd century.

The buildings themselves are heavy piles, neither ugly nor beautiful, simply Roman imperial works to display power, to dominate attention & to hold Syria loyal—They correspond to certain modern baroque architecture—The enterprise is more apparent than the art. How wonderful that such stones were ever quarried, and quarried, transported, and once on the site, lifted to such high places! A half mile away, a great block, 70 ft long, is still seen in the quarry, undetached, but smoothed on all but one face. And Baalbek is a remote town—between the two Lebanon ranges—Among the fragments are columns of red Assuan granite such as I had seen only a month ago, on the road to Shellal; 900 miles away.

Shellal. Ancient village on the bank of the Nile, south of Aswan.

The two days at Baalbek were very pleasant, & I envied the Germans who had worked there for several years. While the sun burned in the valley: the mountains to East & West were covered with snow.

In the early morning I walked to Râs-el-Ain, a beautiful spring, where is a mosque, now abandoned, of Bibars, whose works at Cairo & Damascus are sturdy & dignified—In Baalbek, there is another mosque built of columns & capitals pilfered from the Roman site; & an Arab citadel on the Roman walls, with some very fine vaulted chambers. The Roman substructures are cool, powerful barrels, of admirable masonry at the points of intersection. And the whole ruin, at sundown, shows beautiful yellow tones of weathered stone, like the quarries nearby, with the additional play of light & dark, deeply drilled ornament.

Sultan Bibars al Bunduqdari (ca. 1223–77). Sultan of the Mamluk dynasty, known for his building program.

In the town, in a poor shop which I had entered to buy dates, the owner, thinking me a Frenchman called me brother & cousin, since his father was French. He offered me a good liquor, & much lettuce, as a sign of good will, & gave me extra weight of dates. He knew almost no French. He explained that his father was a soldier—& that he, as a good son, loved all Frenchmen. I meet French soldiers everywhere, on trains, in stations, & in town; usually they are bored by Syria, in which there is little to amuse one—few cafés, & no excitement. When they learn of my itinerary they tell me I am making a "nice promenade." They live in barracks, & travel only to reach another.

With love,

Meyer.

P.S. March 30, i.e., The child would be born to-day. There is a large American Medical School in Beirut—& a beautifully located hospital overlooking the blue bay.

Athens, 20 April 1927

Dearest Lillian:

I came here this afternoon, a whole week behind last month's schedule, & a month behind last year's. This means that I shall stay here only a very short while. I was too long in Constantinople. I had to give up Saloniki. This grieves me terribly [*small drawing of a grim face held in hands in a roundel with domed building behind*]. I had also to give up Bourssa, in Asia-Minor, a half day's ride from Const. Even in Const. I missed much in the two weeks. I never crossed to Scutari, which, every morning & evening, I saw from the ferry.—And in the museum there were many rooms unvisited. And there were mosques, churches, & walls I had planned to see many months ago, but never came to. It was a happy time tho a very inefficient one. The Riefstahls gave me every comfort. I lived in a beautiful suburb, at times so enchanted by sundown or a grey sky, to keep me for hours in a happy soli-

Scutari. Üsküdar, a neighborhood in Constantinople east of the Bosphorus.

Rudolf Meyer Riefstahl (1880–1936). German-born professor of Islamic and medieval art at New York University, who resided in Constantinople from 1927 to 1929.

tude — I had good friends, who often accompanied me to the city & walked with me from site to site, & often lingered for hours while I attended to matters that did not interest them.

I lived in the midst of intrigues of Riefstahl to found an American School of Near Eastern Studies in Constantinople — I was invited to stay with him, introduced to his presumed benefactors, & used as an argument. Finally I was offered a position teaching in this school which does not yet exist. Riefstahl was not candid and it was not until after much questioning that he admitted that there would be only small chance for the independent research that draws me to Const. — & that in the summer there would be no vacation, since it is in the summer that there will be most visitors (endowments). Then I would be interrupted in my researches on Thraco-Phrygian lug-holes to lecture to each fresh ship-load on Byzantine toilets; or similar matters. There are other reasons why R. wishes to have me in Constantinople — but none of these, at present, seem to promise the chance I desire. — It would be wonderful to study a year at Const. Tho the Bosphorus is so obviously important for prehistory: its ancient levels are still unexplored. — And Asia Minor is exceedingly rich in remains — in Mohammedan, especially — If the Institute is established — we will always be able to come there in the summer — but I fear — without much profit — Riefstahl wishes me to teach there a whole year: 1928/29; or arrange to spend a half year in N.Y. & half, in the Near East. This coming fall I will see him in NY. & I will learn more definitively of the "Institute" — which is still a project. The reason R. is so anxious to obtain a written statement of my willingness to teach in the school, before it exists, is that it can be used to convince his influential wealthy friends that the time is ripe & that the intellectual means are at hand — I could give him no statement, especially since he was so vague about the duties involved & the possibilities of investigation — And the non-existence of the school — made the selection of the faculty even more hypothetical — Me, the faculty! What a school of Oriental Studies! When I reproached him that I did not know a single Oriental language, R. replied that neither did he: & yet he is an expert in Oriental rugs & textiles & pottery! & a professor of the subject in NY.U — His father, Wilhelm Meyer was a famous mediaeval scholar & philologist — & a more conscientious man.

Bosphorus. Narrow strait separating Turkish Asia Minor from European Turkey, extending from Constantinople to the Black Sea.

What do you think, darling Lillian, of this chance to live a year in Constantinople & the Near East! If it is only to teach — & not seriously — & without possibility of free enterprise — it is very difficult. For the society of Americans of Constantinople is very poor. — & the preoccupation with small matters in the presence of better objects will be only the more irritating after a journey of 5000 miles. I must wait until I see you — which will not be far off — & we can together see the matter from more sides — For I shall not make such a journey without you.

With love, dear,

Meyer.

Athens, 21 April 1927

Dearest Lillian:

On the Acropolis, much of the nonsense said of the Greeks seems true. Here, the influence of air & setting on people seems obvious, the sharpness makes for clarity: the unchanging blue sky for ideas of the finite & permanent: the high place for serenity & detachment: the beautiful materials of nature for ardor: & the success of the architectural enterprise for social pride. The location is the greater part: Remove every building from it, & it remains remarkable. It could admit no complexity: it could endure no vertical accents; and required no subtleties, or picturesque massing. Now it is known that the exterior (non-spatial) character of Greek architecture is a point in development—traditional—rather than an absolute & peculiar preference—But even to-day, one could only build for exterior effect on the Acropolis—Having attained such a height, & commanding so wide & beautiful a view it would be to lose all gained, to enclose oneself in an elaborately walled space—In the dark Museum on the Acropolis, all sense of the site is lost: in the Erechtheum, it appears between the walls & columns.

Below the hill, in the city, is the church called the Little Metropolis, the smallest cathedral in Europe,—no larger than your house. On this hot sunny day, it is darker & more gloomy within than in the largest Northern churches in rainy weather. Like the Parthenon it is a Greek building. The walls are of older classic & barbarian materials—inscriptions & grave stelae, & ferocious animal fights (like Rostovtzeff's Siberian & South Russian pieces) in stone. But the festival to-day is very happy: crowds in bright colors pass thru it all day. This is the Passion week: & the bells clang continually thruout Athens. It is a joyful holiday to bury & raise Christ. Incense is sold in street carts; the stores are closed for 3 days; no meat is eaten: but enormous vegetable meals are not an ascetic substitute—To see the bright crowds everywhere, it is a pagan holiday. I think there are moving pictures of the Crucifixion & Resurrect. & in the large shop windows are models of Biblical scenes. Tonight there will be a great procession. When Christ rises the kneeling priests will break eggs. In the meantime the museums will be closed—This is a nuisance, for they are too large to be seen in a few days—The archaic pieces in the Acropolis museum are wonderfully strong: they are more "intellectual" & passionate than the "Golden Age" work which I like less & less: The painted stone female figures are much more varied than I had supposed them: & there is such technical perfection in these earlier pieces that the argument from incompetence explains none of their virtues. In the National Museum, too, I saw wonders. The Stela of Aristeon: the Mycenaean metal work, the 6th century vases, surpass the Periclean—which is also fine, but borders on fussiness & an empty dexterity.

Mikhail I. Rostovtzeff (1870–1952). Russian scholar of ancient Greek, Iranian, and Roman history.

I called on Dinsmoor, who is away for the week end: but I saw his little girl—who is more beautiful than ever. She no longer considers Miss Sterret ignorant because she does not speak Greek like herself. She is very grave & corrects the wildness of her little brother who throws an ink bottle at her in reply—She gave me flowers before I left—Mrs. Dinsmoor told me everything about everyone in Greek Archaeology—& even more—she drew up for me lists of restaurants & use-

William B. Dinsmoor (1886–1973). Historian of classical Greek archaeology at Columbia University. Schapiro took his course on Renaissance and modern architecture.

ful stores in Athens — timetables, routes, & hotels in the country — Mr. Dinsmoor after more than 10 years has not finished his book: he demands an unquestionable perfection — I sought out Blegen — but he was gone: & his wife gave me a letter that had been waiting for me several months at Athens (in the American School). It was from Strittmatter, now a Benedictine in Scotland. He is Frater E. Anselm Strittmatter. O. S. B.

Carl Blegen (1887–1971). American archaeologist and assistant director of American School of Classical Studies in Athens until 1927.

Jakey has written me a gay letter, announcing his plans for the next year. He will go to Wisconsin. He is very confident he will do well — even win prizes & scholarships. He wishes to study architecture or medicine — since W. has no school of architecture: it will have to be medicine!! What can one say to that? But he likes his biology — & writes that he is "intensely happy" when he is with you — (May I be home soon, darling; I will be as happy.) He enclosed an old photo of himself — with the remark that now he is "way bigger." He is, & in many ways — (This, — Mary cannot see.) He wishes to take a special course in Wisconsin on some ancient Civilization — & For this he has great enthusiasm — only a little while ago he decried any sort of "intellectual stuff" — & "sentimentality[.]" Now (March 27) all seems well. —

Mary Schapiro (1905–87). Schapiro's sister.

With my love, sweetheart,

Meyer.

*'Academic' prejudice — into which Jakey also slips — he received two A's

---

Keppel, of the Carnegie Corporation — wrote me "I wish I were 30 years younger; I would apply for one of our own fellowships."

Frederick P. Keppel (1875–1943). President of the Carnegie Corporation and former dean of Columbia College.

Patras, 2 May 1927

Dearest Lillian:

At 3 o'clock this morning the boat will arrive in Patras from Piraeus: At 4 it will leave for Brindisi — I must wait in the harbor until the hour: it is better than to sleep & be awakened suddenly & to hurry in the darkness. There is no landing dock: a little row-boat will carry me out to the steamer.

Every morning (but one) this last week I have risen early, with the sun; my room in darkness, to catch a train, or to proceed by auto, early, to Mycene, Tiryns, & Epidaurus — It has always been pleasant; even refreshing, & provoking an élan for a whole day — Rising so soon, I see the rest of the world come after, to fill in the picture: & I can enjoy a few hours of watching — even when pressed for time or engaged by trains & tours. — At Olympia this morning I was awakened even before the sun came up: I lit a candle to see my own face; in a half hour, it burned "invisible & dim" — Mount Cronios was before the window & the dry bed of the Cladeos, which had once risen to inundate the temple precinct.

I rode to Patras with a fat old German doctor, a general practitioner from Berlin. I induced him to travel 3rd class. He is writing a book on Telepathy: metapsychology: & prognostic dreams, of which he has a collection of 8000. He sees in a dream the word "VIPRÉ." He awakens, deeply moved — His maid knocks in agitation on his door: a telephone call to help a man poisoned by veronal: Such poisoning is rare: it is his first case of it; so he consults his books: & searching for veronal—he comes to a paragraph on Viper bites: (spelled VIPÈRE.) This is a prognostic dream. Or he sees a name in a dream:—of an acquaintance: & in the morning paper he finds an article concerning a criminal of the same name: but not the person he knows—etc—etc—He begged me to send him any such experiences—He is collaborating with Gardner Murphy of Columbia Psych. Dep't—on questionnaires relating to telepathy—It came out that he is a neo-vitalist, & a friend of Driesch. He turned the talk to the Jews in America. He is an "Aryan-Mensch," he explained later, & he perceived instantly that I was a Jew. He himself comes of a Jewish family converted 2 generations ago: to Protestantism. But his circle remains Jewish: & he is very proud of his ancestry. Like some other professional Germans I met, he knew the important names in every other field: & every second man mentioned was Jewish: He knows all these names because he reads the 4 worthwhile newspapers of Germany (*Vissische Ztg, Frankfurter Ztg, Berliner Tageblatt, Kölner Ztg*) which give news of work in all the sciences & have literary & scientific supplements of high intellectual standard—Later he drew my picture—which I signed. He invited me to his home in Berlin. He was sorry that 4 years ago I had lived in Brücken Strasse: a most disreputable quarter that he would not recommend to anyone. And if I do visit him I will meet his sister who will be interested to discuss with me the psychology & aesthetics of cast shadows in Italian painting & the correspondence of leaf & tree-form in early Renaissance art.

Gardner Murphy (1895–1979). American psychologist at Columbia University; introduced a course on the history of psychology.
Hans Adolf Eduard Driesch (1867–1941). German biologist and philosopher; the last great spokesman for vitalism.

The old gentleman is so fat he could hardly approach the ticket window at Patras: & I had to buy his ticket for him (to Corinth). He is also partially deaf: I spoke very loud emphatic German to him on the train filled with a Greek audience of laborers, peasant women & babies: many at the breast. When he discovered what an uncertain word of mine was, he roared it out several times in victorious reassurance—But sometimes he was painfully puzzled—Then I thought: this must be the source of his telepathic interests: growing unable to hear orally transmitted thoughts, he is looking for immaterial, soundless—transmission: soul acting upon soul.—But this was my helpless embarrassment grumbling, & reproaching the doctor: who is really very amiable, & I am sure a good man, if tediously metapsychological.

I walked out of Patras in the afternoon to see the fine mountains to the East. At a village crossroads, in a café I saw a boy of 18 drawing a portrait of another Greek, who kept a terribly stiff pose—The boy turned & saw me watching: & tho there were many others around him: he tore his drawing in two: And I guilty, walked away. But I was recalled by the man: & invited to have a coffee with them. I was asked by one who spoke Italian, what work I did, & finally the boy said that he would draw my picture & I his—wagons halted: & drivers came down to watch us work. I made the first drawing: I was very happy to obtain a good likeness, even if artistically poor—The picture was passed around & applauded. While the boy drew my face the Italian speaking man announced the progress to me saying—"gli occhi, orecchi, la bocca" etc. Then some men said it was a poor likeness & some

"While the boy drew my face." This drawing, signed "D. Kaspacos, Patras 2/5/27," is still among the papers that reside with Miriam Schapiro Grosof.

found it perfect. The boy showed me other heads he had drawn: several were very fine & scrupulous—but without over-nicety. He begged to accompany me on the road. On the way we met a priest who had learned of the drawings, & asked to see them. He made me promise to draw him as well, when I returned. I was left with the boy who spoke only Greek which I could not understand. He indicated a monastery several miles off which he would be happy to show me. It was "kallos" (beautiful); & he made gestures of supreme felicity to indicate the beautiful. Often he stopped before trees & houses to repeat these gestures: Once he approached a peasant woman in an orchard & spoke to her, pointing to me. Then she climbed a tree, & came down with hands full of Greek yellow plums for us. The boy had much to say to me. He was unhappy that I could not understand—but when I shook my head & smiled, he patted my back & seemed to indicate that it was all well. I saw a Franciscan monk walking towards us: I asked him to translate my friend's Greek. He wished to know what I thought of him: I told him he was a good boy & a fine draughtsman. This pleased him enormously. But the monk, on learning that I wished to visit the convent in the mountains said it was a five hours walk to the place, & that it hardly merited the journey; there were no mosaics or frescoes, no old building.—

We turned back to the church where I was to draw the priest—The boy explained that he was a student in the Polytechnic & had once sung in the choir; & he repeated bits of liturgy. There were other matters he unhappily could not make clear. He formed gestures strange to me: He abandoned words for a while, using only his hands & face: but soon he whispered the ideas as he gestured: as if I were not to hear them. The priest was all chuckles when I returned. He was a big bearded peasant, in a frame church,—filled with people—for the holiday services. He left the offices, brought two chairs behind the church & asked to pose—He adjusted hair & robe, etc. Then he & my friend quarreled—I think he told the boy that he couldn't draw at all: & the boy threatened him: & the two jumped at each other as if to fight—This was very comical. The priest, for the moment, was in a masquerade costume. A large crowd of women & children gathered to watch this major operation. Every few minutes the "papa" enquired how the face was progressing; & there was a buzz about me. He was pleased with the drawing. I wished to be malicious & make a comical picture: but I intended a limerick & it turned out an ode. The priest broke away for a while to say several prayers. He returned quite unchanged, & quarreled again with the boy. Then the boy offered to draw him. This was easily effected. I had to go then. The boy asked my name & address which I wrote in Greek—Then he gave me his. He is called Dionysos—He kissed my hand as I left. He ran after me & shook my hand for the last time—

His face & figure were much like Whittaker's—Except that Whittaker's missing tooth was missing—

With my love, dear,

Meyer.

P.S. I must tell you of Prof. Hazen of Barnard. We traveled together in the Peloponnesos for 3 days. He picked flowers in the theatre of Epidaurus—Once

Whittaker Chambers (1901–61). Friend of Schapiro's from Columbia College; writer, editor, Communist Party member.

Charles D. Hazen (1868–1941). Professor of history at Barnard College and Columbia University.

he fell into the water at Nauplia: Near Argos he lost his toilet outfit. I met him in the Express office—Since he was trying to find a party visiting Mycene, Tiryns, etc. I suggested that he join mine (which did not really exist)[.] This he could not promise. Then I found 2 architects from Avery: I begged them to join my party (Hazen & myself) & see much at little cost. When they agreed—it was for a 7 day trip, with whole day stops at Epidaurus, Mistra & Bassae, for their work. I was anxious to go the next morning & called Hazen in his hotel & dragged him to the auto office, & got him to join. But he tried to disclaim any responsibility. He intimated that it was not to interfere with our plans that he joined: that he had only a ½ hour to decide, but was a man of slow & careful decision, etc: etc. All thru the trip: he refused to come to any conclusion: & only acted (he implied) out of deference & altruism.

He told us of a "high-born" English lady, believed mad—who at table asked an American professor (to break the ice)—the date of Plutarch's death—Whereupon the wife, in great indignation answered that it was her husband's sabbatical year: & that it was from just such concerns that he had gone to Europe—to rest his aching intellect—

Rome, 10 May 1927

Dearest Lillian:

I have since been to Corfou, Brindisi, Bari, Foggia, Naples, Pompei & Rome—That same night in Patras I finished "Crime & Punishment." In Corfou I lingered & lost my way & reached the boat as the anchor was lifted. In Corfou I met Jews in the streets who addressed me in Hebrew—I was with Santee: we visited two old Byzantine churches in the outskirts of the town. They are practically deserted, lost in the vegetation of surrounding gardens. The parkways along the shore are very charming, no shipping breaks the view—On the boat to Brindisi—I met Rhys Carpenter—again: I had been with him at old Corinth. Then I saw him another time in Rome—At Bari were beautiful Romanesque churches with unhappily remodeled interiors: & a museum in which were casts of the best art of the region: so I was consoled for Altamura, Bitonto & Trani—which I could not visit—Mussolini's name & face were everywhere in Bari—this is his native province—Even the university bears his name on its doorways.

Rhys Carpenter (1889–1980). American archaeologist and art historian at Bryn Mawr College.

Pompei was a full day—which ended wearily: what privacies to invade—& what unlimited rows of houses & decoration—The horseshoe arch noted by DeWald is not a horseshoe arch—but a damaged semi-circular arch. This was a puzzling problem: for the presumed semi ⊙ was not entirely plausible. The baths had magnificent brick-work. The celebrated bordello was a poor mean house with dark cubicles & the barest decoration—a few erotic figures—less insistent than those in the private houses: I was only 3 days in Naples & Pompei—too little time—especially with Paestum, Salerno, Herculaneum, nearby: & the wonderfully rich Naples Museum—The piety in Naples is unbelievably primitive—the religious music excellent like the native operas. The show is run by men, & attended by women—The stone & bronze feet of saints are worn away by endless kissing.

The blood of St January was to liquefy the night I visited the Cathedral—but I could not wait—

At Rome I saw Westermann again. Today we visited the Terme Museum to see the objects found in a Syrian Syncretistic sanctuary on the Janiculum. At the American School Library I saw a copy of Rostovtseff's *Social & Economic History of the Roman Empire,* which appeared when I left NY.—It is an enormous work: & I was sorry to travel when I had this before me—

Now I have so much of Rome before me that I despair of seeing the city in 7 days. More time, I cannot give. I live in a Pension—rather I eat there, but my room is with a neighboring family, who from extreme piety have darkened the house, with heavy curtains & hangings—incense is burned: & the walls covered with sorrowful Christian images—On S Maria Maggiore an inscription says—"Plenary & quotidian indulgence to the living & the defunct." It is easy enough to the defunct—There are tablets which state that a certain sum bequeathed by Signor XYZ in 1650, provides for weekly & Annual masses for his soul—in perpetuity. And in 1927, the shrivelled canons & the idiotic hairy boys pray for him. His skeleton should be exhumed, & dangled before the altar.

But one cardinal has founded a school for the Science of Infancy: in which religion is only a footnote: & in which parents are invited to attend courses on Psychology, Physiological Chemistry, Public Health, Preventive Medicine, Sociology, etc.

Meanwhile the government invites the young men to join the air forces—It is stated in electric lights—like our White Way ads—that Italy's power & supremacy will depend on aeroplanes. I have not seen such patriotism as the Italian, elsewhere—I hear, that except for a few very old men—non-Fascist professors & teachers are expelled—And the land seems unusually prosperous—In the South the fields were in full cultivation: & everywhere public works & construction, evident—The cities, too, which only a few years ago were reported filthy aggregates of slums of ruins, are thoroly modern & clean: & lively—Yet the papers talk of bad times: of unstable prices: lack of confidence etc, and at the same time of vast military projects—Mussolini's head is stenciled on walls, columns, urinals, bridges, & park benches. There is no fanaticism like this one. When Westermann discusses it, he speaks in a whisper tho there is no one about—

White Way. Nickname for Broadway between 42nd and 53rd streets in New York City.

I learned that I will have no mail in Rome. 3 months ago I had given Cairo as my forwarding address to the Rome office. Last week the Rome office sent my mail ahead to Cairo: Cairo—probably to Constantinople, the latter to Athens: & Athens to Rome again. By that time I will be in mid-ocean, approaching NY.

with love, dear,

Meyer.

Florence, 23 May 1927

Dearest Lillian:

I think I will stay another week in Florence—I can rush about and see almost everything in two or three days; but then I will be shamed by my apprehensions—

There are individual pieces which are alone worth a whole morning; and this is a pleasant town to dream in. It is so joyful to stand before Donatello or Brunelleschi—even in the most melancholy mood—if only the thoughts consequent to such perfection are allowed to ramble, to thicken, to move—that the ordinary inspection—which is simply an identifying of things already learned—is a great fraud—I came to like Michaelangelo more and more—& I find that the lapse in my appreciation of him in past years was a theoretical error—an ingrown short-sightedness—But I should not say—"I come to like him."—for I tremble before his work: & I tremble instantly for it imposes itself so quickly. It was so at Rome in the great chapel: & it is so in Florence—everywhere—And Signorelli, in Orvieto, was also magnificent: but this I had expected—

Rabbula Gospels. Florence, Biblioteca Medicea-Laurenziana, MS Plut. I. 56.

To-day, in the Laurentian Library, I made very happy acquaintance—I am working with the Rabula Gospels—a Syriac Ms. of the year 586 AD—an important Ms. for the history of East and West Christian Iconography—& the change from classic to mediaeval styles. An old man sat down near me to inspect an 11th century Greek Ms—with wonderfully minute illuminations—When he saw the Rabula, he said to me in Italian, "That has occupied many people." He could not hear my reply: I learned that he was almost entirely deaf & I wrote my words on a slip of paper. We began to discuss the book. I regretted that its paintings were never completely photographed—that poor line drawings made 60 years ago served as the basis of study: & that the Laurentian authorities refused to permit me to photograph details, since the Italian Gov't was soon to publish the whole work. The old man said—It will not appear for many years—not until after my death—But he had photoed them himself 50 years ago, under a more benevolent administration—Which surprised me. Then he offered to write his name—& asked me to write mine—His was Jean Paul Richter—Mine, dear, you know—(torralum—torralum) Quel honneur! But how amazed I was—for I had supposed him dead at least 25 years! He had been the first to edit the writings of Leonardo—40 years ago—and even earlier, he had worked on Ravenna mosaics—At 4 the library closed—and together we went to the Medici Palace to see the fine processional fresco of Benozzo Gozzoli—On the way he spoke of his friend Kondakoff—(who flourished in the 70s and 60s.) We talked of early Christian arts, of Coptic, of Fiorenzo di Lorenzo, of the capitals of San Miniato, and of the Baptistery mosaics—He was delighted to hear that I had been to Baalbek—He had visited it in 1876, before it was known—& in a time when a horse was the only means of travel to Baalbek. He rode two days in the mountains from Beyrouth—spent three days in Baalbek—& rode two more to return. This was in the pre-snapshot camera period—& he had to draw most painstakingly to record any detail. How simple it is to work now—tho the material seems infinitely more complex! In a year, I have had no such troubles—all was laid out before me.—at most, a little walking or climbing: but the old adventure of toilsome discovery has disappeared.

Jean Paul Richter (1847-1937). German dealer and historian of Italian art and early Christian art and archaeology.

Nikodim P. Kondakov (1844-1925). Russian historian of Byzantine art who studied Byzantine works primarily through iconography.

But discoveries there are, & very happy ones—whether of new Mss, buildings, carvings—or facts & relations that help to explain them. Only there is so much that any preoccupation is an ascetic infliction, that keeps the eyes fixed on one spot—I run thru the Laurentian Library, skipping all but certain works—for I have not the time: & I dare not turn aside except for too brief a moment. Such a splendor shines on the pages of the opened codices, that I beg myself to remain longer. The Rabula is an ugly piece of incompetence: but is all the Syro-Mesopotamian that survives of that early time—& I must devote a few more days to it. And there is an 11th c. French Ms. that is close to Moissac which I must handle afterwards—& then perhaps—I can consider in leisure, the beautiful 14th c. books.

I am well, dear; but I am subject to a thousand changes of thought each day: & I can only say that at this moment I write to you with great joy & in happiness—and with all my love—Meyer

Milan, 6 June 1927

Darling Lillian:

As your term ends, mine does, too—I have been called back to Paris by a letter from Hamann, who has been photographing Mss. for me. But as soon, the summer session will begin, in South France & Spain. I have had to hurry thru North Italy—with the usual promises to return another year: but I was happy to visit Ravenna, Bologna, Padua, Venice, Verona & Milan—I should have stayed longer in Venice & Ravenna—Giotto, Donatello & Tintoretto were especially fine—the last overwhelming in some works—I saw fine Romanesque & Byzantine architecture & beautiful Mss.

I heard at last from Murray after a year's silence—His wife was ill—& he could not write—He advised me not to "scatter" but to "concentrate." In the Bologna Museum, a little boy of 7 or 8[] drew aside a curtain to see a painted shield with St. George & the Dragon: his mother stopped him, saying "That does not interest you"—"Everything interests me," he replied—In a few minutes, the museum closed—

with my love, sweetheart—

Meyer—

Paris, 13 June 1927

Dearest Lillian:

I was very happy to read that Sophie is coming—But when she arrives I will no longer be in Paris—since I leave in a few days—This is unfortunate—but it is now too late to change my plans—I will write her in NY. & again in Paris—

Sophie Milgram (1905–68). Lillian's younger sister.

She must be sure that she travels with a friend—otherwise there will be many vexations—It must be very lonely for a tourist in a foreign land—without the language & without friends—& especially for a girl—But if she is with another she will live much more cheaply & easily & never be lost—2 girls can travel 3rd class in Italy—but never—one—2 girls can shake off the crowd of peddlers, beggars, guides, & agents who pester at the stations—but never one—And of course when there is so much to see & enjoy—the company of a friend is very sweet.

I came from Milan a few days ago—called by a letter from Hamann who wishes to finish work at the BN. But he arrived only to-day. In the meantime I have been working in the library with the last few Moissac Mss—& some fine books from St. Germain-des-Près—

I was crazy to reach Paris. I rode 17 hours from Milan—crossing Switzerland—& lovely country, with all manner of grandeur & picturesqueness—& quiet villages that seem uninhabited—The Italian lakes were very beautiful & I did not regret that I had so suddenly changed my route—giving up the Riviera by which I had entered Italy.

And Paris was such a happy entry—as if it were my home I saw again—I had to slap the first acquaintance I met in the streets—but it was old Omont—almost 80—& his beard quite stringy—But he greeted me as joyfully as I greeted him—& we walked along the Avenue de l'Opera—very gay—He spoke of the Near East Missions of the French Scientists in the 17th & 18th century—on which he has published 2 large volumes—& treated me as the very last of them. In the library I found Rand again, & many of the same faces—I learned that Enlart had died—& that Deschamps had succeeded him as director of the Trocadero. I was sorry to have returned late to see Enlart. I had taken special photos in the East of works in which he was interested. Before I left, in January, he had given me addresses of friends in Syria—

Pauline "Polly" Rush Fadiman. A friend of Lillian's from Barnard College and wife of Clifton "Kip" Fadiman.

To-morrow Kip arrives in Paris—Polly has already been here several months—A boy whom I knew very well in high-school—has also come to the city—I expect Herman in a few days—Is not this like a return from a vacation the opening of a school year—when we meet on the same campus?—It is so for me—

with love, dear—

Meyer—

P.S. I will not be home on time for the opening of school—perhaps not until two or three weeks after—At least it seems so now—when my plans are so much larger than my vision—

Paris, 22 June 1927

Dearest Lillian:

If I returned earlier, I could also go to the beach with you—but in the middle of October it may be too late—Yet we can walk and see the ocean which in autumn, in the grey day, is very fine.

On the walls of the Medical School, a few blocks from me, are posted notices of summer courses. There will be a series of conferences in the hospitals on "Recent Work on the Liver" by a dozen or more men: and another series on the Bile Ducts (the "biliary ways.") and others, I cannot now recall—All the lectures are indicated, & seem so rich and esoteric (including your "syphilis & cirrhosis["]) that it is a great pity you cannot attend them. But I think stenographic reports are made of these conferences & published—I have seen in the bookstores many such small volumes reproducing various courses in the medical schools & hospitals—The

German students complain that the hospitals are insufficient, & work difficult—like my friend Karl last summer: with his bitter contrast of the 75 people he cut in one day in Vienna and the meager half-dozen in Paris.

You made a happy calculation when you supposed that I might need the $100—But I am well provided for. I have been sent the first two month's stipend of next year's allowance, since I am remaining in Europe August & September. This will cover all my expenses—I have lived more cheaply than I had supposed: travel & photography & books have been the great expense. In fact, the Carnegie people gave me about 500 dollars too much; since at the end of 1 year, I had spent on travel and food and lodging (both Atlantic trips included) less than $1500—And it was never intended that travel include so much time in the Near East, when the student's problem was Occidental: & that it should provide for several hundred volumes, 2 cameras, and thousands of photos—

I enclose one, a snapshot, taken with the smaller camera, of the recumbent head of a gigantic figure of Ramses II, in Memphis. A house has been built around the statue to protect it. It was abandoned on this spot after great efforts to drag and roll it to Cairo—At least once, dear, behold it, horizontal. It was impossible to photo the whole figure—It was everywhere in this house—

In some ways you are like him, darling, tho less assured—

Meyer.

Paris, 25 June 1927

Dearest Lillian:

When you tell me that it will soon be a pleasure for me to dress: I think it will be an even greater pleasure to undress. For I will be very anxious to take off the red, yellow & blue bags & hats you describe—It is already two months that a great rent in my trousers (a little below the left knee) has been crying to be repaired: It is still a hole: & will be for many months. How many tailors I pass in one day: how many windows with new suits; cleaner hats than the present relic thru whose hole the hat racks penetrate with such deliberate charm—& yet I alter nothing: I choose no new suit or hat, even after I have told myself—To-day I will buy a new hat—To-day I will buy a new hat—without the slightest argument or contradiction. It is evident that I do not wish a new hat. I have not worn the present hat the full six years which render a hat, a part of the body itself—a genuine organ that functions, ~~unconsci~~ me unconscious (terrible slip—these, Lillian)[.]

The rapid color changes you describe in clothing fashions only illustrate the theory of the celebrated Kondakov (v. 2nd French ed. Travinsky 1887) that in art as in life. The last steps of progressive degenerescence are the most rapid—the most colorful—the most striking in their originality: yet the least fruitful. Shall I then commit myself to a contemporary theory: declare myself a child of the age—& enamored of the efflorescence of putrescence—wear yellow trousers, red vest, green jacket & purple hat with salmon pink zigzag stripes? Or go in mourning for my unhappy age—in a smart dark suit of very durable Scotch crepe-de-chine—

"2nd French ed. Travinsky 1887." Nikodim P. Kondakov, *Histoire de l'art byzantin considéré principalement dans les miniatures*, trans. Florentin Trawinski, 2 vols. (Paris: Librairie de l'Art, 1886–91).

3 buttoned with knotched lapels? The hose are the man—& these too must be considered: but before such complexity, I welcome this late hour which demands sleep & no clothes——

With all my love, dear—

Meyer.

P.S. I hear from Jakey—that on July 2 you leave for camp—Oh how delighted I was to hear this—But I stop to wonder if this is a mere 48 hour plunge in the water, among 10,000 4th of July vacations—or a whole summer in the land, with little children, and a lake—and boats, & restful days—with some leisure for the unforgettable "medicine"—Which is it, darling?—I can only hope, the last.

Barcelona, 20 July 1927

Dear Lillian:

Please forgive me this long silence—I was indifferent & could not write. But I could have said something, if only a few words: I let days pass awaiting an occasion—a better mood—a letter from you which might rouse me.

I left Paris July 2, and traveled South slowly, stopping in Bourges, Brive, Beaulieu, Souillac, Carennac, Collonges, Martel, Cahors, until I came to Toulouse—There I remained 3 days—I was with an architect, La Farge—who told me much about his grand uncle—Henry Adams. We visited churches together and analyzed construction & design like 2 collaborators on the same problem. He left for Moissac; I for Carcas[s]onne, Narbonne, & Perpignan—He plans to repeat my Near Eastern trip to Egypt, Palestine, Amman & Syria.

Henry Adams La Farge (1902–85). American architect and grandson of painter John La Farge, a friend of Henry Adams.

On July 14, I walked to Cuxa from Prades, & to Codalet, to see the fragments of the old monastery left by George Grey Barnard—On the hot holiday, peasants were still at work in the fields:

George Grey Barnard (1863–1938). Sculptor and proponent of showing sculpture in its original surroundings who bought and sold medieval sculptures dug up in the French countryside, including Saint-Michel-de-Cuxa.

My first days in Spain were great thrills: The landscape, the buildings & people were little different from those I had seen the last days in France—for Perpignan, Cuxa, Prades, & Elne, are, like Gerona & Ripoll, Catalonian towns—But here the remains are richer, more imposing—almost stuffily furnished with imagination—The landscape, the mountains are closer to the cities & small towns. They are seen from the streets: the contrasts of mountain & valley & river beds & forests are not lost in distances—I think I ought to stay longer in Spain: but there is little time.

I will not go farther south than Toledo—It is very hot in Barcelona. In the mountains, in Vich & Ripoll, pleasanter: but still hot in midday—as in the worst of NY. summer.

I speak a miserable broken Spanish—am understood & tolerated: as no American would tolerate as bad an English: & the priests especially[] are kind & quick to follow my thought. Sometimes there are Spaniards who talk French, & everything becomes easy:

I will write soon, dear Lillian—

With my love,

Meyer

Barcelona, 21 July 1927

No, dear, I did not guess that you were camp physician. Tho I had wished it. But I still do not know for how long—whether for 2 weeks, like the interns who come one after the other—or for the whole summer: You will care for the children, all of whom will love you—may they not be ill to come to such a sentiment—(a formal idea of mine—really, I do not know them, form no image of either their sufferings or your ministrations) & you will live more happily in the country. What detestable summers you have spent in the city—while I frolicked with the boys & girls or bit myself all over with gloomy reflections in "adult" (!) camps. There was always a time in mid-summer—after 2 or 3 weeks of healthy rapture for the change of air, the sports & the thoughtless mechanics of our routine—when I thought this camp a horrible prison—& longed to leave it. I do not remember if I made it clear to you in the letters I wrote you then. I found fault with every detail: I do not think I alone—for there were common complaints, strikes & committees to annoy the management. But afterwards in the city we agreed that it was best to return & that nowhere else could we have such gay & cheaply paid for—indulgence—I cannot think of it now as a place where I will work with a crowd—but as a repose in a desert or a forest with some discomforts & a great relaxation. The assurance of sun-rise & sunset is real, where there is a routine fixed by another: & very pleasant if without duties & with few restrictions.

I doubt these days spent en[?] voyage. & my doubt is so embroiled in accidents of temperature, of comfort, of variety that I cannot insist on any philosophy drawn from it. And without such insistence, there is no action—no change for worse or for better that does not spring from other fortuities. & I continue to waver & exploit my own capabilities—There are so many comforts for pride that always some hope remains—& the most bitter self-criticism is submerged in one instant of fulfilled variety—

It strikes midnight at this moment. I should have been in bed 2 hours ago according to plans made earlier in the evening—as years ago I should have been in Hartley dormitory when I was with you in our poor sweet garden—

Hartley dormitory. Residence hall at Columbia College.

But if I do rise earlier—at 7 to be at the Archives at 8, what shall I be, or do? I came to-day at 9 & found the place closed: & it was not until the afternoon that I learned that it is a holiday—some festival pertaining to the Queen of Spain—who figures so often in bawdy college verses—to fit a rhyme.—A Catalan boy led me from place to place—anxious to find the Archives for me, & knowing as little of their location as I who am a stranger. But after he left me, he wrote me his name & address—& I gave him mine. Surely I will not see him: as he will not see me: & I can only wonder if he did not half wish me to call upon him—as I for a moment thought that perhaps in a lonely night in Barcelona, his company—tho mute & troubled by our lack of even one common language—might comfort me. He is a medical student—as I learned from the books he carried & a few words of Catalan that I grasped in the confusion of tongues—I know what will happen tomorrow—if I do visit the Archives: & see the manuscripts from the Abbey of S. Maria de Ripoll—I will find again pages I have seen in photographs & which

Paris, BnF MS Latin 2077. Ninth-century manuscript from Moissac. **Paris, BnF MS Latin 1820.** Eighth-century manuscript from the Abbaye Saint-Mesmin de Micy.

are already familiar, but also others which will excite me enormously because the forms of letters (paleography, is the more noble & consecrated word), certain ornamented initials—& several unreproduced & unknown miniatures will show a relationship to Paris BN. latin 2077, or 1820, & to various sculptures in Catalonia & Languedoc—Then I will be very happy: write furiously rapid notes & copy details—& perhaps photo them—Then I will day dream more complex relations—I will hold threads in more directions—& the work I have done in Paris will seem even more significant. I am sure I will tell Senor Alloch & other interested Catalans of these rapports of Mss. in Moissac & Ripoll—showing clearly the derivative character of the latter: & I will be both publicly (the 12 men who understand these matters) & self honored.

The minuteness of such work becomes so ridiculous—in the light of Barcelona—among the slums & narrow stinking streets & harbor, and the crowded Ramblas which one thinks the very highway of urbanity—that I despair of its seriousness—Once, 100 years ago, the poet with a taste for human history or the arts, sat on rocks in wild landscapes (Chateaubriand's Caledonian bard) or mediated ruins: it's made of scraps or leavings of history a poem for a given mood—If he saw a Ripoll Ms. he did not say that the total absence of Visigothic a, t, & f forms pointed to an earlier penetration of French culture in this region—but that the minute regularity of script was the unvaried beating of a devout heart—& that such cardiac religiosity outlived the passions & frenzies of contemporary kings & delighted generations unborn (adoration of the egs.)

I know that after 1000 monographs have exhausted a million details, their blurred image will make a fine picture for the few people who are taken by such things. May they be taken by other things.

The professional habit becomes so strong that vanity is reinforced each moment by the simple success of its preoccupations. The humility of unpaid, unsung scholarship is a foolish tale: I am overwhelmed by the libraries of the world which surely contain 10,000,000 monographs—& the books, stores & quais, & the pages rotting in warehouses—which no search for proposed truth or man's happiness designed, but the professional practice of printing, broadcasting personal details. What business-man has the circulation of a poor thesis? the discussion, the review, the endless citation & recollection of his existence in footnotes & polemics? These may have happy results—give us telephones or a more just view of man's character. But disinterestedness is not their prime distinction.

Some days ago I saw in the Annuaire of the Catalan Institute a volume of beautiful photos of textiles, of carvings, of architecture, of miniatures & pottery—& I was so filled by these objects that I wondered if there could be a happier scientific devotion than to such things—But I remember that I reacted so to the printed representations of them: & not to the works themselves: For with them I feel otherwise: Sometimes I approach gaily & talk ecstatically to myself & bring myself to tears & regrets—but as often I detect a peculiar length of the ears in one figure, a deformed uncial M (ɱ) in a border inscription, & relate A to B to C to D. & do not regard the works in themselves—as art until the bell rings & I am about to leave. I am professionalized, dear, sweet Lillian: I am a monster of measurements, plans, transverse sections, squinches, arabesques & orthostatic courses—What will I say to you when I return? that the "Nil Formidetis" of a Santo Domingo de Silos miniature is a non-textual variant, & that since it occurs in a French script, but in a lectionary written in a Visigothic, hand, it is a later addition, & disproves the contentions of the celebrated Schlichtgeroll & his whole misguided school—

And if I am asked—My dear man, do not lose sight of your proportions, of your noble Jewish tradition—what is the value of such a point?—what light does it shed on our future? what new happiness does it bring to the great mass of suffering mankind? Then with one eye shut, I will adroitly reply—My dear colleague (for we are all colleagues, in this business)—you stand too close to the truth to see the whole of it: & the little you can see from your place[] is so tiny, so insignificant that you must question its value & the labor devoted to its discovery. But at a distance of 1 kilometre (the scientific distance) or better 2, or 3 kilometres—you will see 1000 details form a perfect pattern in which will rejoice your eyes—& which will lift man from a brutish ignorance to a sublime mastery of his own life—((& of nature)—no distinction)[.] It is only from the complete probity of such details that the whole derives its force—But the colleague who reads only text books & outlines of science is insistent. How can the Silos inscription affect him? he asks.

And then I shut the other eye & say rapidly to keep him from following me, that—

If the inscription is as I say—a later addition: then likewise the miniature: if the miniature is later: then the relief in Silos copied from it & with the identical inscription, is of the middle 12th century & not of the 11th as Schlichtgeroll would have it. Now if Schlichtgeroll is correct it means that only the initial stages of Romanesque art were rich, fruitful, original. & that Spain preceded France in such creations & furnished her with every motif—(This has an undoubted interest to the patriots of these 2 countries). In which case that gloomy school of morphological historians who believe in inevitable curves of archaism[,] maturity & decay, is correct, & we to-day are all damned: But if the inscription "Nil Formidetis" is a non-textual variant—then by a processus of logic (too long to develop for non-technical minds!) Silos sculpture is of the middle 12th century & as rich & archaic & inventive, at a time when elsewhere the Romanesque styles are decadent: Hence the "archaic, maturity, decay" curve is not a single line, is not a simple determined form: & the history of the arts & the human spirits do not confirm the predictions of contemporary pessimists & politicians. And further it is possible to determine why Silos forms are archaic & novel at this later time, why they escape the sad destiny of their neighbors—so that we to-day can take courage from this fact & improve ourselves—& not despair.—& we can restore empirically some details of the Silos "situation" & revive[?] ourselves—

This will calm any colleague. But he must not be shown the inscription or the Silos works: or the long arguments on the matter—for they will quicken any prediction of our decay. And I should add that in few discussions of the subject are those beautiful carvings of Silos properly reproduced, or their artistic character—

"Nil Formidetis." From the speech by the angel to the Maries, found on the relief of the Maries at the tomb in the cloister of Silos; see Meyer Schapiro, "From Mozarabic to Romanesque at Silos," in idem, *Romanesque Art* (New York: G. Braziller, 1976), 94 n. 179. Schapiro wrote to Arthur Kingsley Porter about this specific problem in a letter dated 24 July 1927 and about the more general difficulties he was having in a letter dated 10 November 1927.

Schlichtgeroll. In German, *schlicht* means "plain, simple" and *Geröll* means "rubble, gravel, garbage." Thus, *Schlichtgeröll* means "plain garbage."

which is their most valuable part, analyzed. And if the colleague is obstinate or at all a man of sense—he will say that it is not any paleographic data which will strengthen or depress our world—& that it is naïve to presume that man's energies are turned one way or another by such problematic & abstruse books—It may be that the Romantic revolution in philosophy & literature played a great part in 19th century socialism & nationalism & in the supposed emancipation—spiritually—of modern man. & that this revolution in ideas was determined in great part by historical studies—by the development of the idea of progress—& by travel—but there were more profound economic causes—& men fished for ideas or confirmations—& found the waters well stocked—we continually breed these facts & suppositions—for whoever loves such a diet. But after modern methods of breeding, the product is unpalatable, too bony, refractory, hard,—& with too little actual digestible substance—One must pick the flesh from a hundred to fill one plate: & the bones uneaten, are hard to dispose of. They are true offspring—

Works may surpass their motives: but the pettiness of most researches—at this moment—give an even poorer notion of motives.

July 22

Darling Lillian:

This, being early morning I cannot well subscribe to all I wrote above. In a half hour I will be to the Archives, & split hairs—why do we despise "hair-splitting[”]? The word itself should inspire us—as the very summit of dexterity & detachment. What can one do with a split hair? what future life is there in it? But the process of its "becoming" is wonderful—a spectacle, only the elect can assist at, & a feat that demands the subtlety of every touch & the most ingenious attentiveness to immeasurable parts. Some day the hair-splitters will come into their own. As Mortimer Adler has hoped—when philosophy abandons its moral or dogmatic ends—only dialectic will remain—And the supermen will split curled, frizzled & wavy hairs, hitherto unsplit. Some use may be discovered for the split fragments. Perhaps they will be a rare hors-d'oeuvre—And this science will be justified: & relapse into its old state of a practical problem.

Meyer

Mortimer J. Adler (1902–2001). American philosopher who taught at Columbia University until he earned his PhD in 1928. From a letter from Clifton Fadiman dated 28 December 1926, it is clear that Schapiro knew Adler at Columbia; Schapiro's observation here is a criticism of Adler.

Saragossa, 24 July 1927

Dearest Lillian—

The last day in Barcelona was quite other than I supposed in my despair. I was only 2 hours in the Archives when I had finished the Mss. & found them a poor lot—for there was little to discover: the best had long ago been chewed down to a well known fact. But the catalogue drawn up by Garcia in German was very interesting, and I learned what a poor proportion of the original library of 250 books (in the 12th c.) I was handling: & how partial must be any judgment. The archives reading room was a terribly hot & informal place. An enormous priest smoked a cigar—He leaned often towards me to see what books I was studying. I yearned to know if he wore trousers under his cassock, or simply flannel underwear or per-

"catalogue . . . by Garcia." Zacharías García Villada, *Bibliotheca Patrum Latinorum Hispaniensis, II* (Vienna: A. Hölder, 1915).

haps nothing but a cross and a Bible—There was such a barking of dogs and yelling of children in the streets that the handful (Goliath's hand) of readers swore & shook their heads & looked about for some imaginary justice to end this clamor. But I was half glad: I was pleased that besides minuscules, there were children & dogs in the world—& I ran outside in great joy 3 steps at a time—when Ripollensis 192 was completed—But I regretted Beers, the German who in 2 years classified & catalogued 1500 Mss. in Spain, & then died a premature death—shortly after a monumental Sitzungsbericht of the Wiener-Akademie der Wissenschaft—phil-hist. Klasse—What a loss to Palaeography!

Rudolf Beer (1863–1913). German paleographer who specialized in Latin, Spanish, and German works.

Once outside, children & dogs had ceased—There were so many of them that all distinction ended—they were like the grasses of the field—or the clouds, or the windows with the washing & bedding—all common objects, at least someone's joy or despair—but for the rest of creation—anonymous.

In the afternoon I rode to Tarrasa, 20 miles away; & after a half-hour of wandering in the town, continually misdirected, misunderstood, & misunderstanding—I found the group of 3 churches I was seeking. One was a Visigothic, 8th c. building—still beautiful in its bareness & unhabitation & wonderful to think of & study: for its plan, an exceptional one, is found in Etschmiadzin (Armenia), Germigny-des-Près (France) & in Milan in the Carolingian period.

The grouping of 3 such ancient buildings reminded me of the Bologna St. Stefano group which I had enjoyed immensely & to which I had come twice. In Tarrasa were 12th c. frescoes of the deepest & most beautifully saturated colors, such as the late Renaissance employed, but here without shadows, simply on flat figures. There were also Gothic & Renaiss. paintings—almost as fine.—Later I passed a Gothic church in Tarrasa—a poor thing beside the others, tho many times as large & more richly furnished—Two men were carving the capitals of the West portal which had never been finished: & I was astonished that the labor of the 2 was identical to the smallest leaf-lobe—& that no difference in design could suggest 2 different hands. Yet it is the official working method in anthropology & archaeology: to presume that identical products spring from identical hands, & that different hands, however much under the same influence, produce at least somewhat different results. But here, of course, is another factor—the modern mechanical atelier training, the fixed patterns, the use of casts & moulds, electric drills: & the laborer—status of ornament & stone-cutters. It was a comical reflection on the thought "Style is the Man" to see these 2 workers—one [*drawing of two men on a scaffold before a round-arched building (fig. 4)*] enormously fat & red and short & the other, a skinny efficient man, with his hat over his eyes.

I stopped too often to buy ice-cream sandwiches—& before I realized it I was late for the train to Barcelona. I ran & caught it. Since I had no ticket I had to pay a fine: & since this fine was annoying I decided to stop on the way home (!) at San Cugat del Vallès (Saint Cucufat of the Valley) where is a beautiful Romanesque cloister, the only one in Catalonia, whose author & sculptor has signed his name to his work. I found it closed—An idiot boy, remarkably hairy, guessed my intention, & found the concierge for me—He ran limping, tho not lame—chased, &

Sant Cugat del Vallès. Named after Saint Cucuphas, who is said to have been martyred on the spot now occupied by its medieval monastery.

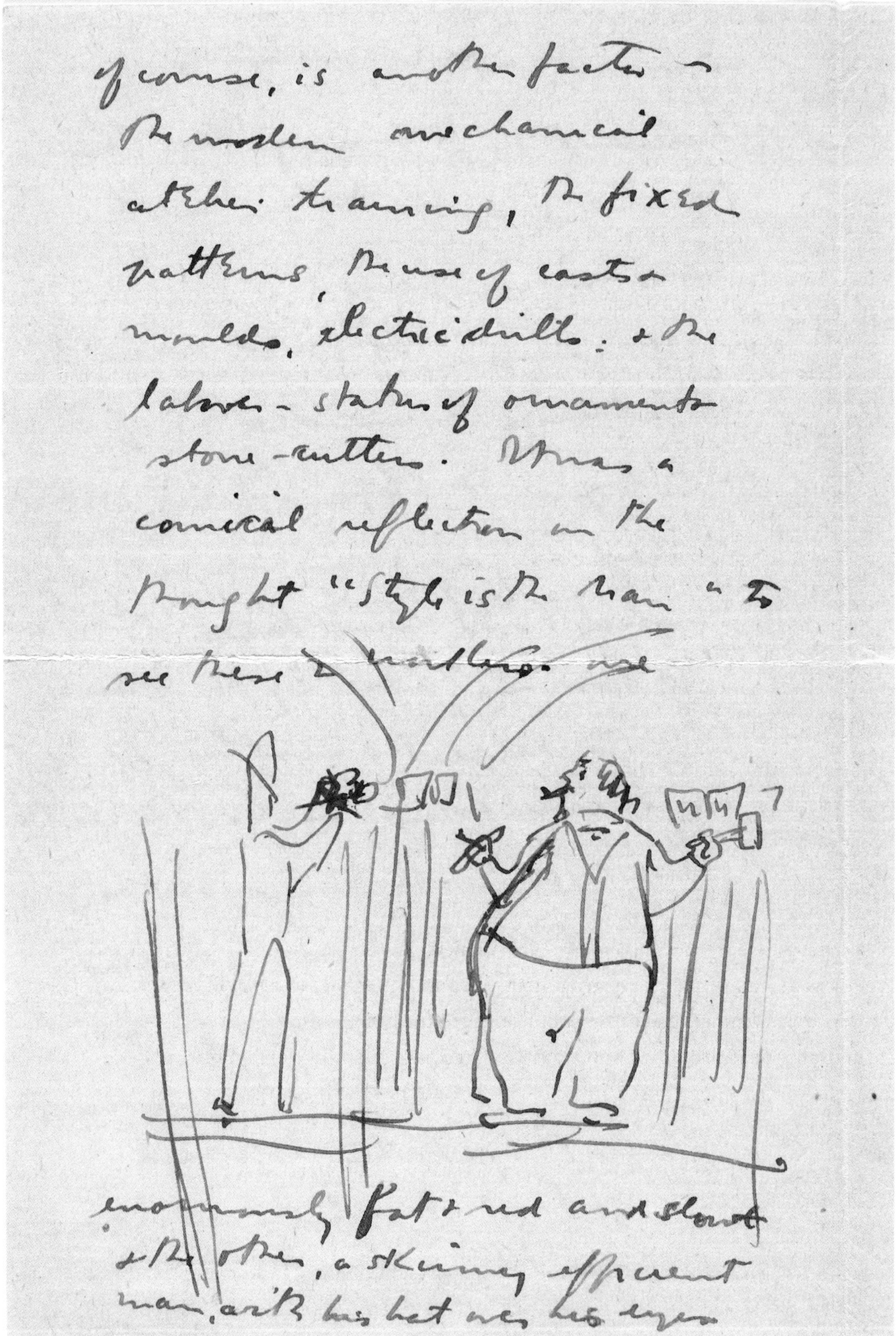

of course, is another factor — the modern mechanical atelier training, the fixed patterns, the use of casts & moulds, electric drills: & the labor-status of ornamental stone-cutters. It was a comical reflection on the thought "style is the man" to see these 2 [illegible] workers are

enormously fat & red and stout & the other, a skinny efficient man, with his hat over his eyes

Fig. 4. Two men on a scaffold before a round-arched building, Saragossa, 24 July 1927

barked at, the dogs he passed, & smiled most ingratiatingly to me. In the meantime I ate a good part of a watermelon to prepare myself for this coming spiritual adventure. I was pleased by Arnold Catell's cloister: & tho I had thought to look, & take no notes, I wrote for almost 2 hours, photoed, & drew. Children played by the central fountain. The shabbiness of the galleries disappeared: & the whole cloister was a rich garden & a pure work—The church adjoining was equally fine—Later I walked behind: & how astonished I was by the garden around the apse—with flowers absent from the cloister: and beside a small shady park of parallel rows of trees on a terrace—From its parapet I saw the whole country which was quiet & simple, but so cut by roads & minor valleys to make a modern picture—The church tower, above the park, had Moorish proportions—but no Moorish details—a subtlety (really my own) that pleased me—

Arnaldo Cadell (act. ca. 1190–1207). Spanish sculptor who signed the cloister.

Returning to the station was a path thru poor quarters—of working people—Since I was in khaki & dusty, I felt easier, more sympathetic—& regretted my hat—for no one here wears a hat.

I reached Barcelona after 9 PM. ate too large a meal—made out rain schedules for a week ahead, chatted with the pension owner—& went to sleep—

The next morning was in Tarragona.—of which I could write a great deal, dear, but now I can not, since it is 11:30, in Saragossa, & tomorrow I must take an early train to Huesca—

But how can I refrain, dear Lillian, from saying that in Tarragona—climbing the steps from the lower city to the upper, I saw the beach & the blue sea: & that at noon when the cathedral & cloister were closed, I bathed—the first ocean swim in almost two years. It was very warm, in and out of water: the tide was low—only few people were on the beach—At two I made my meal on the bath-pavillion, of cheese & peaches & tomatoes and bread and beer—all excellent. Where were you then, sweetheart?—I returned too late to the town. Both museums were closed: & one concierge asleep—not to be awakened—I found, instead, an early Moorish remain that brought Amman back to me: & I lingered for hours in the cloister of Tarragona Cathedral—beautiful like San Cugat's & Gerona's. Then I rode all night, 11 hours to Saragossa.—whence I write—my dear,—& whence I leave, hence, for Tardienta—Huesca (v. supra)[,] Jaca, S. Juan de la Peña—cloisters all—God begotten—Meyer

Madrid, 1 August 1927

Dear Lillian—

I come from Gómez-Moreno, who was most affable & easy: & gave me more in an hour than I had found for weeks in travel & study. There was little information: but it was all surprising & original. I was amazed by his freedom: others have been terribly secretive & suspicious of questions: he was always laughing & amused by his own discoveries. He looks the perfect father: & also, curiously, like the sensual indolent Moors of the picture books & stories. I came at the last moment, as he was preparing to leave for his vacation, but he showed in no way either urgency or his watch: & remained with me a whole hour. Later we walked in the park. Perhaps I will see him again in Santiago.

Manuel Gómez-Moreno (1870–1970). Spanish professor of Arabic and Christian medieval archaeology at the Universidad de Madrid.

Waiting for him, I had spent two beautiful hours in a private museum of decorative art—of which he is director—It is impossible to speak of so many objects—They occupy little rooms, are all exquisite, finished,—of many materials—swords & helmets, & pots & textiles & rugs & books, & iron & wood work. There are Moorish, Visigoth, Gothic, & Mudejar pieces—It is sinful to speak hereafter of "mere decoration" or of "surface effects." Ornament & texture are capable of as much variety as music—but variety is not their distinction: but their imaginative richness, named coldly. We dream so much in terms of human beings & living shapes, that these works become miraculous, inconceivably created—or by minds quite different from ours. How far can we prolong a fantasy of polygons, or a blue white & gold combination?—Figure arts, tho much more complex, seem, for the moment—easier.

A week ago, I came to Jaca, for one day, to see a tomb, described by Porter. But the Bishop refused me admission, since an order from Rome forbid men visitors in a convent. I thought then to leave Jaca—disconsolate. But I remained six days, & have not been so happy often on this voyage.

I met a group of Spanish students & professors, of the University of Saragossa Summer Session, which by a wise choice is held at Jaca—a small town of 5000, high in the Pyrenees, cool, & in a lovely country—mountains on all sides, tree shaded woods, parks, & Romanesque churches all around in neighboring villages. The Spaniards were so good to me, I was very unhappy to leave: & unhappier still, that leaving, I would not return for many years. Some may come to NY, & some will write to me.

One day, I climbed Mt. Pano to see the monastery, now deserted, in its cave, between precipices, under an enormous overhanging rock—S. Juan de la Peña. I ought to write you a whole book of this trip & the cloister—dear—certainly you will love to be there. The going is as fine as its end: & there are even the pleasures of contemplative melancholy—an achieved weariness,—& a sad human spectacle—For a while I was absorbed in the mean business of copying inscriptions & after the high mood of enlarged panoramic visions, & this elevated solitude—I grovelled in controversies & epigraphic interpretations—& believe me, dear, I was most wickedly ecstatic to discover that a most distinguished elder in my profession had misread a stone 200 years & had thereby been induced into a brilliantly supported, & apparently impregnable theory. I made some measurements, studied the cloister: experimented successfully with another theory of the proportions of base circumferences in columns. This last is very neat: & I will learn in a few months, if sound—

There were also two trips to Santa Cruz de la Serós, 10 miles from Jaca—a most wonderful church of which I shall send you pictures. The sacristan was a good-natured peasant who seemed overjoyed by the problem of holding the other end of a tape—I did not finish work the 1st trip: & in the 2nd, there was no auto to take me to Santa Cruz, & I walked the 20 miles—a poor way to enjoy landscape. The peasants on the road, offered me wine & water, & looked after when I was some distance away.

One whole day I spent in the cathedral of Jaca, and another in its archives, where were donations of the 11th & 12th centuries signed by the Kings of Aragon: in arabic. (Their coins also bore arabic characters)—& written in a script whose changes from visigothic—to "French" hand were nicely discernable over a period of 75 years, & were paralleled by changes in costume in the miniatures: & in the technique of drawing—

The cathedral was especially interesting—for its construction is unique in Aragon: & has been subject to many wild explanations. The classic plan of it, reproduced in the manuals, is inaccurate: & a description of all details still lacking. I came to another conclusion after I had drawn & measured: & found the "alternate system" of supports was purely perfunctory & artistic, & corresponded to no existing structural system & that these probably never were groin vaults—I was delighted when Gómez-Moreno agreed—He had come to the same conclusion on purely logical grounds—without examination of the building—from his knowledge of the whole region: & by comparison with simpler works.

In Jaca I was with 2 doctors—brothers Noguera, who keep a sanatorium in the Pyrenees, to which I have an eternal invitation. Noguera Sr. gave a lecture in which he utilized the experiments of Pavlov on conditioned reflex, for surgery of the stomach—But I could not follow him in Spanish—Little children in the audience—slept, cried, played or picked their (own) noses—& older minds, looked very anxious & thoughtful—

Ramón y Cajal, after whom are named many streets in Spain (in Jaca, too)[,] was in Jaca at the time. But he is old & infirm & not to be visited.

I met the doctor who originated the theory that El Greco was astigmatic, & that the distortions of his art can be reproduced by special lenses. He has one pair thru which the fat figures of Rubens become ascetic & elongated: & another in which El Greco approaches Rubens: & others which will make of common human types these 2 extremes. But I unfortunately, did not keep the appointment, being busy with architecture, & arrived 2 hours too late for the good doctor—He looks like both Gómez-Moreno & Santayana—When I discussed the astigmatic problem with him, he said nothing, but smiled most knowingly, as if all I had said, had long ago been considered—

This is a vicious method of approaching social phenomena, to explain religion by mouth infections, architecture by religion: design by personal idiosyncrasies. The doctor agreed that most people were astigmatic: but that El Greco's art was very uncommon. I think it would be interesting to demonstrate the doctor's thesis by good photos comparing the results of various vision: & then to show the actual causes; 2 parallel & 2 plausible explanations—He admitted that the "sporadic" recurrence of elongated & inhumanly proportioned forms in many cultures & many periods must have an explanation other than astigmatism, but he is firm on El Greco. He neglects Tintoretto, the teacher of El Greco, who employed similar distortions, & the whole baroque movement: & finally, El Greco's origin in Crete where flourished in his time a Byzantine school which employed extreme elongation: if El Greco were astigmatic as is said, then his pictures would not show it:

Santiago Ramón y Cajal (1852–1934). Spanish doctor, awarded the Nobel Prize in Physiology and Medicine in 1906.

"I met the doctor . . ." Germán Beritens, an ophthalmologist in Jaca, first expounded this theory in 1913.

for to El Greco's eyes his picture must be "normal" to give him his anastigmatic impression:—unless the flat surfaces are very differently seen than masses.—And always there is the irregular appearance of these distortions in El Greco—the absence of any given time sequence, the coexistence in the same work of both long & normal, straight & bent forms, etc., etc. Perhaps Natalie—still likes El Greco—as she did 2 years ago when we walked in Central Park—& when she laughed so boisterously that a boy who passed, stopped in amazement, & turned a hand-spring—"Madame, you fill me with unholy glee."

The day after to-morrow I will visit Toledo, & see El Greco, the Jewish mediaeval synagogues, & the Arab buildings. But I cannot think of them now: there is so much that comes between. To day the Prado was closed: & in the Archaeological Museum, I finished only a few rooms—all too absorbing for this short stay.

José Camón Aznar (1898–1979). Spanish critic and art historian.

I am sorry that when I visit Salamanca, José Camón, whom I met in Jaca, & who teaches in the University of Salamanca, will not be there.—But he will connive to reach America in a year or two. What a time we had explaining matters to each other: for tho he reads French & German, he speaks neither: & understands their spoken words only with great effort: & my Spanish is still insufficient: & so mingled with Italian: that to day, in speaking Italian, with GM, I often lapsed into bad Spanish—But Camón & I understand each other—(or presumed so: or accepted a smile or a gesture as a full meaning) & were never overcome by these language difficulties. And what things we talked of—for 2 people dumb to each other. I met him at Santa Cruz de la Serós, in the company of a Saragossa lawyer, who, without shame, & with much humility calls himself,—a "dilettante"—Camón is very nervous, rose in his seat in fright when the auto sped, or another car approached: & was overcome with anxiety because of a forthcoming lecture—He declared himself—radical—very radical—anti-religious—but his ideas are full of Catholic theology: & his whole manner & appearance that of the neurotic mystics—who are not concerned with ethics or institutions—but with original sin, sacrifice, ascetic vengeance upon one's self, & a mad love of Christ as the ideal of suffering. He introduced me to Gómez-Moreno—& to the El Greco-doctor & to others, & will send me Spanish literature forever after.

There is much more to write, dear Lillian,—but wait a day or two. No word from Sophie: She did not call up my friend at Paris. But when I have your explanation, she will be going home! & soon—me—with love,

Meyer.

Segovia, 4 August 1927

Dearest Lillian:

I came here to-night at 10:30, from Madrid. For two long hours it was twilight on the route—I did not know where to sit, thru which window to look, it was so beautiful on either side. Between Cercedilla & Tablada (real patent-medicine names) we were on a mountain ridge, with limitless plains below us, and arid vistas, as fine as those of Syria. At each station crowds were seated at little tables, drinking & awaiting travellers. These are poor summer resorts, a little cooler than

Madrid: the gatherings are so cheerful, & gay & in such fair settings, with clusters, of houses & trees, I think of the Venetian pictures which celebrate the bourgeois picnics of the Renaissance—Only here are no fine colors & rich garments—but more life, to compensate. The very change from Madrid was happy. There I was undecided—whether to leave or stay; because of the heat, the very long day becomes very short—since all stores & schools & libraries & museums are closed from 2 to 4: The Prado & Museo Archeol. not open at all in the afternoon, the library of the Royal Academy closed for the summer, etc. And to walk in the streets is impossible in this sun. The night becomes the day: Supper is not served before 10 at night—and breakfast is usually between 9 & 10 AM.

I had no great regret to leave Madrid—tho there remains much to see. In the distance it seemed strangely populous for there is desert all around: on the same level. My last impressions here were as of Paris & Toulouse & Dijon & Rome—of railroad stations, & poor squatters' suburbs between factories—nothing of the glamour of the morning in the Prado—the parks & splendid avenues with rich ugly houses.

On the train, I was in great joy—to be going once more—& at once felt a cinder in my eye. I did not mind the tunnels, the embankments & passages thru long narrow mountain ways with narrow railway perspectives, or blank stone walls. I think everyone leaned out of the windows the whole way to Segovia. At one station I descended for a drink, & instead of the water I asked for, I received a terrible liquor, which left me dizzy for sometime after. But the wind & the moving train cleared my head—tho at one moment I wished to sleep. I began to read: I was soon brought back to the country—I dream often of weeks freely spent in the country at home—in which I will do nothing—really nothing: but walk & be with you. And as I construct this Elysian vacation: I introduce a book or two—& finally the repose has become a long labor: & the solitude & nature a more efficient place for work. I see myself with you on every hill which commands a view & in every quiet spot—& under all trees that are beautiful. This Castillian landscape had little that I have not seen at home: & I could relive it in anticipation without a long voyage. Once I thought that I would work on Romanesque architecture of Aragon—as an excuse for spending several months in the neighborhood of Jaca—& visiting S. Juan de la Peña again: & Santa Cruz de la Serós.

Small stretches of the trip excited me as bits of El Greco & Titian this morning in the Prado—I think the evening coolness, and the one cloud, and the still faint crescent moon over a world that was all below me, receding in one plane, alternately fertile & populous and arid desert—were the very opposite of Madrid, where I only saw tall houses and an endless stream of people in cafés & shops & narrow streets & driven by the heat—But when I entered Segovia I rode into the town square—which was again a small Madrid; a band played—; under the arcades and out into the square cafés and seated crowds; and children dancing & as much animation as in a city ten times the size of this—Here I was delighted: I had no sooner found a room than I ran down to the square & walked about, finally sat down, & drank coffee till midnight (Hooray! I have found some ink!)

The cathedral apse is at one end, magnificently staged—at least in this uncertain light—For one moment a passing cloud, defined its silhouette: & the whole square was the more vivid & merry for the sombre mass behind it.

Now I wish to write more and more, dear Lillian. What a calamity to travel two summers away—& to leave for ourselves only the cold indoor seasons! I remember how sweet have been the autumn days: & what warmth there is in winter streets at night. Here is something else which is good. In 4 years, have I spent one summer with you? I become as quickly impatient to return, as sorry that I must leave, with so many things undone; at one moment I regret sadly every bit of idleness or relaxation, & another, the compulsion to work which keeps me from lingering—I am again, in the train—with 2 different views from the two sides of the windows—troubled that in gazing thru one, I see nothing of the other, & vainly striving for a midway seat, which when found, is useless, for the angle is unpleasant, & the full extent of the desired object is not seen.

Yesterday I rode to Toledo—What is one day in Toledo—an annoying limitation: an endless regret for time—In the afternoon most of the churches were closed—But now I recall that I saw marvelous works everywhere—that I learned much & delighted in my own deductions, and enjoyed the picturesque, & coldly, colorless, broken landscape of the city & the Tagus, as the pictures & buildings—I visited the two synagogues—one, so thoroly restored as to limit my interest—but its proportions were astounding, an unvaulted Gothic narrowness set on low squat columns & horseshoe arches; & the other, of Simon Levi, a beautiful chamber—with the original stucco & inscriptions, & ceiling—& the tombs of the noble Spaniards who had despoiled the Jews & installed Christian services in this heretical hangout. What a pride could be ours—if we knew these things as our culture & felt within us the continuity not merely of the inscriptions, but of the rich fascinating ornament in which these Hebrew characters are set—But they are Moorish work (rather Persian) & we have not the capacity to recreate them: nor do we possess even a descendant of these forms or their idea. In the Casa de Nesa, I saw more Moorish wall & stucco—as magnificently spun. Tho much more intricate than the Christian decoration the Moorish does not produce the effect of extravagance of architecture, or wealth expended, of gold & precious things; & these chambers & the synagogues remain bare simple buildings, beside the churches nearby. Their exteriors are unornamented: the masses undeveloped: only the surfaces are enlivened: & by a repeated motive, hopeless to follow in detail, which, from a distance is a large simple pattern.

The Mozarab church of S. Cristo de la Luz kept me several hours—for it has a great variety of construction: & a most beautiful south wall. From the photos I had judged it a large building—It is tiny. The exterior arcades are proportioned to effect an endless movement & variety. One half the building is pure Arab—the other mixed, Roman, and Byzantine & Persian—I wandered around the walls of Toledo, thru the old gates—which are a great thrill to me, & show that the Moors could also mass, & work finely with voluminous towers and walls. In one church I jumped to see apsidal fenestration identical with that of the Pantokrator in Constantinople—the street was no different from the oriental—Beyond the north walls, the surrounding country passes into desert banded with horizontal stretches of sparse trees—a very mournful scene below the sandy slopes—I came to this on a grey day—the first in Spain. To the west was a wonderful bend of the river, mountains, & a rocky descent among jutting houses, whose angles were so surprising & harmonious I sat & drew the scene—Later, near the Alcantara bridge was another view equally exciting—without warning, mountains rose from a plain: the river turned twice; & on high rocks—gloomy & jagged, stood the city—El Greco painted this—his finest landscape—I was to his house, once the home of Simon Levi—furnished with Moorish & Christian fittings—Next to it in the Greco Museum, were 20 of his pictures—but not the very best—yet El Greco—& to me, wonderful—I am always astonished by traces of naivete in his works which are executed with such rapid assurance & knowledge. I saw the *Burial of Orgasz* in the church of St. Tomé—A man was copying it,—most blasphemously—The best of El Greco is in the Prado, beside Titian & Rubens—I thought to cry out with joy at some pieces—You should have been there: & I would have kissed you wildly instead: & my meaning would have been clear—I did not know what to look at—or why to stand & gaze—what to think. I poo-pooh the analytical method afterward—tho it is a great satisfaction to follow complex rhythmical coordinations—& I think Miss Mullen an officious fool to recommend that in the approach to works of art, random & "aimless" movements be diminished by "education" & only the "essentials["] attended to, as a result of the Barnes & John Dewey analytical focus—

Why can not Natalie come to see the "Espolio"? & the Resurrection, & the perfect portraits in the Prado? I must convince her that it is not mere vanity to come—& that it is within her dreadful personal limitations—

The Titians, too,———What a grand person!—In Venice, in the Accademia, there is a figure of himself in the large picture of the *Presentation of the Virgin.*—He is a bystander in profile—who gives a coin to a beggar. In the Prado, his self-portrait as a very old man, is also in profile. I am happy to think that he lived to 99 ("Science," it may be said, questions this: since it is based on his own statement & contradicts by 4 or 5 years another statement of his)—just as more than the ideal mathematics pleased me when I read that Fontenelle lived to 100—This longevity is a metaphor in moral justification. Titian was a supremely good man: The change from his early to later works shows a most noble earnestness; a steadily increasing richness in all characters that are beautiful & strong—the greatest freedom in subject & technique—& delight in all pleasures—in sensual figures and in sad religious images—This is to me a purely moral good.

And what shall I say after, of the mind the intelligence the sensibility the great logic of the pictures & the color, & the passion for beautiful surface & the deep harmonious juxtapositions—on every inch he painted—There is so much of him in the Prado—the collectivity adds, richness, fertility, imagination—to his qualities—Velásquez is far below—only a few portraits are satisfying—the development is one direction: it is not reenforced: it does not grow more thoughtful, or

Mary Mullen (?–1957). American art educator and trustee at the Barnes Foundation.

Albert C. Barnes (1872–1951). American collector who displayed works of art not according to style, school, or period, but in such a manner that an overall decorative effect was created.

John Dewey (1859–1952). American philosopher, psychologist, and education reformer who taught at Columbia University. Schapiro took Dewey's course "Philosophy 191: Types of Philosophical Thought" in winter 1923.

more capable—or more ambitious: only the dexterity is marvelous. And surely, Velásquez, when he paints his own portrait, represents himself, frontally—painting a picture—

And then there are Goya, Rubens—a wonderfully subtle, quiet unassuming Giorgione, Bosch, & Spanish primitives—in the one Prado. I do not write of the Archeological Museum where are also treasures—much from South & Central America & the best of mediaeval Spain. The Iberian cultures produced great sculptures—which the moderns will imitate when they are better known. The prehistoric collections are too rich for my short stay; & the Arab I could see only too hastily—

It is two AM. All the church bells of Segovia are now playing—You, too, are still awake. Tell me darling—what you do & where you are? I shall go to sleep.

Your, Meyer.

Santiago de Compostela, 9 August 1927

Dearest Lillian;

A whole day spoiled because of rain. What I wished to study here is out-of-doors. There is plenty in doors, but I grow impatient, stand for a while in the rain & finally return. It means I must stay here to-morrow, perhaps a third day: for that one exterior wall is very complex—and there are chapels, indoors, whose details are invisible in this darkness.

Yesterday was a long ride of 24 hours from Salamanca to Pontevedra (21 hours more precisely)—It was quite pleasant—I wonder now at the hypersensitiveness of a year ago when I was annoyed by the prospect of a 3 or 4 hour trip. In Spain a 3 or 4 hour trip is a little journey, a few miles—the distance between adjacent cities. I slept between Salamanca & Astorga—The sunrise was fine & mysterious—as many months ago in the South of Palestine near Gaza—Figures alighted in the darkness, carrying great bundles, and moved heavily from place to place, in a dim gas light among sleeping groups of men, women and children—This was at each station for the whole hour of sunrise; the newcomers more distinct, fresher, as the car approached the sun, and the land changing with them—

At Astorga there was a change of trains—I had a great bowl of coffee, which has never been so warm—and little round sponge cakes of the region, called "mantecadas" ("mantecado" is ice cream: I refused the "mantecado" when it was mentioned!) I was sorry I could not stop in Astorga—It was the home of Beatus, the 8th c. monk who wrote the Apocalypse Commentary, which was so beautifully illustrated in the early middle ages. There are also Romanesque buildings that I glimpsed in the distance. At Monforte-Lemos I changed trains again; at Redondela, a third time. Now there were only peasants in the cars; for over 200 miles, no cities, but little villages in the mountains of Asturias and Galicia. I saw many women of surprisingly Mongoloid appearance—and everywhere the greatest variety of types for a mountain-peasant population. There were some with straight black hair, like the Breton women in features—and some of fine blond type—some who recalled Near Easterners—very few like the Castillans from whom I had just come—I passed the night in Pontevedra, a most beautiful town near the ocean. For a whole hour we rode along the shore, past fine bays and inlets—I regretted to descend when I was most weary, & the scene, the happiest of the whole journey.

In Pontevedra before sundown, I saw a church festival, the choir boys lighting altar candles to form a splendid cross & border [*drawing of a cross of dots surrounded by a border of dashes in a butterfly shape*] and the peasants and townspeople entering to kneel and observe—The streets were not merely crooked in plan: they rose and fell: & their houses changed proportions rapidly, but preserved a most delicate white and black color—The outer walls are carried by very low arcades, barely 8 feet high—When the women walk under the houses—on the sidewalks, they take the water pots from their heads, for there is no room under these low arches. By the river all was fragrant,—gardens, bridge, trees, and small houses. A woman was struggling with a pig to force him into the yard—Some children followed me for several blocks—I entered a debased, gaudy baroque church—but seeing much humility in all the show I not only forgave it: I loved it & thought nothing else so fitted for this town & this mood. But I had been riding from Salamanca a whole day & night: I had descended towards evening—in a quiet spot—Later from the balcony of my room I saw the water above the station, and the mountains far beyond—When I lay down to rest at 10, after dinner—preparatory to the writing of a letter—I did not awake till early morning. I slept in my clothes.

I must tell you of Segovia, Ávila & Salamanca—a wonderful △, which I will visit again. At Segovia I was rushed: there was too much to see: When the Moors were expelled at the beginning of the 12th c. there was a great fever of Christian building in Segovia & Ávila & there are to-day more fine churches than can be seen in one day, in the two towns. Most of them are closed after 9 in the morning: & little boys were sent to fetch the respective sacristans—who are pleased by the prospect of a tip—but annoyed that they must wait a half hour or an hour for it in my case—Some are shrewd: and dust the furniture and polish/grease the religious machinery while I work—At Segovia, one of the finest churches is now the ceramic atelier & home of Daniel Zuloaga (the uncle of the painter). His products are cheap, wretched parodies of the good models of the Moors. The Roman aqueduct was a splendid vision; what a walk to follow it a whole mile into the town, growing taller and taller with the descent of the road, until its head is almost invisible, and it has changed from one to three superposed arcades. In the country outside Segovia, I walked to the Temple of the True Cross, which stands alone in a field, in view of the Alcázar, a long & many-towered castle perched on a sharp-prowed rock with the effect of a high rapid ship. Inside the cathedral is a collection of printed books of the 15th c.—far more beautiful than the Mss. of the time.—I remember these more clearly than the building itself—I rode to Ávila by autobus—saw many country churches I could not stop to enter, came to the town before sundown—walked around the walls, visited San Vincente—a marvel (by French architects & sculptors), ate too much & had a belly-ache. The next day at Ávila was a great joy—The next, at Salamanca, it rained miserably—but I

Daniel Zuloaga (1852–1921). Painter and ceramicist whose home and studio were in the church of San Juan de los Caballeros; uncle of Ignazio Zuloaga (1870–1945).

saw everything (almost) rapidly & with many consolations—in the company of an English boy, an Oxford student of French literature—& a passionate photographer—consuming no less than 50 films in 3 hours, and regretting that he had forgotten to stock up properly, this being Sunday, & the stores closed. We agreed the New Cathedral (16th c.) was a mess of plateresque presumptions & confused design—the old (ah! 12th) cathedral, the perfection of Romanesque & beyond which nothing—In his excitement, he forgot to focus, & employed infinity on nearby objects—Later he saw a Dominican in white & black—& begged him to stand still for a portrait—We crossed the river to obtain a view of all Salamanca, on the hill with its Gothic silhouettes and domes—& truly it was wonderful—& I regretted that I had likewise not stocked up & that my last film had been wasted on an already familiar portal. I drew, instead, a small sketch, flimsy & without depth.—but, as the critics, the scholars, the family, the friends, the journals, the enemies, the teachers, say—when a more choice word is lacking—when a more precise sentiment is shocking, to one's proper pride or to the other's—"interesting"—I therefore enclose it.

We visited the old university: I was delighted to come upon the name of my friend José Camón Aznar on the bulletin board—It was announced that another had been substituted for him, to examine students. The older lecture halls are theological designs; they have very little light; tho covered by a flat ceiling of wood rafters, great depressed arches hang across the rooms creating more darkness—[*a small drawing of the room*] In one room the seats are arranged in two groups, one around the lecturer's table, as if a jury and the others before him, as if an audience—Dark pictures and tapestries make the room even more gloomy—No science could be taught here: for who can encourage observation & precision in such shadows? These must be the Halls of Law and Philosophy and Letters & Theology. Outside all is different—Richly carved corridors, grotesques and a profusion of ornament, a cloister with great light windows, fine courtyards, etc. Nearby, in the houses we saw delicious patios—rich in flowers, old stone, fountains, and shadowed corridors—In the evening we talked about America—against which he has the most violent prejudices, begotten in ignorance—not only of America, but also of England. He reproached Americans for not being Oxonian gentlemen of leisure, taste, & liberty to[?] horror of mass education—of business, of organization, of science. Absorbed in French literature, his favorite is Rabelais; he has read no Frenchman, post-1700, except one or two school classics of the 18th c. He takes only literature and language courses in Oxford—tho still an undergraduate—& believes that the system of free or wide studies in several subjects is wrong—(not Oxonian) & that compulsory Math, science, history & philosophy of most American schools—a tyranny. "One learns these things before 18" he said—one fails to learn them before 18 & one has a great horror of them afterwards—We became good friends before the night—I left de Gourmont's "Sixtine" with him—I had found it in Barcelona: since to mail it home would cost more than the book itself (15 cents), and since I was tired of dragging it about all Spain, my bag being more than full, & my pockets bursting—I dropped it in the hands of Nasan, who had never heard of de Gourmont—but was

Remy de Gourmont (1858–1915). French novelist, journalist, and art critic.

excited by him — when he heard a few anecdotes & some bibliography. He spends many summers in Spain. — How fortunate this English residence which permits easy fortnight trips on the continent!

So I come to this end, dear sweetheart — that in a month or 5 weeks I will be short of funds — and in rags. My passage home is fortunately paid. Will you not send me 100 dollars — if you have them — if not, will you speak to Mary, who will ask my father: since it will be too late to write me & for me to write in turn to my father. Please do not cable, since it is a needless expense — but send by money order to American Express Co. I will surely not need the money before Sept. 15–20. — & most likely not more than 50 to 60 dollars.

I fear that you may not be at home when this reaches you, & you will be put to great trouble to arrange the matter in the country. I still do not know if you are in camp or in the city. You did not tell me if you are doctor for the whole summer or for a few weeks between stenography; I cannot guess, since in camps I have been at, there were both permanent & transient physicians. And it was Chester Street you wrote on the back of the envelope — a precaution, or your coming address in a few weeks? I can only hope that you will have all summer in the country & that in addition to preventing the infection, and curing the aches of 100 children, you will have your own repose and pleasure: & that you will not find it necessary to work in September before school opens. Joey once said that the 4th year was the easiest! I look forward to your 4th year — and mine — Mine seems the beginning of my studies. Sometimes I find it difficult to recall what matters even occupied me in 2 years of graduate work — what actual instruction there was — what I have learned — You remember how I fussed over the pre-history of the Near-East, Greece & the Balkans. I recall absolutely nothing of it. A few days ago I found that I could not remember several Chinese names. This was very depressing. I looked like a distressed Chinaman at the moment — all yellow & slant-eyed. And when I return it will be increasingly difficult to resume these subjects, for so many new things have come up in the past year —

Chester Street. Lillian's home address in Brooklyn.

Tell me, shall I be glad to return? I alternatively jump & sigh. As I ride towards France (Oviedo, León, Burgos) I know I am riding home —; but I wish more time in South France — And I am happy that I approach home — I dream most luxuriantly of you.

Meyer.

[*On a separate sheet: a drawing of Salamanca*]

León, 14 August 1927

Dearest Lillian:

I am in such a hurry to return, everywhere I stumble — At Santiago, I yielded & remained three days: at León, likewise three days — really four, since I will visit Sahagún — in the neighborhood — which was never on my program. I will reach France too late to do all the work for my thesis, Murray will be furious — & I, very sad & disappointed. I need three more months in South France; I have little more than one month left. I do not think of the matter at all, until some particular trouble or frustration makes me melancholy—& occupies my whole mind—then everything sad, unpleasant, objectionable, is recalled to confirm the moment's pessimism; & difficulties I have repressed with some simple consolation or reasoned indifference, return to plague me—I came to León very buoyant & full of plans, but I was only to stay one day—The ride from Santiago occupied a whole day—from 6 in the morning until 10 at night: This was very pleasant—with Santiago behind, I was relieved of a burden, since I had been careless & incomplete there, & had come to no clear idea of the building. It may be likewise in León. My ideas were so upset by what I saw the first day, I had to remain a second to reorder them: & the second day leaves me more puzzled than before. A Canon who has studied San Isidoro for many years contradicted my notions flatly & with great conviction—He thought I would agree with him—for others had been converted—Ideas, if professionalized, become precious personal property—; a decline in value produces serious emotions: I could think of nothing else for several hours. Today I worked till my eyes were weary—without solution. I did not see that the day was beautiful, that it was Sunday, & the people better dressed & gayer until I had left the building—

Bravo. Perhaps León antiquarian Clemente Bravo Guarida.

I was addressed by a Spaniard named Bravo—a friend of Gómez-Moreno—who is also interested in these problems—He too has ideas contradicting mine; but his reasons are all bad, tho the conclusions possible—I will see him again—to-night, & we will fight it out on the diagrams—

I walked late this afternoon to the cathedral, which is beautiful, & took me from this vexatious business—I think the earlier preoccupations were good, since they left me in a mood in which the architecture was wonderfully relaxing or quieting—There was no desire to know—or to study; & every detail had some charm for me: & I noticed what usually escapes me. The air of the interior, the quality of the space, the darkness & half-shadow, the scale of the few others in the building, beside the rising shafts—& exquisiteness in plateresque & flamboyant works which I dislike—There were two peasants wandering (in such buildings one can wander, remain in one room, & yet change walls at every step) in the aisles, peeping hurriedly into chapels, & whispering. Their simplicity is different from that of the cathedral, tho built by men of their faith & with tools like their own. I rarely think of the builders except as technicians & designers—but to day, the interior appeared so fantastic & foreign to any mind. I know in our world—I was brought to think of persons, & to the character which made these things. Perhaps as in the animal kingdom where forms utterly strange to us receive common mechanical explanations—no peculiarity of mind need be invoked to explain these buildings—but technical problems & liturgical needs, alone—But then the question is shifted. For conditions which produced such works, surely affected the men who built them & lived in them: & the style, mechanical in origin, was acquiesced in & became conscious—yet the growth was continuous—there is no interval for a quiescence—no conscious repetition without an actual change in the style.—We must conceive, then, both work & man as changing together—which is too difficult. Or we may abstract from all the works—qualities, habits of mind & hand, ideas & call them, the mind of the culture—give it thought processes, feelings, animate it completely on the pattern of a single man: remembering always that this huge mind which contains & does all things, is not the model of the little ones & may be strange to most of them. There was a happy collusion of my mood (reduced to innocence by fatigue & the thoughts of the past few days) with the objects about me. I was practically alone with them. The statues & pictures & capitals & windows were in an immense space, limited & undefinable—all mine, in shadow & light—Then I returned to wish, that which had annoyed me & made these things a little distasteful—I thought that nothing could be happier than to give onesself completely to these objects, to study them minutely, know every detail—living whole years with them—There would be no method—no school of thought—no simple approach which criticized the others—Besides the perfection of craftsmanship & thought, the peculiarities of individual minds—the possible moods in which a man 300 years ago made the Virgin[] look proudly at the angel Gabriel—as an amply gowned Roman matron; & another 400 years earlier, attenuated all figures & gave them sorrowful staccato gestures—& another, a little before, carved Adam, Eve, Christ, Lazarus, Moses, angels, devils, as fat goitrous smiling people these moods[] too must be recreated, to prolong the day dream that accompanies love of the work. I was entirely submissive—repeating romantic heresies of another age, & ideas I usually laugh at in others—we have all the vices & sentiments in us. This I will forget soon.

I wished also to carve & paint—and in thinking of future summers, I have omitted travel—& gone to the country to make statues & pictures. This—several times in the last few weeks—I think often of your tools, which were the joy of a summer & then abandoned—perhaps rusty & dull by this time. I will carve much more freely & boldly: I began too soon, & therefore ended too soon. Now it is more difficult to work, since it is to resume something left behind—And I wish also a hundred thousand other things—all because of this voyage. I know I shall soon be with you, darling—

Meyer.

Burgos, 20 August 1927

I have just returned from Santo Domingo de Silos, a Benedictine monastery where I spent four days—What four days! I have not been so happy this whole voyage—The life is so good, I can well join my homely upright friends & remain forever in this cloister—It is surely healthful & sane—It is also beautiful: & beside the world around it[,] it is free from superstition, religion, strife, stupidity, wastefulness, disease, & bad manners—The religion is a reverent habit which gives a great dignity to everything done. There is no excess—no sermonizing—inquisitiveness, or self-torture—I have not eaten better in Spain, than in S. D. S. The food is grown within the monastery—There is beautiful fruit, delicious honey, & wine, & Benedictine liqueur beyond words—One is rich here—The library is very rich too, and the cloister sculptures—of the 11th c. are the finest works of Spanish Romanesque art, without any parallel, & strangely isolated in history—

There is also a treasure of mediaeval metal-work and Mss., noble monks, generous life — fine talk & companionship & apparently the perfection of freedoms — one sings the Gregorian chants — & the mass is very simple & beautiful — I should write much more of S. D. S. — but I will tell you instead, dear —

your Meyer.

This is frightfully scrawled — but I must catch a train. I am no longer in the cloister —

Toulouse, 25 August 1927

My Dearest Lillian:

I return to Toulouse which is no longer as interesting to me. This should be the beginning & not the end. Because of Spain, the objects I handled are not new — but have different meanings — To-day I re-examined St. Sernin, my old notes in hand. They are very primitive & insufficient — I should have seen Spain long ago, and have traveled in its provinces as I did in France. At Santiago, León, & Silos, I had to change completely[] ideas I had formed at home: & there were many apologies to make for dogmatic criticisms of past years.

This is far from your beautiful letter, dear — in which you swim in the sun and in the darkness. I swim only in the darkness: & mistake flashes for fixed stars. I often disturb the water with my flapping. When I dive there is a great splashing, which subsides quickly; my mouth is always full of water —

I wrote you of how beautiful was the monastery at Silos. I saw little of its exterior or the surrounding country — The course of life is so pleasant and orderly within: & the work suggested by the buildings, the manuscripts, and the carvings, so absorbing, I had no wish to leave or to explore beyond. The monks were, every one, gracious and quiet; there was no touch of morbidity or suffering or extreme asceticism in them. I was embarrassed by their prayers which were brief and simple, but in which I could not join — I was embarrassed by my own lack of faith: for it seemed, in my non-participation — a criticism of these men, an estrangement, that was really only formal. The short chanting before and after meals was beautiful, a reverent thanks and acceptance — which surely I owed more than the others — In the mass, all was subdued: no shrill and over-resonant music (& no jingling of coins) as in the cities, but simple chants of the middle ages. The mass was a meeting of pious musicians — The church itself, an 18th c. baroque building, is an unfortunate hall for these services — The cloister outside is miraculous, with more in common with the chanting and the Benedictine life.

Thruout the meals, which are excellent & served in a fine refectory, there is silence, except for a man who sits in a pulpit & reads chapters of church history. After lunch, after a brief prayer in the Chapel of Santo Domingo, the silence is relaxed — but in amusing gradation, lest a sharp transition indicate a suppressed desire, and a criticism of the restraint imposed. As we descend the steps of the chapel, we offer by signs the precedence to each other, gesture and smile, like dumb men; prolonging this talk till we are in the cloister where the first words are uttered. Then for a half hour we sit in the garden or a small chamber, and drink coffee and a delicious cordial, prepared by the monks. I return to the cloister to continue work which was never finished. Several of the monks have studied the same questions: They are very fond of American students, because it was an American who first demonstrated that these sculptures are not tributary to French art, but are of the 11th century, preceding French work by 40 or more years, & testifying to the great culture of the abbey in this barbaric period. The abbot is chauvinist in his attachment. He denounced the French with ferocity and seemed ready to devour Mâle and Deschamps. But Porter is the hero of the cloister—not only for his science, but his generosity: He has enriched the library with his 10 vol. work on Romanesque art, and has given the monks photos of over 100 marvelous miniatures of a Beatus Commentary on the Apocalypse, written at Silos in 1100, and now in the British Museum—Their gratitude overflows, and refreshes Americans who follow Porter.

"The abbot." Luciano Serrano (1879–?) was a Spanish historian and the abbot of Silos; he began restoring the cloister soon after becoming abbot in 1919.

At night I was awake till very late—in the company of a Harvard instructor, who had been in Silos a whole month, studying architecture and Mozarab liturgy—He spoke mainly of Porter, his special love. Between admirations, he killed the flies which swarmed in his room, but never infested mine—He knew Rand, and confirmed all I like in him. After the first night there was no discussion of architecture, for he was mainly occupied with liturgy; & none of liturgy, for he knew so many people.

"Harvard instructor." Identified by Schapiro as Walter Whitehill (1905–78) in a letter to Lillian (6 January 1928).

A Padre Justo was ready to examine every point with me. He was very agile for a monk, leaped & climbed on vaults like a schoolboy. He is homely and honest and tender and disinterested beyond all students I have met. In the monastery he has access to few foreign books of the last 20 years—& to practically no good journals—The library is very rich, but in theology & church history. Comparative studies are impossible. Tho he knows Silos itself better than any more learned man he is very humble and defers to others, submitting all his observations to them.

Justo Perez de Urbel (1895–1979). Benedictine monk at the Monasterio de Santo Domingo de Silos. Author of many scholarly volumes, he later became the first abbot at Valle de los Caídos.

Outside Silos the whole world changed, as if I had lost an important object. On the way to Silos, the chauffeur sang endlessly, in a beautiful sorrowing voice, and addressed whoever he passed on the road, hailed peasants and children, & blew kisses to the girls. But returning four days later, he limped, & seemed woebegone. In the Burgos cathedral I was refused admission to the cloister: in the provincial library, the attendant said the Ms. I wished to see did not exist; & finally drew it forth with much grumbling—He refused to give me another. I missed a train, remained the afternoon in Burgos, walked to the convent of Las Huelgas nearby, where I could not see the best things, since in a nunnery no man may enter. (But you, dear, can see Silos)—I missed the evening train, since 2nd & 3rd class had been omitted from the "Rapido" & in the morning I was compelled to travel 1st class (a nuisance, & an extortion) since 2nd & 3rd were likewise absent. After 15 hours of riding—Toulouse—I had Giraudoux's "Eglantine" to read—a story of a girl who loved an old Jew and an old French noble—an ingeniously poetic novel—

Jean Giraudoux (1882–1944). French novelist, essayist, diplomat, and playwright.

I embrace you in thought, dear Lillian, & hope to be with you, very soon—

Meyer.

Moissac, 8 September 1927

Dearest Lillian:

I return to Moissac after a long absence, & I find so much now that was not here before—because I have been elsewhere—that I must remain here until the very end of my time—& then leave for home.

Komméja was alive when I entered—I say "was"—for he is historic—to me-like the abbaye & the cloister—& I think of my excitement to see him after such long uncertainty & expectation: He had not answered my letters & I had had no news of him from others. I soon learned that he had been very ill, had been operated on several times, & was now confined to the house, with only the rarest departures. But I do not think he is unhappy: Each afternoon when I come to him he is busy writing; he is assembling his old papers & notes, to put in order what no one will understand when he is gone. His great complaints are that he must eat—a suffering—& that no one in the region is working, & the best sites, unexplored, the most "curious" problems unsolved—He is sorry that, as we begin to know each other, we must part. Yesterday, for the first time he called me by name—To-day his only contemporary in Moissac died. There is another friend, still older, who totters about, & tells me,—"Poor Momméja, he will be gone soon: he no longer rises from his bed"—and I dare not tell him that I have just left his rival ancient, writing a new book at 75. And Momméja says of Dugué that he is totally unreliable—that his memory is gone, & he has only a few months to live. But when I asked Dugué for the plans of excavations he directed 20 years ago, he not only brought me the papers & photos, but offered to go with me to the church, & explain the details on the very ground—I declined his offer—he was pitifully insistent: I trembled while walking with him: he might fall at any moment. And when he wished to climb the tower the better to enforce a point, I had no response: this man is beyond good & evil, neither young nor old, alive or dead—At one time I had to carry him. He remarked then, that he climbed this staircase; so dark & narrow, three times a day, only last year. I was cruelly annoyed when he opened the plans before me—they were the limit of incompetence and wasted labor; there was nothing to say. He had an answer for every question & realized no difficulties—With his keys he opened a side entrance to the cloister, barred by furniture, and closed with iron rods. There was a more accessible way he would not take—I learned many new things from him—he was very happy to be with his former occupations again, & moved without warning from place to place & made brief speeches in all—

After 10 days together, there is little of Moissac to discuss—with Momméja—for he has given me his notes to read—He tells me of his friends, among whom were Anatole France and Cartailhac—& of his own experience; and recounts endless stories and facts of the region. To-day he explained why so many natives were buccaneers & explorers in the 17th century (one founded Detroit); the directions of population shifts in the Tarn and Garonne country—the religious wars, geographical changes in the centuries, agriculture, and the history of a family—Yesterday I remarked on his table a small carved box with Merovingian ornament, but a modern provincial work. And I learned from him that it had belonged to Jean Baptiste Pérès, the man, who 100 years ago had proved that Napoleon had never existed, & was a solar myth. It was amusing that he could not remember Pérès' name: (I had to recall it to him.) the more so, since he had written several essays on his life & works. But I was the more surprised, when he drew out from his papers an article on a book by Pérès which proved that the life of Napoleon is predicted in the Bible, foreshadowed in the Book of Macchabees which is its exact parallel. And then followed an hour of stories of Pérès' life, & of his family, which Momméja knew well, at Malause, near Moissac, and a discussion of Apocalyptic exegesis in the 17th & 18th century & in recent times—on the difference between French & English apocalyptic interpretations—on theological theories of history, & again on Pérès, who was surely, a strange mind & personality. This was an interest of Momméja I had not suspected. I liked his sympathy for a man so different from himself. Pérès was a Jansenist & in great earnest, & wrote enormous tracts that are still unpublished. His book on the Biblical prediction of Napoleon, his most serious work, is forgotten: the other, a slight fragment is well known, tho I have not seen the author's name quoted beside the common use of his idea. Momméja wrote that no more attention was paid to this second edition (of the Napoleon Macchabee parallel) than to the first, according to the inflexible law that imposes on each one, the expiation of his own happiness. Happiness, for Pérès[,] was the unexpected, disconcerting success of his "Napoleon never existed["]: the expiation was the unreasonable distain for all his other publications.[] Even his biographer did not know of the second Napoleonic parallel. It is as ingenious as the first. Pérès, besides theology, wrote on celestial mechanics; and published the trajectories of all meteorites fallen in the department of Lot-et-Garonne.

Jean Baptiste Pérès (1752?–1840). French physicist known for his satirical pamphlet *Comme quoi Napoléon n'a jamais existé; ou, Grand erratum, source d'un nombre infini d'errata à noter dans l'histoire du XIXe siècle* (1827).

Momméja has given me accounts of Bladé, the original of the Abbé Jerome Coignard, whom he knew for many years in Agen. He enjoys the reminiscences as much as I do, & for several days prehistoric archaeology has not been mentioned. He had little to say of Glozel, which is now a subject of controversy. You remember, dear, I wrote of it last year, when I met Reinach. R. is now firmly convinced of the authenticity of the Glozel finds, & of their Neolithic character; Jullian, as certain that they are Gallo-Roman. He does not consider the inscribed bricks the earliest alphabet, preceding the Phoenician by 2000 years, but a Latin cursive of a sorcerer. When challenged to read it he was for a while embarrassed—& finally chose an "easy" brick & read an incantation in it—with one obscene word which he did not translate. A charming incident was the testimony of Prof. Brinkman, of Bergen, a paleontologist—on the animal incised on a bone fragment, [] Loth published a letter from Brinkman, & said "Brinkman, who sees reindeers every day, declares it a reindeer"! Then Jullian came forth & blew on his trumpet the names of classical & mediaeval writers who mention reindeers in North and Central France in post Azilian times. Likewise with every detail. The exchange of letters is becoming bitter. The papers enjoy the perplexity, the enormous historical perspectives, the ironical interchanges of opinion, the conversions, &

Jean-François Bladé (1827–1900). French author of books on popular culture, medieval history, and the geography of southwest France.
Jerome Coignard. Character in Anatole France's *La rotisserie de la reine pédauque* (1893).

M. C. August Brinkmann (1878–1940). Norwegian paleontologist and chief zoologist at Bergen Museum, Norway.
Joseph Marie Loth (1847–1934). French linguist and historian.

the minute science which contradicts itself, & yet is not unintelligible to the lay reader. I am impatient for the study of parallel sites. As long as there is only one example of the Glozel culture, it is subject to many uncertainties: but other sites with similar artifacts will end the chronological controversy & turn more attention to the problem of the alphabet & art & pottery & their relations with the Eastern cultures.

Meanwhile, at Agen, where Momméja excavated for more than twenty years, there is a Prune Congress, of the Society of Agriculture of the Agenais, and the Society for the Promotion of the Culture of the Prune. The prune is Agen's chief export, its main source of wealth—Tho I am less than 20 miles from Agen, I have not eaten a prune in the 10 days in Moissac. I shall eat many at home. (transition!)—like Jack Rush—would that this were home—and that we could sit together in the beautiful cloister, which is more and more beautiful each day, & is a transfigured Romanesque garden, giving charm to the sunlight and the shade, making silence golden, and revery, an untroubled happiness. If this were home then I could sit in it also in the evening; & feel no oppressive change as I leave it to return to my hotel. When I have worked an afternoon, across repeated striking of bells, and have heard the last at 7, I awake in so perfect a twilight, I feel,—I enter a new world,—now is the time to remain & not to go. The mediaeval color of the capitals has long faded—now a delicate pink survives, that, with the shadowed green of unorganized flowers and vegetation, forms a polychromy as sweet as the most sentimental memory of imagined ancient tones. In the most glaring sunlight a deep shade is assured under the arcades, and behind the cedars, which rise out of the court high above the red cloister roofs. How delighted I was to look down into the cloister from the church tower—while everything around burned bright in the sun, the cloister remained a shadowed spot, deep set, in trees and buildings, with only a few arches apparent between the foliage. It is so below; always the cloister is cooler, more fragrant, detached from the accidents of the world about. Few people visit it. When I stop to meditate a capital or the trees or the declining perspective of arches, dark spots, I wish to sacrifice the day or the hour for this luxurious contemplation—Sunlight, which is elsewhere the background, may here be regarded in itself—I think sometimes of Greece, thru which I passed so hastily; I have bright memories of it; and I conjure scenes which I had beheld for a passing moment, & I try to fix them for a longer time. For a little while I attained, without premeditation, the mood, in which Greece was glorious & its ancient works and landscape the embodiments of supreme health. I blinked inwardly before its sunlight, and I exulted in the remembered blue sea, seen on the road to Eleusis, the Argive prehistoric citadels, (where a friend befouled the ancient gallery, & laughed as I photoed him[]) & the day at Epidaurus.—In Olympia I climbed Kronios, descended into the shade again, walked among ruins, also in shadow, & in the Museum, which is sunnier than the temples, beheld the great pediment figures of white marble. I have almost forgotten Paris & Italy—I remember only the sun,—Greece & Egypt and Syria;—& because I am remembering, I soon recall the others,—memory, the mother of musings—

Jacob "Jack" Rush. Friend of Schapiro's from Columbia University.

This is so different from another habit which confronts a new fact with a hundred others; for which Constantinople is a peculiar arch or plan, & Baalbek, a detail of ornament—Work, work, I shall begin again; once in N.Y.

Meyer: to his dear

Lillian.

Moissac, 15 September 1927

Dearest Lillian:

I have not heard from you almost a whole month, & I am uneasy for many things which I dare not recall to myself at this moment—I know that I will soon be home & that it is of no use to write in this way; But I wait day after day: I promise myself some word; I put off my own letters for a while, expecting to hear from you—I should certainly not speak so, after my own silence of a whole month—but I cannot attribute my reasons to you: & I am so near home that I am more than ordinarily impatient. I have a great hunger for society now that I approach it. One whole day, in the cloister, I did nothing but talk to visitors. I did not finish even one capital from early morning till evening. I have come to know other people in Moissac—beside Momméja—but I see very little of them—One is a doctor, Foissac, whose wealth has made him independent of practice—& he has given his time to literature. He writes novels, poems, criticism, of which I have read nothing. I am told they are very fine. But we talk of America, which interests him enormously—now that he is too old to travel—His admiration of New York is remarkable for a European, in that there is no slur reserved for "materialism," lack of art, & the unhealthy life of New York. At 60 he demands details like a child. He knew Jules Laforgue, as a student, but had only too little to say of him: Of all strange & contrary things, Laforgue wished to be like Taine—Laforgue was a torturesome writer, coined words, & mythologized his own miseries. Foissac said that before consumption attacked Laforgue, he was very robust, gay, witty & elegant: later, his depression was disheartening to everyone: Foissac himself has no eccentricities, but a colorless charm & ease. He fears the Bolsheviki: he asked me to tell the people back home that they are a great menace, & that our whole civilization (books & pictures, etc) may perish by them.

Ernest Foissac (act. 1890–1929). French doctor and writer whose works included translations and novels.

Jules Laforgue (1860–87). French Symbolist poet.

Hippolyte Adolphe Taine (1828–93). French critic and historian.

Occasionally I see a brother & sister, Belbèze, of a very picturesque family; the father, a general, was found drunk early one morning in a mud-patch.—Tho already an old man, he took orders, and became a priest, terrorized by his own misgivings: His wife ended her days in a mad-house—One daughter, a sick, bleary woman of 40, lives alone in a great house, once the Palace of the abbots of Moissac—Her brothers, army officers, forbid her to admit any stranger to the house, lest the valuable collection of pictures, & sculpture (stolen by the father from various monasteries of the region) be carried off. I applied many times without success, each time learning from this unfortunate woman, more of the family history—Finally, one brother arrived & I gained admission. But it was no simple admission. The Commandant wished my opinion of various objects that he was to sell: & questioned me about Americans interested in such objects. I was annoyed

Belbèze. Important family in Moissac; nothing further could be located on its members. See Meyer Schapiro, *Romanesque Art* (New York: George Braziller, 1977), 259 n. 68.

that a figure I asked to see was not to be found—tho it no longer belonged to the family—but was an "Historic Monument," of the State, in their keeping. They have sold it, contrary to the law—They will do likewise with the other pieces of the collection—I met two "archeologists" at the house, very evidently dealers, and one of them dishonest—There was a scheme to excavate the neighboring property to find the tombs of Moissac abbots which must be rich in jewelry & crosiers & chalices & ecclesiastical treasures—But from the old plans, I judge, the funeral chapel is not on the property, but 4 or 5 metres underneath the street, & perhaps long ago despoiled—

The house is in great disorder; littered with fine old furniture, engravings, pottery, thousands of books on strategy, horsemanship & theology, and 3 grand paintings, of the 16th century, that are unknown outside of this house—In the house is a 12th century chapel, with the original frescoes: & in the beautiful garden, enclosed by high walls, are fragments of sculpture from the cloister & the abbey portal.

Mlle Belbèze who is suspicious of all strangers, fears dealers, & mistrusts her brother who is a fool, since he is an army officer, & a Southerner, & a person without calm—She & her brother are anxious to sell the collection independently of each other—for some personal profit not to be shared—Neither has the remotest knowledge of the provenance of the objects, their value, or the market. When asked the name of an artist, she returned with an encyclopedia, & searched under P—for a half hour, while I guessed at the name she had in mind. I could not guess her intention, for it was too remote from the wildest possibility. I think I have complicated matters by telling Mlle Belbèze that she possessed an engraving by Lucas van Leyden & that one of the large pictures is an excellent South German Renaissance work. I am now asked to publish the whole collection—since in this way it will receive notice, & attract American buyers. But now it is too late for me to study these things in Moissac. I applied last November & was refused. It will be wonderful if I finish the Romanesque work in the week that is left. Daily I learn of more interesting objects in the surrounding country, which I must visit in years to come. And Moissac itself becomes more fascinating—Its artistic remains can be studied as comparative religion, as folk lore—as design, as technique, as folk-psychology, as history, costume, furniture, artifacts—physical types, and even as architecture—for there are so many buildings, domestic, civil, military & religious, represented in the capitals—The architecture of Moissac also furnishes three interesting architectural problems—still unresolved—One pertains to the church that preceded the present one, & which can not only be reconstructed from existing fragments, but can be placed precisely in time & in the history of its type: It was probably the very first example of domed architecture in France—imported from the Orient—earlier than the Cathedral of Cahors, of which Rey wrote a remarkable monograph. There is also in Moissac a very primitive cross-rib vault, preceding by two decades the North French examples which led to the Gothic. But in the South no Gothic forms developed from this construction, which, carried to the North produced such marvelous changes—In addition

Moissac has military architecture of the 12th century in fine presentation. I never supposed such richness here when I undertook this study—Nor the manuscript illuminations, which constitute a subject apart.

Momméja told me to-day of an abbé of Cahors, who, to gain access to the Mss of de Foulhiac, jealously guarded by his descendants, & closed to all scholars, offered the owner pornographic literature, which was instantly devoured. It is thus that we have to-day some of our most interesting information on the Roman province of Quercy.

I learned also that a certain Devals who made fine studies of Roman roads & communication, was totally bald, & that he spent the last 50 years (sic) of his life with an old servant, named Delilah—Devals was stricken as he descended from a train. The president of the Archeological Society, the Canon Pottier, administered extreme unction, on the spot—Later Pottier said that he "waxed Devals' boots"—a bold remark for a canon: Momméja despises Devals, because in his list of some hundred or more roads, he overlooked one: & because D. accepted as a Roman sword, a 16th century misericord unearthed by Momméja as a boy of 14. But I have seen an admirable study by Devals in which he identifies by philological analysis of modern place names, the settlements of the barbarian invaders, & proves by toponymical documents the W to G, and "orum" to "ou" changes—

Oh, dearest Lillian, a few weeks!

Meyer.

Raymond de Foulhiac (1622–79). French canon of the Cathédrale Saint-Étienne de Cahors; employed by Jean-Baptiste Colbert (1619–83) to research precious manuscripts in Quercy; copied numerous charters of Moissac and other unpublished manuscripts in the Cahors library. **Jean-Ursule Devals** (1814–74). French archaeologist and historian.

Fernand Pottier (1838–1924). French archaeologist who excavated Moissac with Dugué from 1901 to 1903.

Cahors, 22 September 1927

Dearest Lillian:

This is the last night in the South: & I do not regret to spend it in Cahors. When it grew dark in the city where I was compelled to work until the last moment of light[,] I returned to the station; but on the way I saw the Pont Valentre's towers in the distance, & I spent the hour on the bridge which was never more beautiful to me. I have not sung for many years; as a little boy, I would lie awake in bed in the evening and sing aloud for a whole hour. This again to-night—I do not know when I began to sing. I surprised myself, but unconsciously returned to the same fragmentary tunes, of sentimental melancholy—which I did not feel—& vociferous, loud, endless expression which became my actual mood. I thought to photo in the darkness the tower silhouettes, and the hills which give to the river at this point all the charm of a mountain lake. But it grew darker & darker as I planned—the last white clouds disappeared, & I gave up. Huntsmen with black & white dogs passed me, who stood in one place—I walked up & down the bridge many times, always astonished that there were towers & crenellations & the fantastic staircase—There is a dam below, & a great sound of rushing water that makes it an even more portentous event to cross the bridge in the night & to pass from the city into a wilder nature,—the steep hills of the other side, with no lights or houses, & a narrow road along the bank.

Earlier in the afternoon I walked another bridge; the galleries of the cathedral—to see the exterior of the upper windows. The sacristan remained behind, mistrusting his own vertigo. I was so delighted by what I saw that I photoed badly twice in succession. I would have jumped from the height—if it were not dangerous, I was so happy to see these few details,—which I had predicted to myself at Moissac. From the highest turret of the building I took beautiful views. In the 14th c. an open work parapet was constructed—without any religious or practical architectural use—for the pleasures of vista: Every sight is framed by arches—on one side the 2 domes & the tower before them: on another the river & the hills: on another the city & the valley. The domes tho immense, are the humblest domes of the world—It is not such forms that have given "cupola" its meaning of preten[s]ion & pride.

Moissac, which I left last night, once had similar domes—Last night, I saw the abbey church for the first time by starlight & the few street illuminations—There was such richness of sky, the piled forms of the tower & porch & buttresses, in a most powerful impressive light & dark seemed the great heavens, & the numerous stars, the world that depended on them. I saw the portal for the very first time, I thought—since I recognized no figures or sacred imagery—but only the finely serried lines & masses—another architecture. Last night was the building's true destiny: & all the days I have beheld it, & worried in it, imperfect accidents of a strange world—How could I leave it? I could not turn back to see it a last time—The train was a half hour late; there were almost no regrets—I wished I could stay another day, & not night: to check up a few details & renew controversies—

With my love, dearest Lillian—

Meyer.

October 8th

Travel Notebooks, 1926-1927

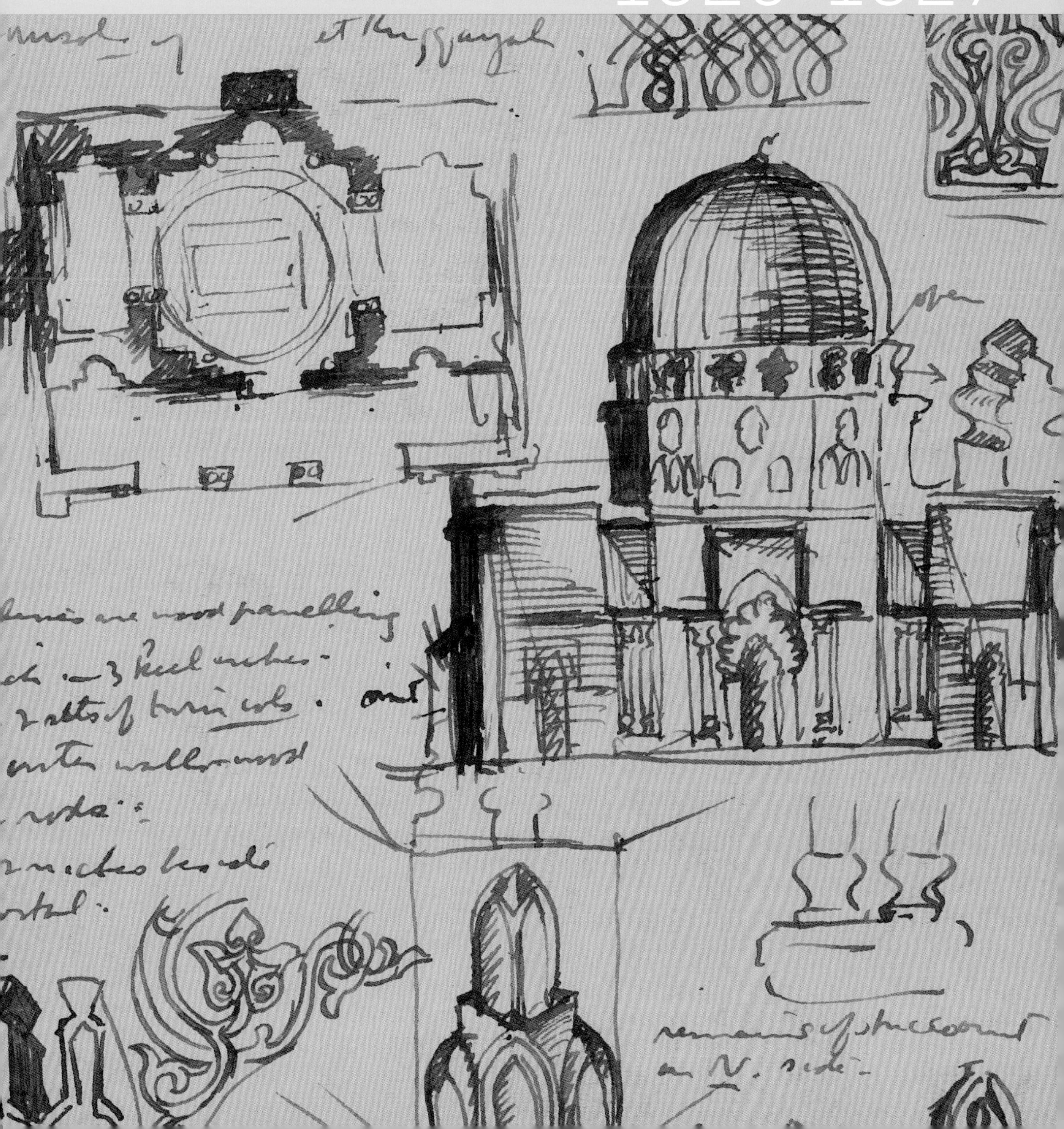

Travel Notebooks, 1926–1927

Note on the Travel Notebooks

Schapiro bought both loose-leaf and bound notebooks as needed and filled them with notes and drawings of the sites that he visited. He sometimes removed pages from the bound notebooks, thus enabling him to rearrange pages for further study — their original purpose, after all. In the 1980s, and perhaps earlier, attempts were made to order and paginate some of the notebooks. After examining the loose pages, it was evident to me that most pages were not in chronological order and that errors had been made in the pagination. While the pagination does not reflect the chronological order of the pages, where available it remains the best way to identify individual pages. Bound notebooks that remain intact preserve the original order of their pages; all loose pages are presumed to be out of order.

In attempting to put the notebook pages in chronological order, I have consulted several sources: letters to Lillian and other family members, as well as lists of dates and other notations on the notebook pages themselves, especially those pages from the beginning of Schapiro's trip. (For an itinerary, see p. 232.) Most drawings are either labeled with a place-name or easily identifiable. In consultation with the itinerary, the pages can be put in approximate chronological order—approximate because many sights or towns are described on multiple pages. In such cases, the order of pages may be determined only by internal evidence, which is usually unavailable.

Of the places illustrated here, Schapiro visited two more than once: Toulouse and Moissac. The drawings of Toulouse are probably from his first, longer visit, when he was able to devote more time to them. Schapiro's notes from Moissac are more difficult to order because he consulted them repeatedly. He made two visits to Moissac, one in 1926, one in 1927. Some of the pages from these visits are dated. By correlating the papers and inks used on dated pages with those used on undated pages, it is possible to establish which pages are from each visit. The drawings from Moissac included in this book are only from the cloister. The captions for the drawings of the cloister at Moissac include the numbers that Schapiro used. His published work on Moissac uses a sequence from 1 to 76, starting from the east side of the southwest pier and running counterclockwise, and includes the pier capitals. The identification of each capital is Schapiro's. The plan of the cloister, including his numbering and identifications, appears before the itinerary; see p. 230.

Schapiro arranged his notes on manuscripts held at the Bibliothèque nationale de France by manuscript number and consulted and amended them for decades. Several facts determine the order of the manuscript drawings. His letters to Lillian indicated that he studied the manuscripts from Cluny and then the manuscripts from Moissac from November 1926 to January 1927 and again in June 1927. Likewise, these letters date his initial interest in Edward Rand's system of hair and flesh sides to December 1926. In an unsent letter of 12 January 1927 to his advisor S. Butler Murray, he estimated that he had finished his study of sixty of the hundred Moissac manuscripts.

The travel notebooks are now housed at the Columbia University Rare Book and Manuscript Library along with the rest of Schapiro's papers. At the time of publication they had not been systematically catalogued and coded.

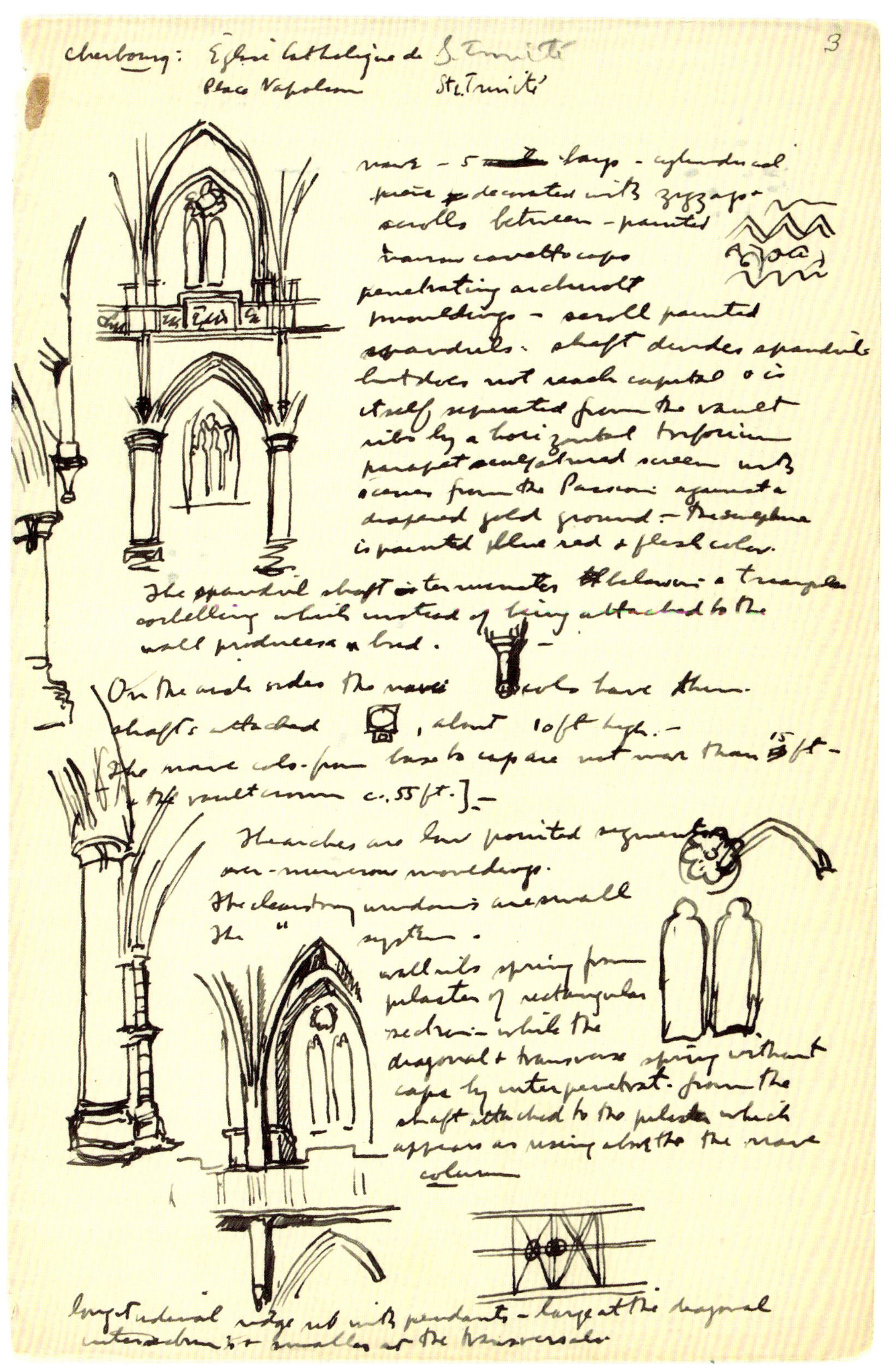

No. 1. Cherbourg, Église de Sainte-Trinité, 10 July 1926

Interior elevations and details of nave

Black ink and pencil on paper

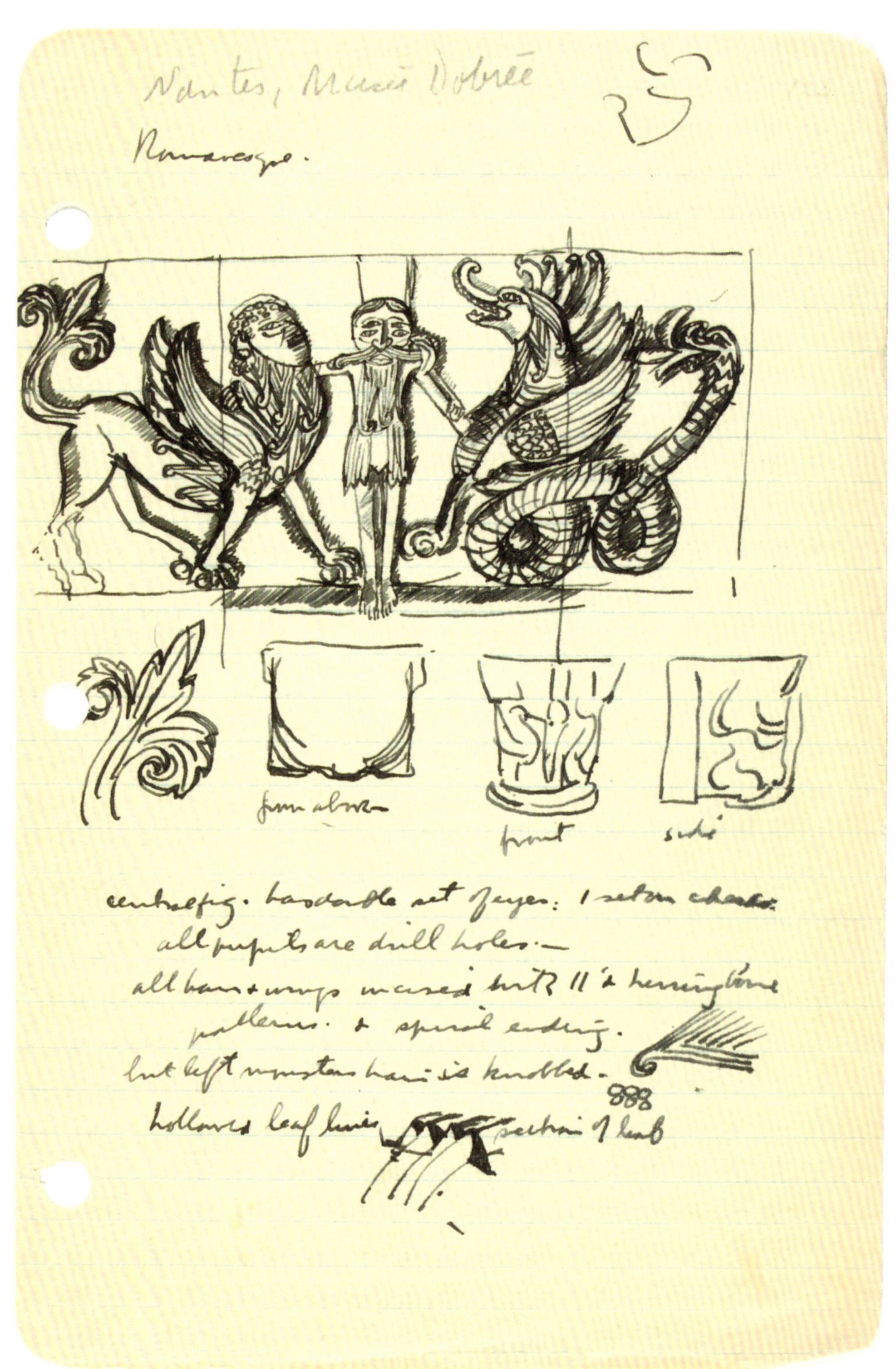

No. 2. Nantes, Musée Dobrée, 17 July 1926
Three faces, plan, and details of a capital from the choir of Cathédrale de Nantes
Black ink and pencil on paper

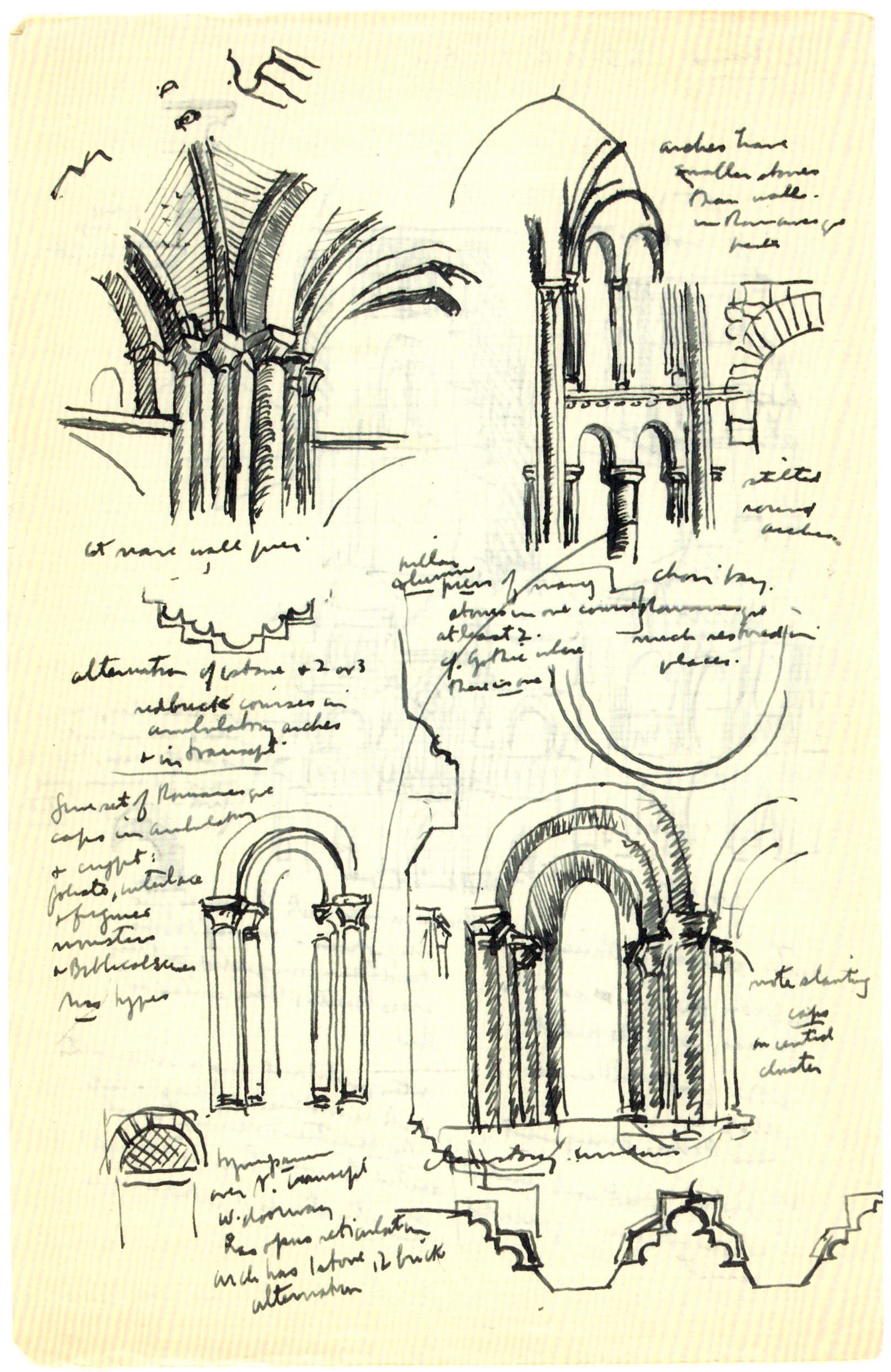

No. 3. Le Mans, Église de Notre-Dame-de-la-Couture, 23 July 1926

Details of arches and nave wall pier

Black ink on paper

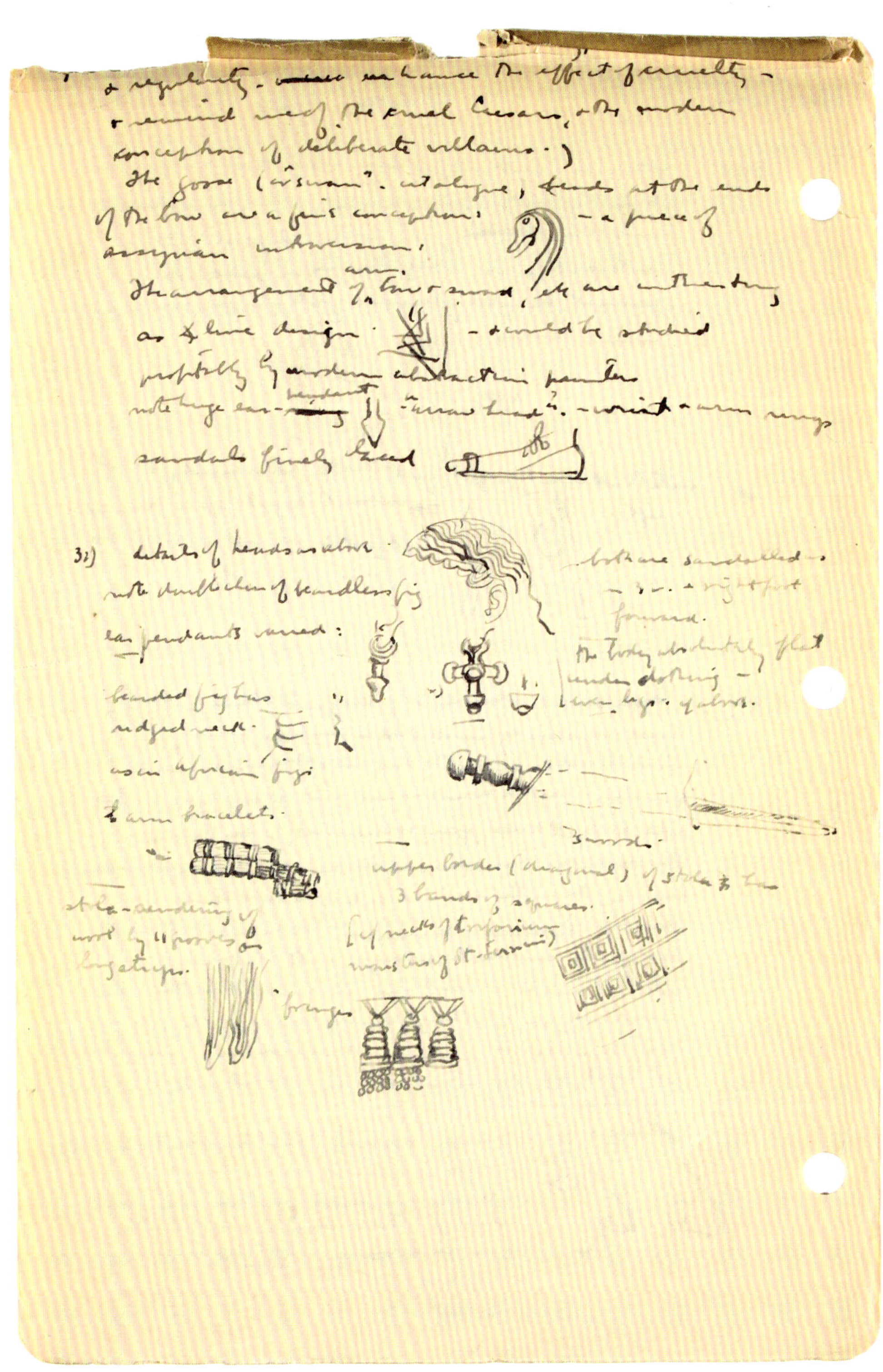

No. 4. Paris, Musée du Louvre, August 1926
Details of relief sculpture in the Assyrian collection
Black ink on paper

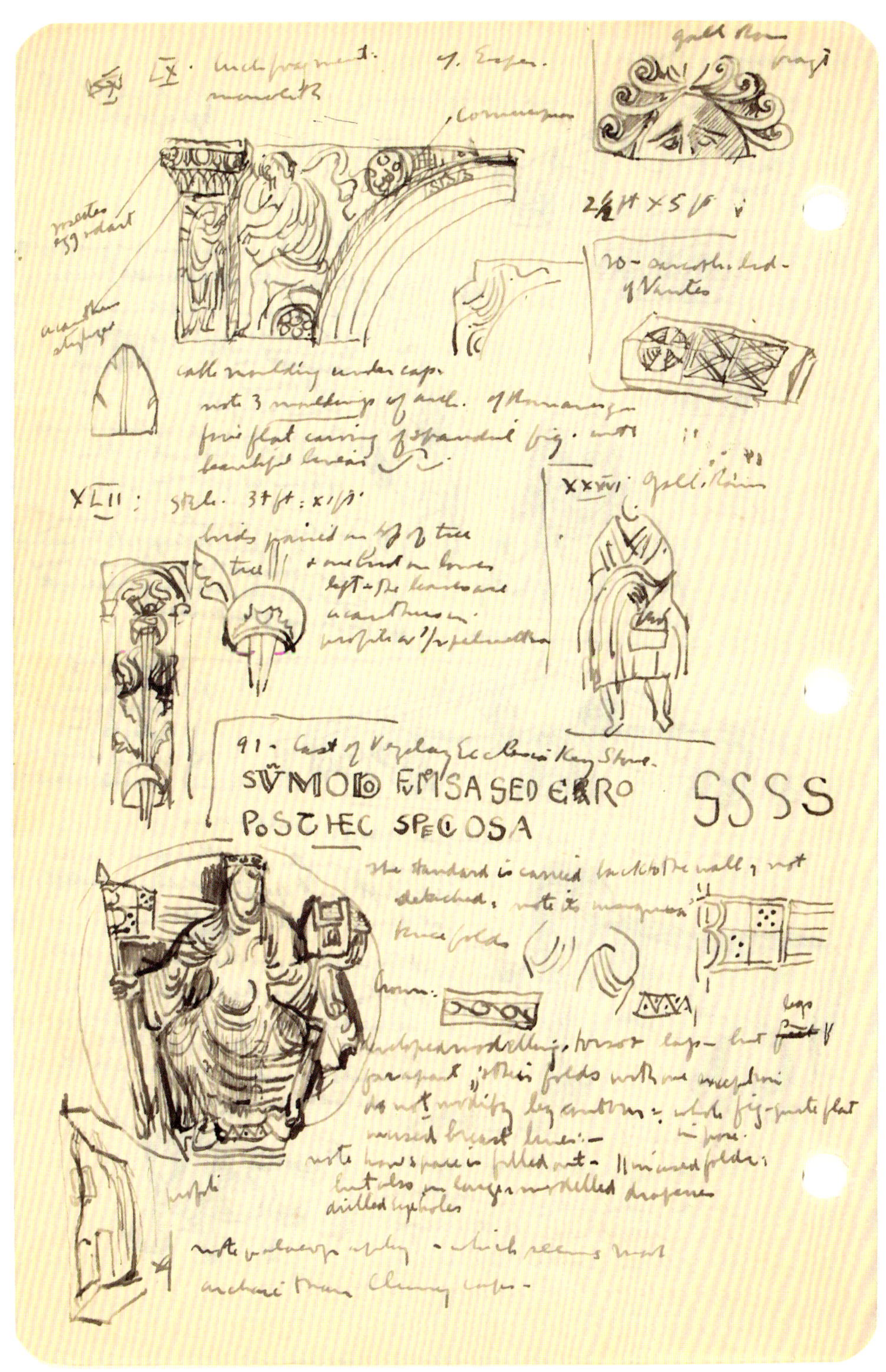

No. 5. Auxerre, Musée d'Auxerre, 4 September 1926

Gallo-Roman sculpture and cast from the Basilique Sainte-Madeleine, Vézelay

Black ink on paper

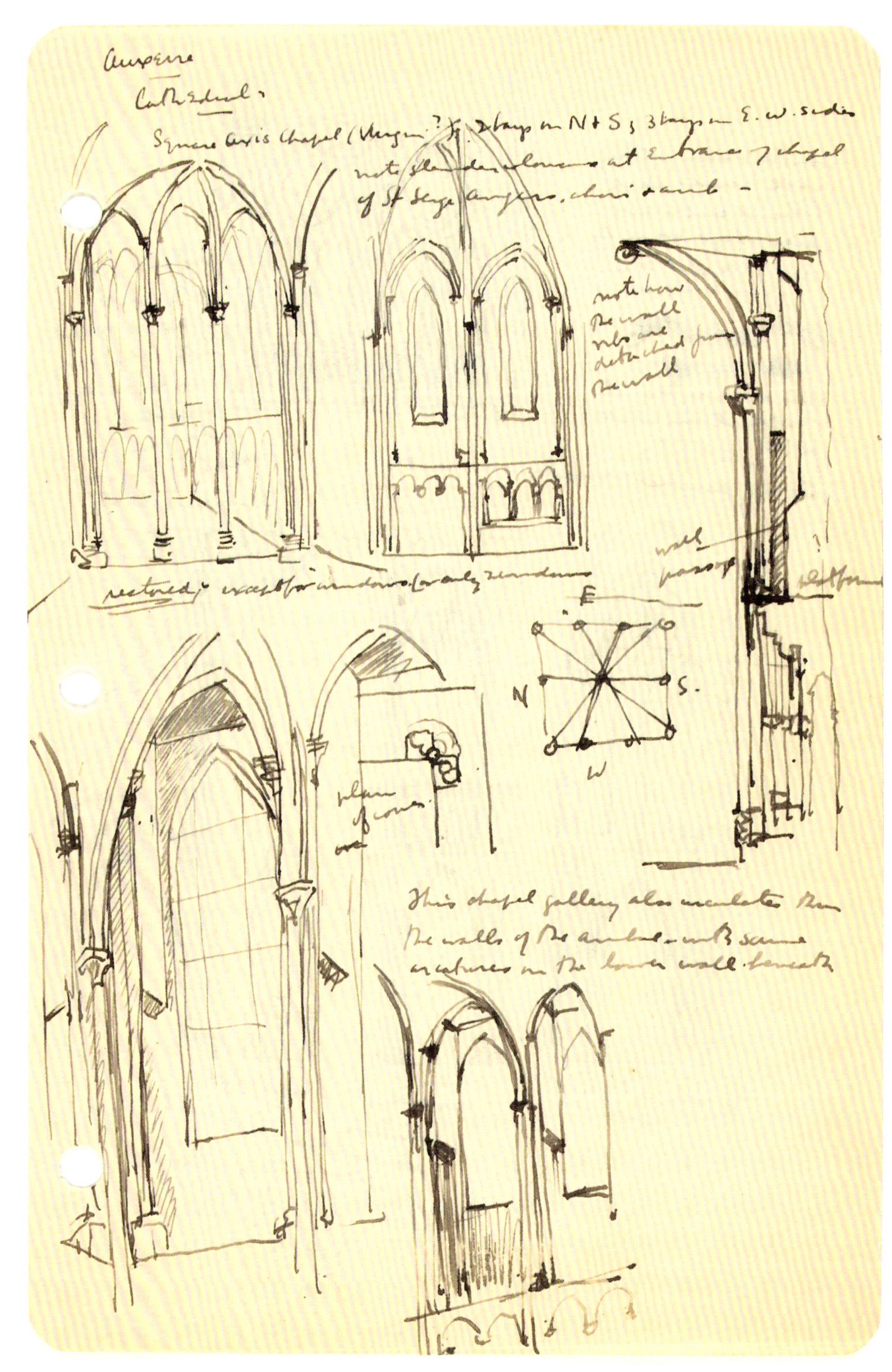

No. 6. Auxerre, Cathédrale de Saint-Étienne, 4 September 1926

Elevations of choir chapels

Black ink on paper

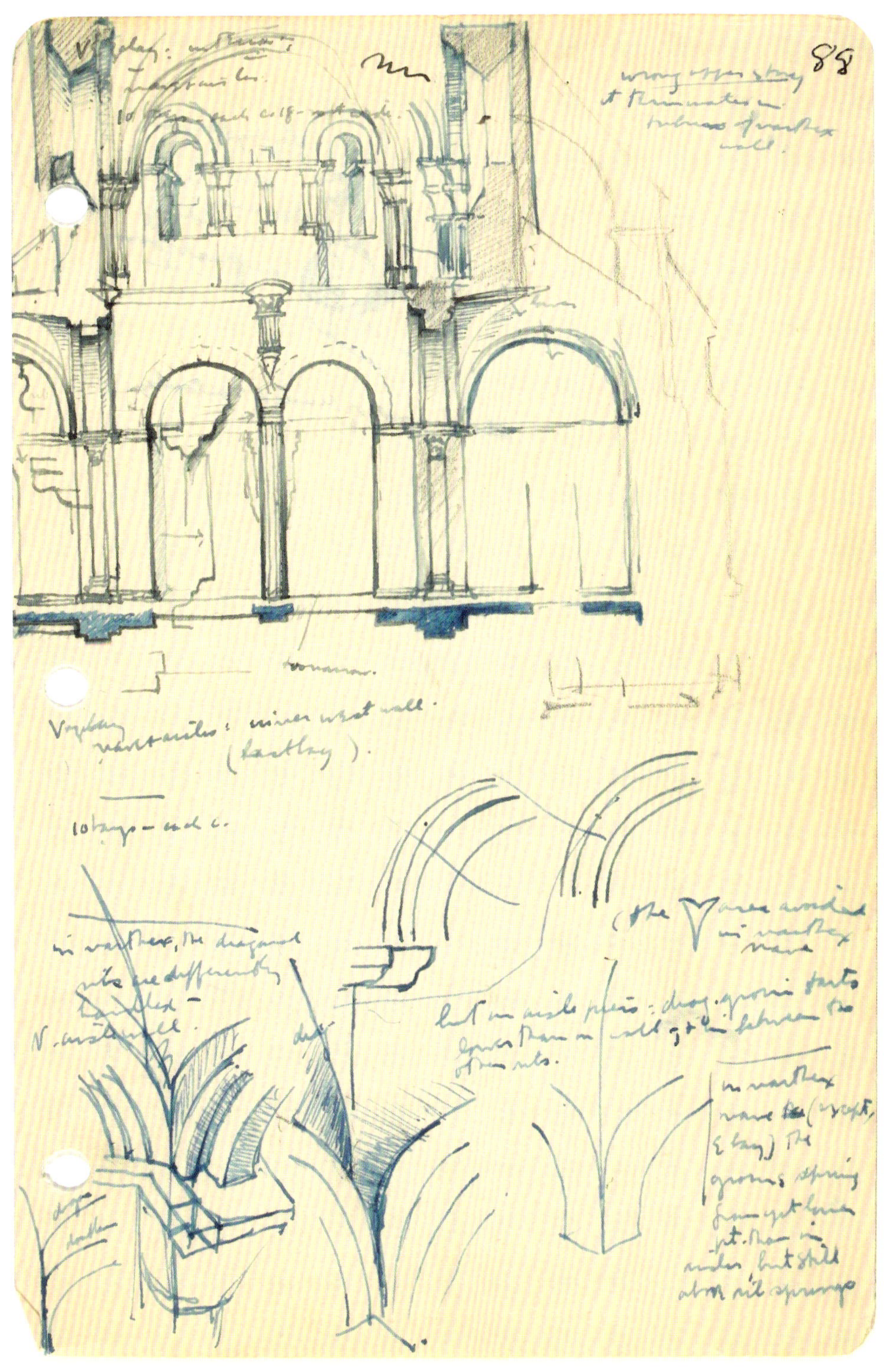

No. 7. Vézelay, Basilique de Sainte-Madeleine, 5 or 6 September 1926

Elevation of inner west wall and details of vaults

Blue ink and pencil on paper

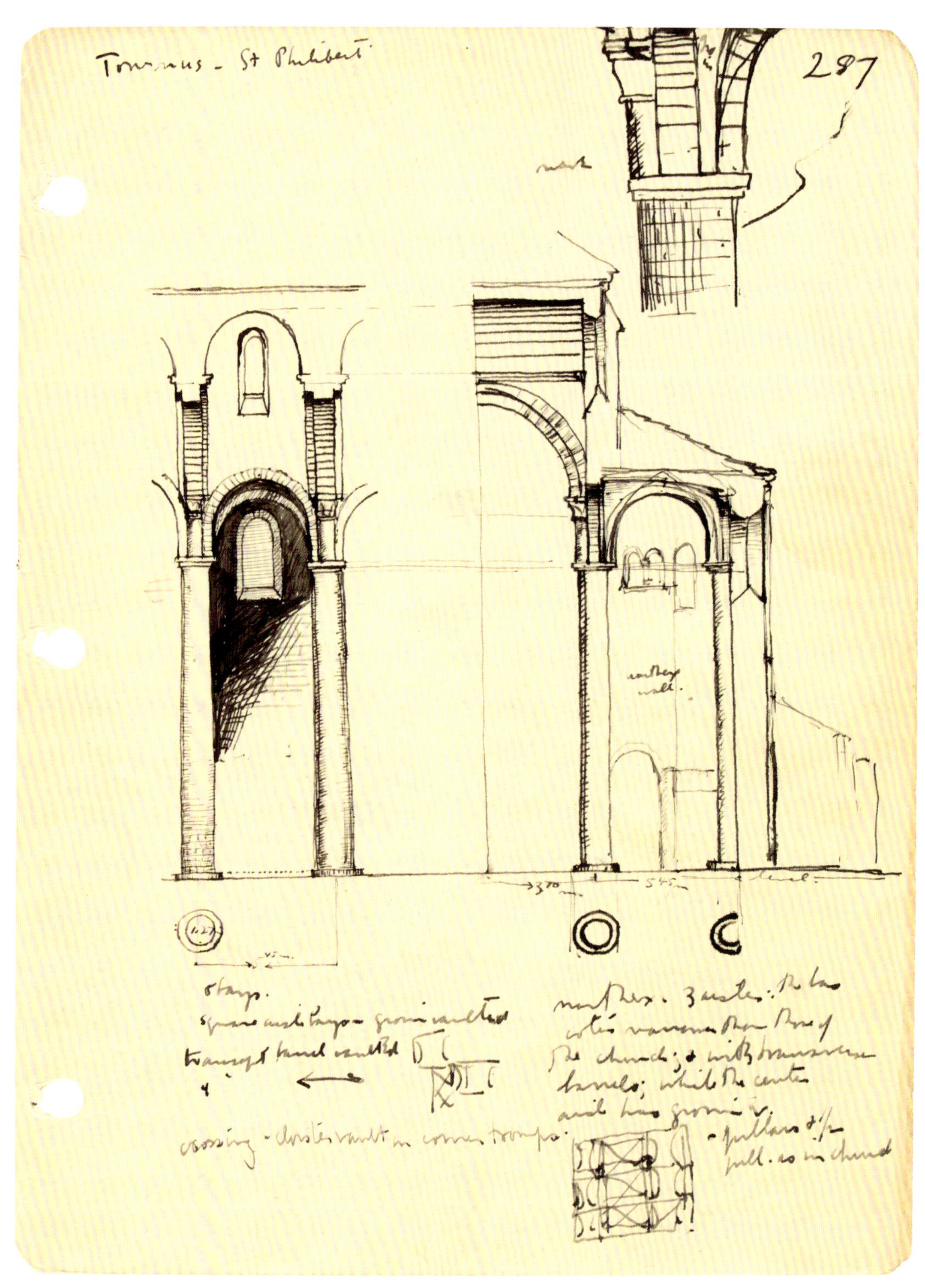

No. 8. Tournus, Église de Saint-Philibert, 11 September 1926

Nave elevation and section with vault detail

Black ink on paper

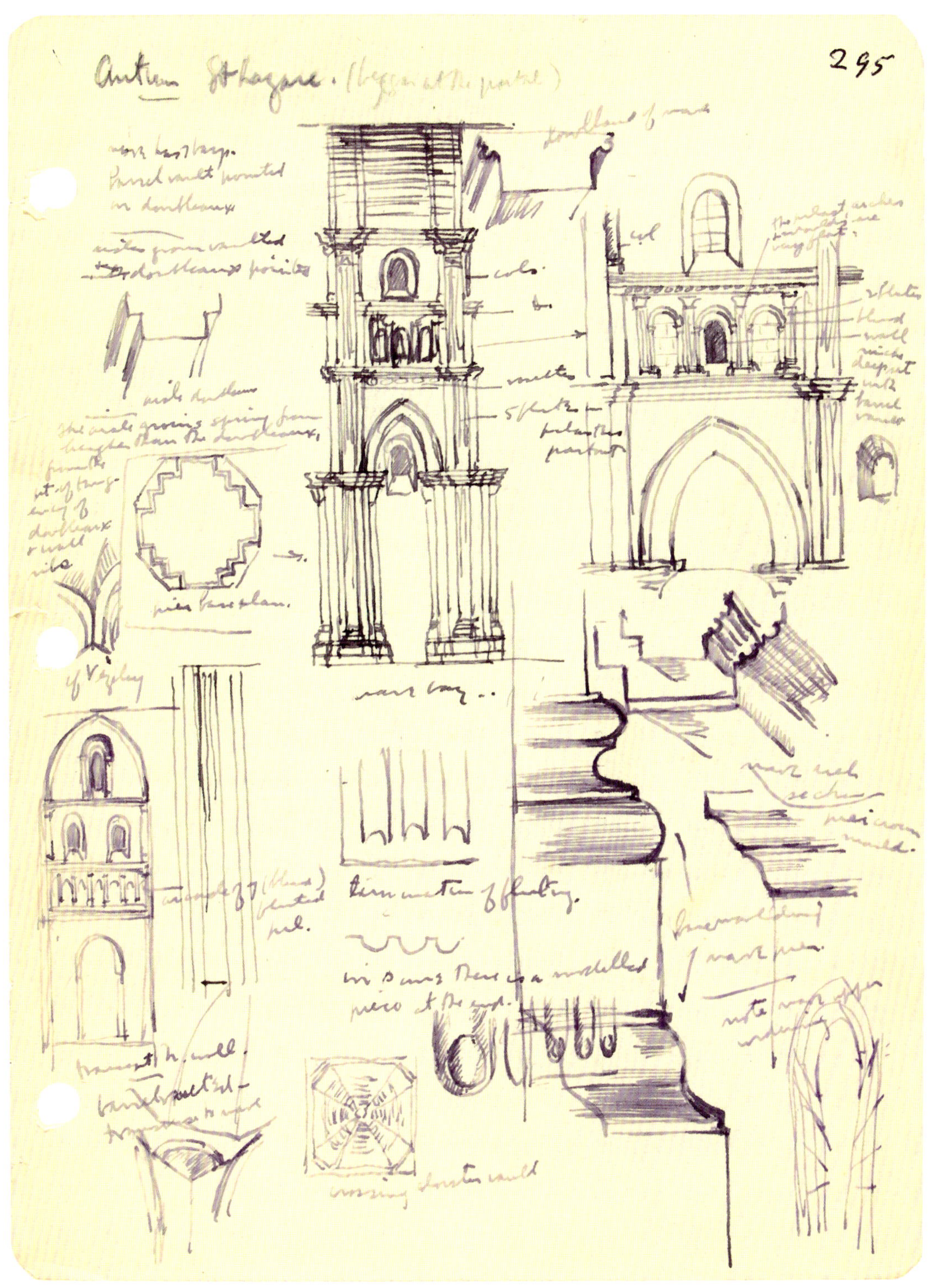

No. 9. Autun, Cathédrale de Saint-Lazare, 11–12 September 1926

Elevations and details of interior

Purple ink and pencil on paper

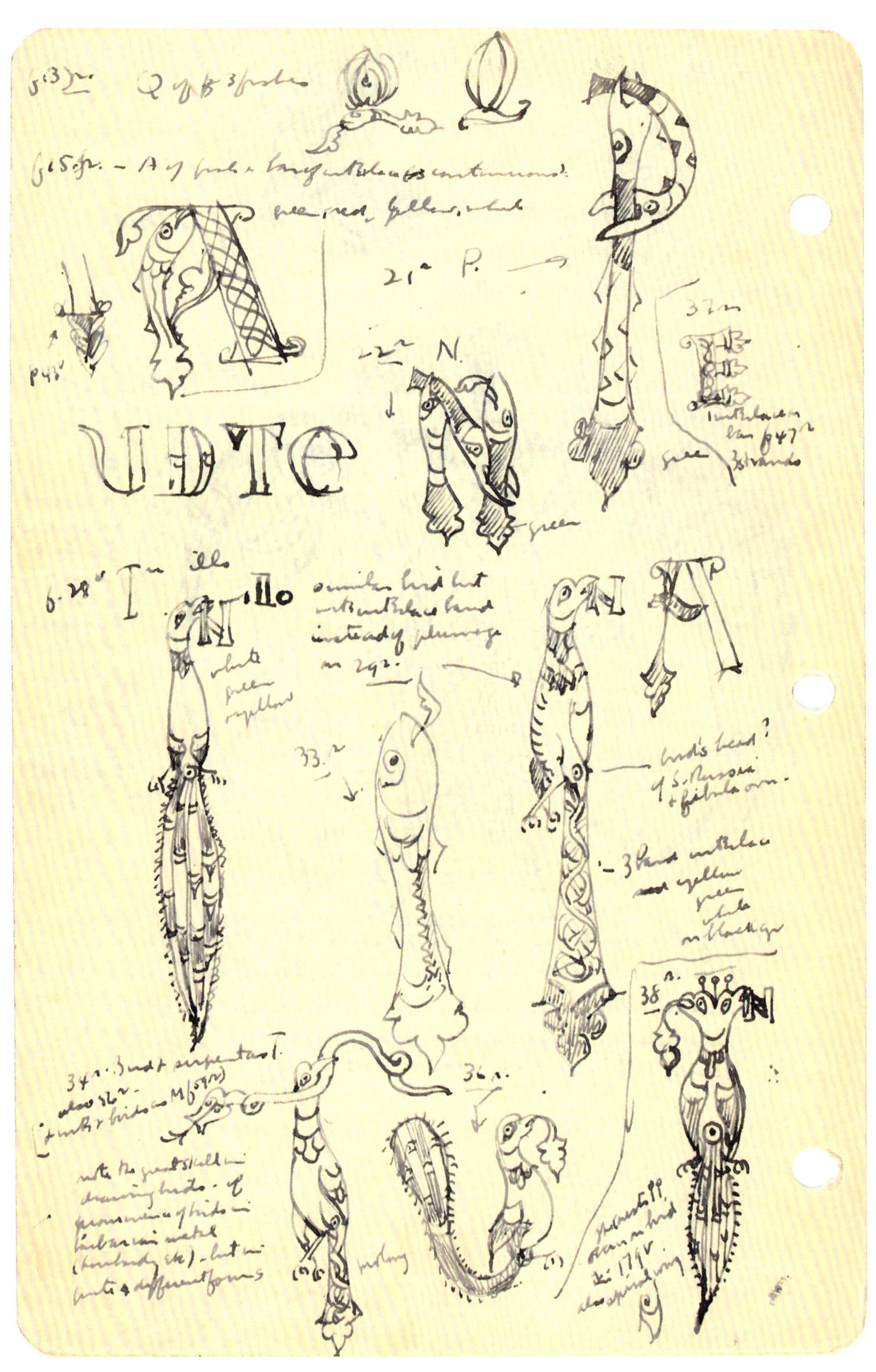

No. 10. Autun, Bibliothèque municipale, MS Lat. 3, 11–12 September 1926

Initials with stylized fish and bird figures from "Gundohinus Gospels"

Black ink on paper

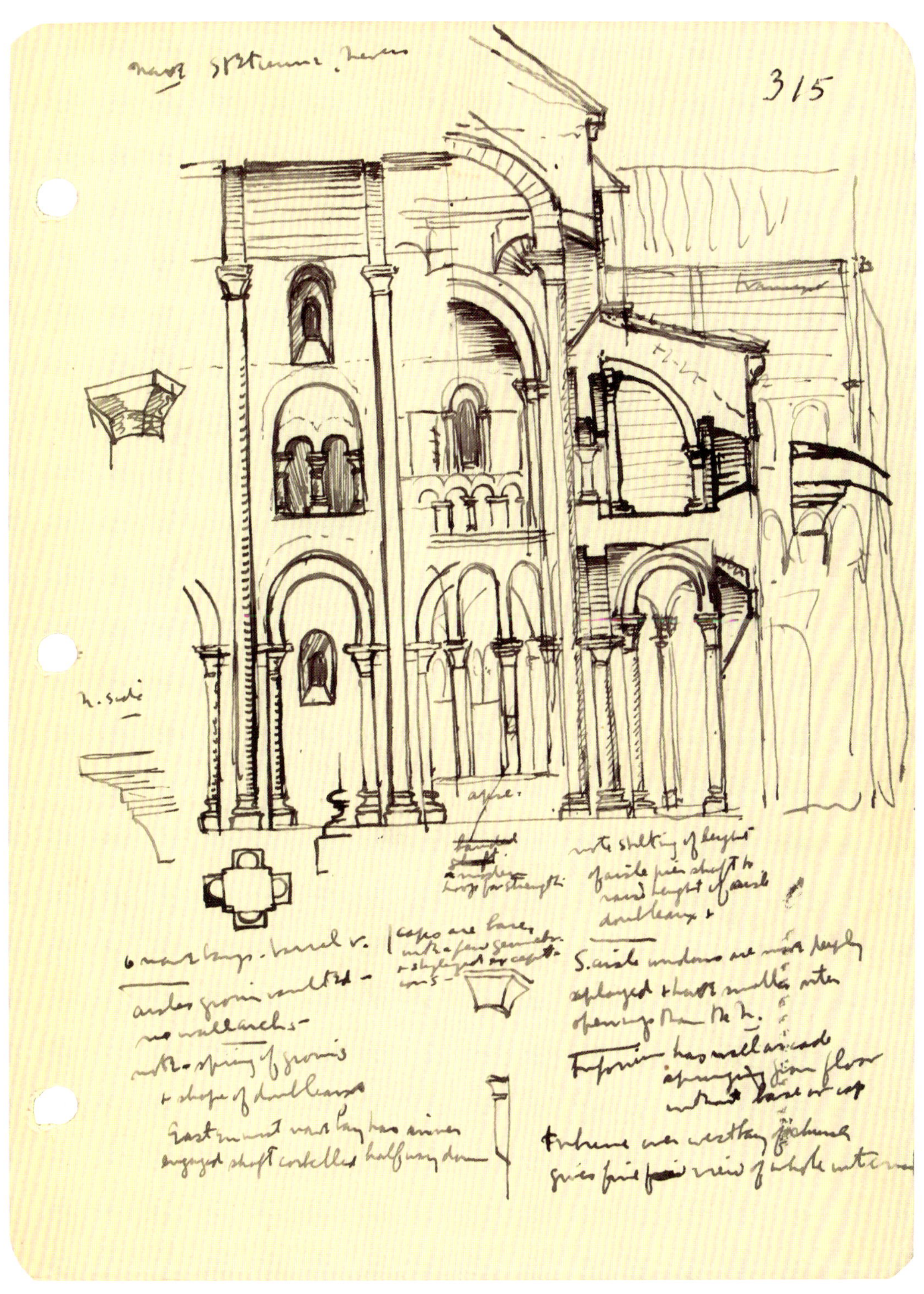

No. 11. Nevers, Église de Saint-Étienne, 14 September 1926

Nave section and elevation

Black ink on paper

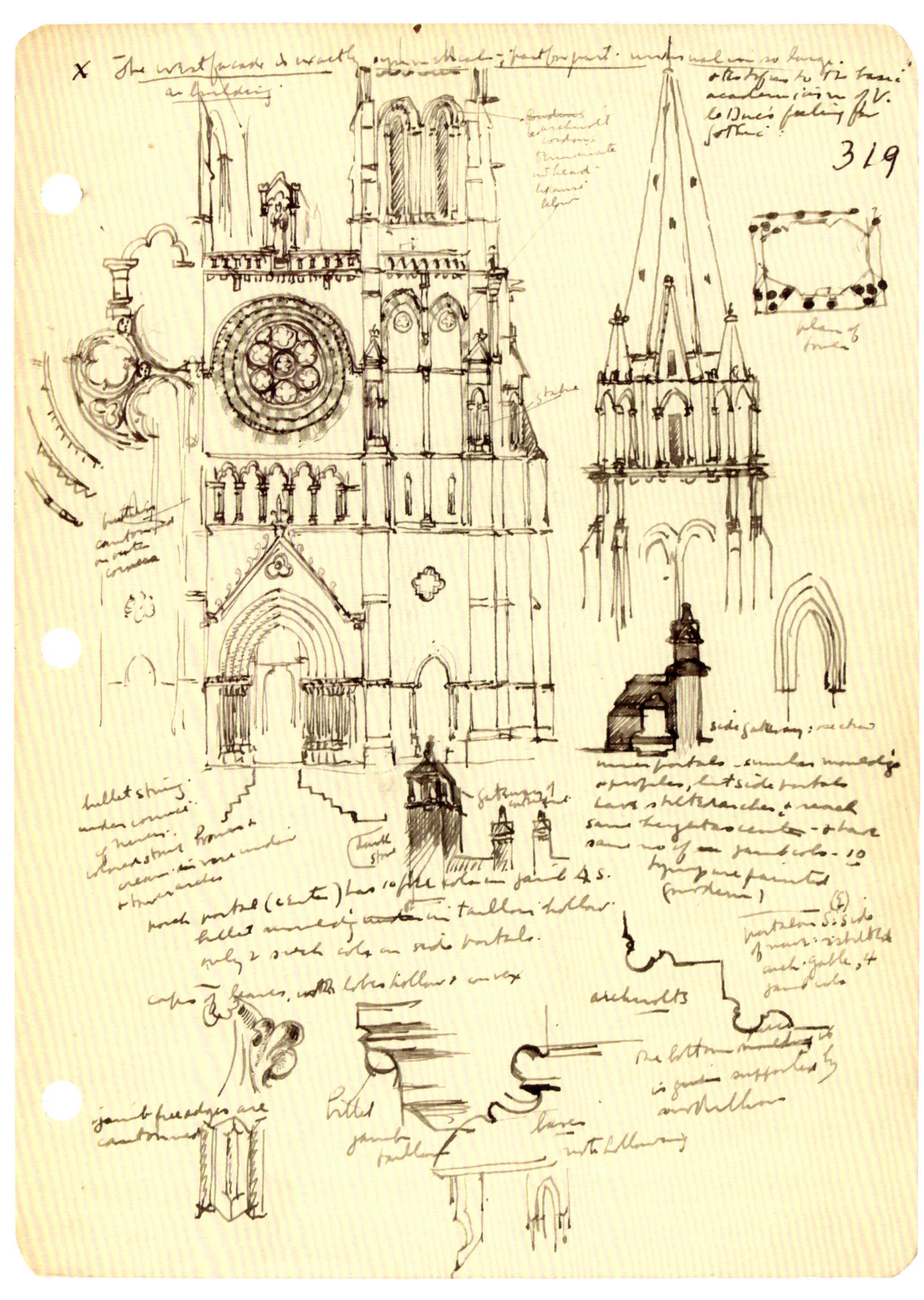

No. 12. Moulins, Cathédrale de Notre-Dame, 15 September 1926

West façade and exterior details

Black ink and pencil on paper

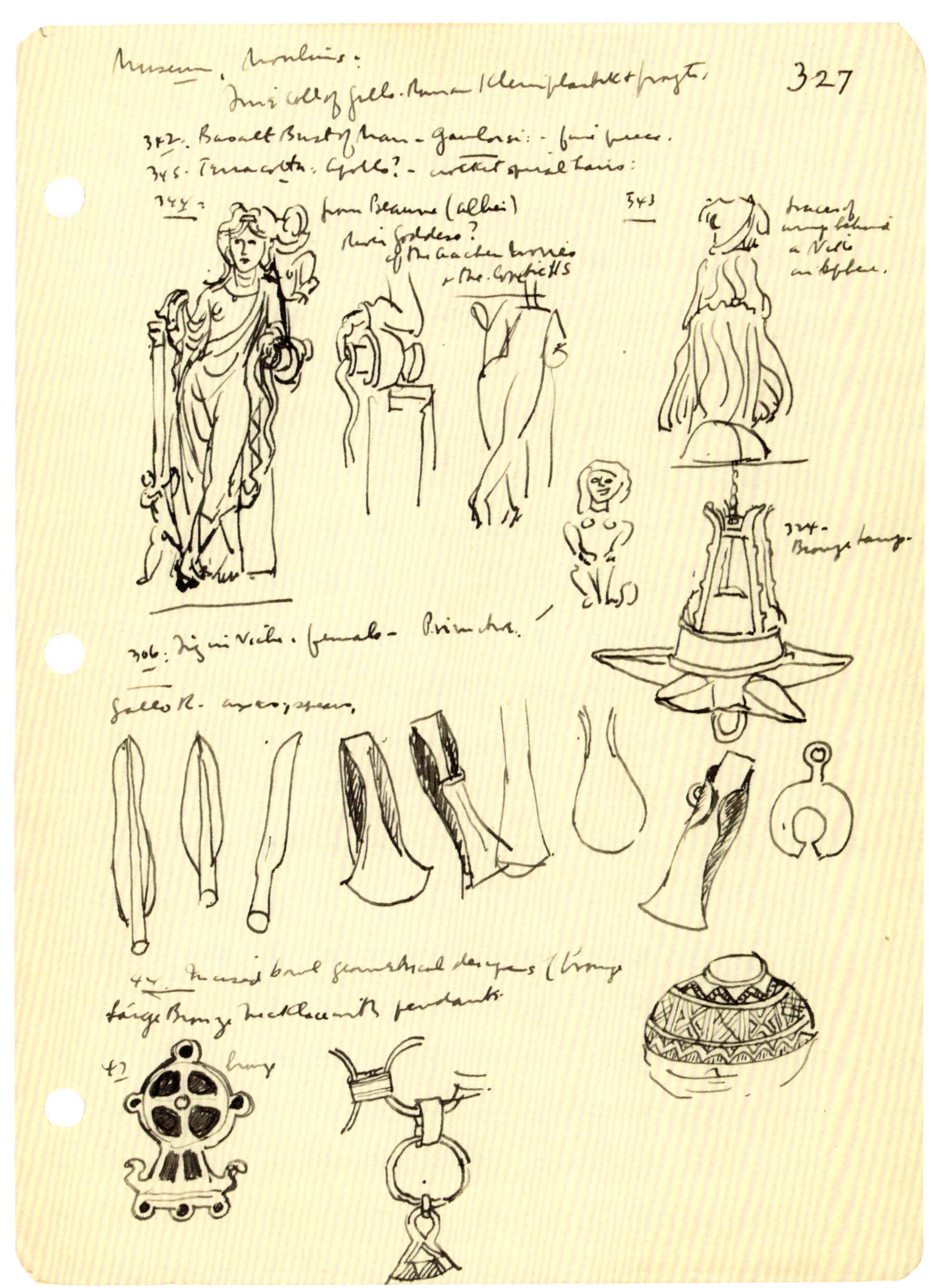

No. 13. Moulins, Musée Anne de Beaujeu, 15 September 1926

Gallo-Roman objects

Black ink on paper

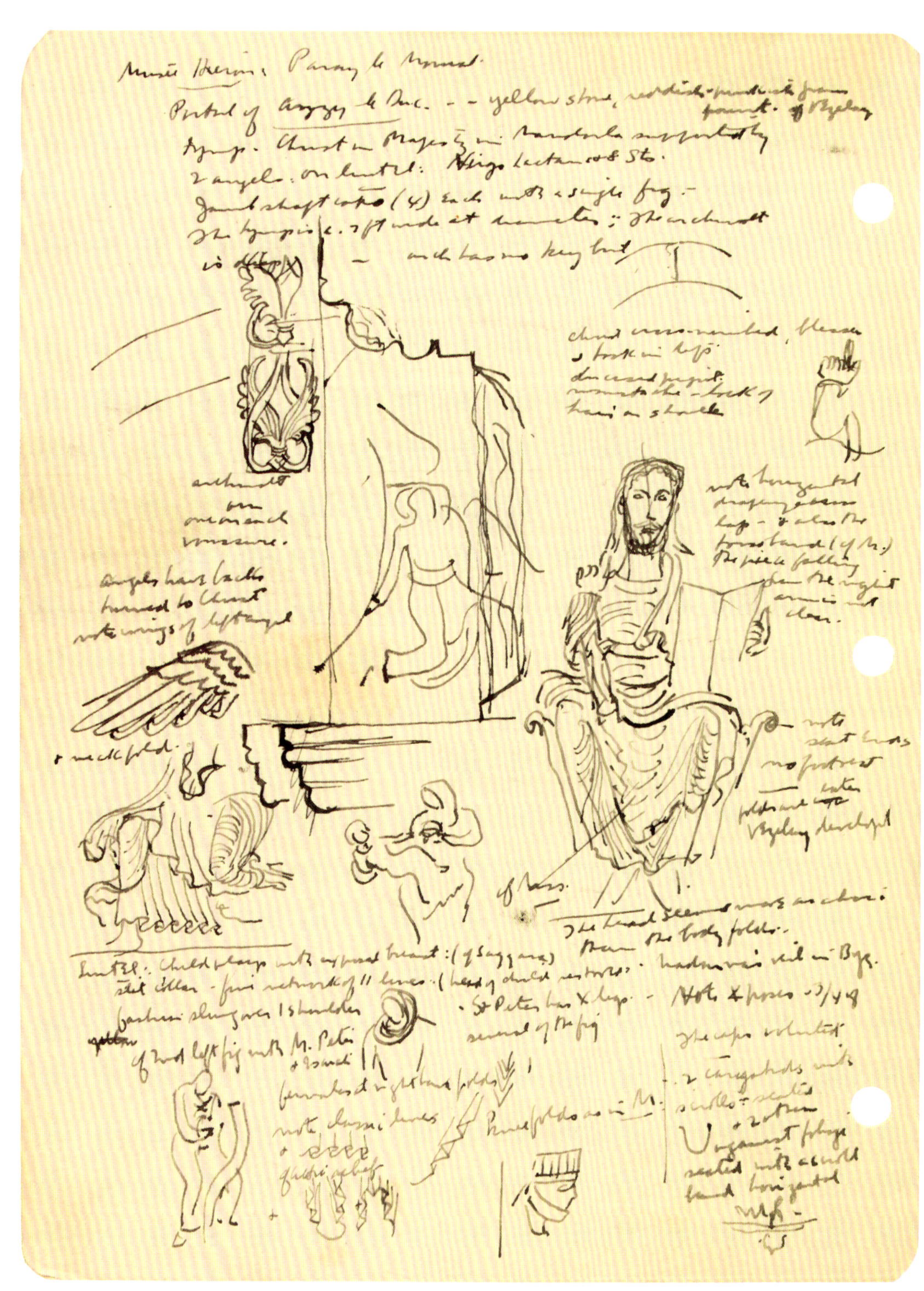

No. 14. Paray-le-Monial, Musée eucharistique du Hiéron, 16 September 1926

Details of tympanum from the priory of Anzy-le-Duc

Black ink on paper

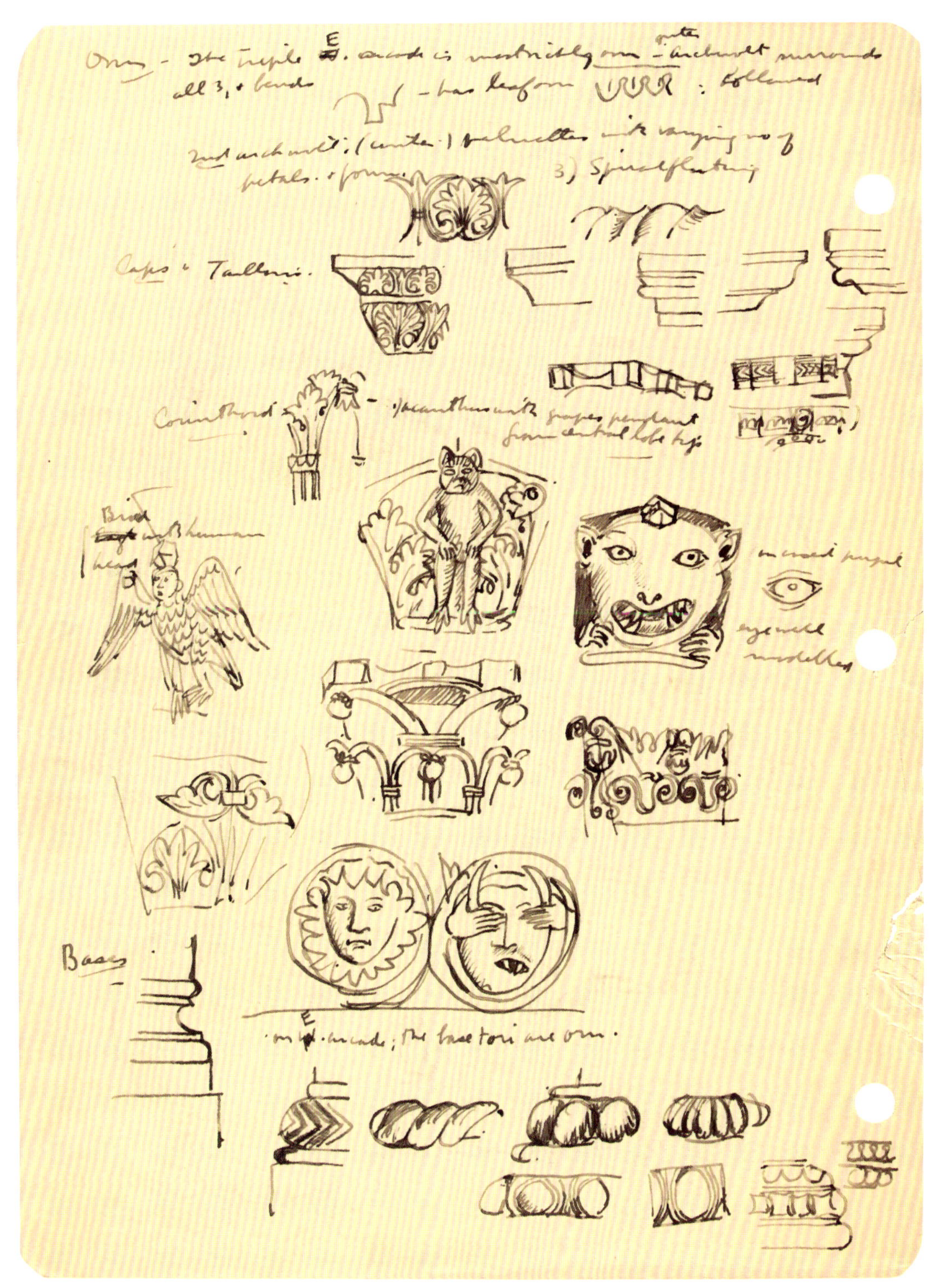

No. 15. Charlieu, ruins of the Abbaye Bénédictine, 19 September 1926

Details of cloister capitals, tailloirs, and bases

Black ink on paper

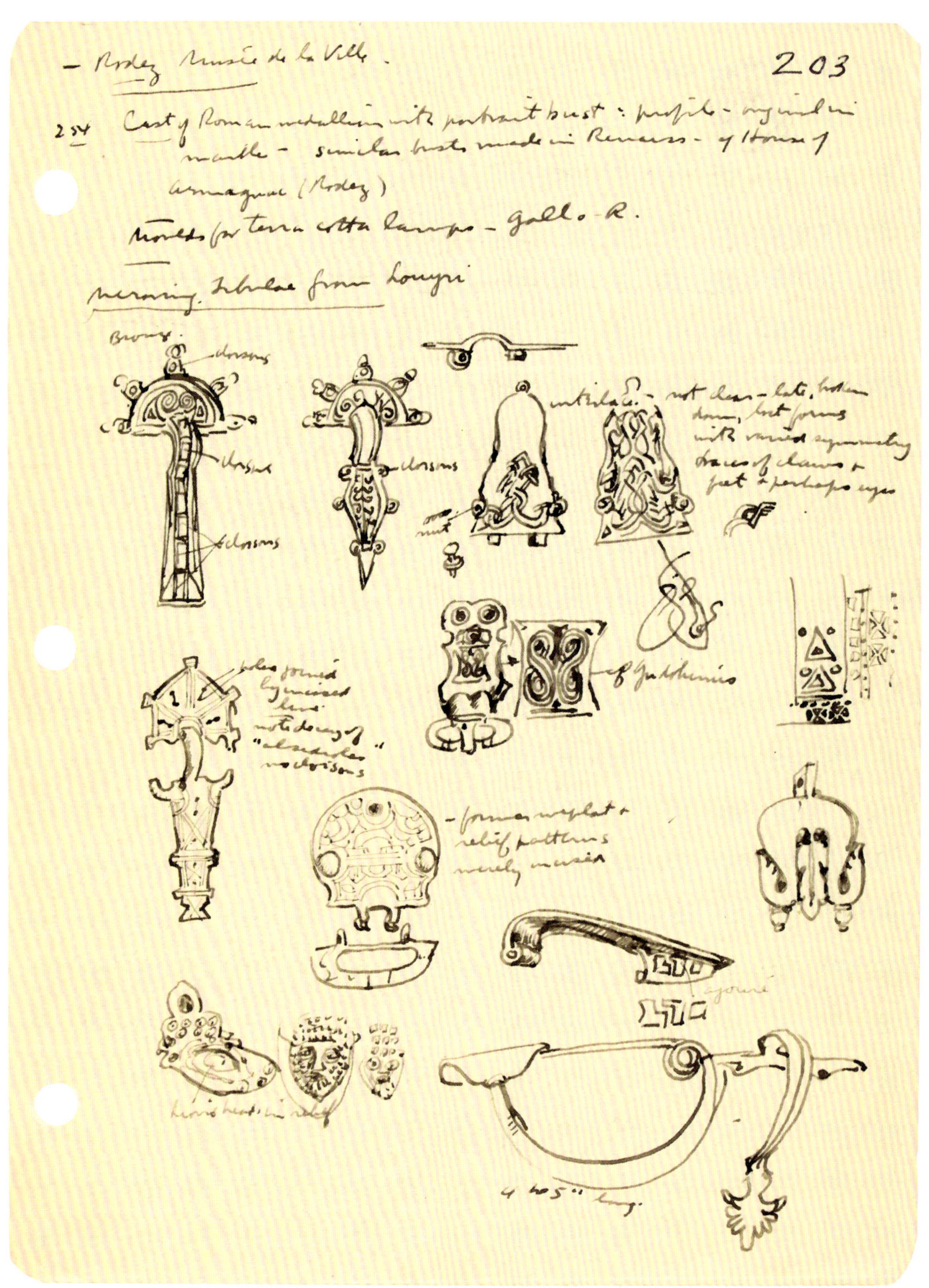

No. 16. Rodez, Musée de la Ville, 24 September 1926

Merovingian fibulae

Black ink on paper

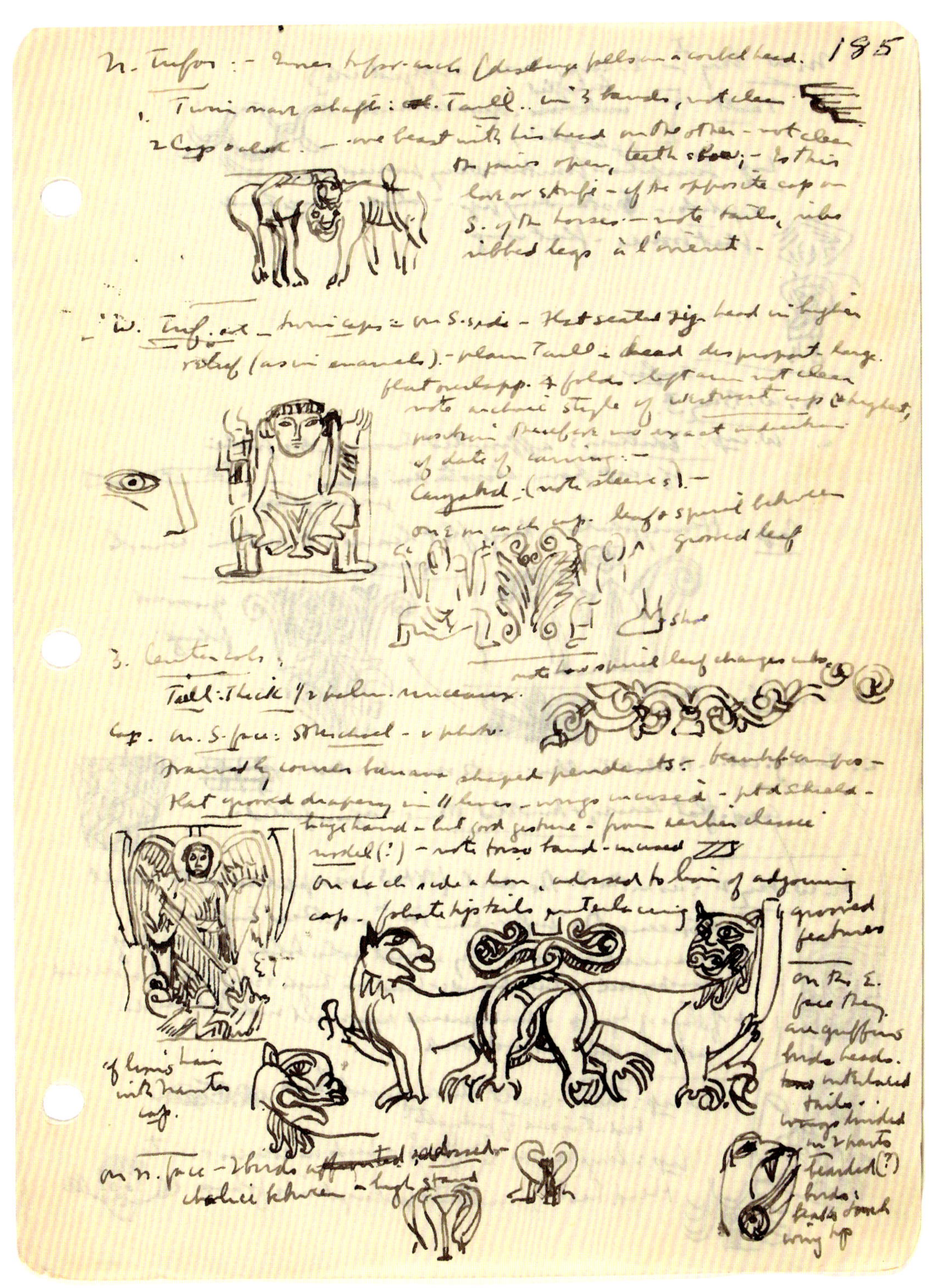

No. 17. Conques, Abbatiale de Sainte-Foy, 26–28 September 1926

Capitals in triforium: lions, caryatid, and Saint Michael

Black ink on paper

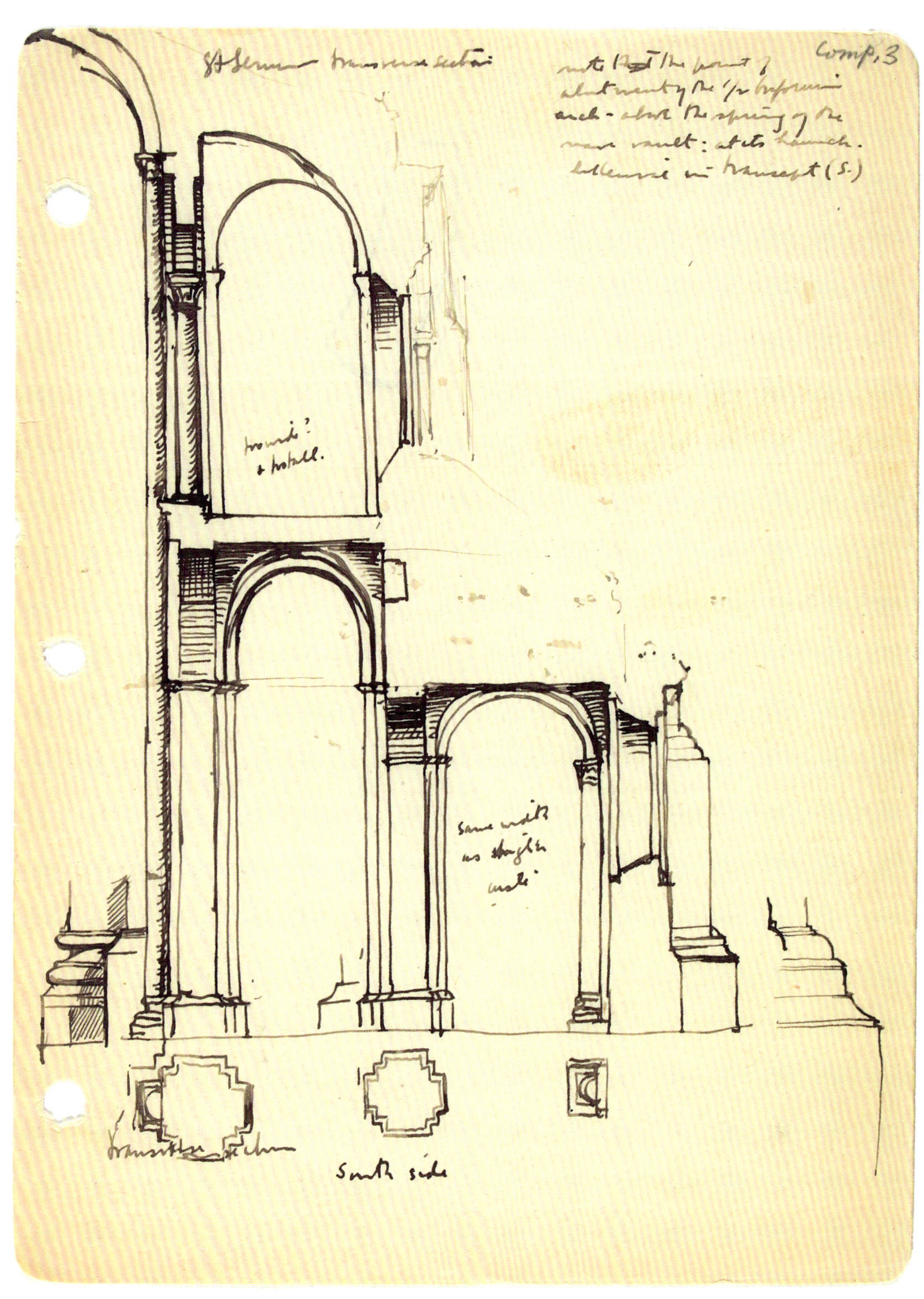

No. 18. Toulouse, Basilique de Saint-Sernin, 2–26 October 1926

Section of nave

Black ink on paper

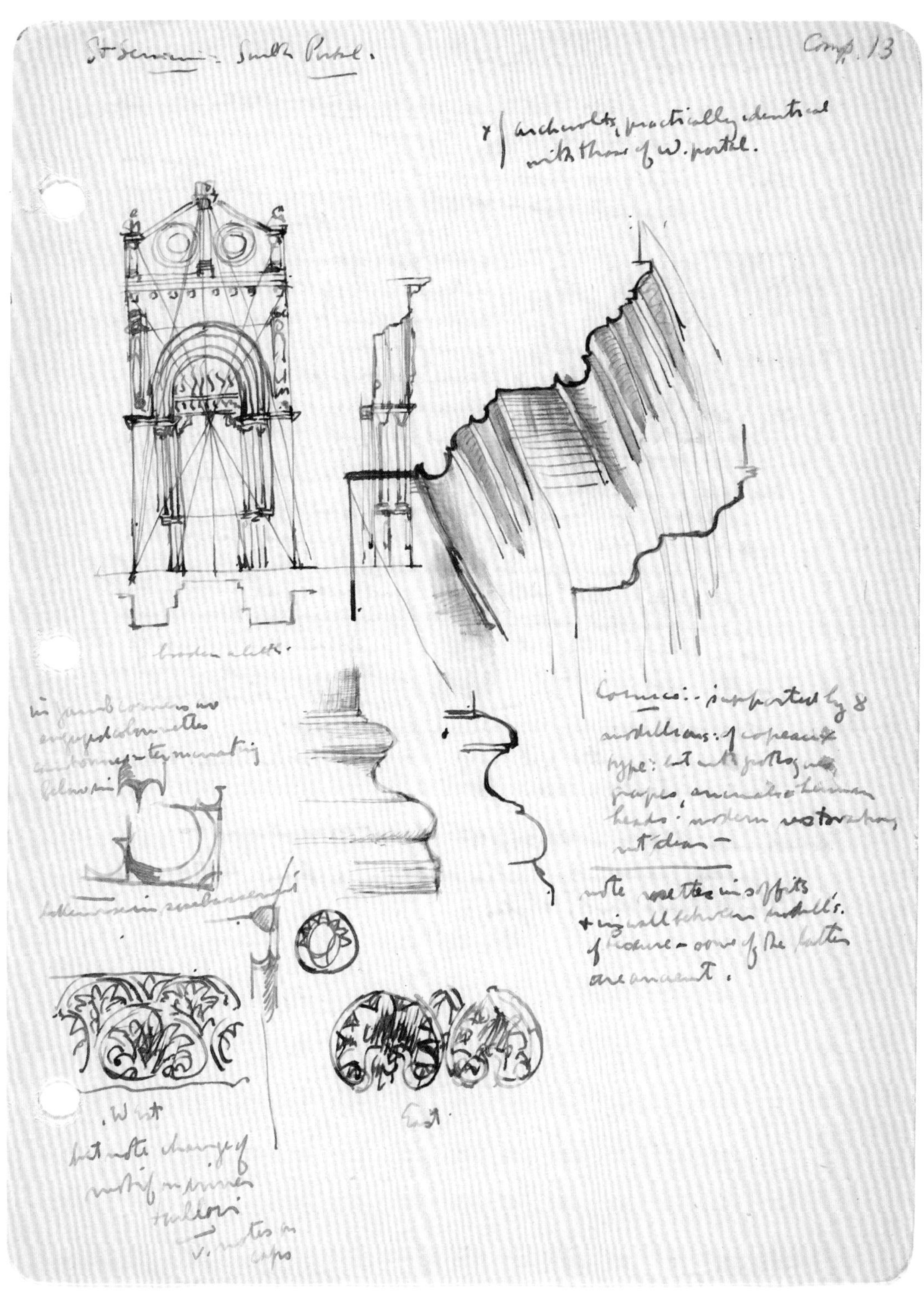

No. 19. Toulouse, Basilique de Saint-Sernin, 2–26 October 1926

Elevation and details of south portal

Black ink on paper

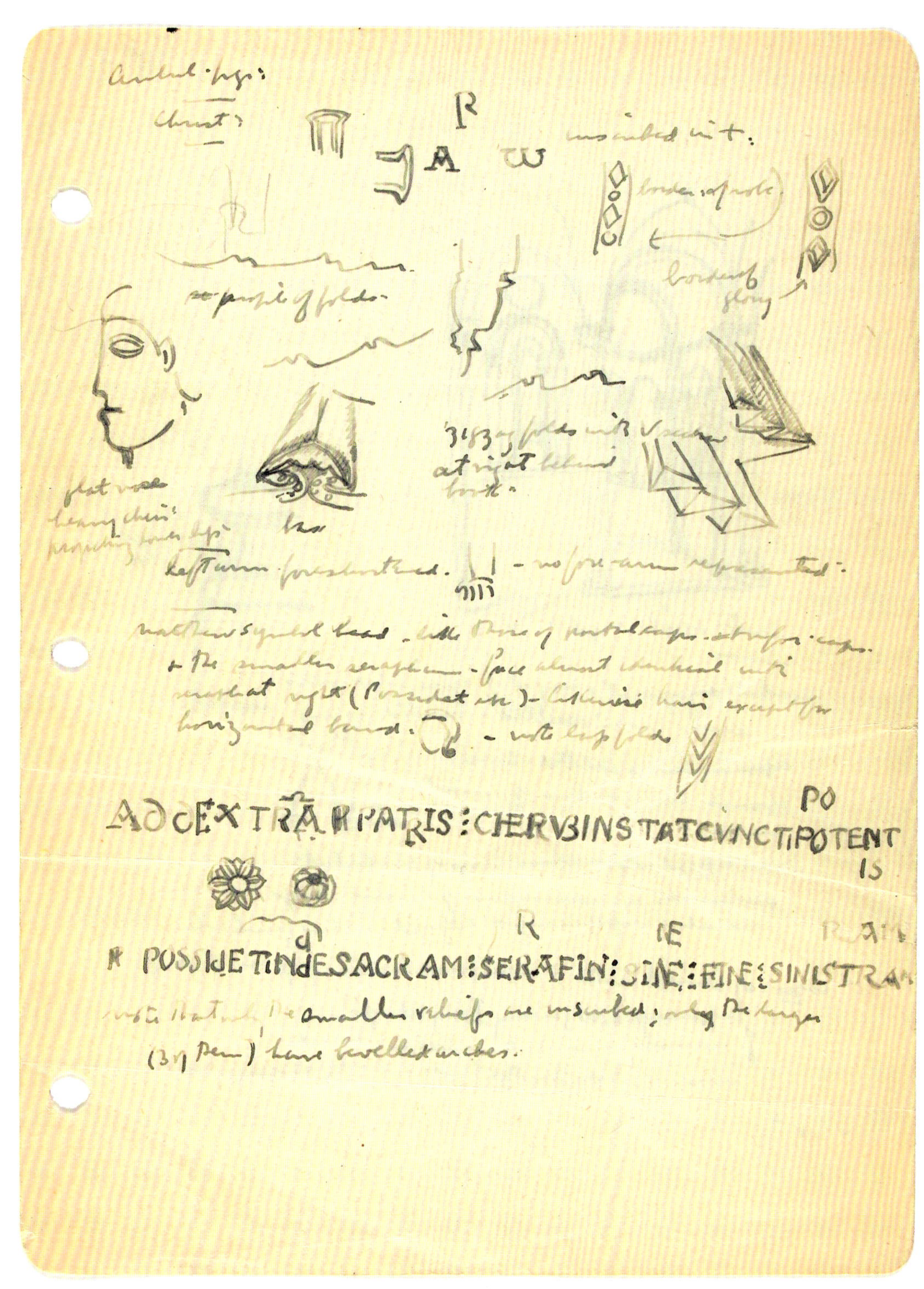

No. 20. Toulouse, Basilique de Saint-Sernin, 2–26 October 1926

Details of sculpture and inscriptions in ambulatory

Black ink on paper

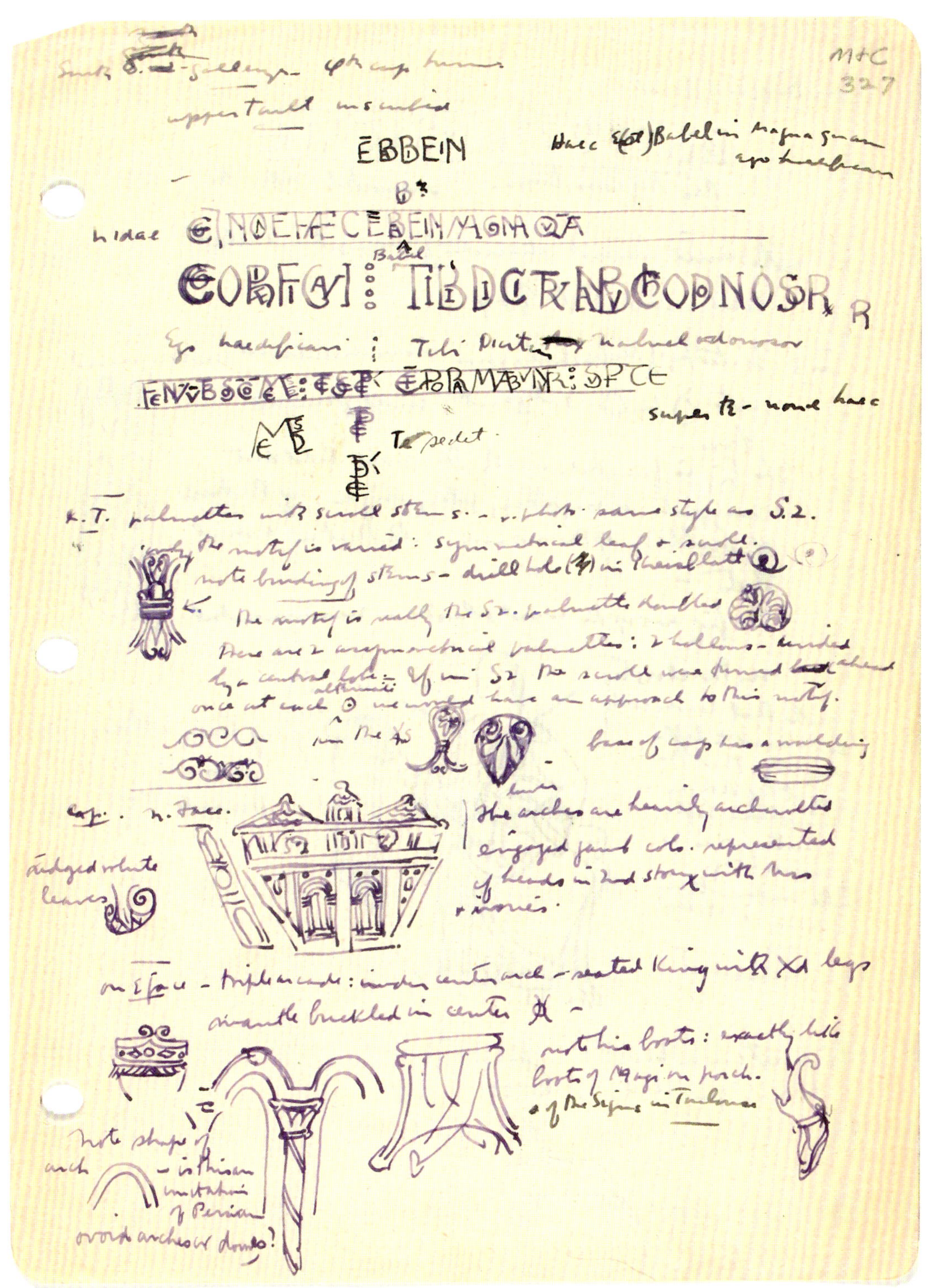

No. 21. Moissac, Abbaye de Saint-Pierre, 28 October–5 November 1926

Tailloir inscriptions and details of Capital 5, Nebuchadnezzar as a beast

Purple ink and black ink on paper

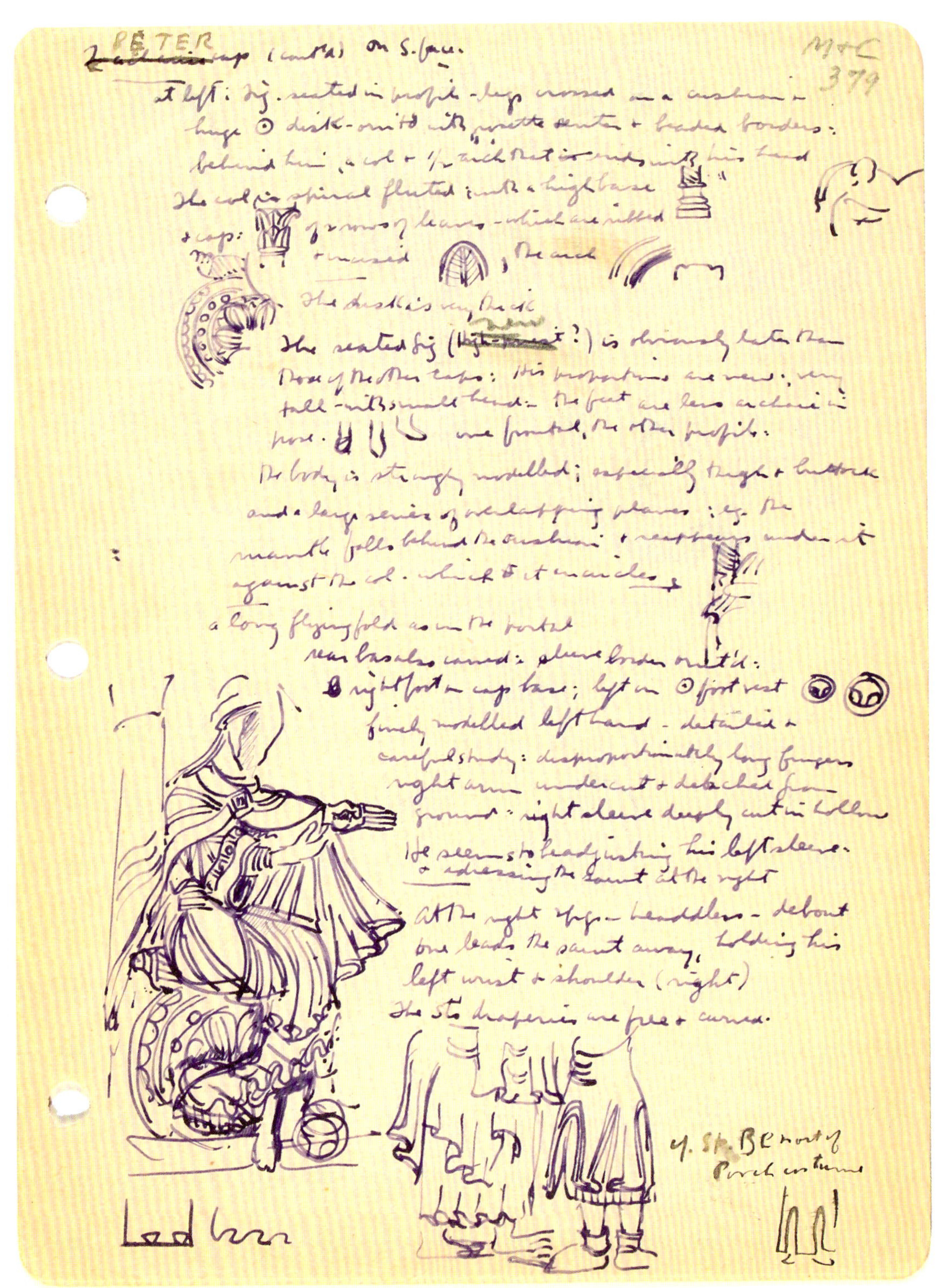

M+C 379

PETER caps (contd) on S. face.

At left: fig. seated in profile – legs crossed on a cushion – large ⊙ disk-ornt'd with rosette center + beaded borders: behind him, a col + ½ arch that it ends with his head. The col is spiral fluted with a high base + cap: grooves of leaves – which are ribbed + incised, the arch

The disk is very thick

The seated fig ([illegible]?) is obviously later than those of the other caps: his proportions are new; very tall – with small head – the feet are less archaic in pose. one frontal, the other profile.

The body is strongly modelled; especially thigh + buttock and a large series of overlapping planes: e.g. the mantle falls behind the cushion + reappears under it against the col. which it encircles

a long flying fold as in the portal

near base also curved: sleeve border ornt'd.

right foot on cap base; left on ⊙ foot rest

finely modelled left hand – detailed + careful study: disproportionately long fingers

right arm undercut + detached from ground: right sleeve deeply cut in hollow

He seems to be adjusting his left sleeve + addressing the saint at the right

At the right of fig – headless – debout one leads the saint away, holding his left wrist + shoulder (right)

The St's draperies are free + curved.

cf. St. Benoit Porch costume

No. 22. Moissac, Abbaye de Saint-Pierre, 28 October–5 November 1926

Details of south face of Capital 17, Deliverance of Peter

Purple ink, black ink, and pencil on paper

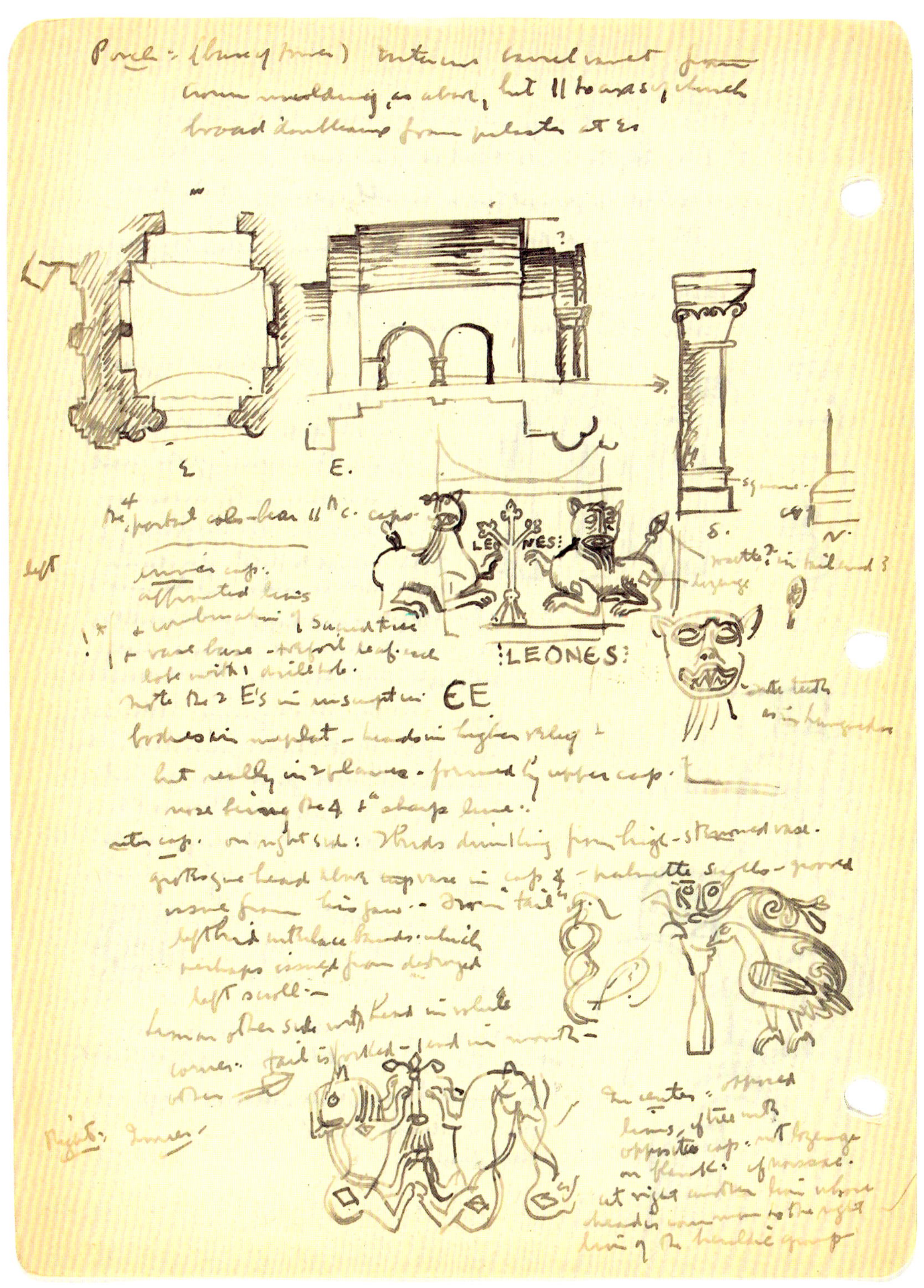

No. 23. Poitiers, Église de Saint-Porchaire, 9–14 November 1926

Plan, section, and details of tower

Black ink on paper

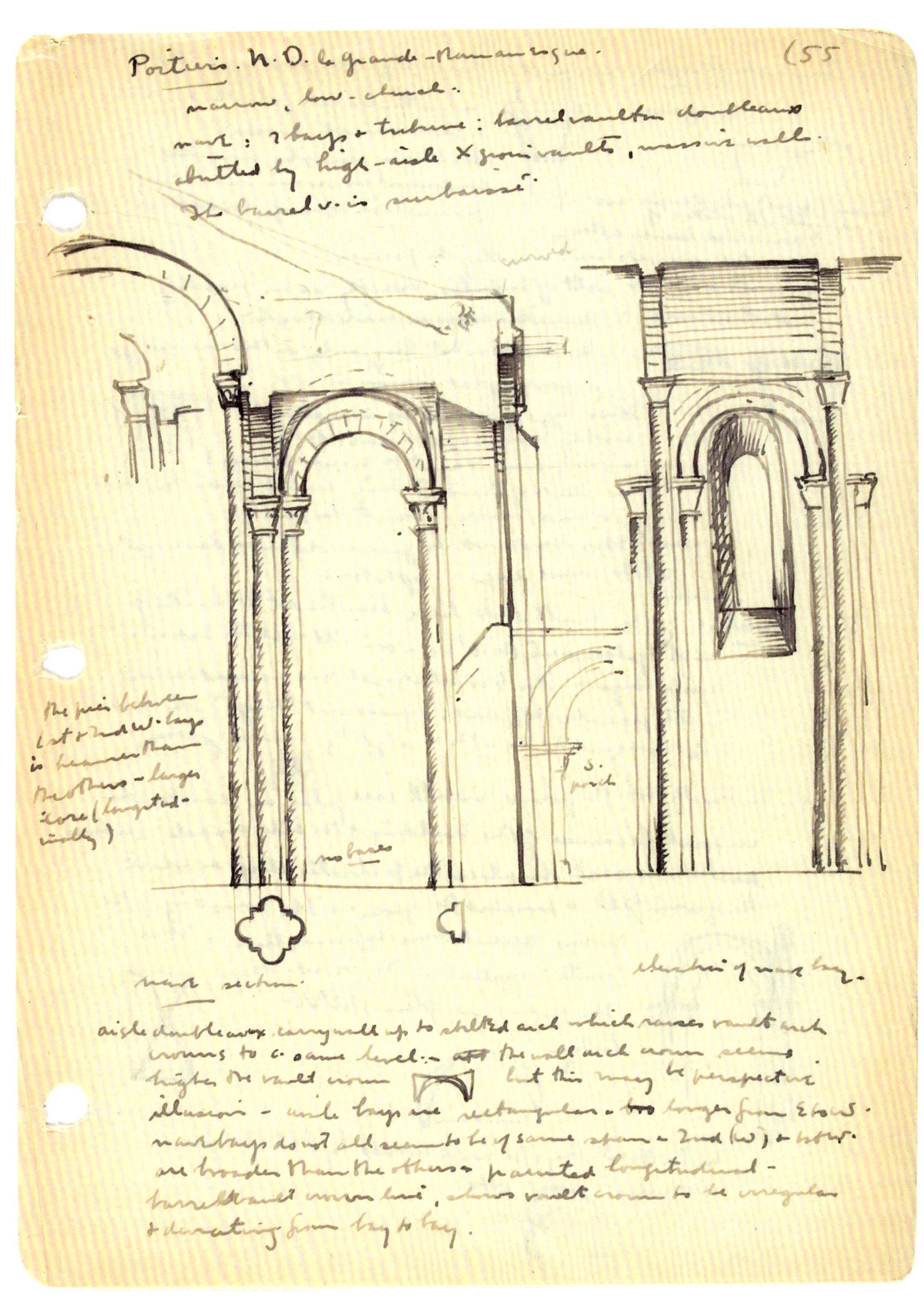

No. 24. Poitiers, Église de Notre-Dame-la-Grande, 11 November 1926

Section and elevation of nave

Black ink and pencil on paper

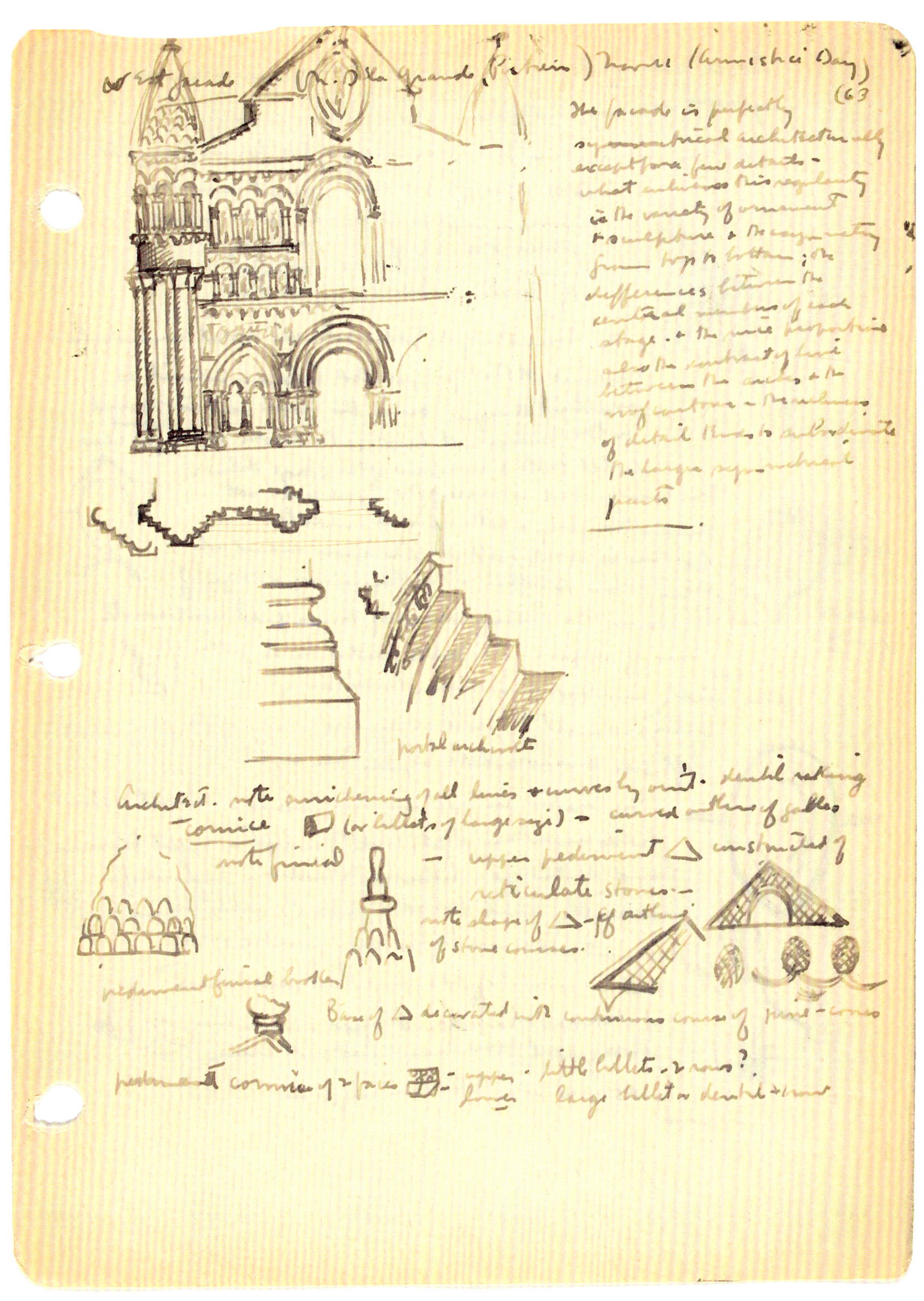

No. 25. Poitiers, Église de Notre-Dame-la-Grande, 11 November 1926

Elevation and details of west façade

Black ink on paper

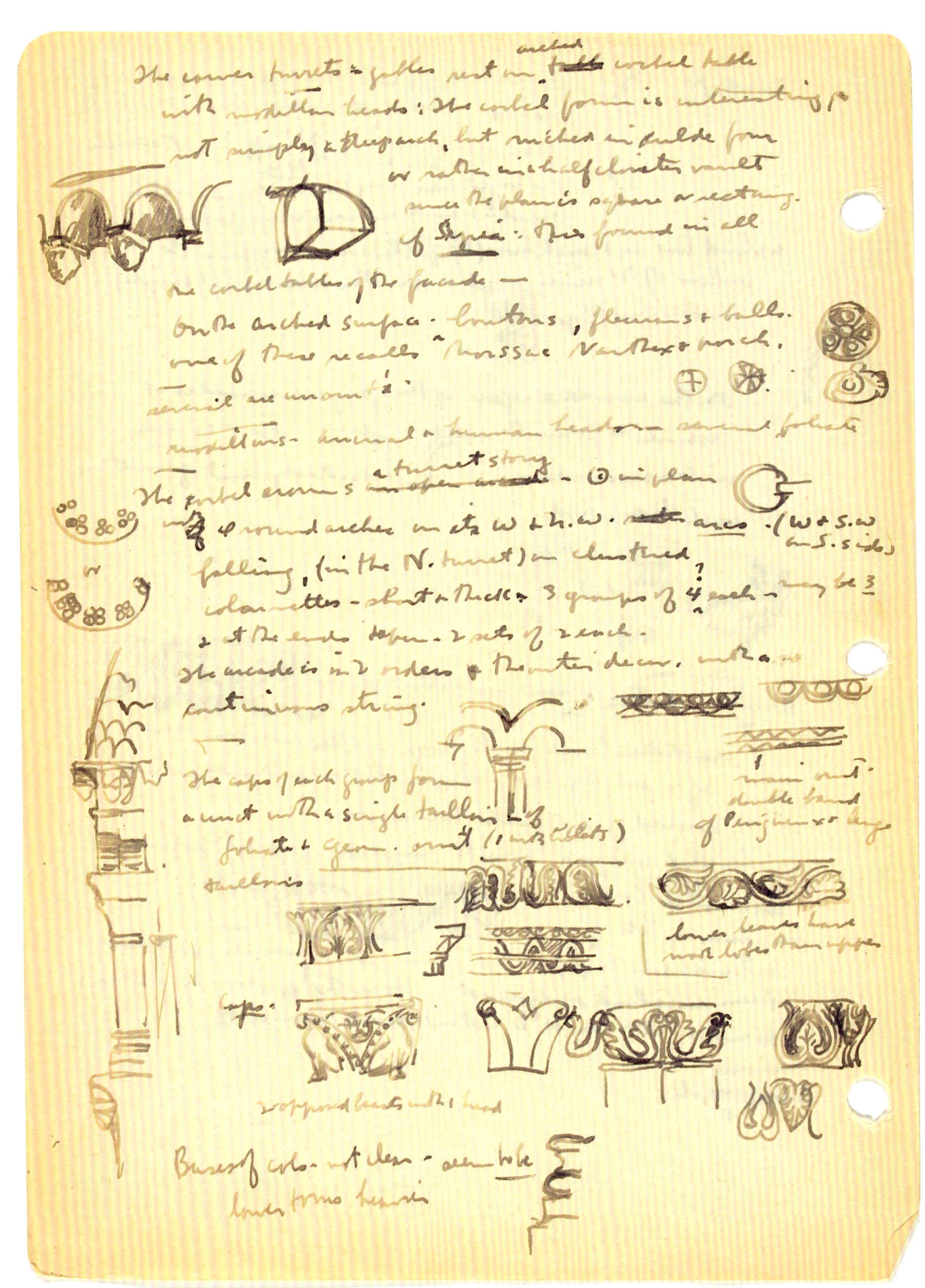

No. 26. Poitiers, Église de Notre-Dame-la-Grande, 11 November 1926

Details of west façade

Black ink on paper

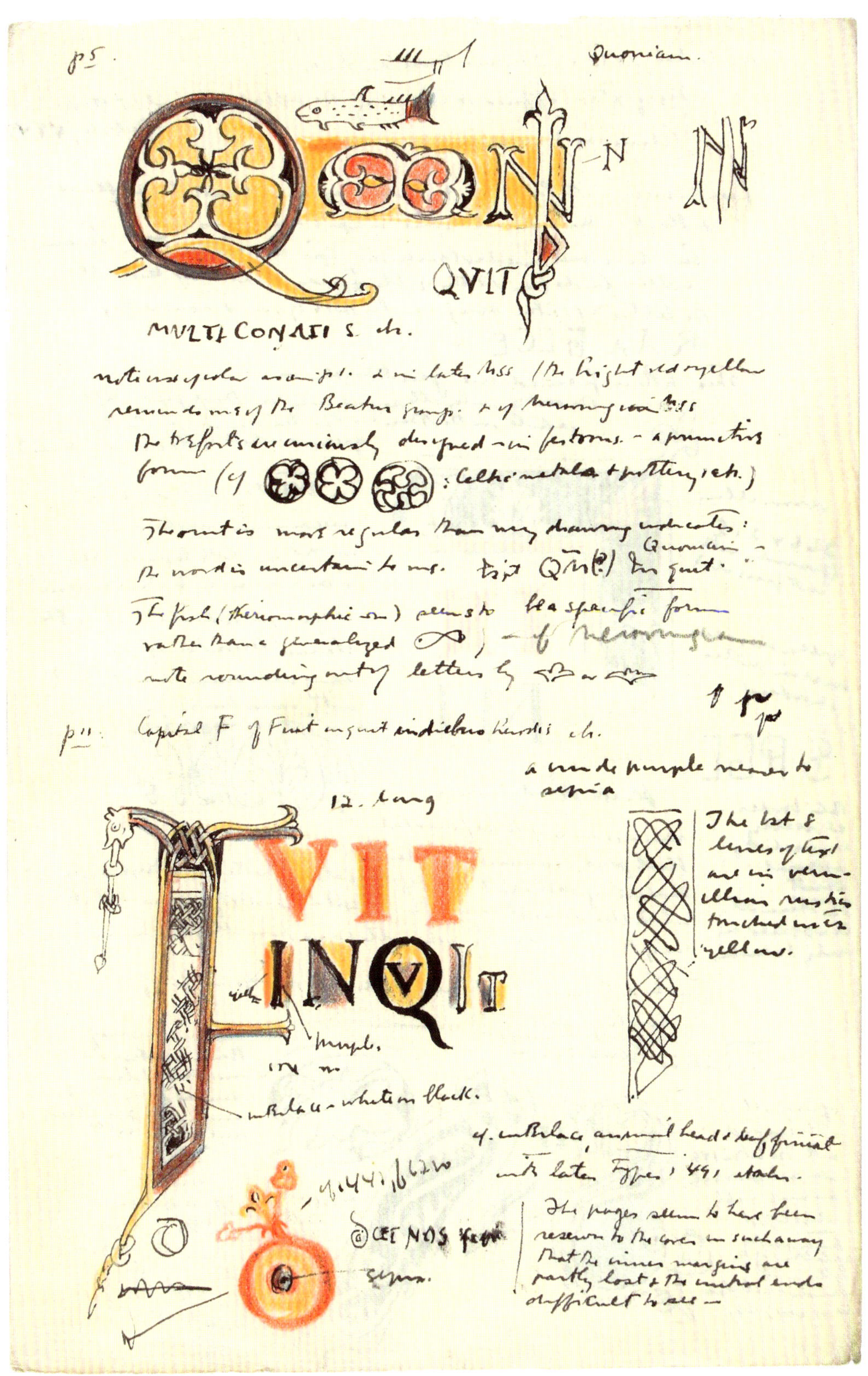

No. 27. Paris, Bibliothèque nationale de France, MS n.a.l. 1438, November 1926

Initials and opening words from folios from "St. Ambrose on Luke"

Black ink, pencil, and colored pencil on paper

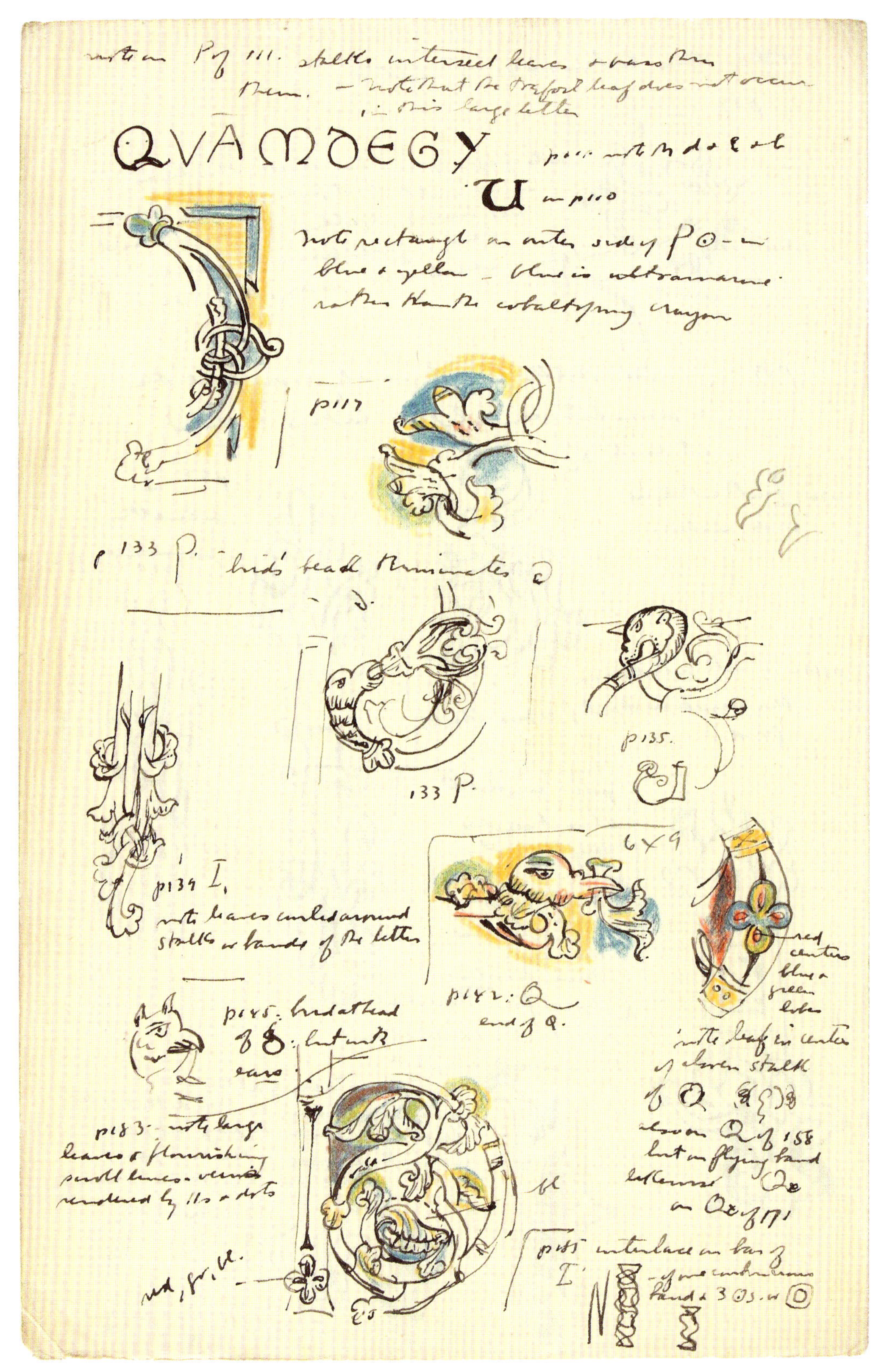

No. 28. Paris, Bibliothèque nationale de France, MS n.a.l. 1491, November 1926

Initials from folios 117, 133, 135, 139, 142, 145, 183, 185 from "Dialogues of St. Gregory, Lives of the Fathers"

Black ink and colored pencil on paper

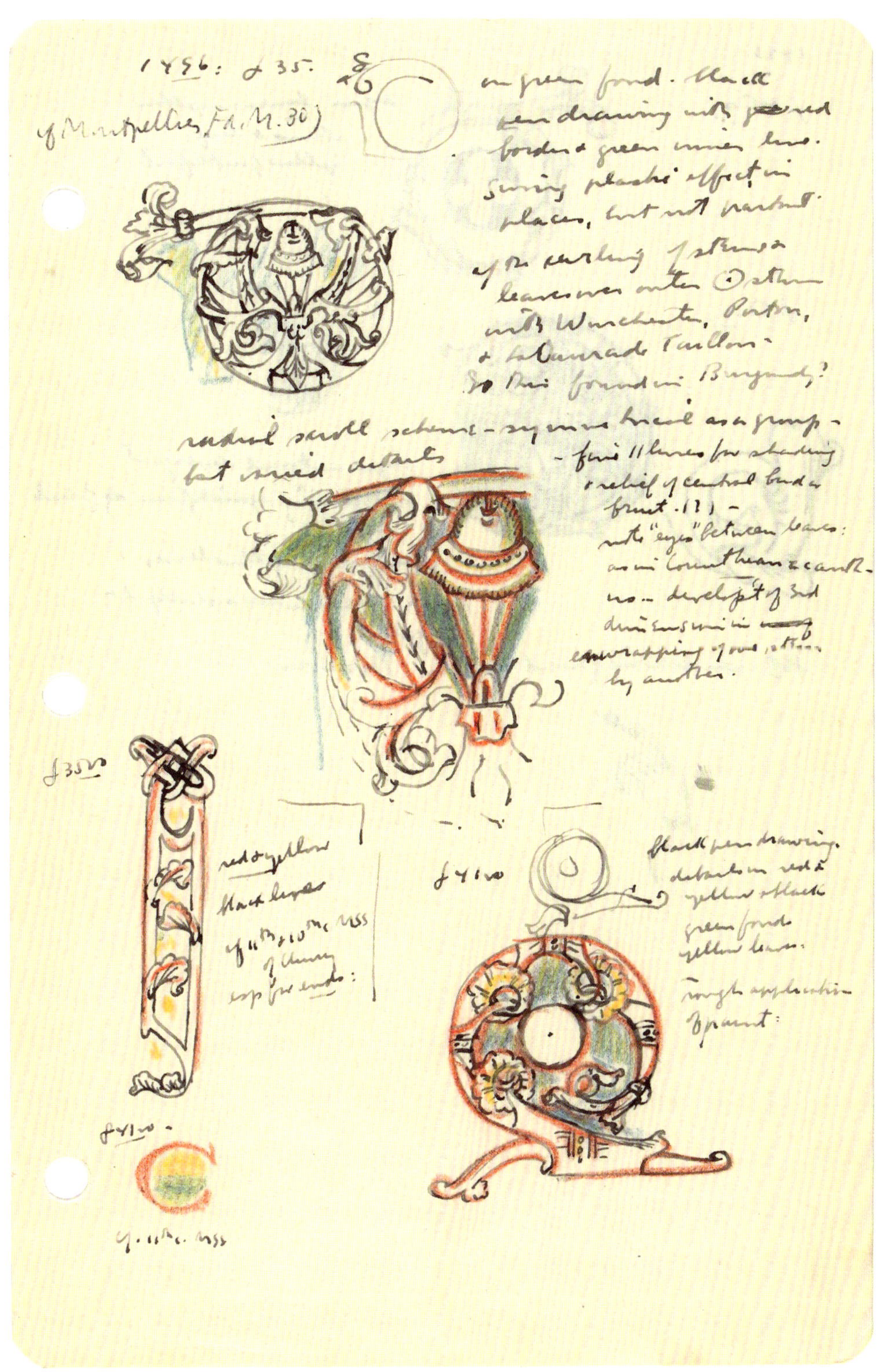

No. 29. Paris, Bibliothèque nationale de France, MS n.a.l. 1496, November–December 1926

Initials from folios 35r, 35v, 41v from "Lives and Works of Cluny's Abbots"

Black ink and colored pencil on paper

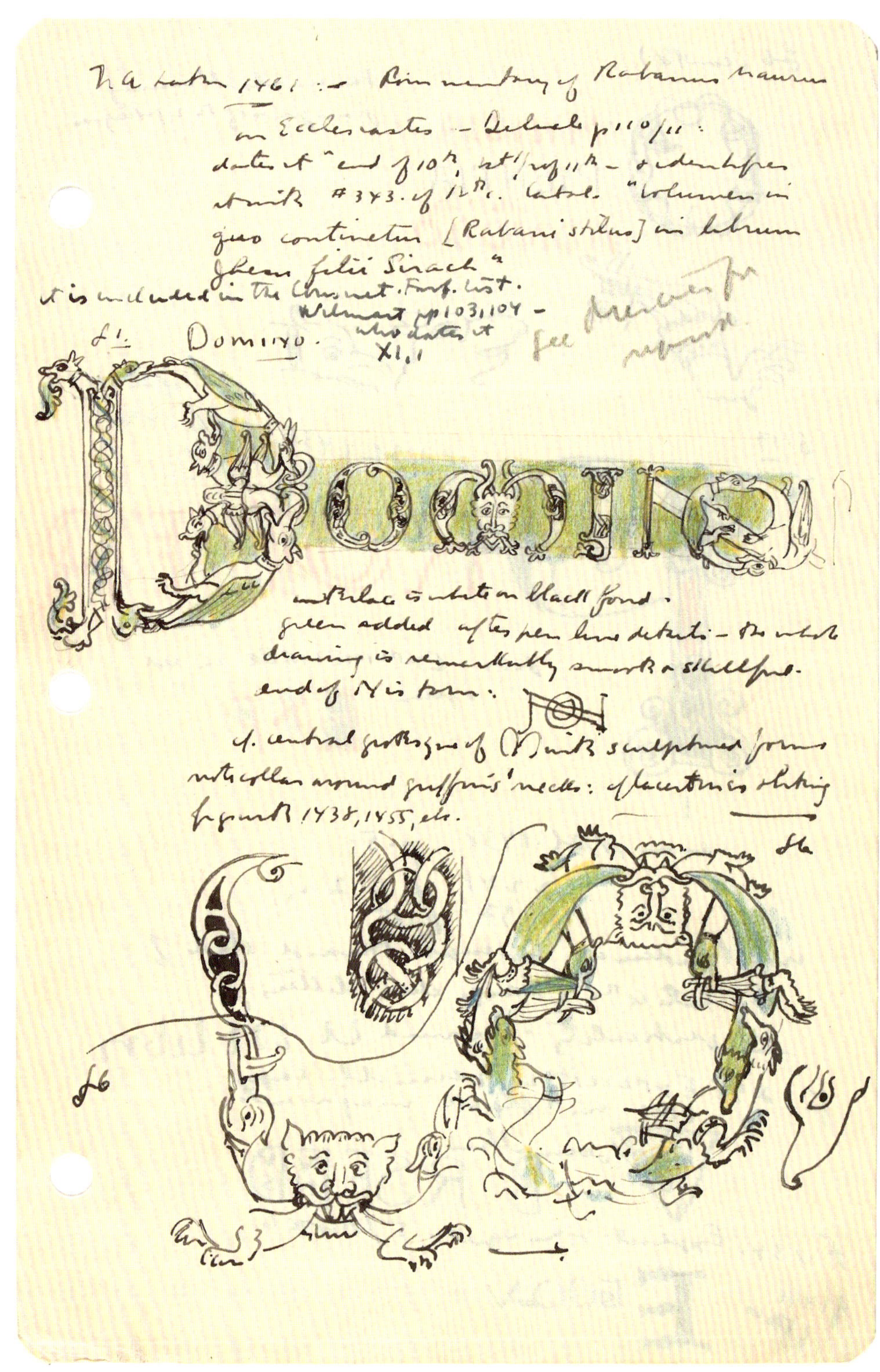

No. 30. Paris, Bibliothèque nationale de France, MS n.a.l. 1461, November–December 1926

Opening word on folio 1r and details of 6r from the "Commentary of Rabanus Maurus on Ecclesiastes"

Black ink, blue ink, pencil, and colored pencil on paper

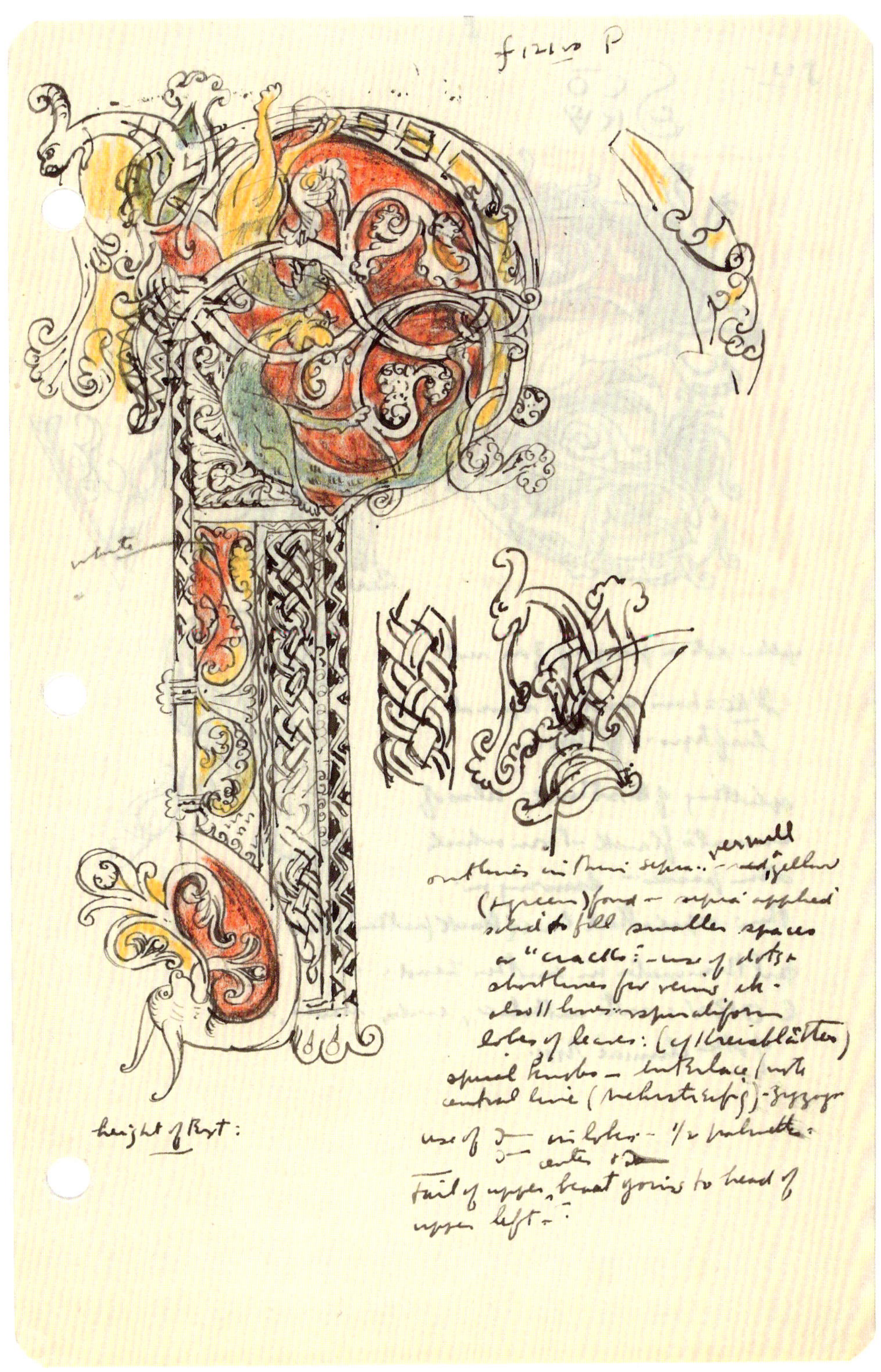

No. 31. Paris, Bibliothèque nationale de France, MS Lat. 3779, November–December 1926

Initial P from folio 121v from "The Lives of Saints and Several Homilies"

Black ink, pencil, and colored pencil on paper

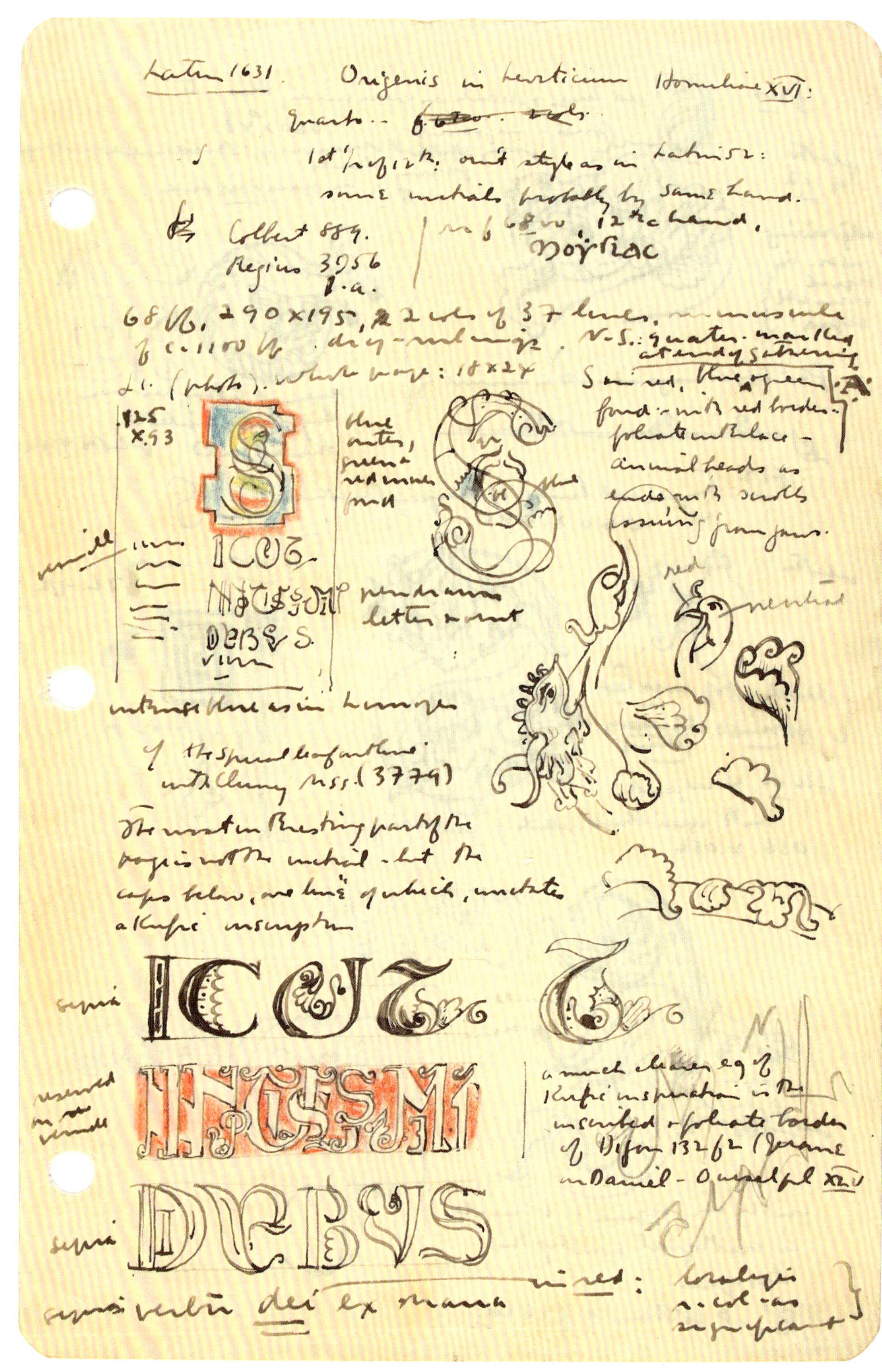

No. 32. Paris, Bibliothèque nationale de France, MS Lat. 1631, December 1926

Initial *S*, details, and display capitals from folio 1r from "Origen's Homilies on Leviticus"

Black ink, pencil, and colored pencil on paper

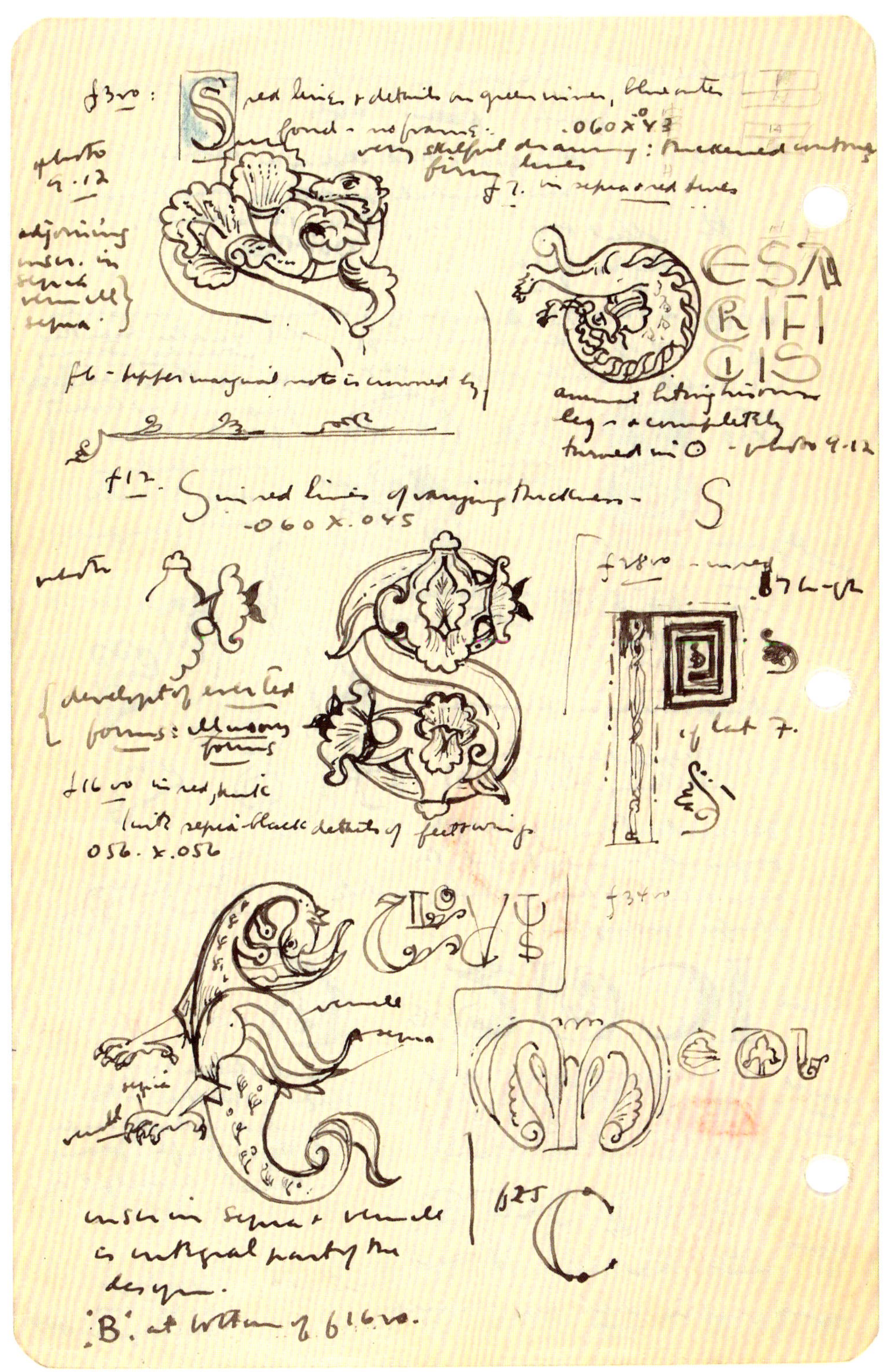

No. 33. Paris, Bibliothèque nationale de France, MS Lat. 1631, December 1926

Initials from folios 3v, 6r, 7r, 12r, 28v, 16v, 34v, and 25r from "Origen's Homilies on Leviticus"

Black ink and colored pencil on paper

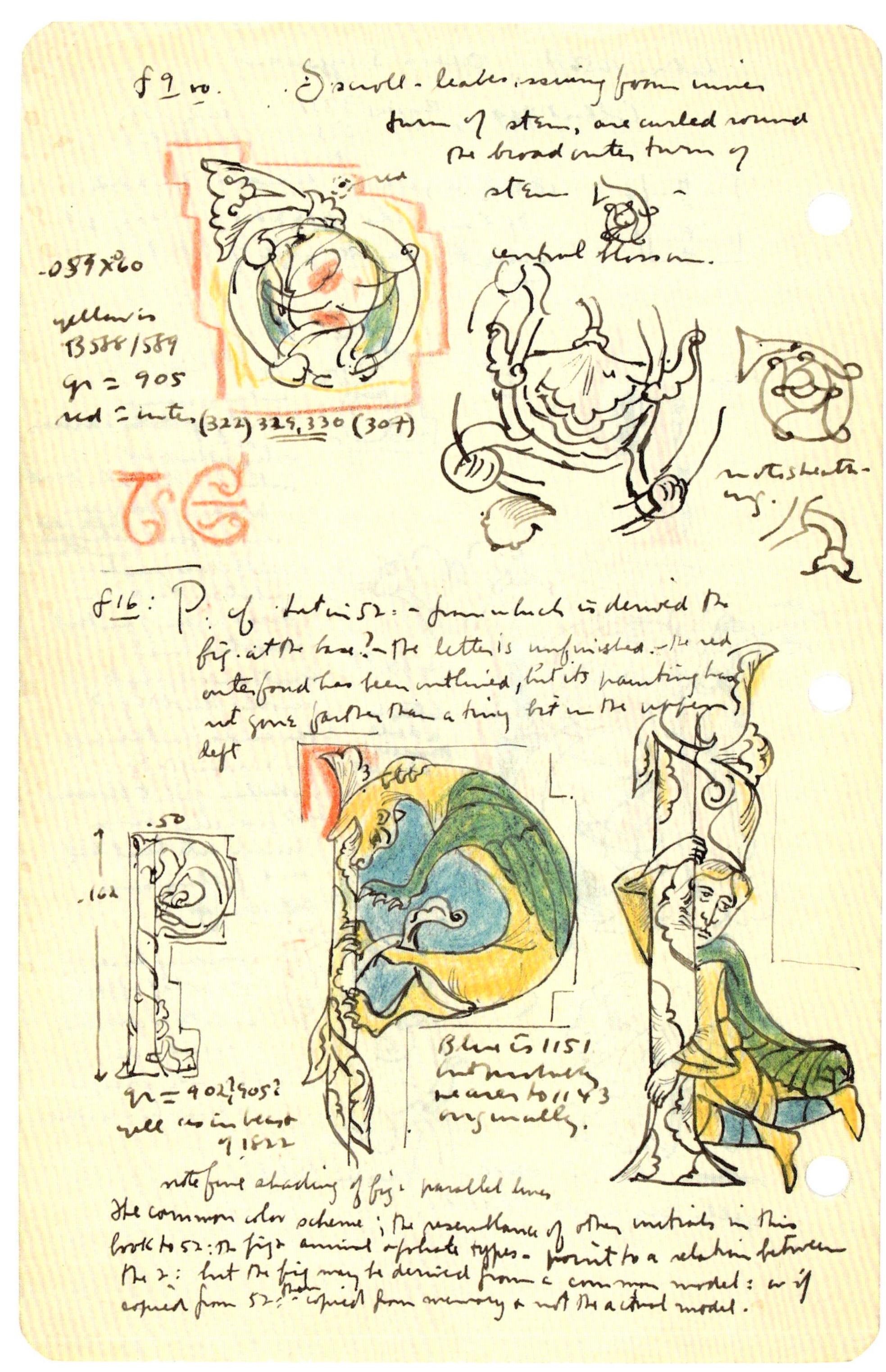

No. 34. Paris, Bibliothèque nationale de France, MS Lat. 1656A, December 1926–January 1927 or June 1927

Initials from folios 9v and 16r from "Works of S. Cyprianus"

Black ink and colored pencil on paper

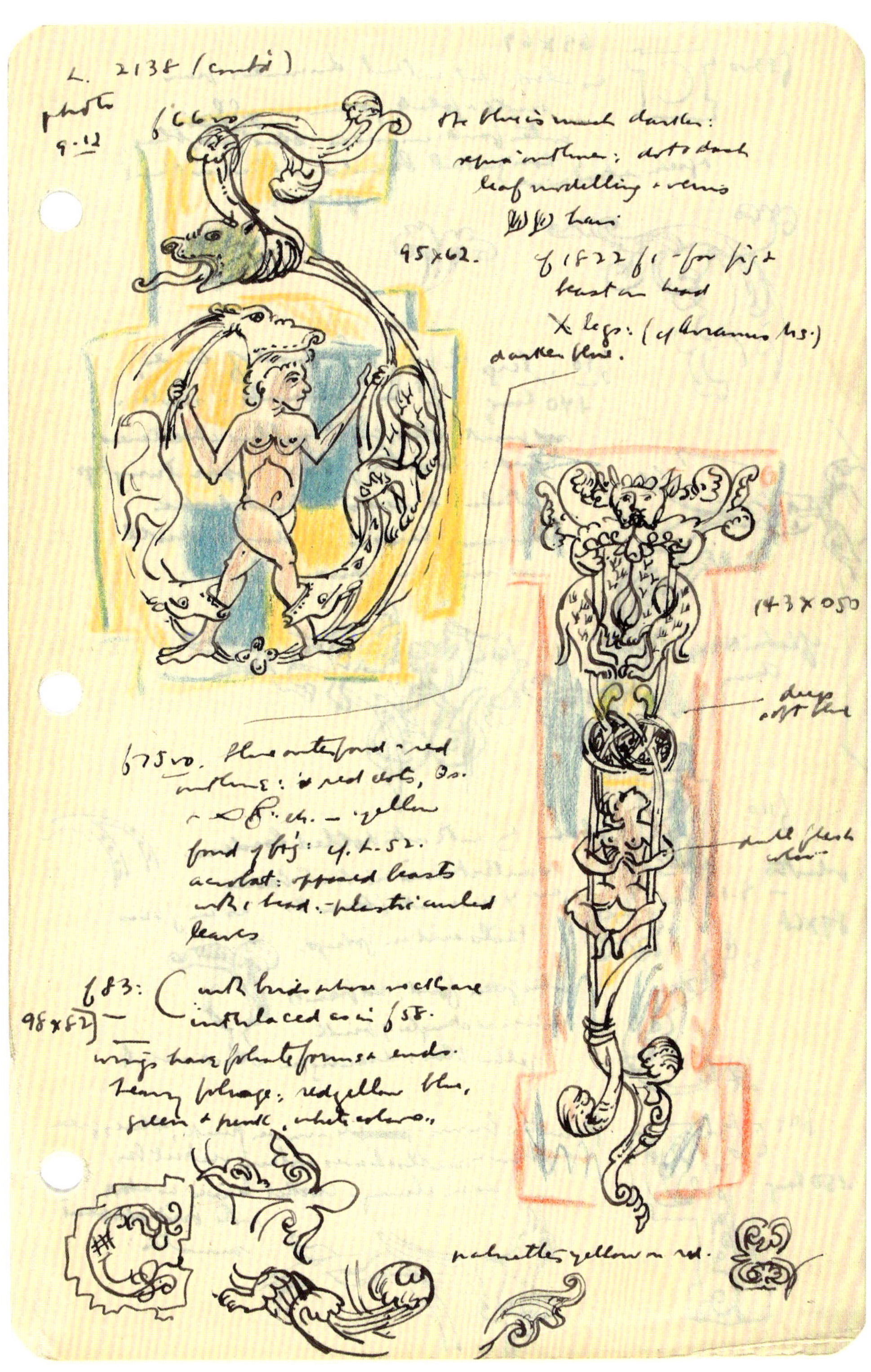

No. 35. Paris, Bibliothèque nationale de France, MS Lat. 2138, December 1926–January 1927 or June 1927

Initials from folios 66v, 75v, and 83r from "Cassiani's Conferences"

Black ink and colored pencil on paper

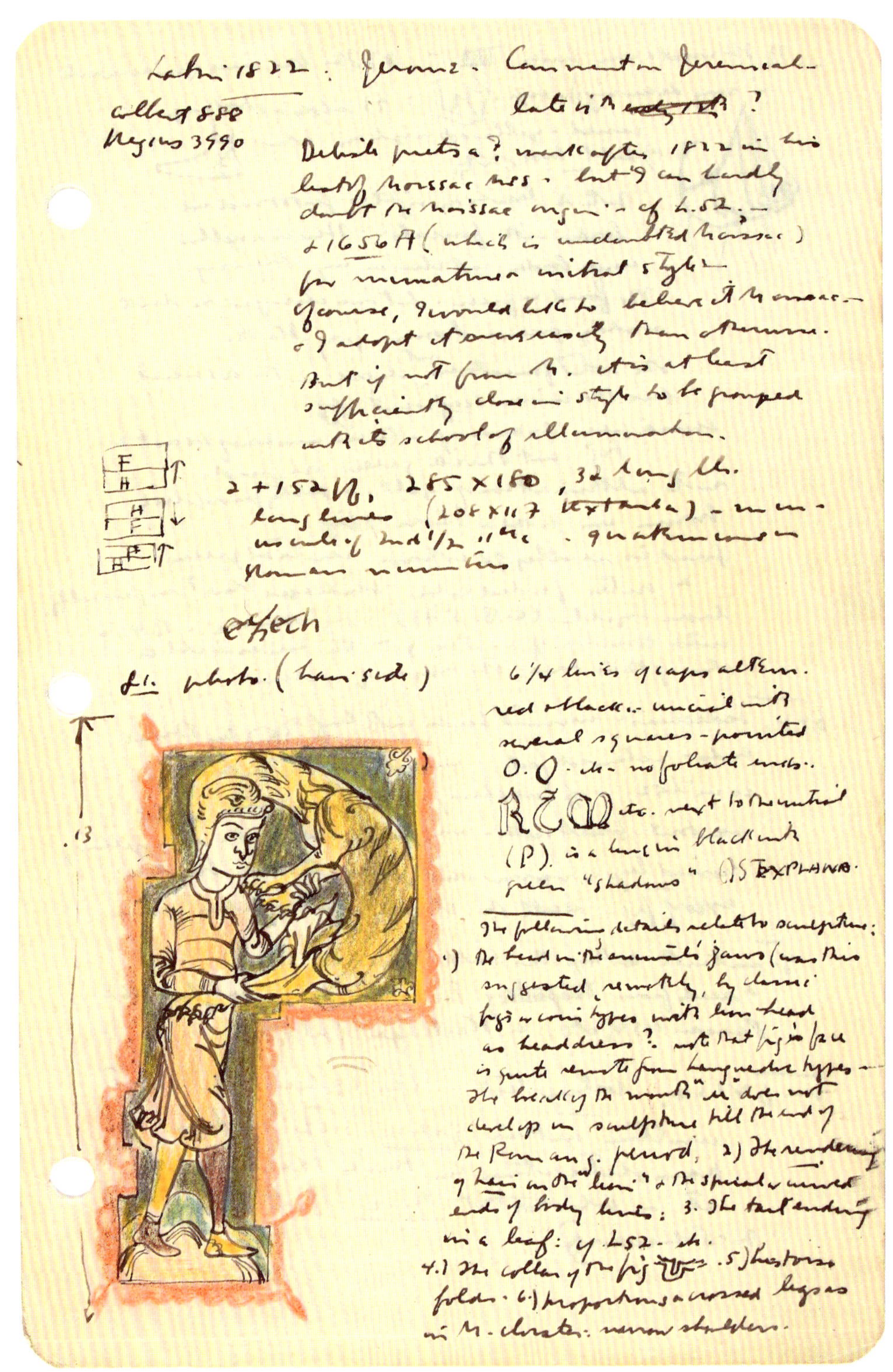

No. 36. Paris, Bibliothèque nationale de France, MS Lat. 1822, December 1926–January 1927 or June 1927

Initial from folio 1r from Saint Jerome's "Commentary on Jeremiah"

Black ink and colored pencil on paper

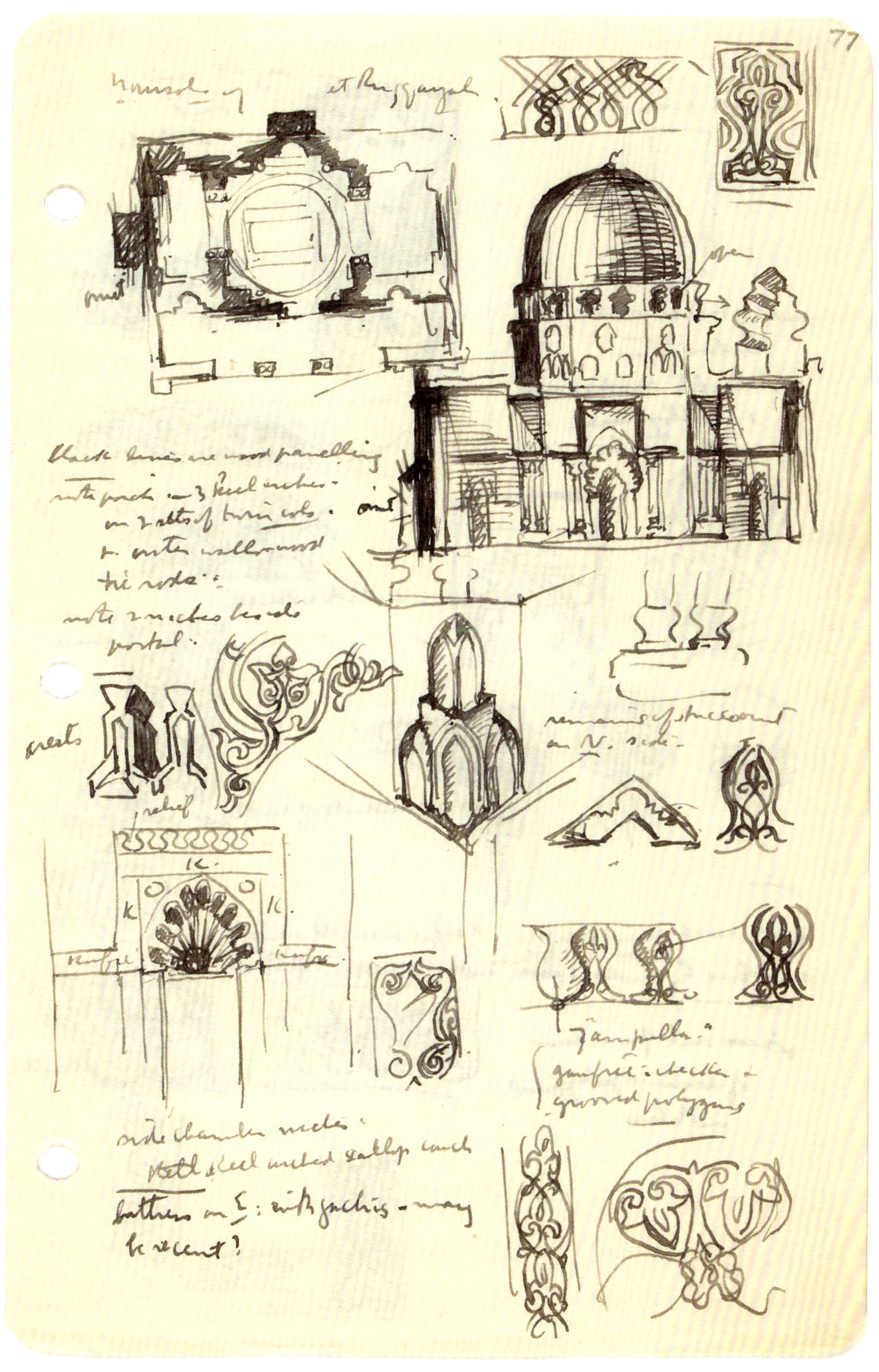

No. 37. Cairo, Mausoleum of Al-Sayeda Ruqquyah, 12–22? February 1927

Plan, section, and details

Black ink on paper

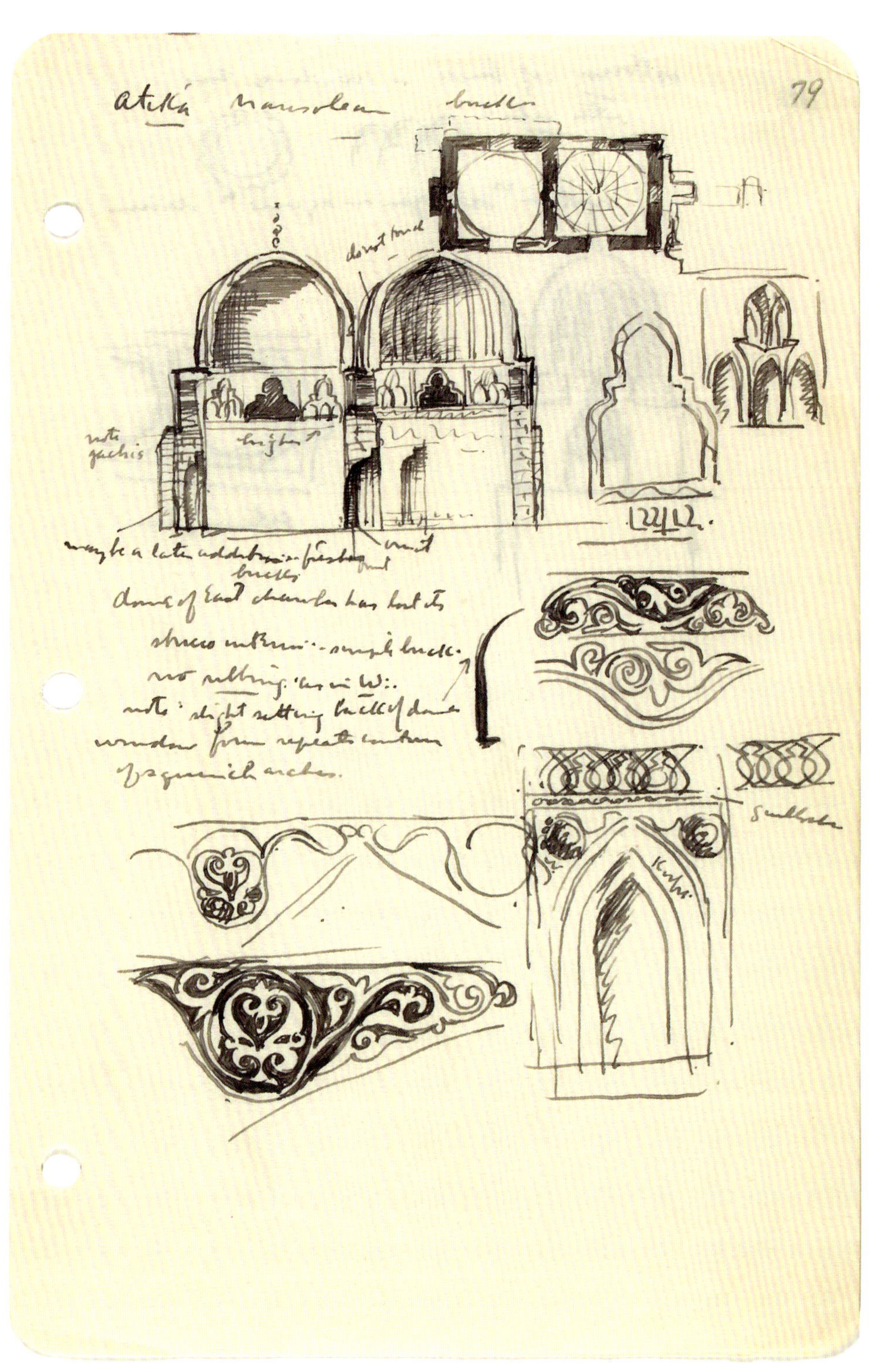

No. 38. Cairo, Mausoleum of Atteca, 12–22? February 1927

Plan, section, and details

Black ink on paper

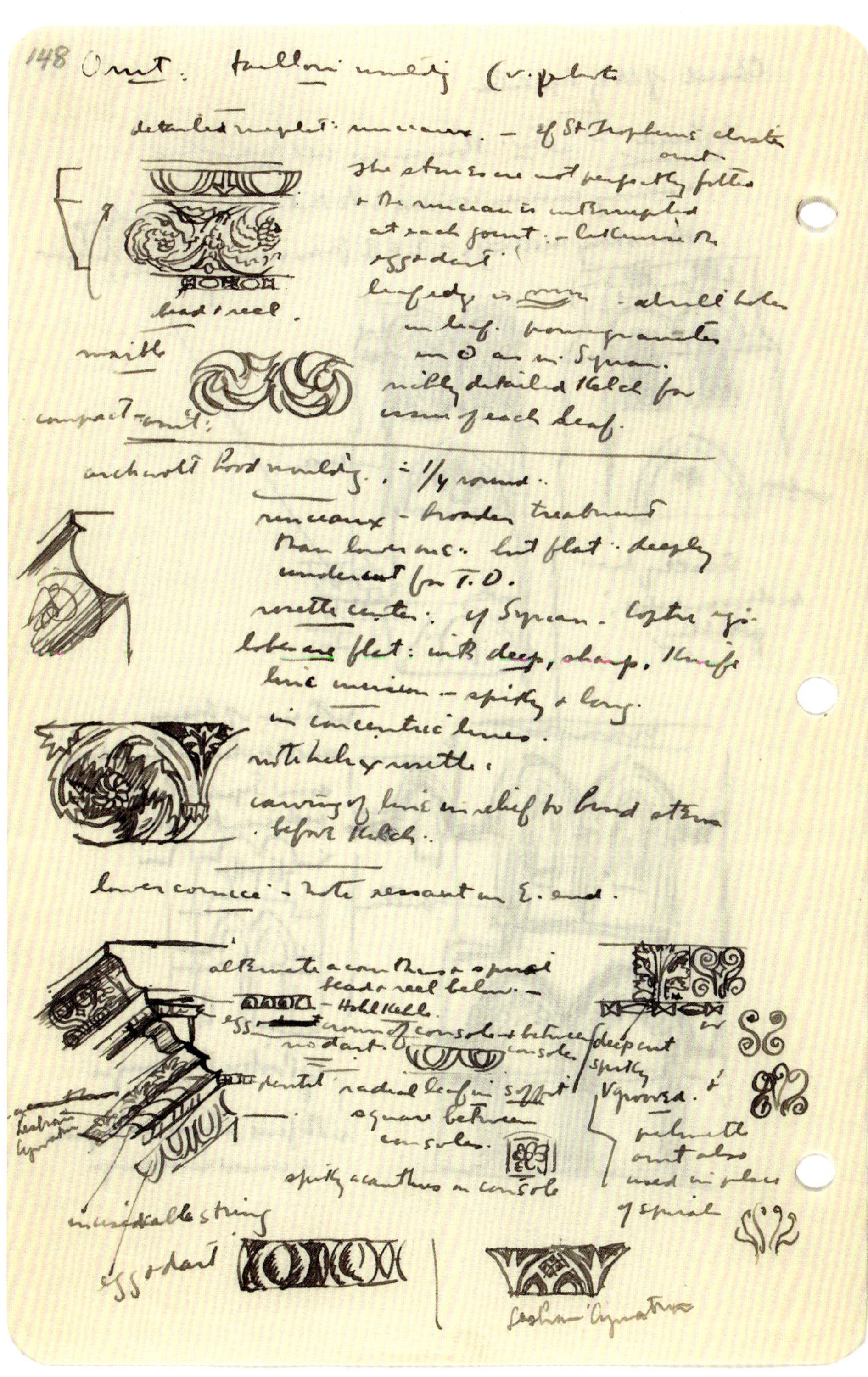

No. 39. Jerusalem, Church of the Holy Sepulchre, 11–17 March 1927

Archivolt molding, lower cornice, and tailloir

Black ink on paper

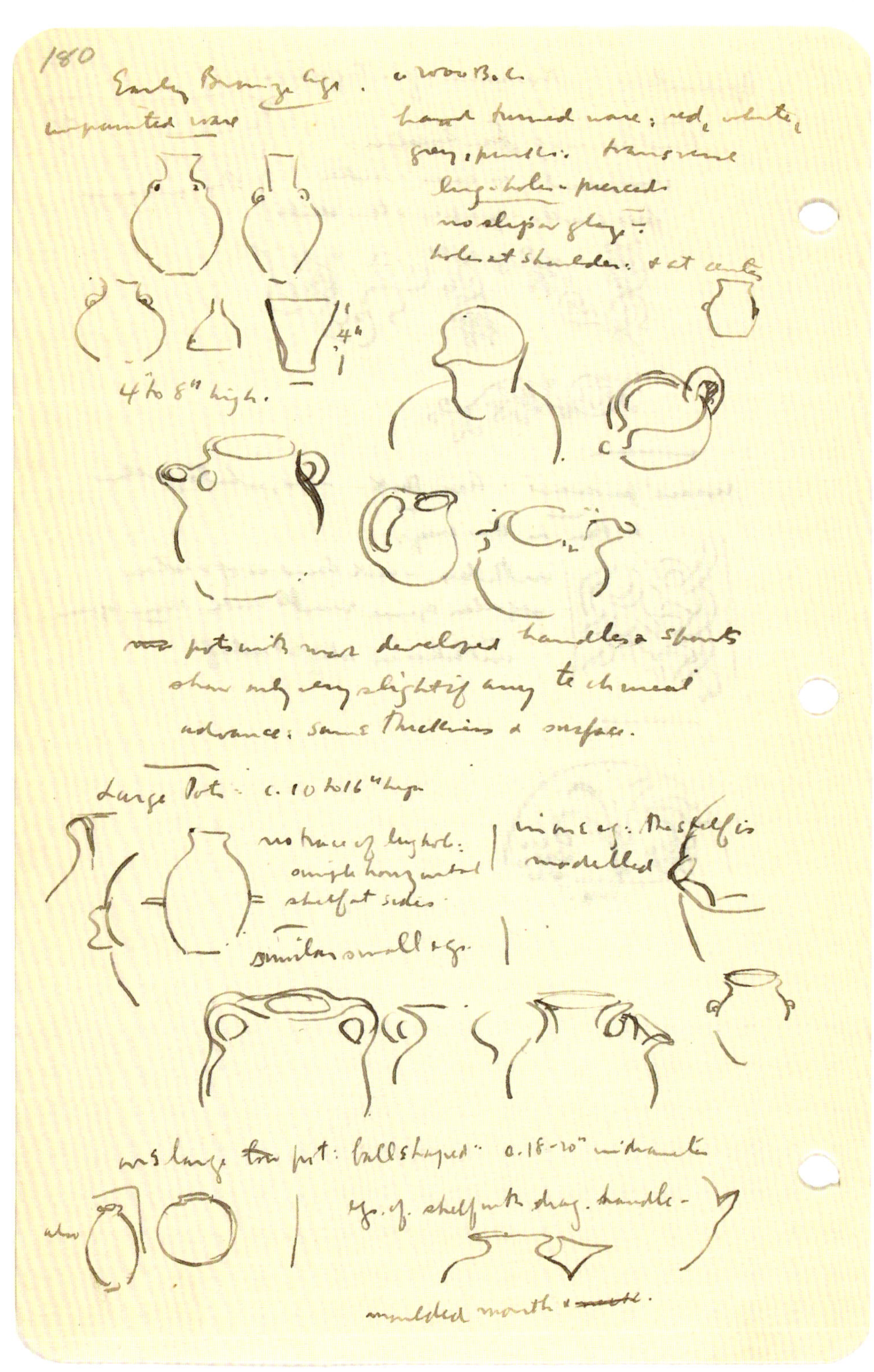

No. 40. Jerusalem, Museum of Antiquities, 11–17 March 1927

Bronze Age jugs and vessels

Black ink on paper

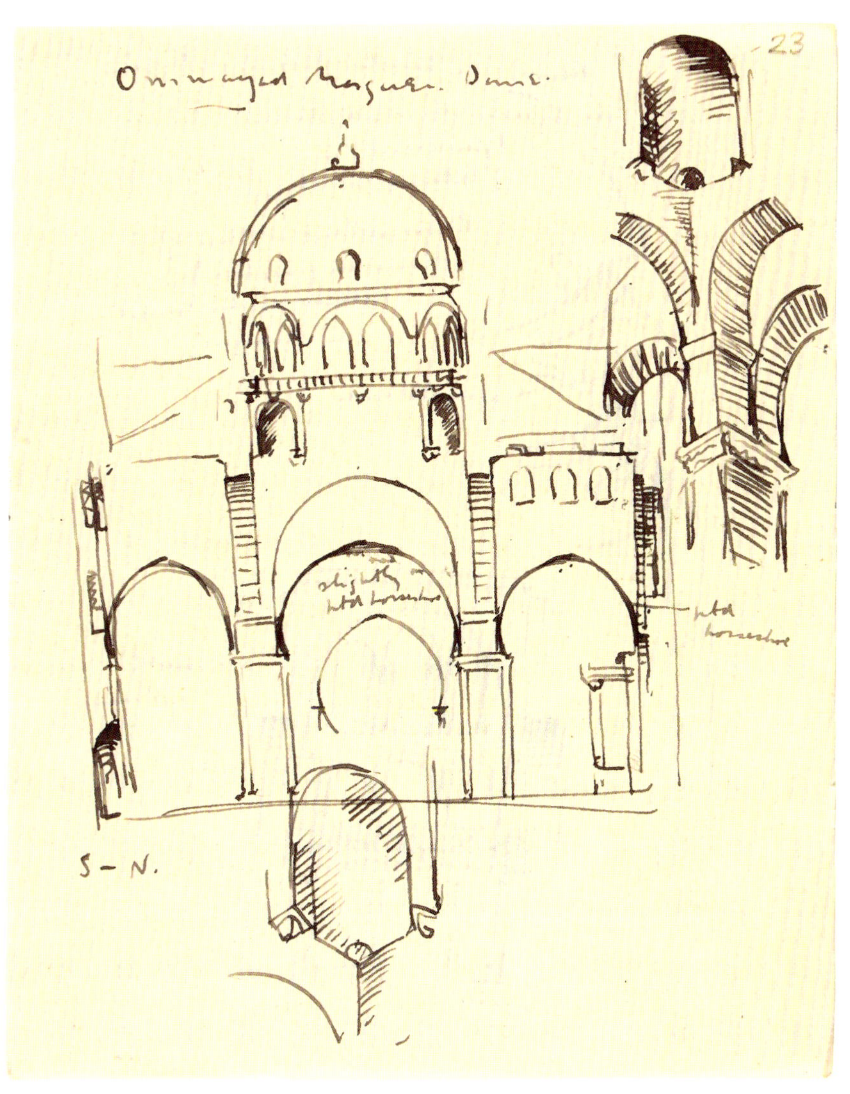

No. 41. Damascus, Umayyad Mosque, 23–27 March 1927

Elevation at crossing and detail of dome vaults

Black ink on paper

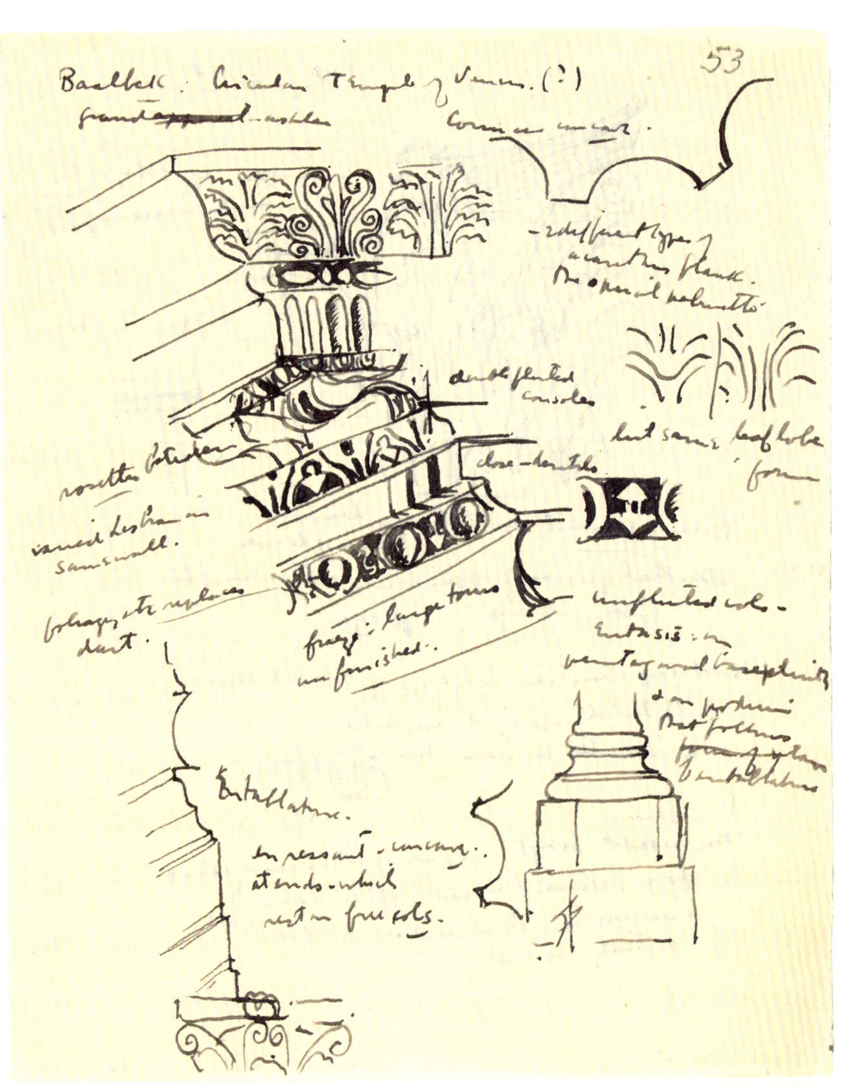

No. 42. Baalbek, Temple of Venus, 28 March 1927

Details of moldings

Black ink on paper

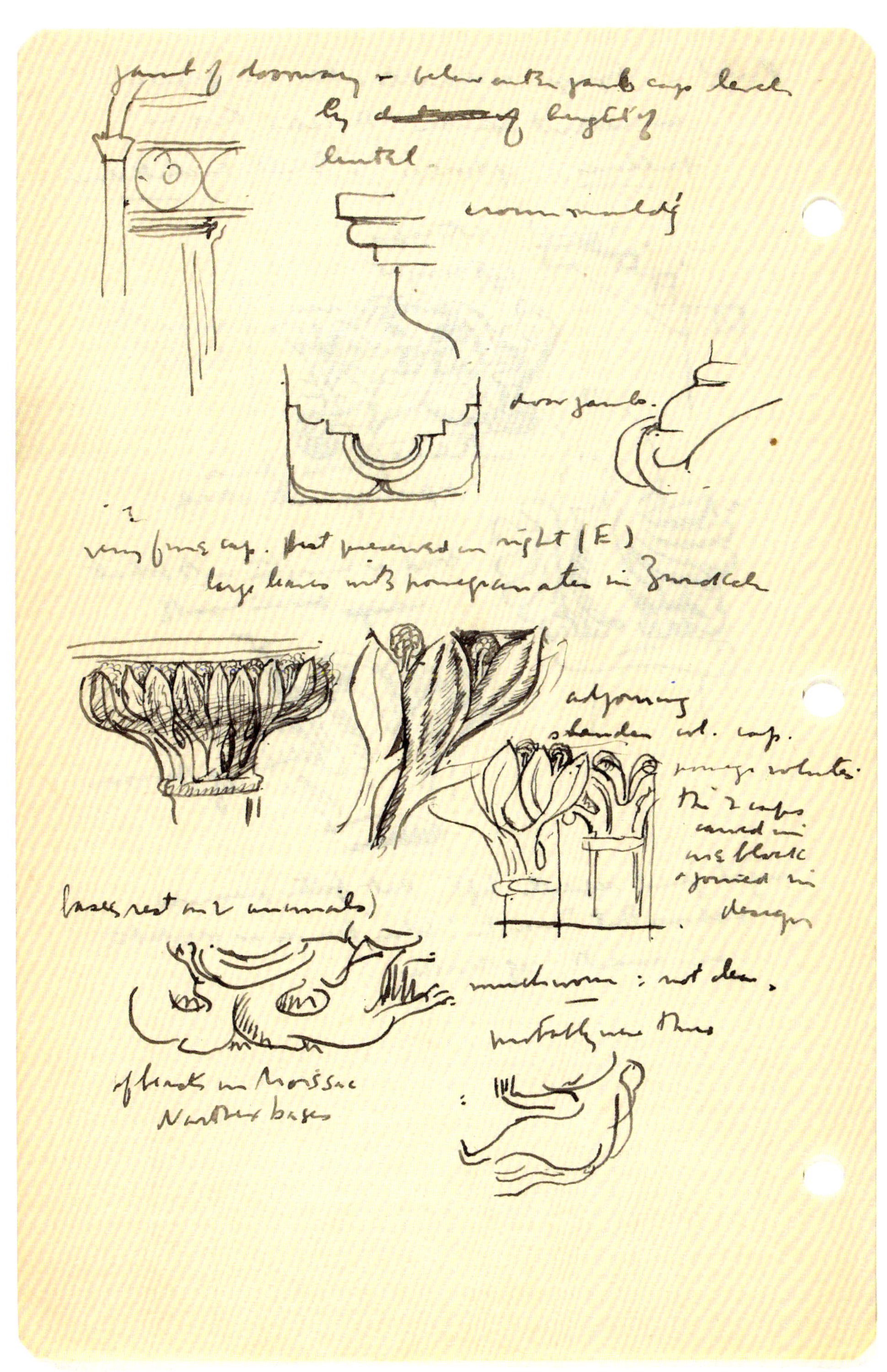

No. 43. Beaulieu, Église de Saint-Pierre, 4–6 July 1927

Details of doorway

Black ink on paper

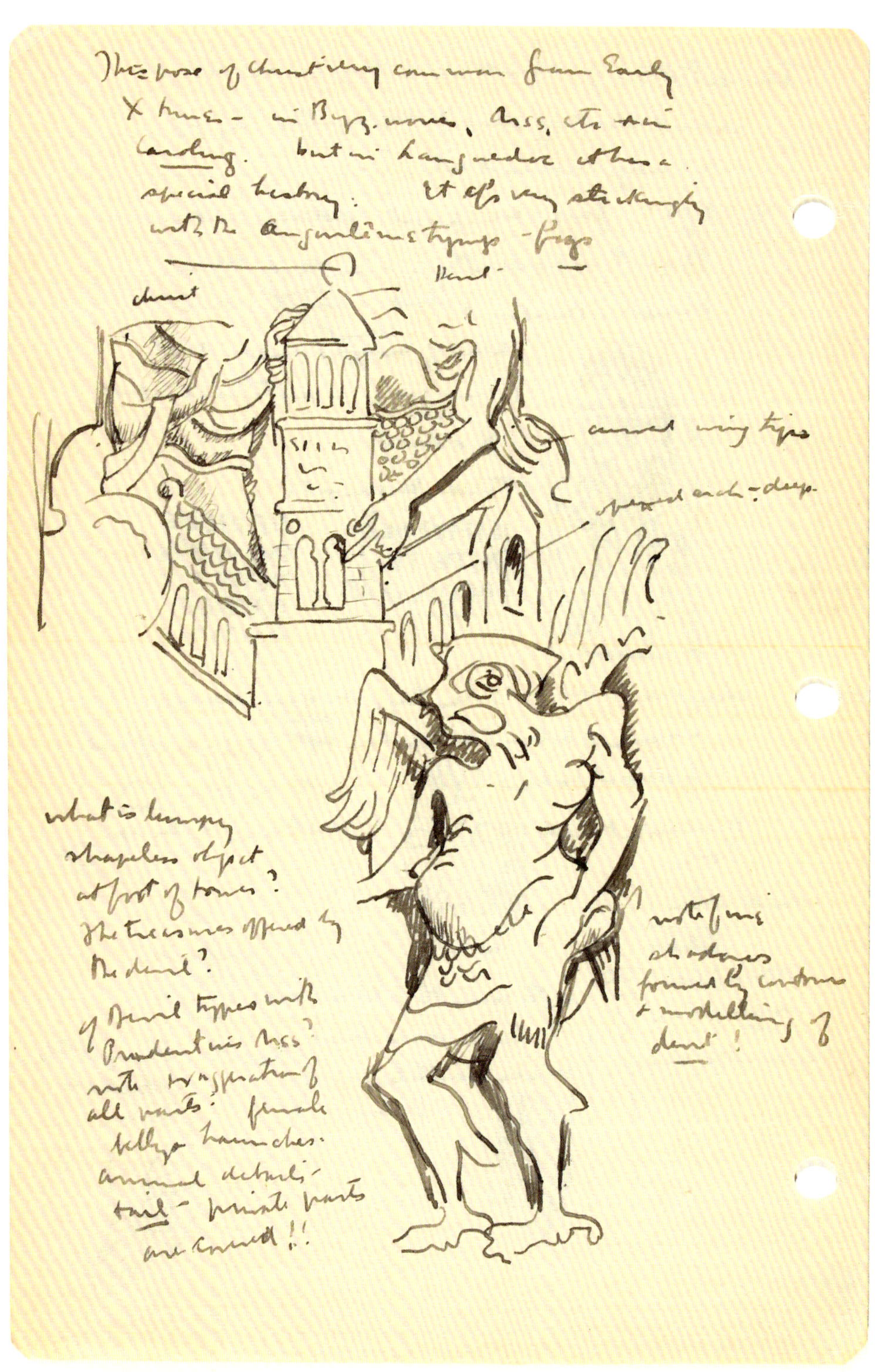

No. 44. Beaulieu, Église de Saint-Pierre, 4–6 July 1927

Details of doorway

Black ink on paper

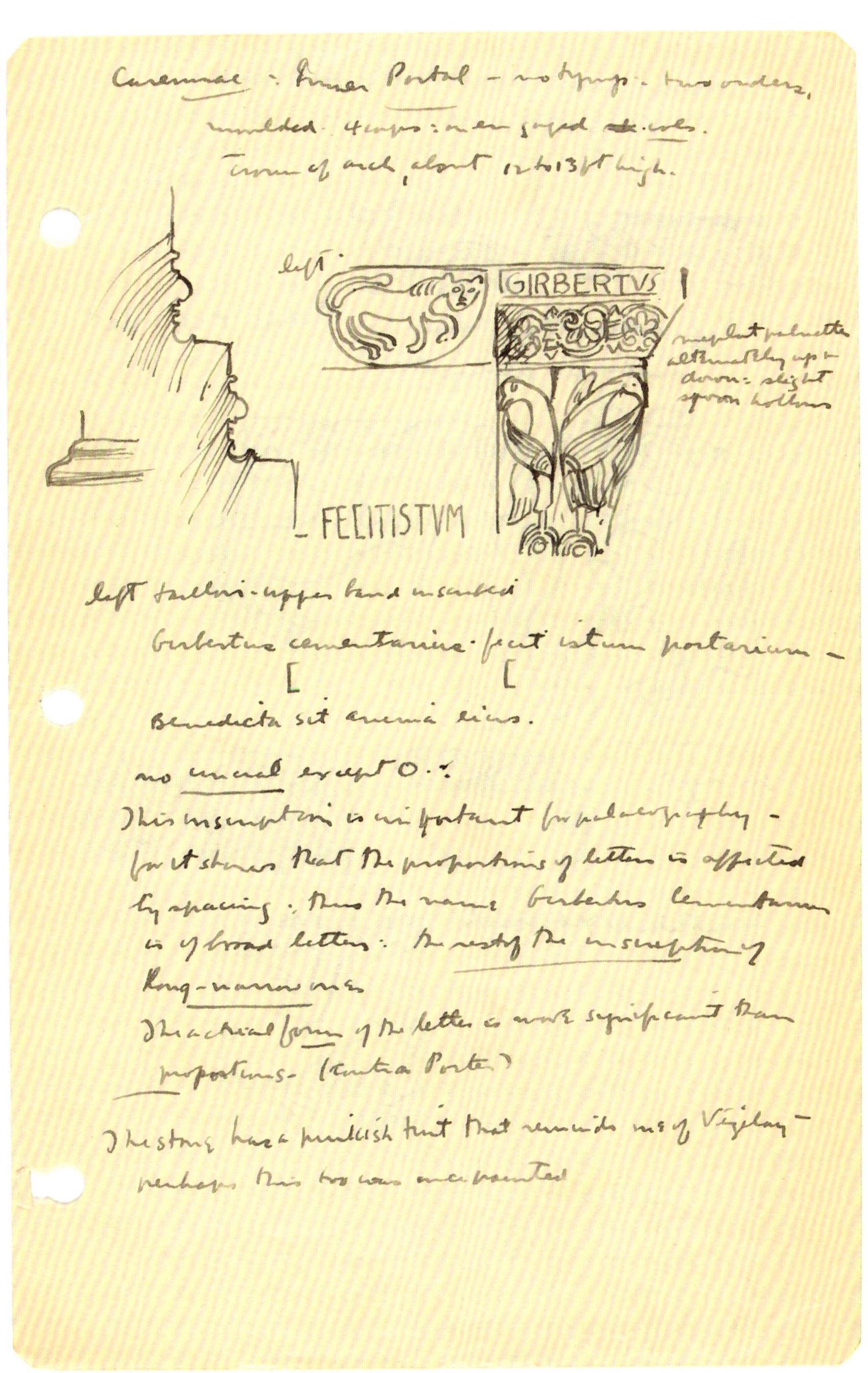
Carennac: Inner Portal – no tymp. – two orders, moulded. 4 caps: on engaged cols. Crown of arch, about 12 to 13 ft high.

left tailloir – upper band inscribed

Girbertus cementarius · fecit istum portarium –

Benedicta sit anima eius.

no uncial except O.?

This inscription is important for palaeography – for it shows that the proportions of letters is affected by spacing: thus the name Girbertus cementarius is of broad letters: the rest of the inscription of long-narrow ones

The actual form of the letter is more significant than proportions – (contra Porter)

The stone has a pinkish tint that reminds me of Vézelay – perhaps this too was once painted

No. 45. Carennac, Église de Saint-Pierre, 7 July 1927

Details of porch portal

Black ink on paper

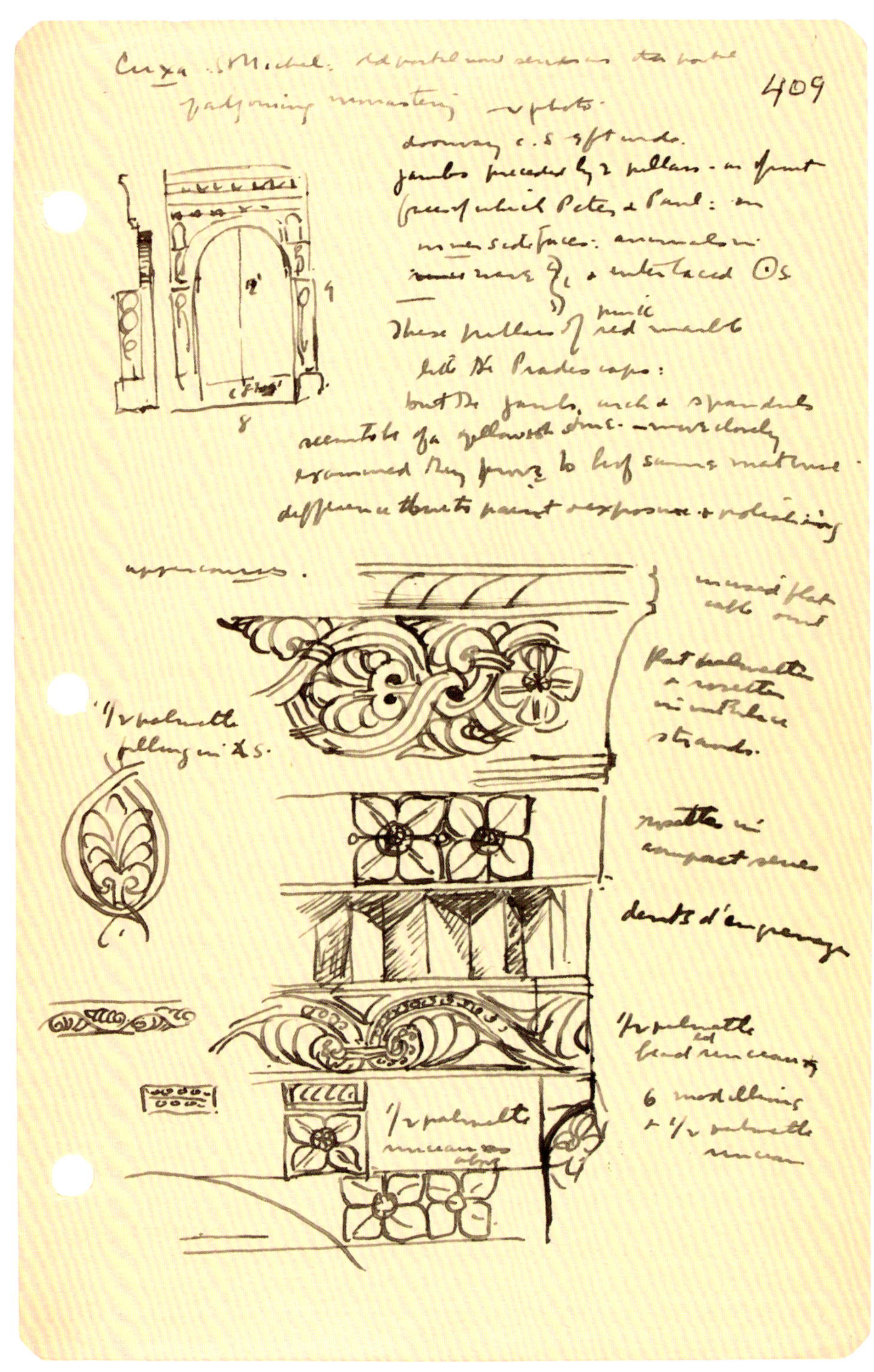

No. 46. Cuxa, Abbaye de Saint-Michel-de-Cuxa, 14 July 1927

Portal and details

Black ink on paper

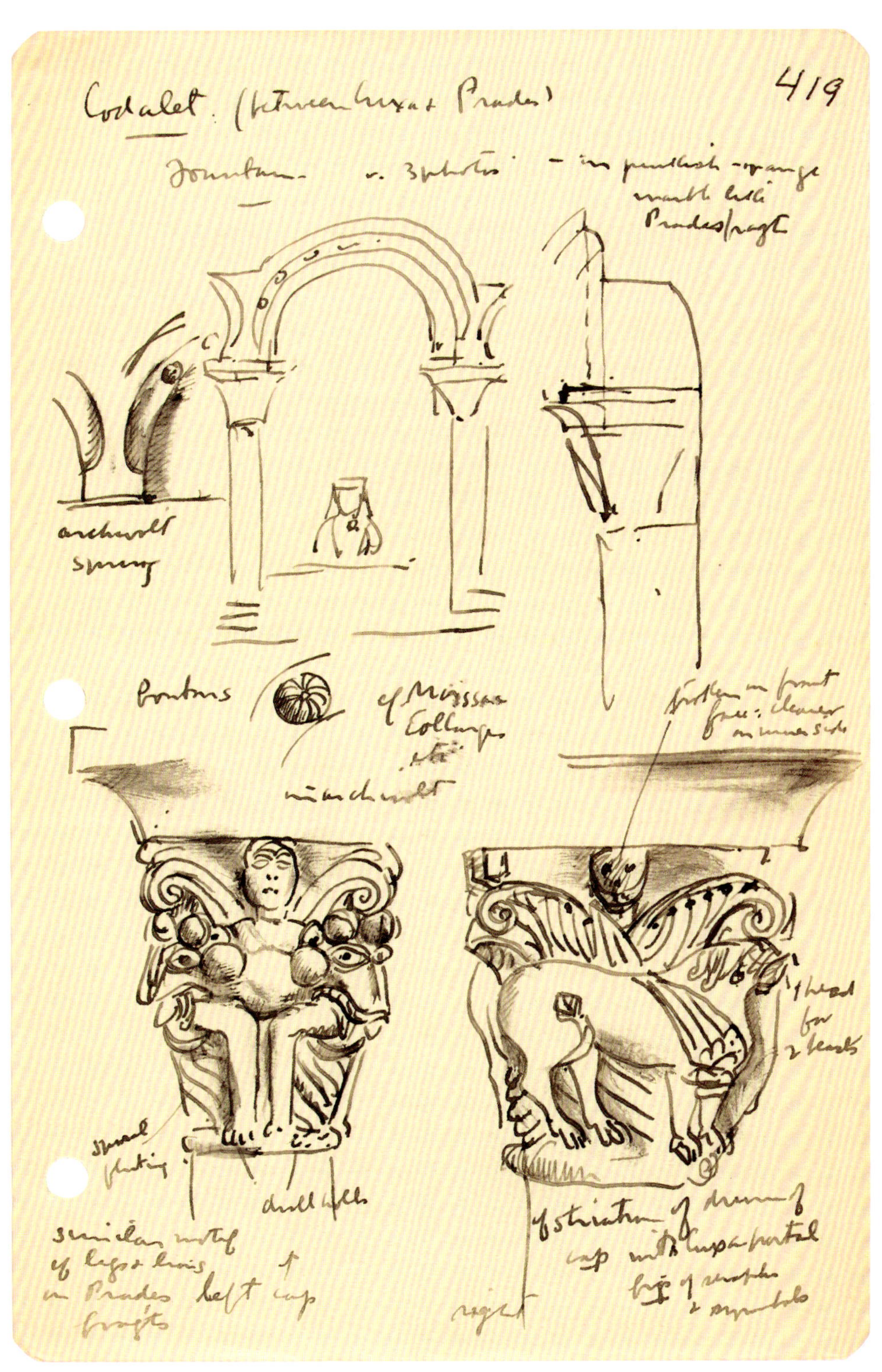

No. 47. Codalet, Église paroissiale de Saint-Félix, 14 July 1927

Details of fountain

Black ink on paper

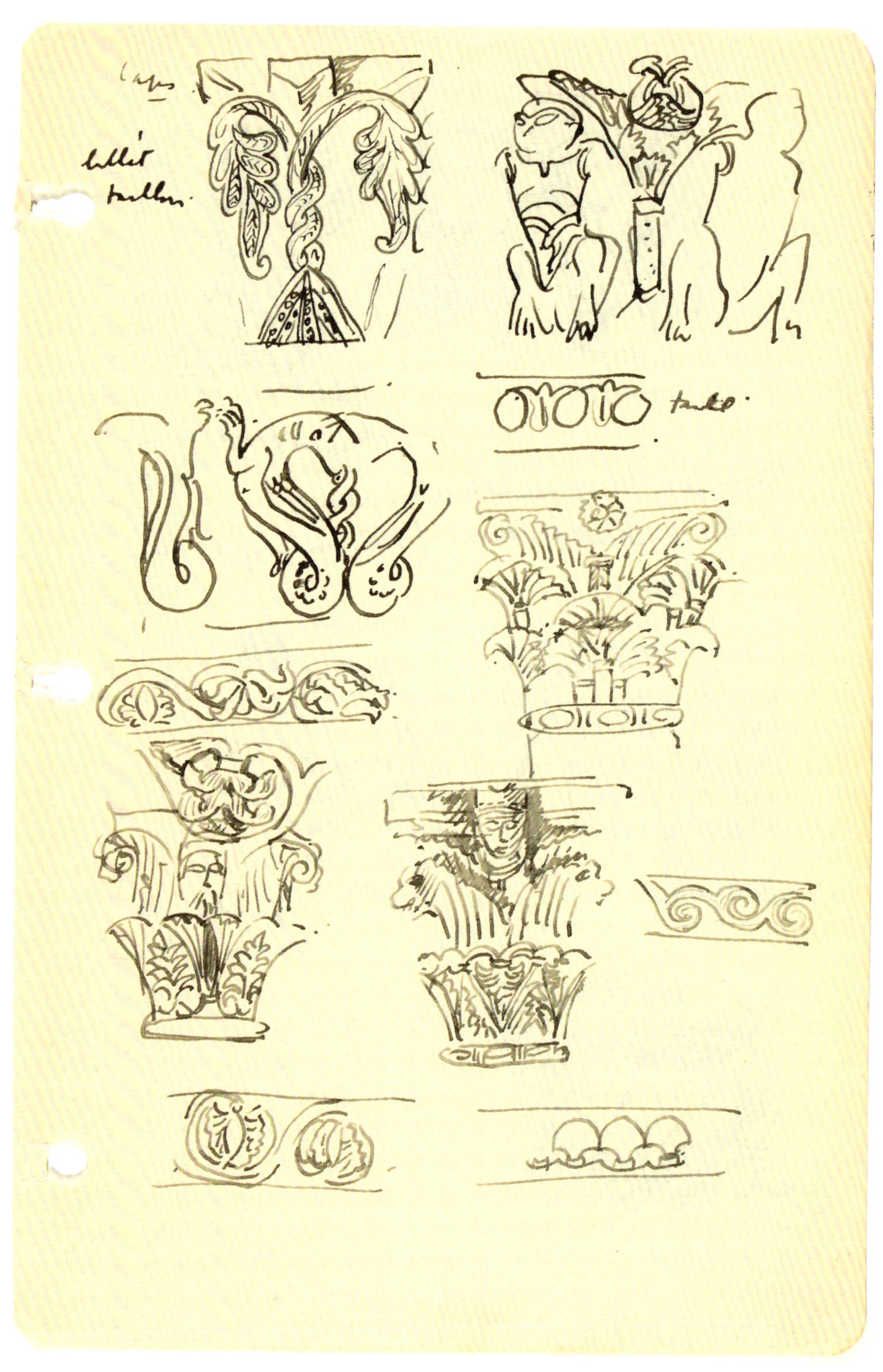

No. 48. Ripoll, Monasterio de Santa Maria, 19 July 1927

Capitals of cloister

Black ink on paper

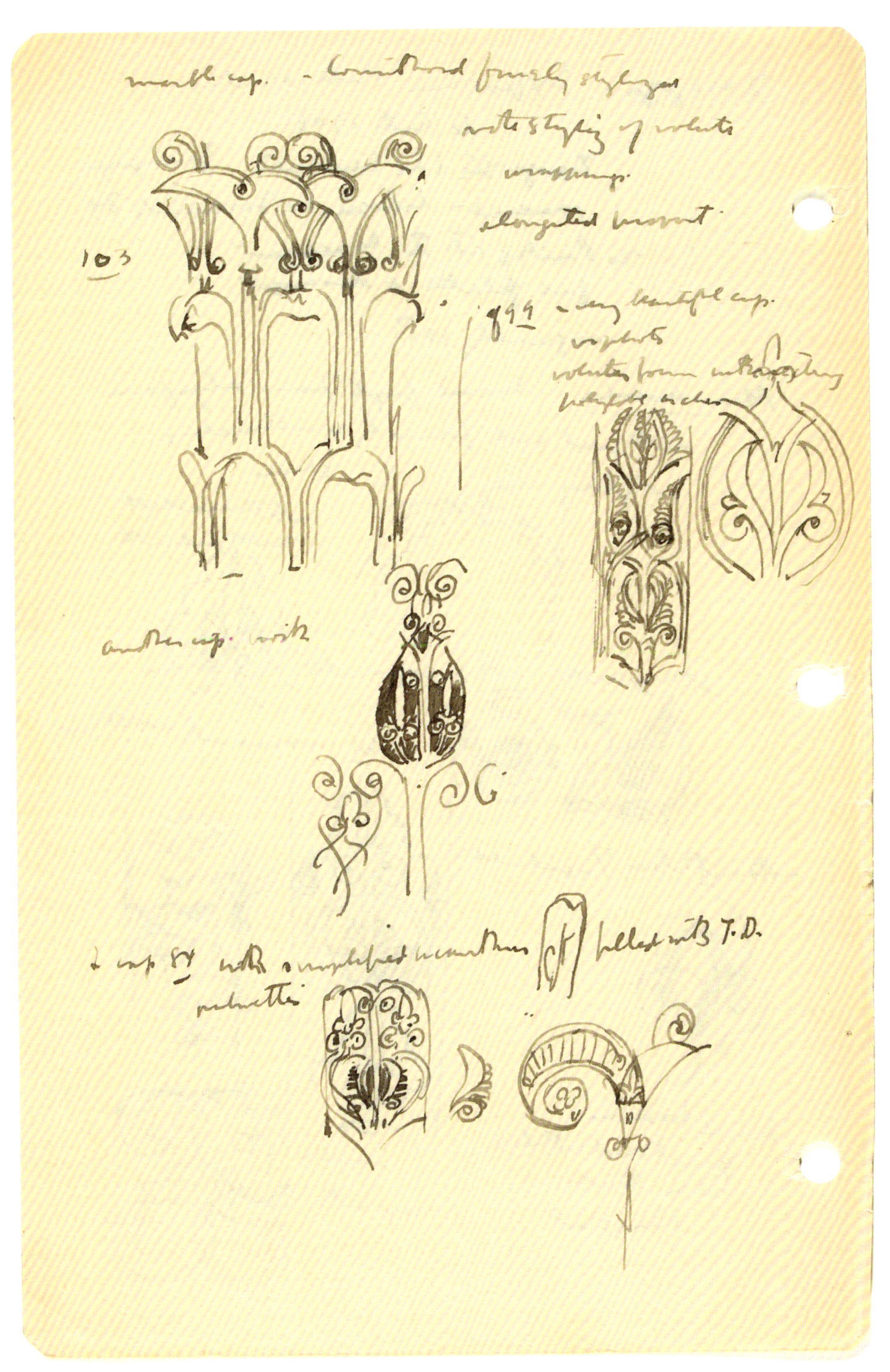

No. 49. Saragossa, Museo Arqueológico, 24 July 1927

Details of capitals

Black ink on paper

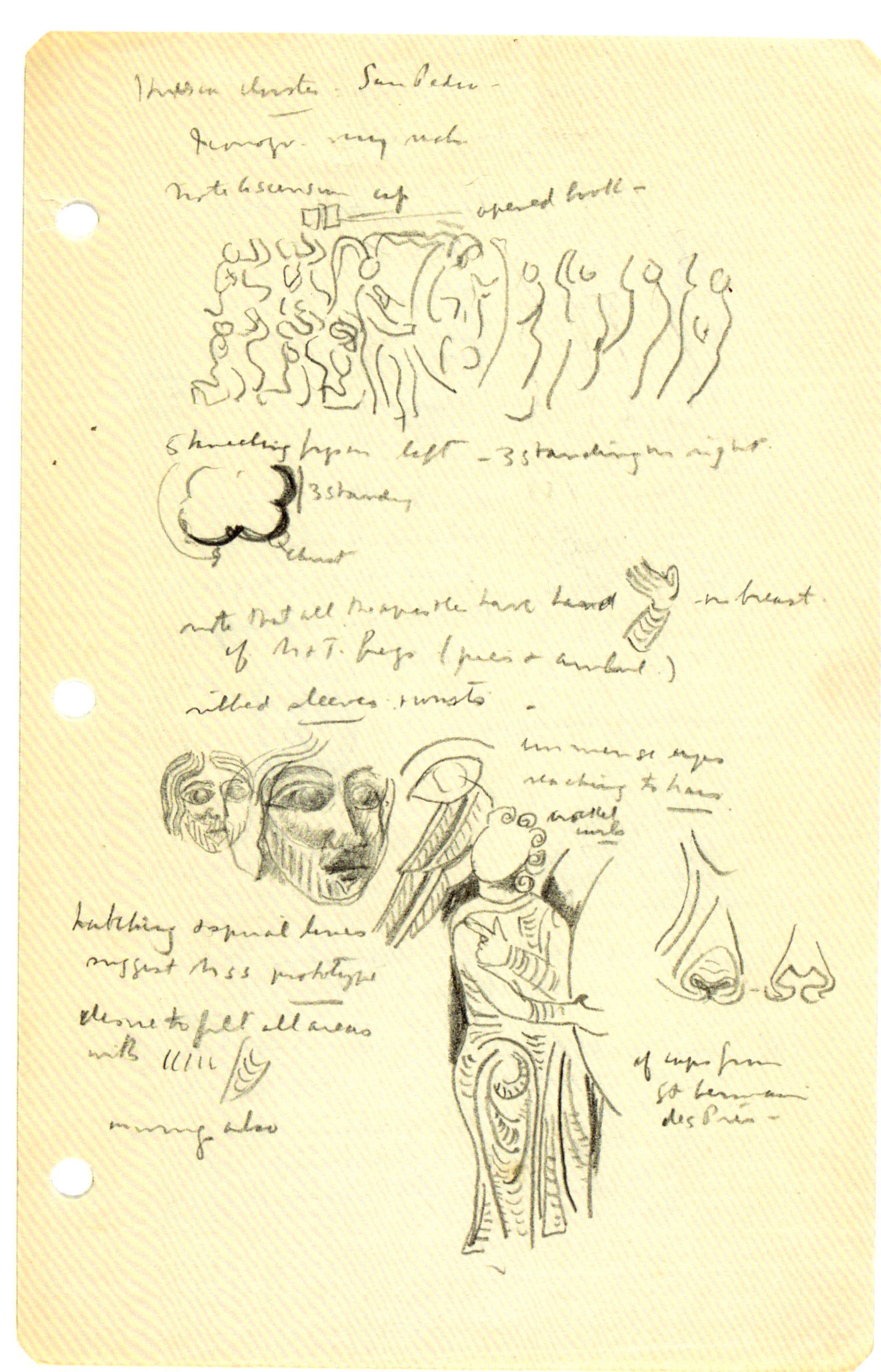

No. 50. Huesca, Iglesia de San Pedro el Viejo, 25 July 1927

Details of cloister capital depicting the ascension of Christ

Pencil on paper

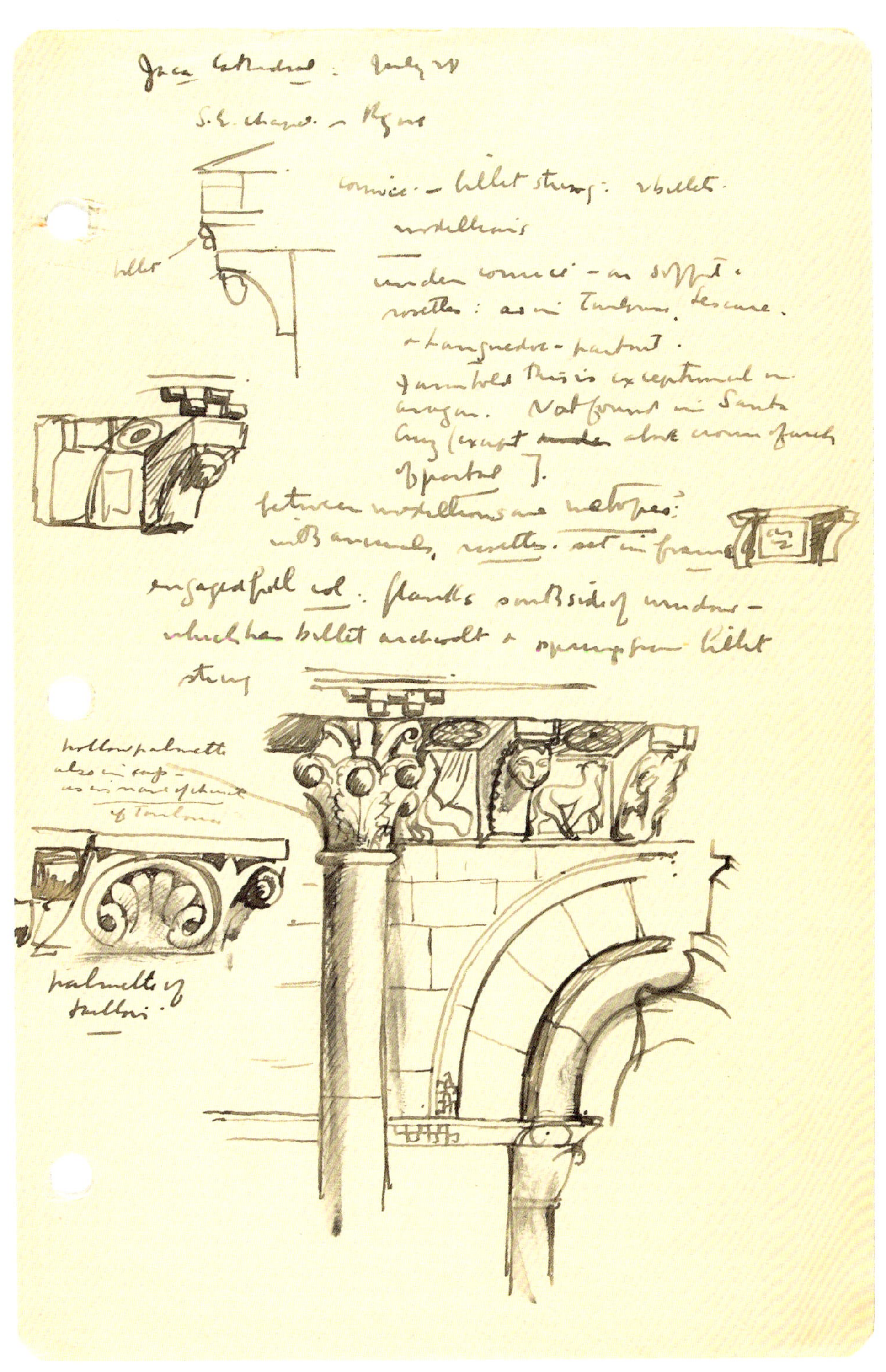

No. 51. Jaca, Catedral de Jaca, 28 July 1927

Details of cornice sculpture on exterior of south chapel on east end

Black ink on paper

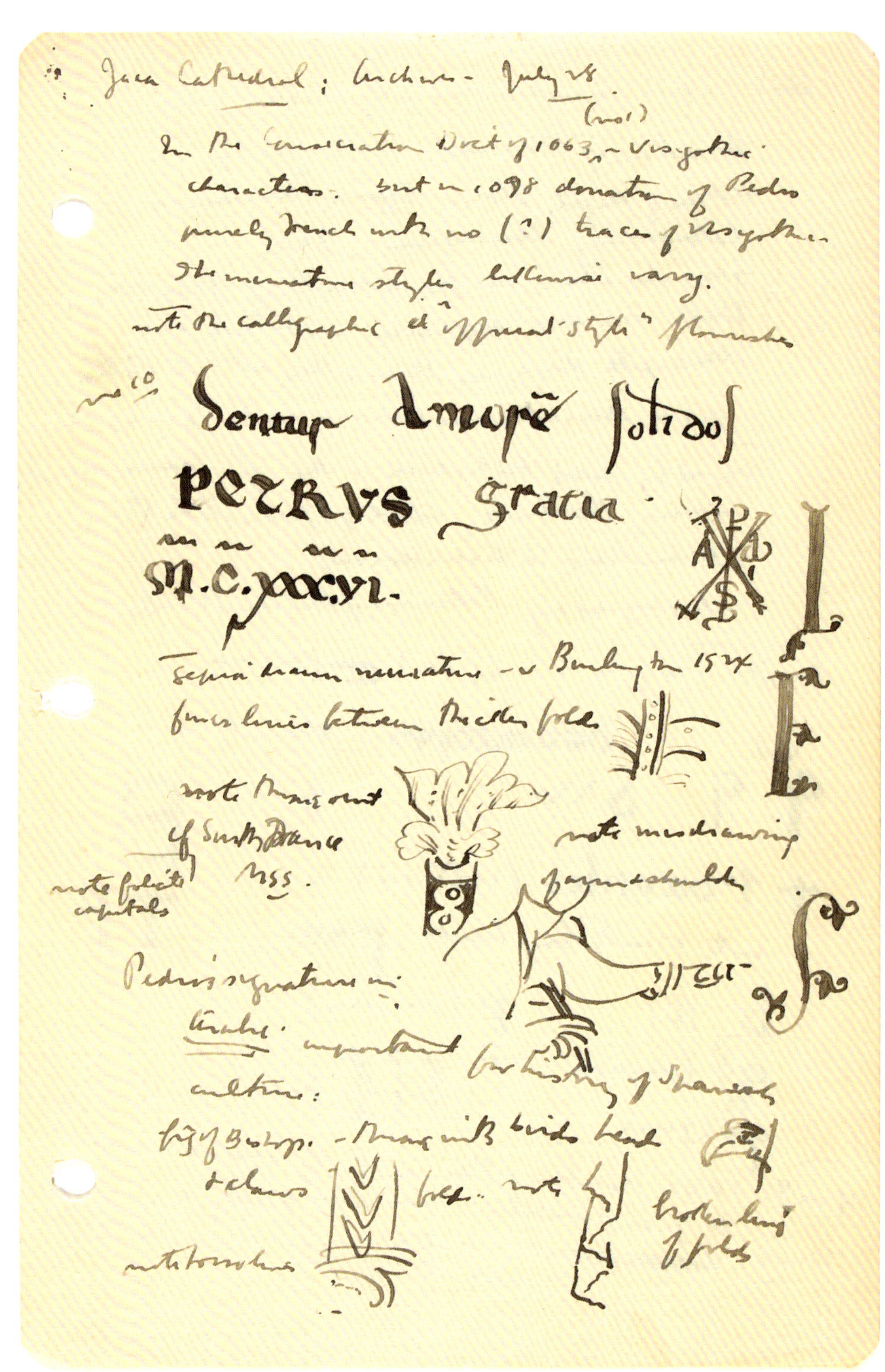

No. 52. Jaca, Archivo de Catedral de Jaca, Leg. 1, Docs. Reales 10, E, 28 July 1927

Details of a legal document showing the donation in 1098 made by Pedro I of Aragon

Black ink on paper

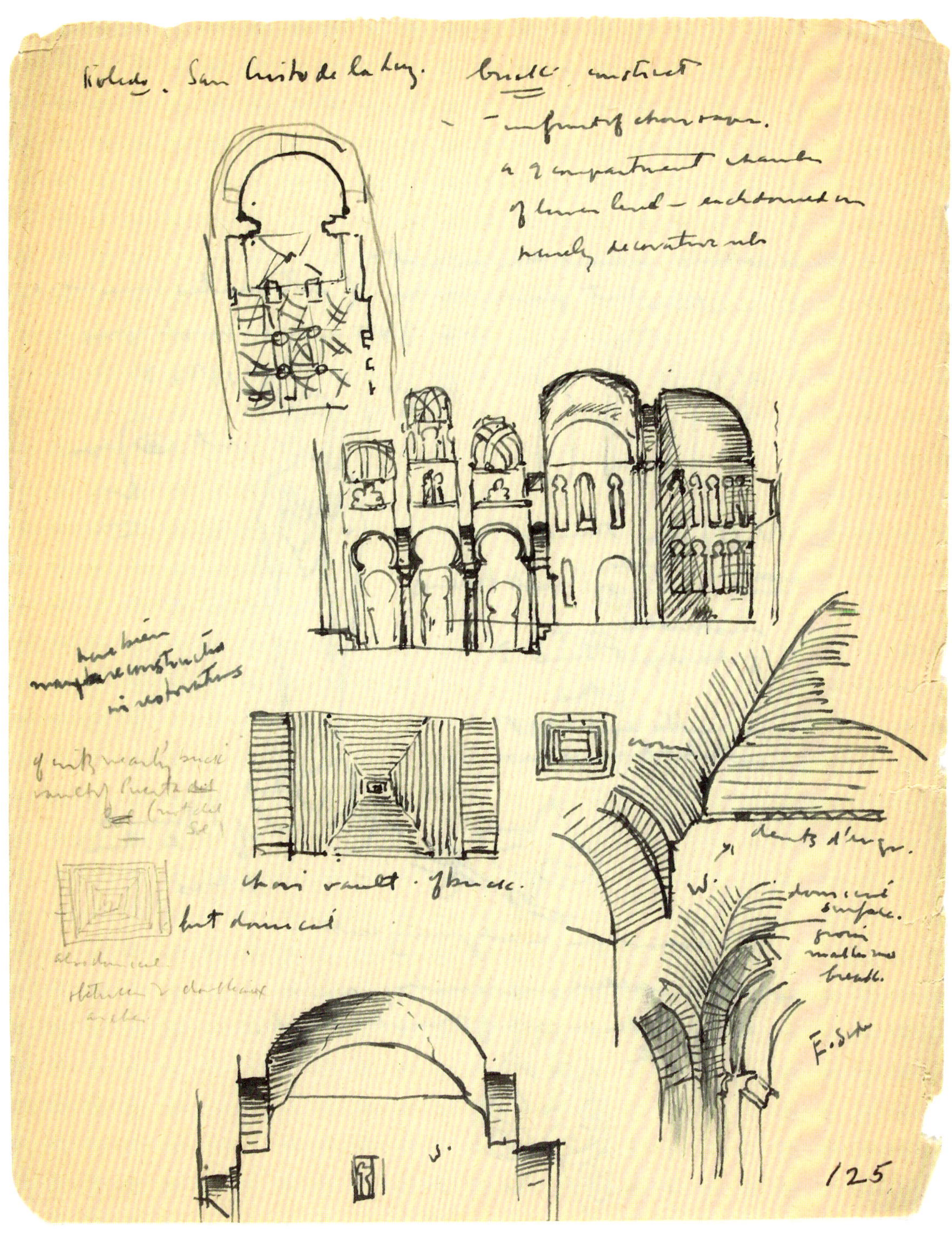

No. 53. Toledo, Mezquita del Cristo de la Luz, 3 August 1927

Plan, longitudinal section, and details of vaulting

Black ink and pencil on paper

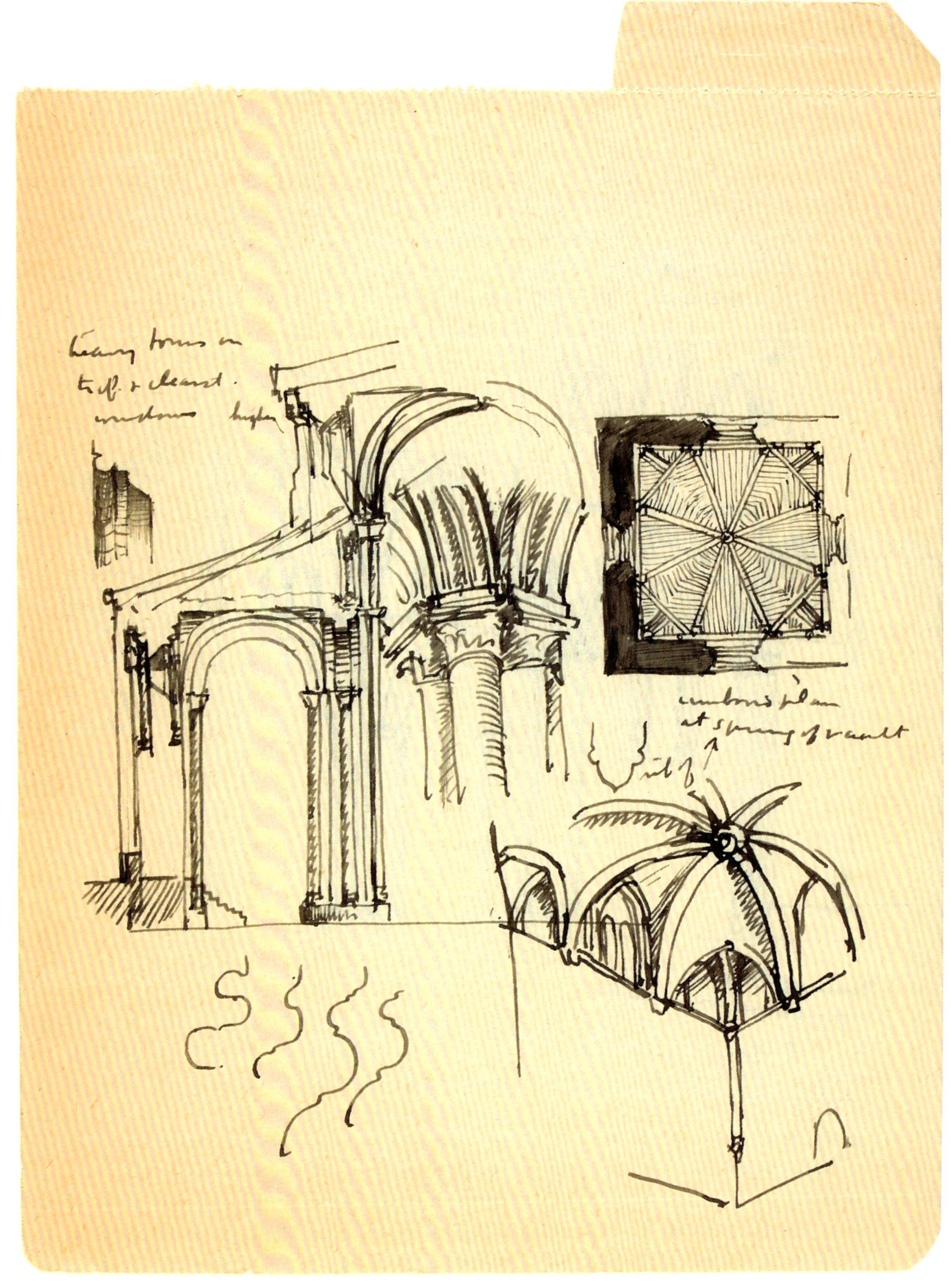

No. 54. Ávila, Iglesia de San Vicente, 5 August 1927

Cross section and details of crossing vaulting

Black ink on paper

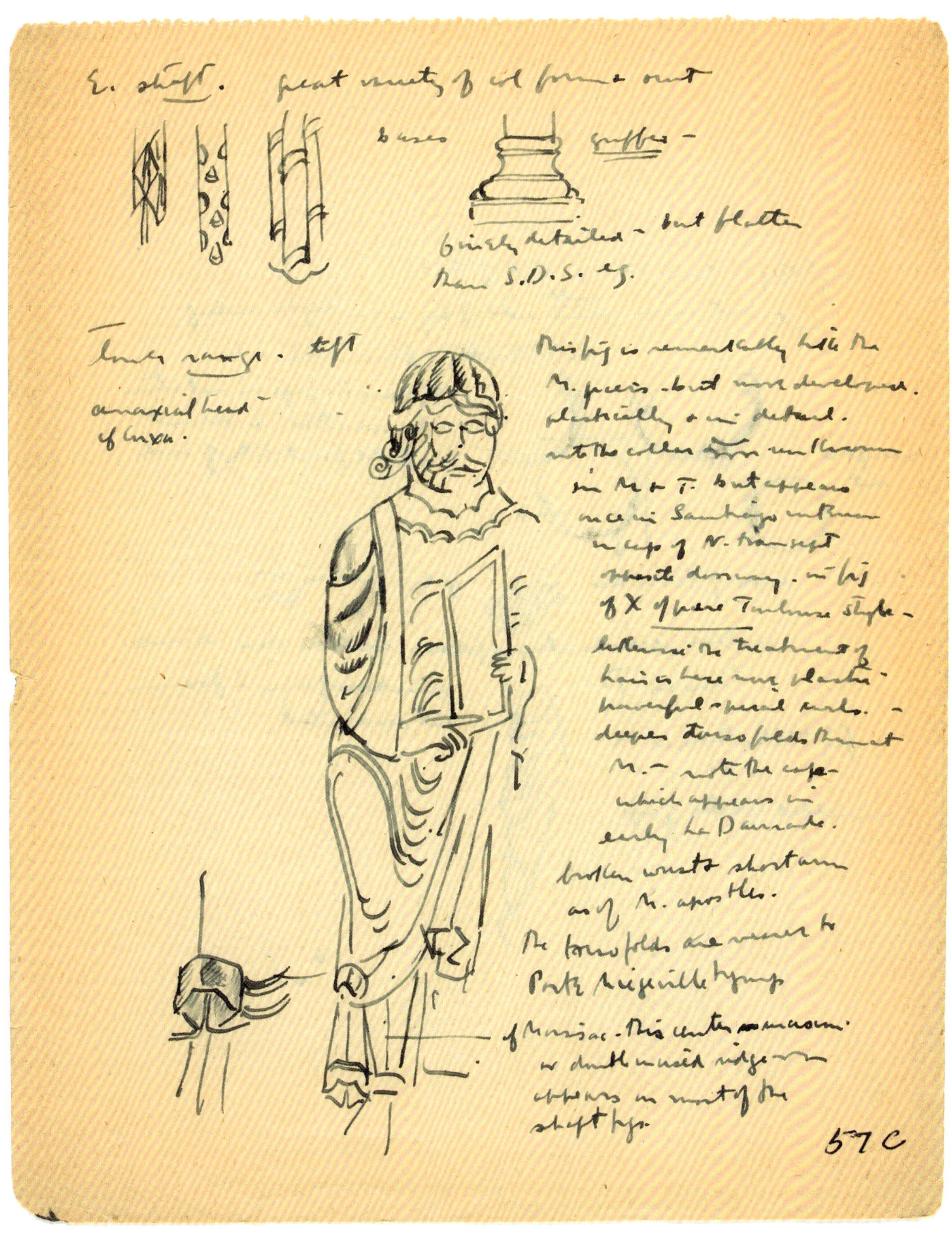

No. 55. Santiago de Compostela, Catedral de Santiago de Compostela, 9–11 August 1927

Column details and figure from the portal Puerta de las Platerías

Black ink on paper

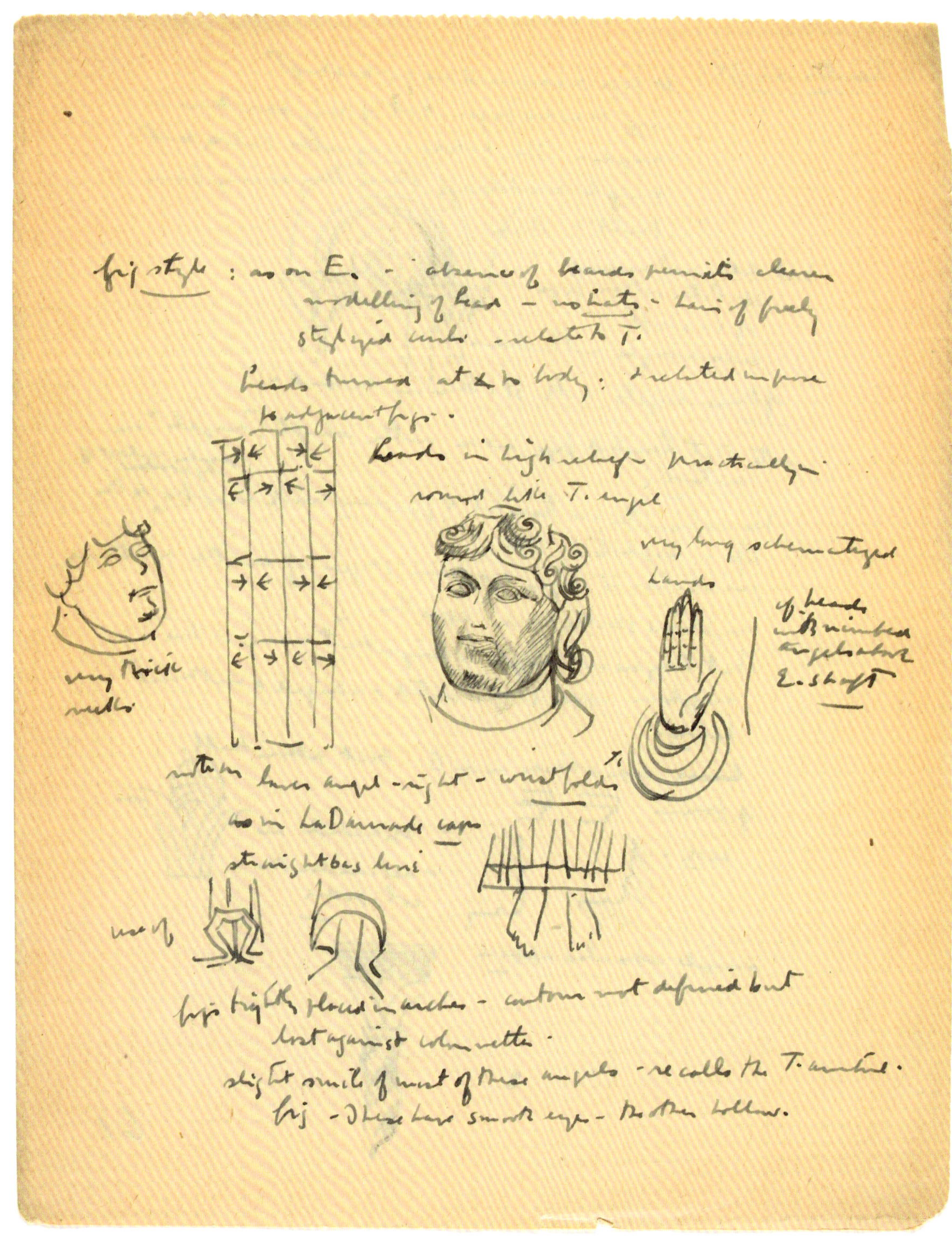

No. 56. Santiago de Compostela, Catedral de Santiago de Compostela, 9–11 August 1927

Details of head, hand, and feet of a figure from the portal Puerta de las Platerías

Black ink on paper

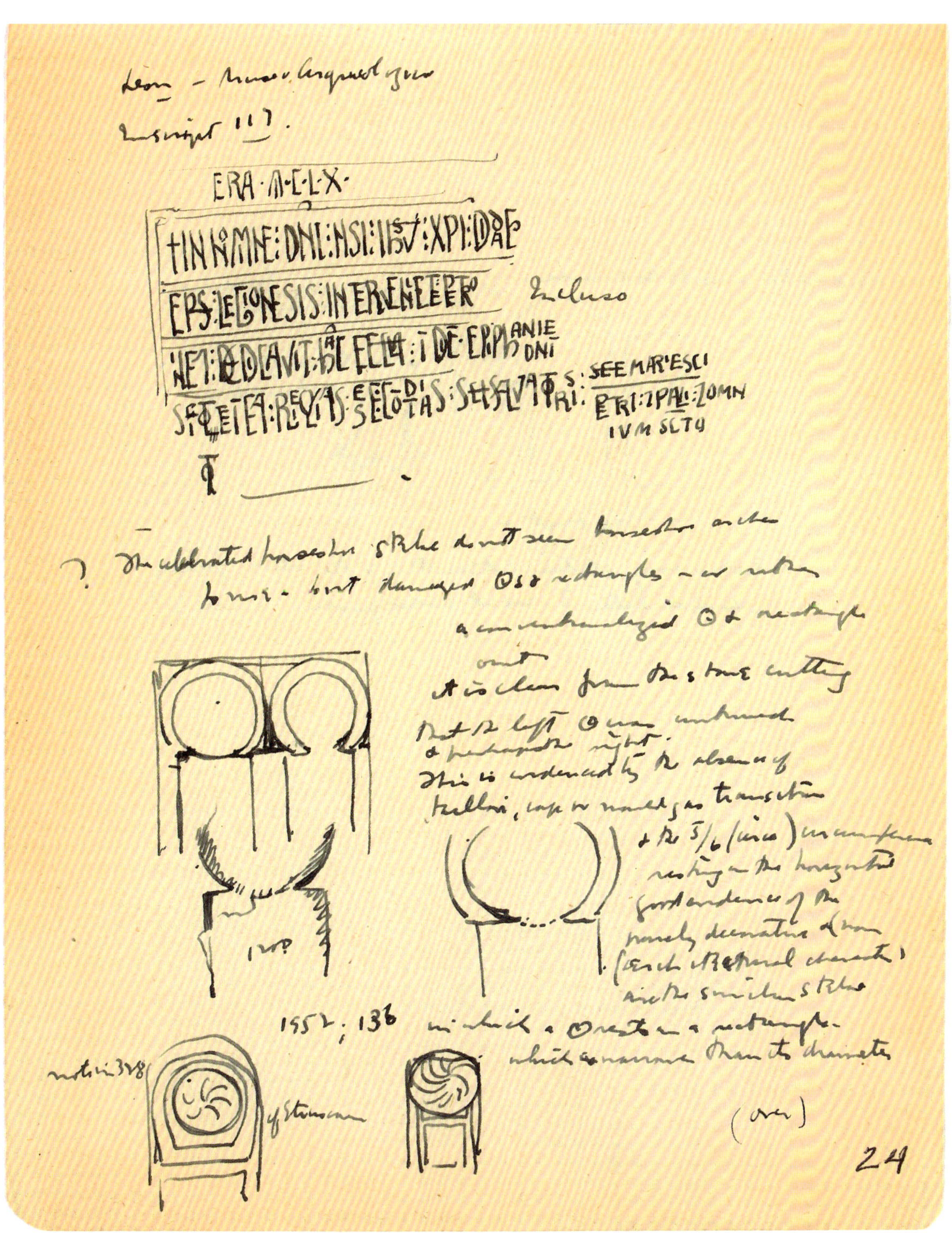

No. 57. León, Museo Arqueológico, 12–14 August 1927

Inscription and stele

Black ink on paper

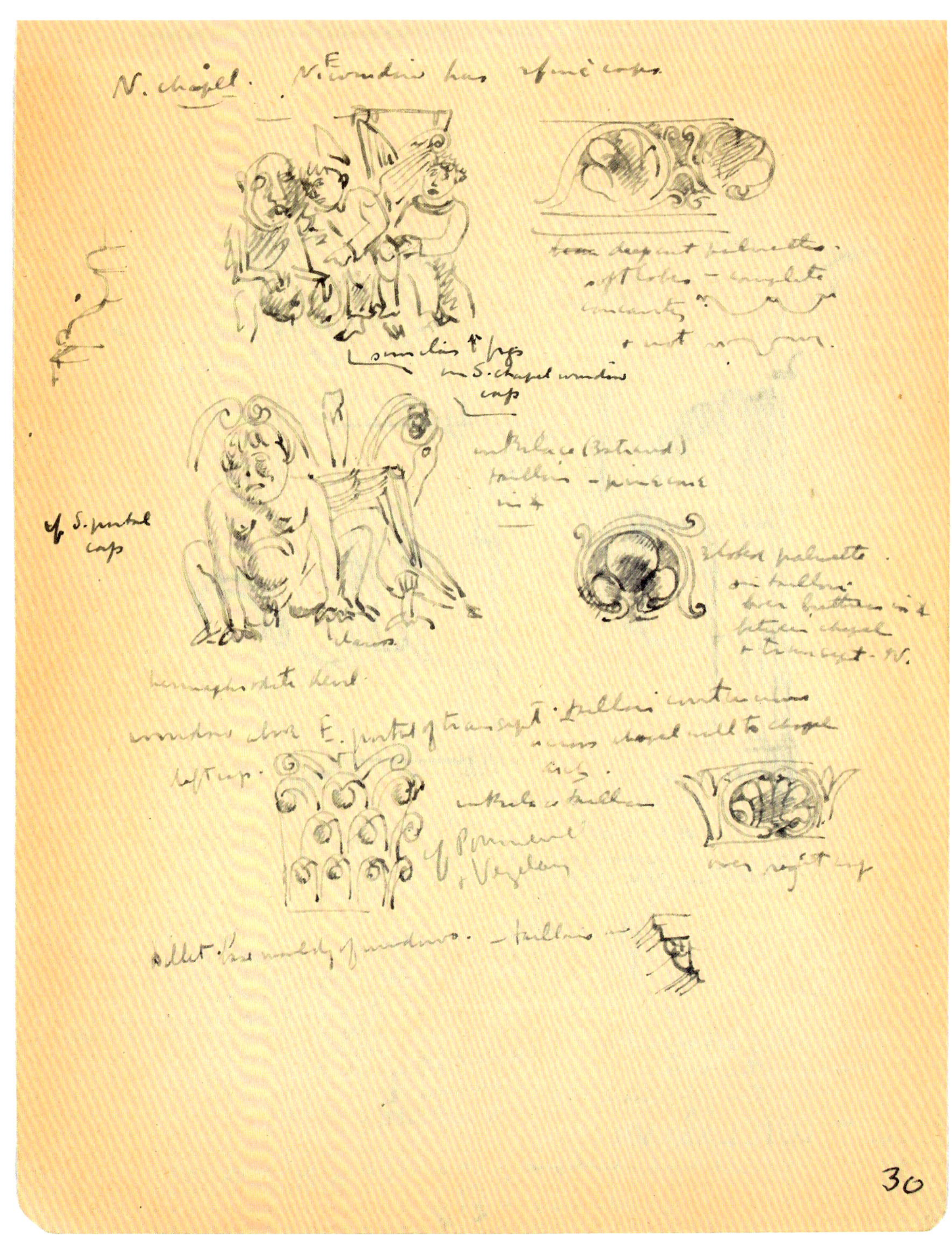

No. 58. León, Basílica de San Isidoro, 12–14 August 1927

Details of interior capitals

Black ink and pencil on paper

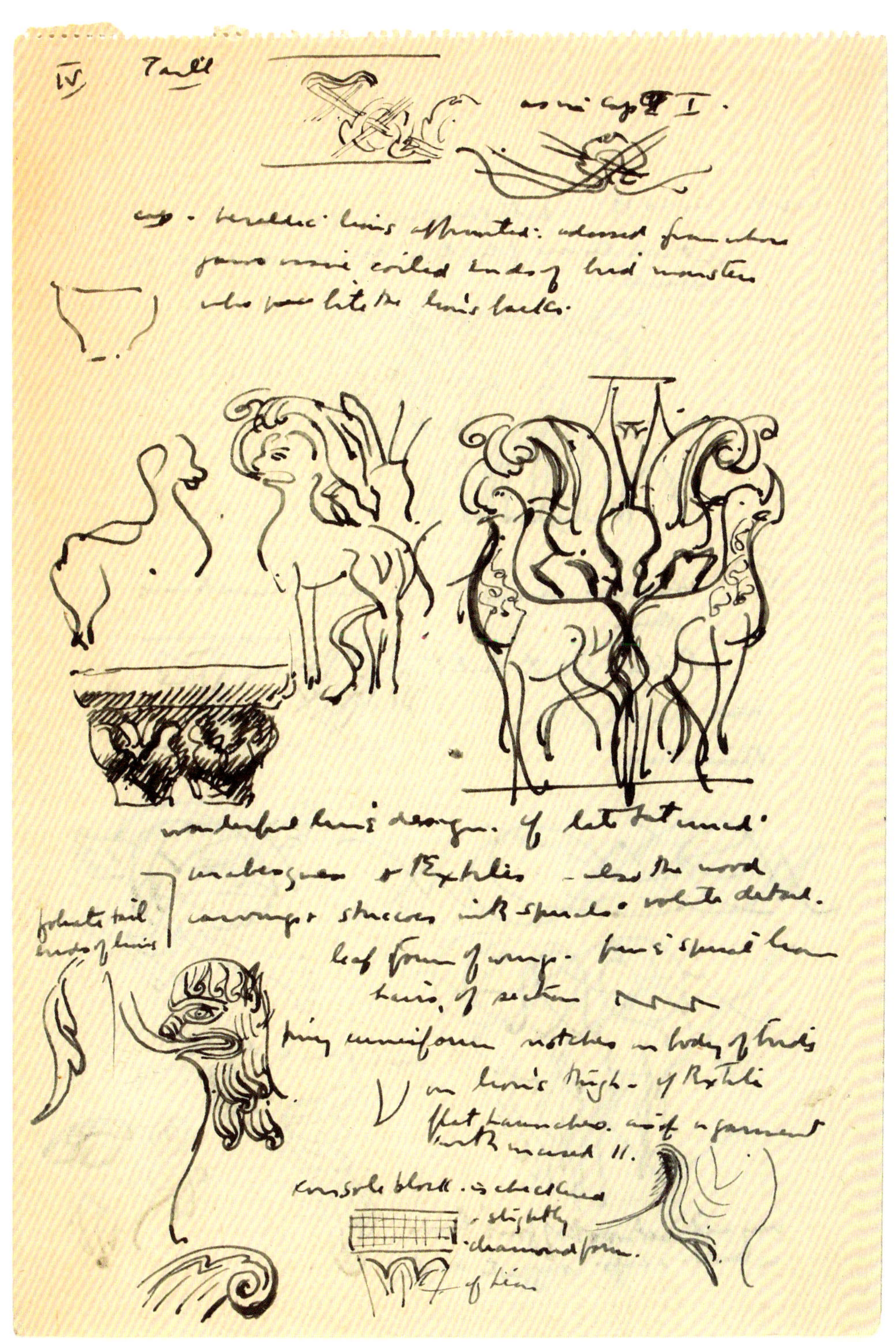

No. 59. Santo Domingo de Silos, Monasterio de Santo Domingo de Silos, 16?–19? August 1927

Details of cloister capitals

Black ink on paper

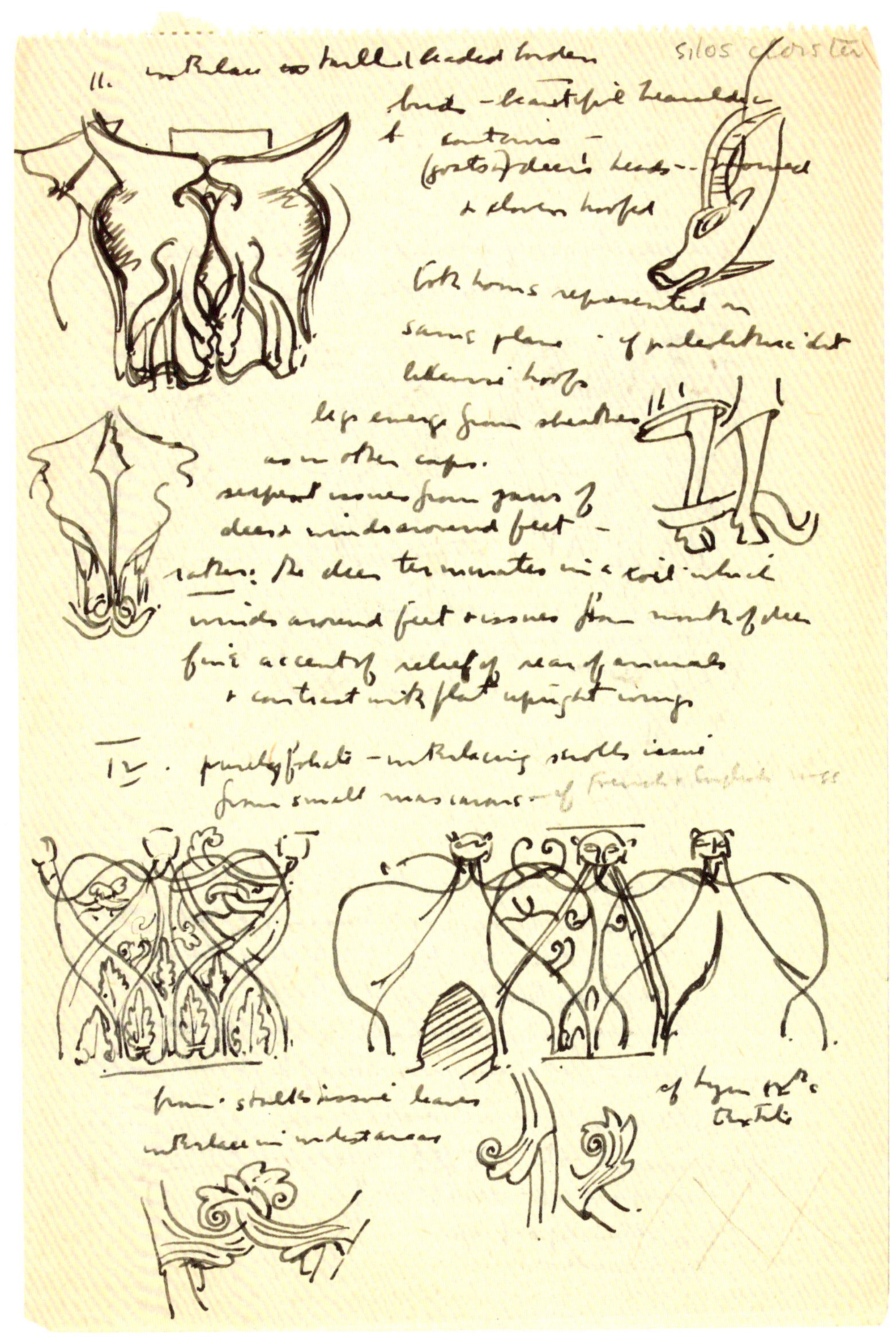

No. 60. Santo Domingo de Silos, Monasterio de Santo Domingo de Silos, 16?–19? August 1927

Details of cloister capitals

Black ink and pencil on paper

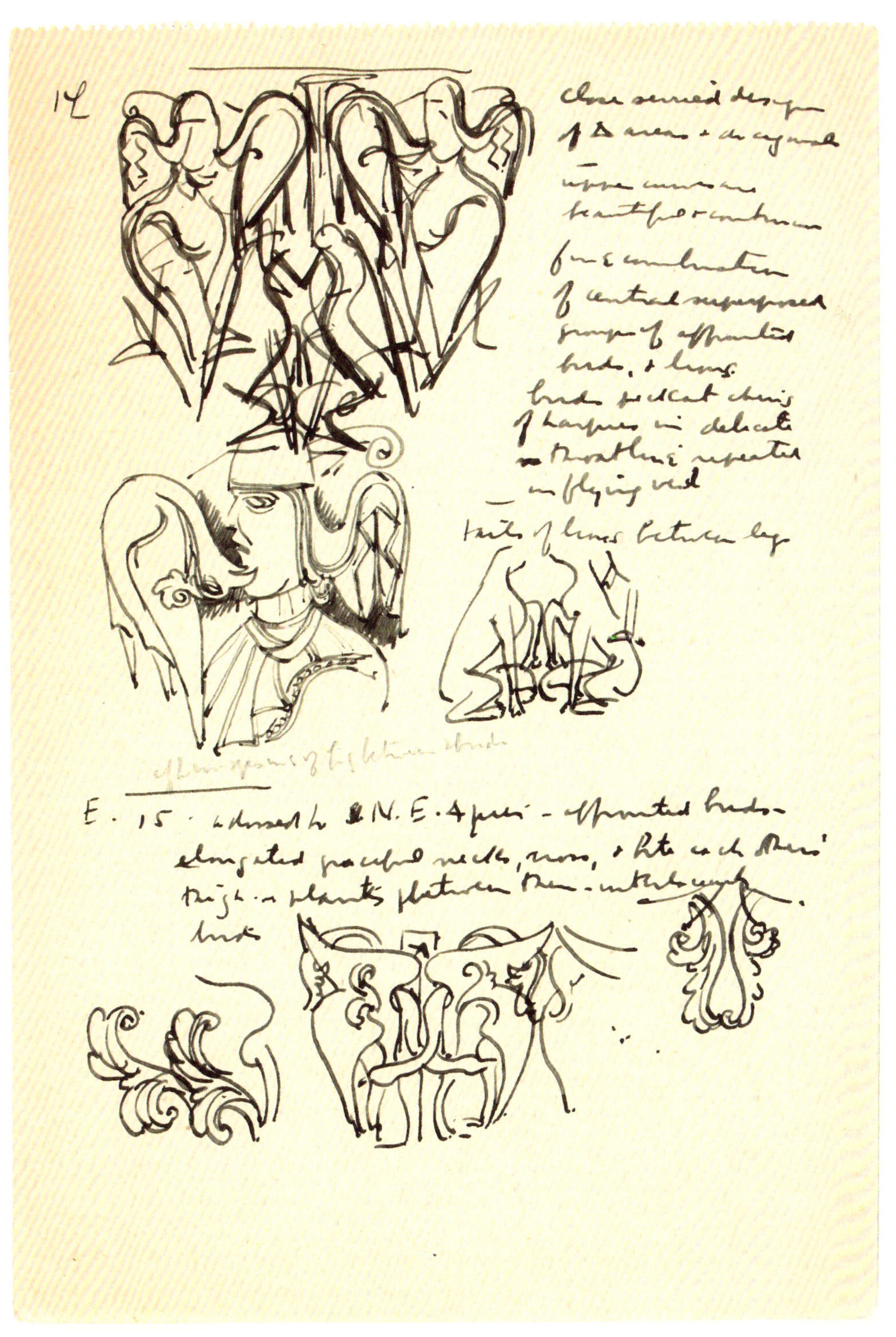

No. 61. Santo Domingo de Silos, Monasterio de Santo Domingo de Silos, 16?–19? August 1927
Details of cloister capitals
Black ink and pencil on paper

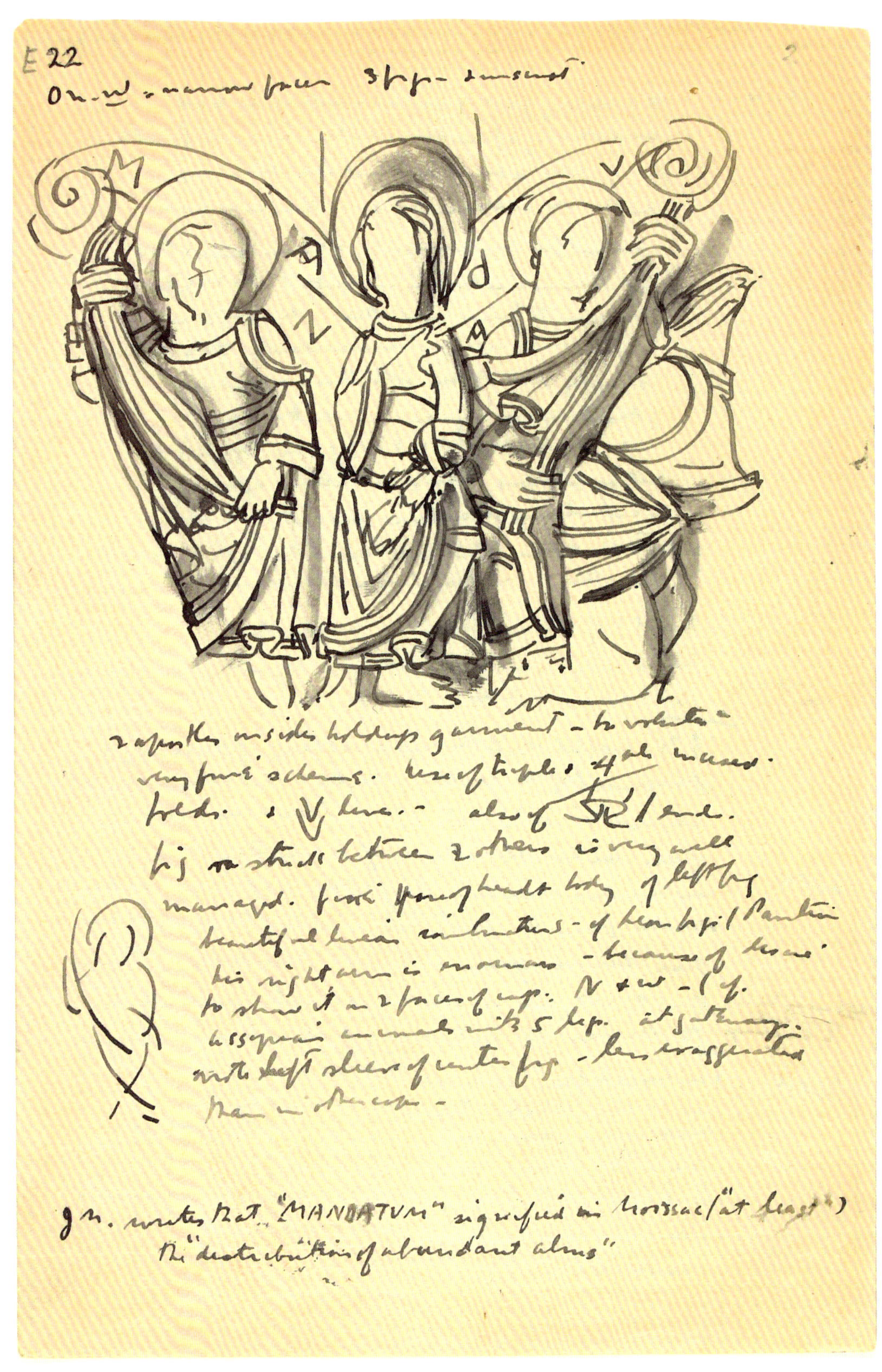

No. 62. Moissac, Abbaye de Saint-Pierre, 31 August–3 September 1927

West face of Capital 25, Washing of Feet

Black ink on paper

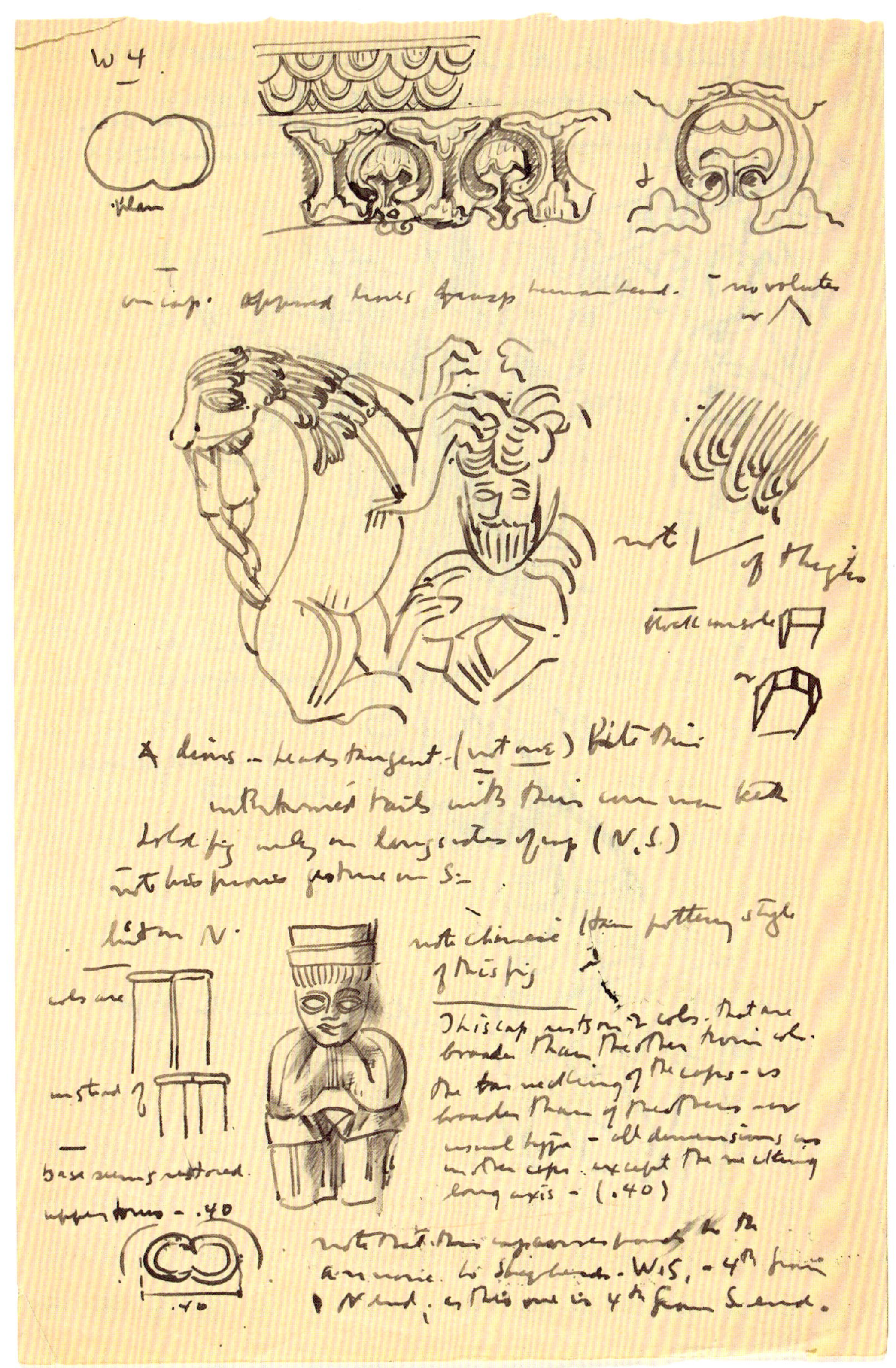

No. 63. Moissac, Abbaye de Saint-Pierre, 31 August–3 September 1927

Details of tailloir, north face, and south face of Capital 72, Lions and Figures

Black ink on paper

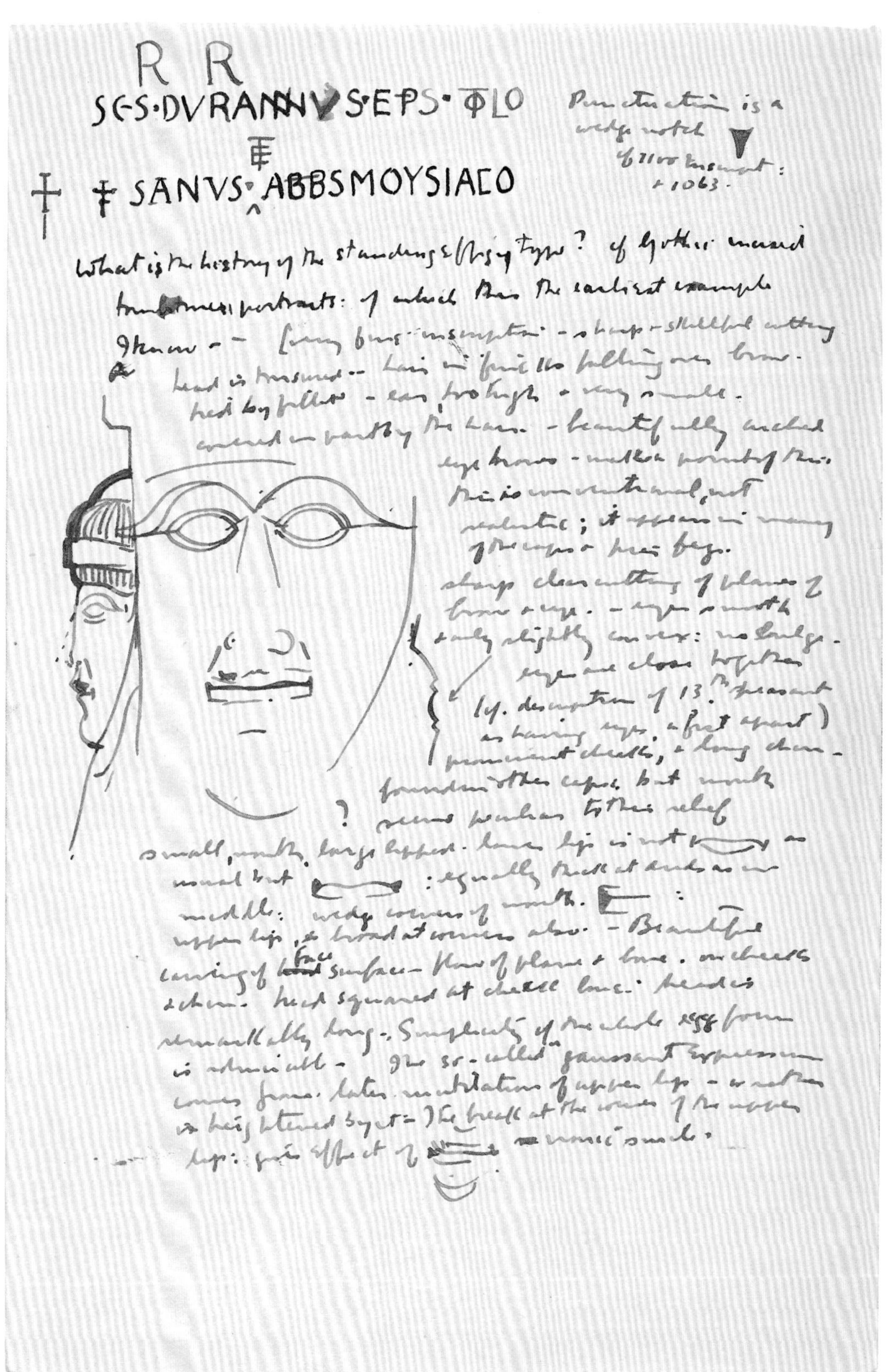

No. 64. Moissac, Abbaye de Saint-Pierre, 31 August–3 September 1927

Details of inscription and Abbot Durand's head on east pier

Black ink on paper

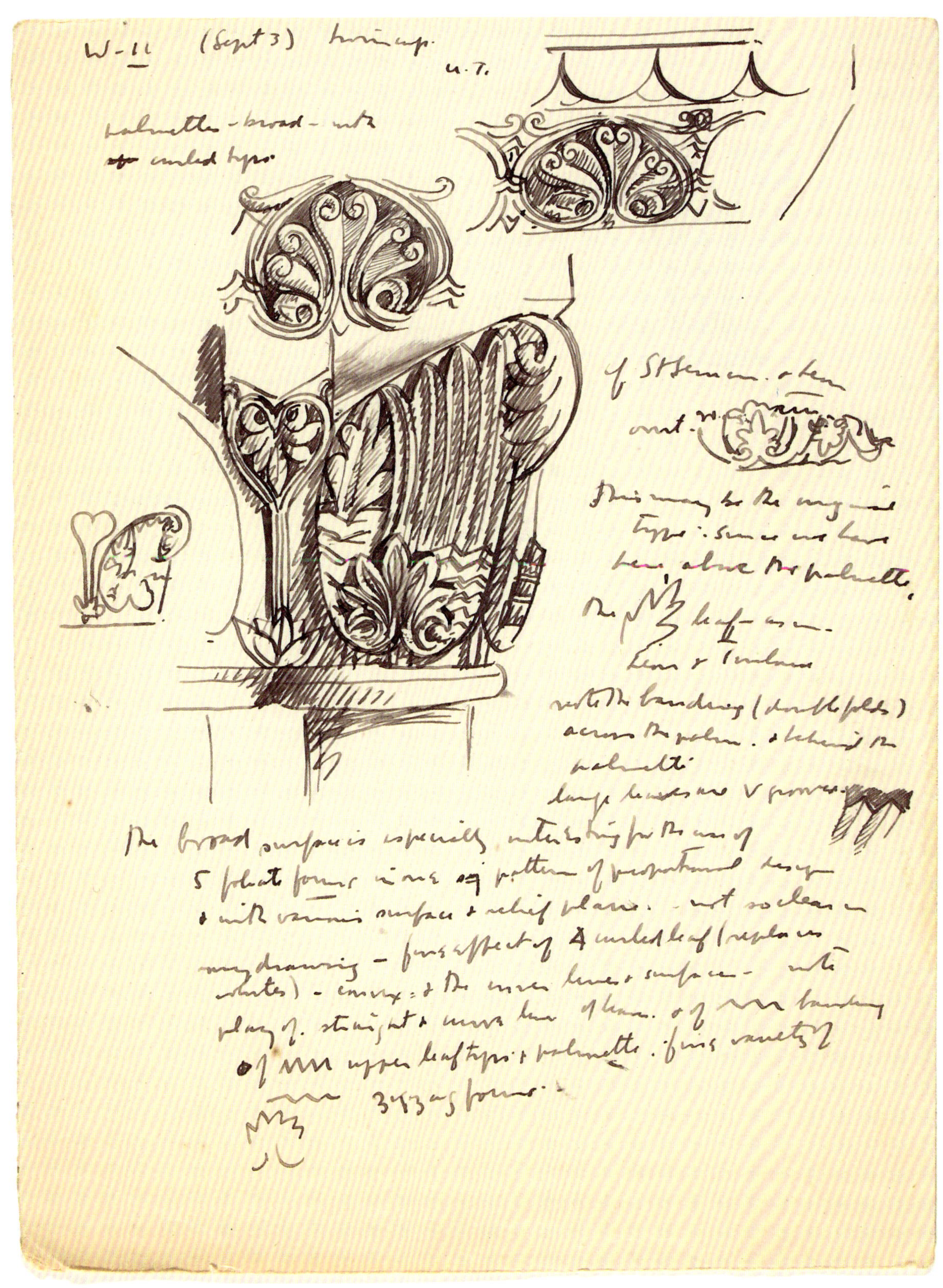

No. 65. Moissac, Abbaye de Saint-Pierre, 3 September 1927

Detail of tailloir and north or south face of Capital 65, Foliage

Black ink on paper

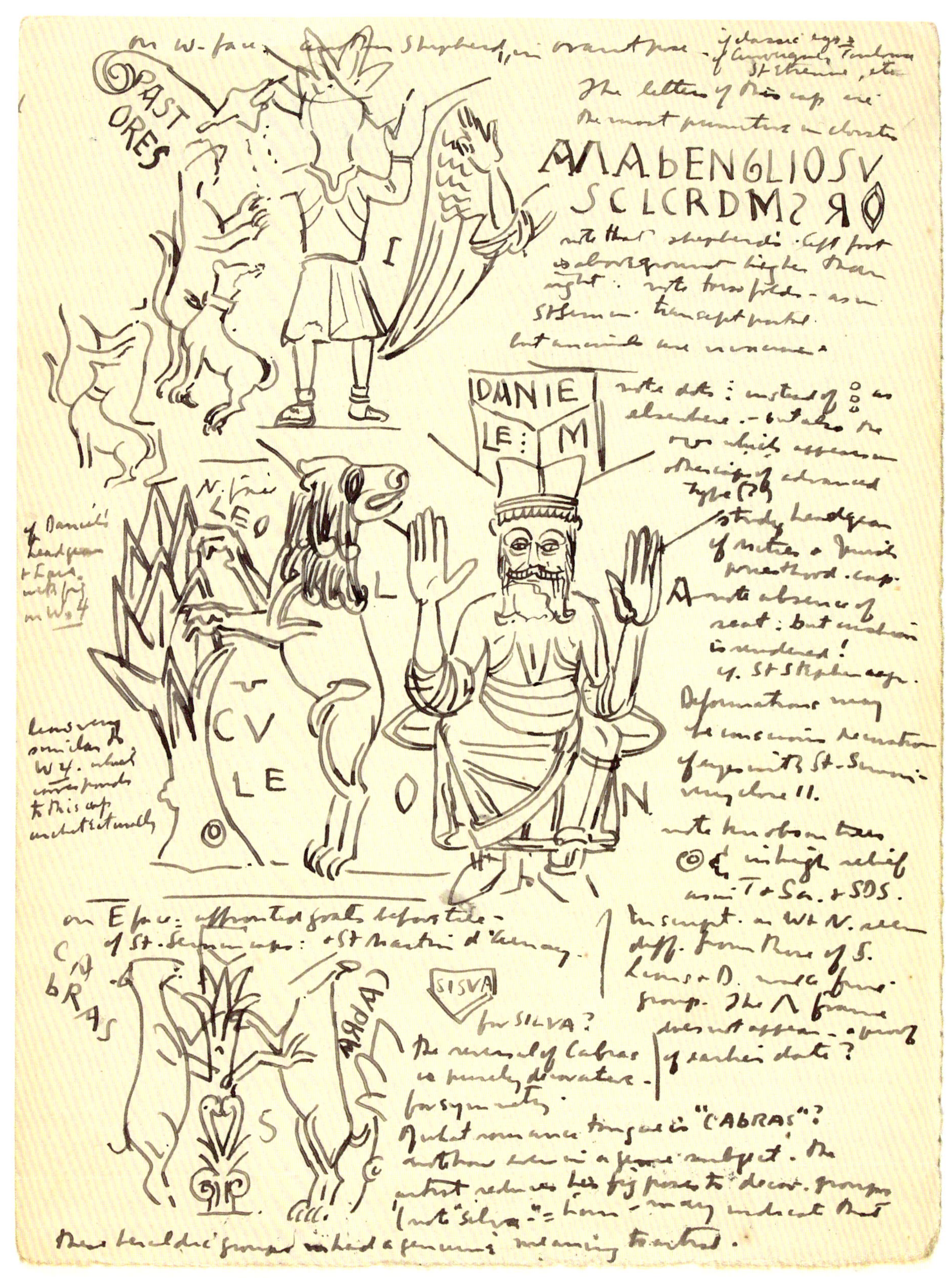

No. 66. Moissac, Abbaye de Saint-Pierre, 3–18 September 1927
Details of three faces of Capital 61, Daniel in the Lions' Den and Annunciation to the Shepherds
Black ink on paper

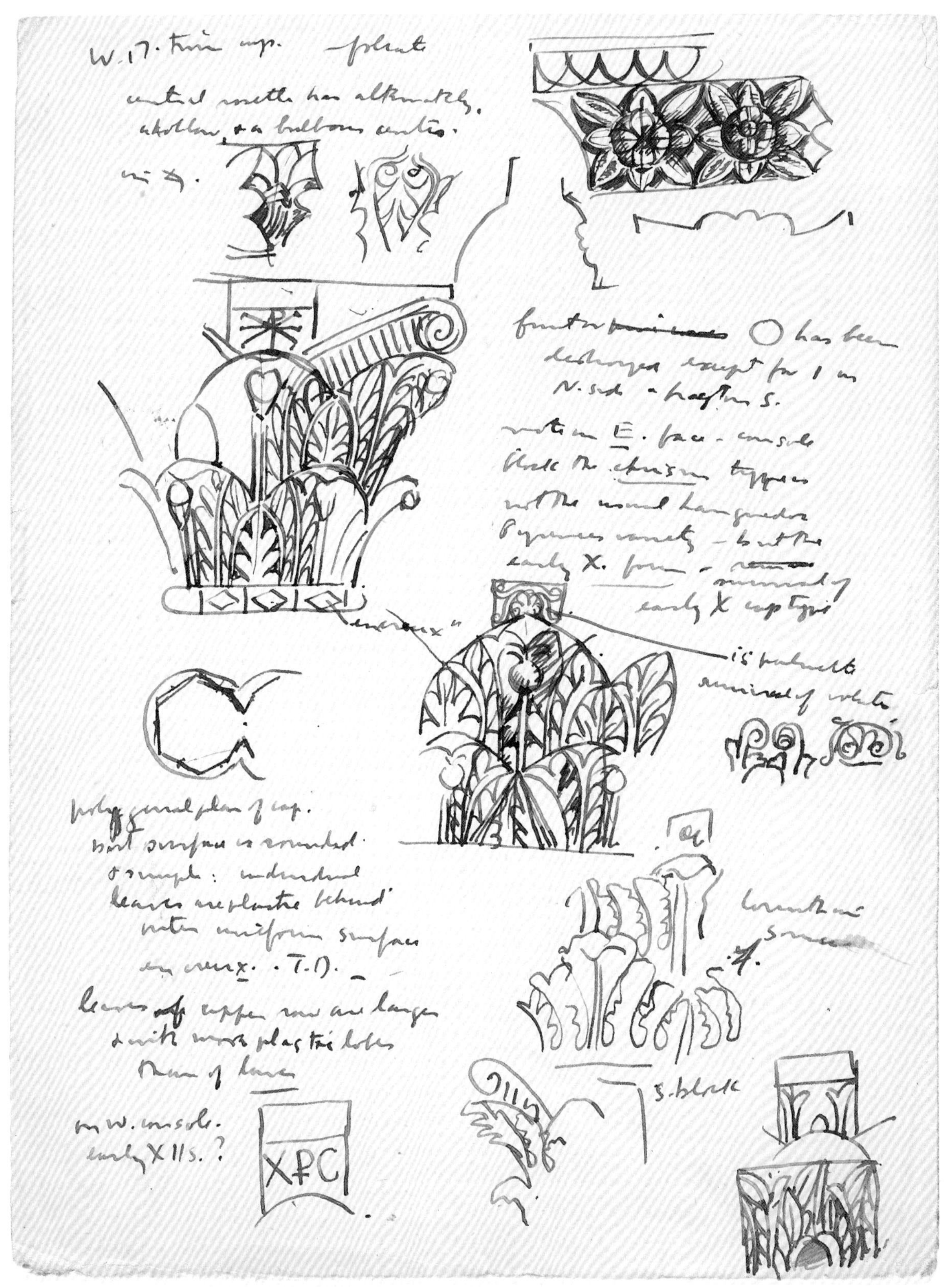

No. 67. Moissac, Abbaye de Saint-Pierre, 3–18 September 1927

Details of tailloir and capital of Capital 59, Foliage

Black ink on paper

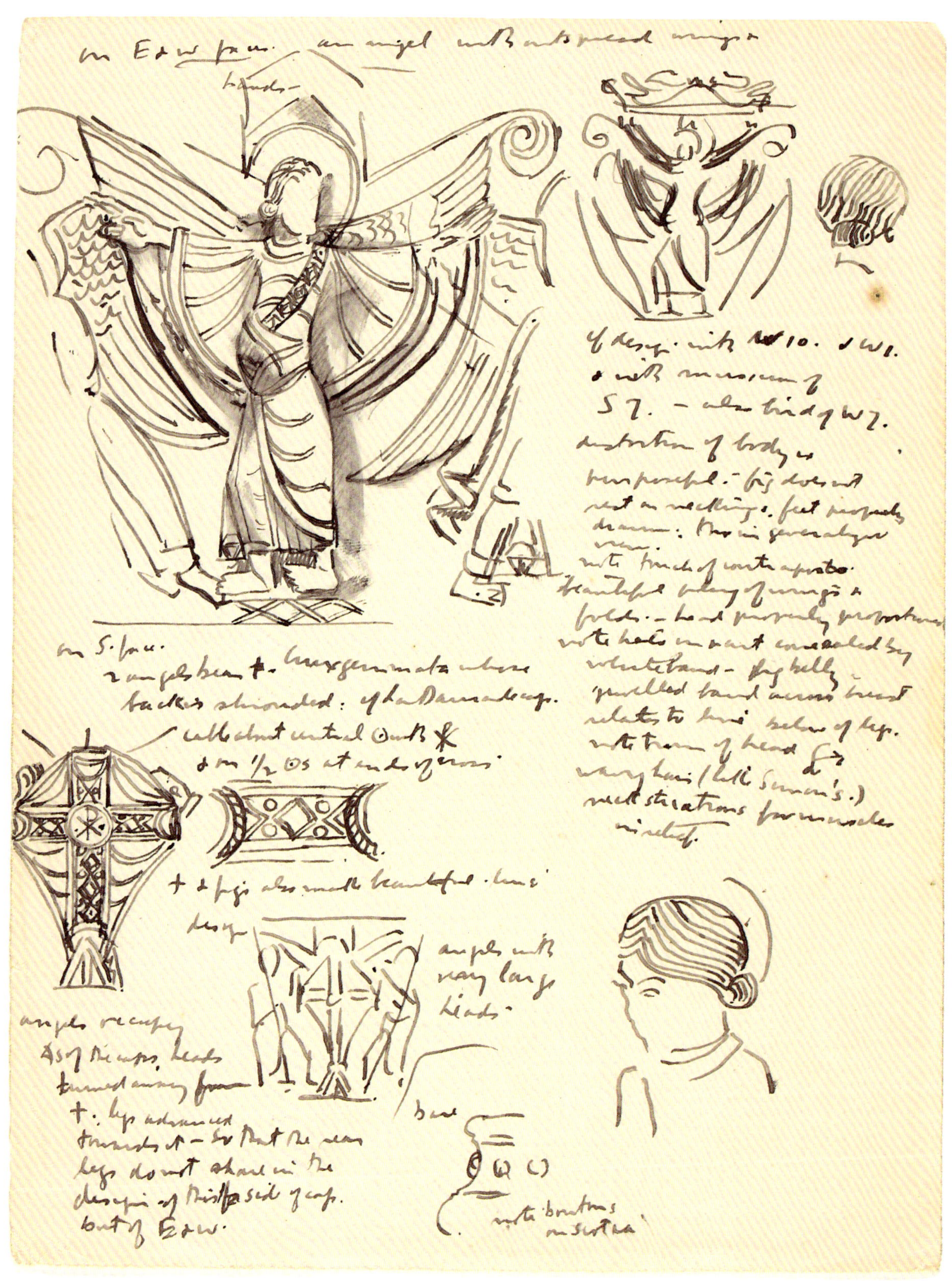

No. 68. Moissac, Abbaye de Saint-Pierre, 3–18 September 1927

Details of east and south faces of Capital 58, Angels with Cross

Black ink on paper

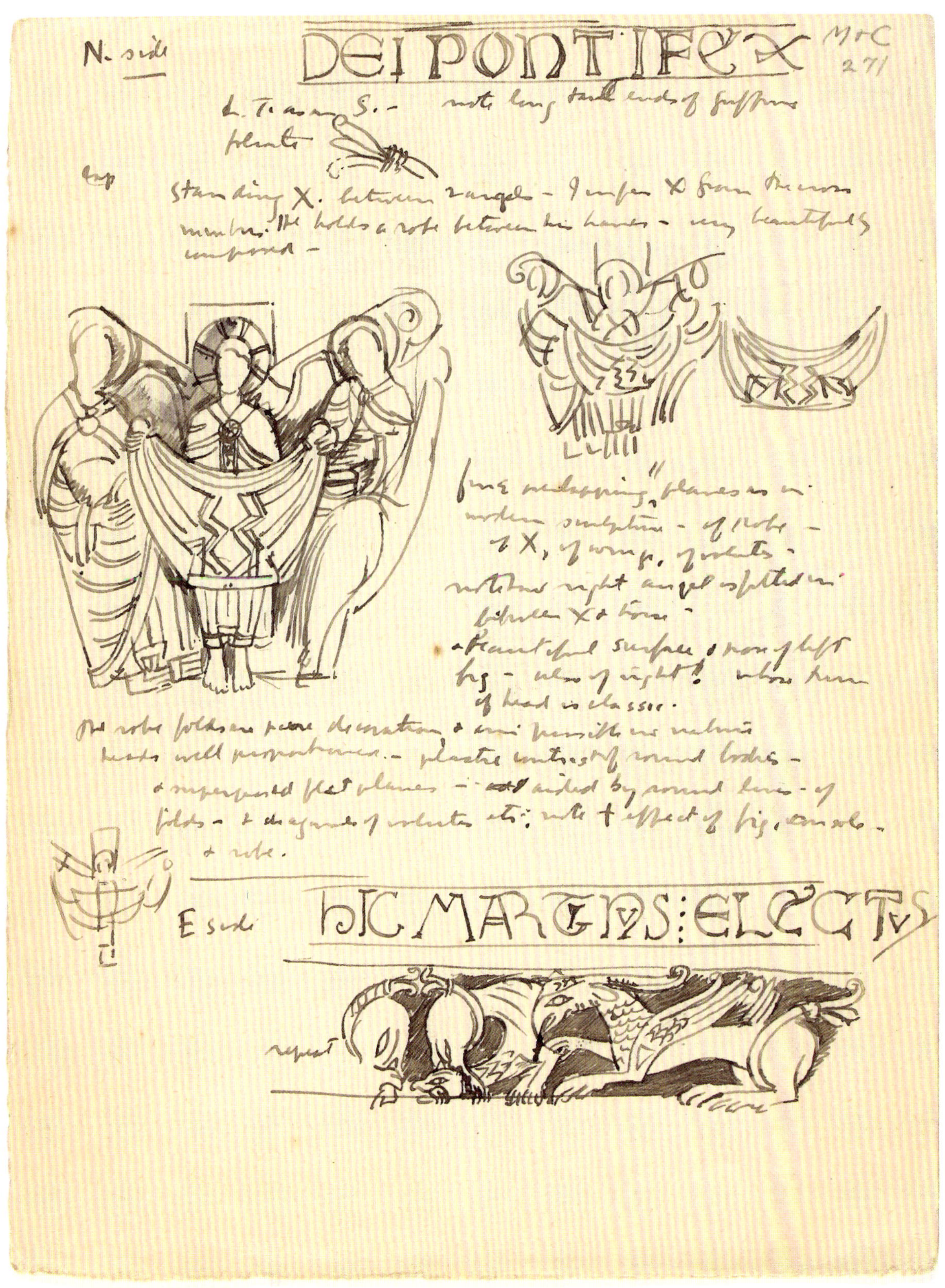

No. 69. Moissac, Abbaye de Saint-Pierre, 5 September 1927

North face and tailloirs of north and east faces of Capital 54, Martin and the Beggar and the Miracle of Martin

Black ink on paper

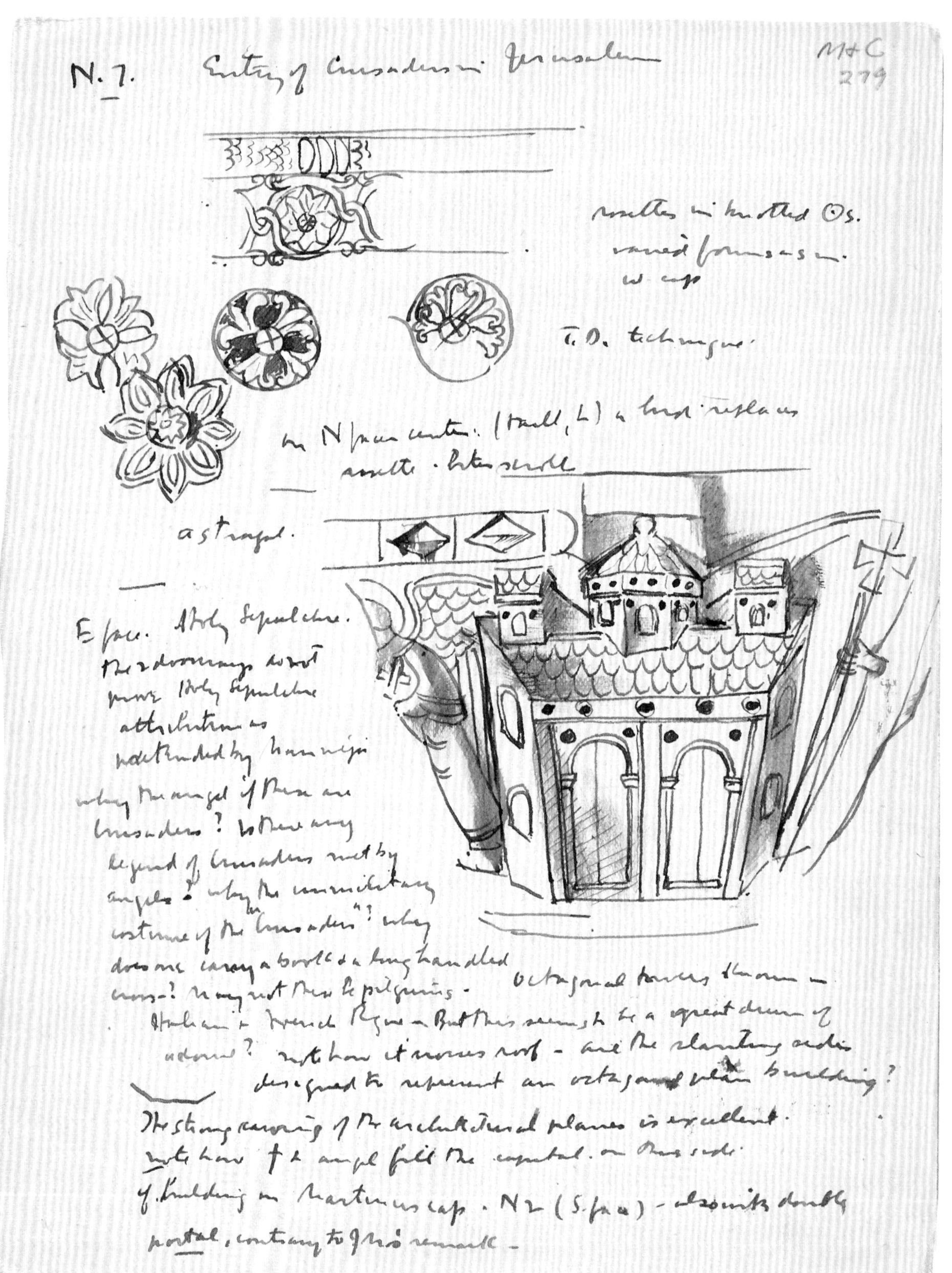

No. 70. Moissac, Abbaye de Saint-Pierre, 3–18 September 1927

Tailloir and details of east face of Capital 49, Crusaders before Jerusalem

Black ink on paper

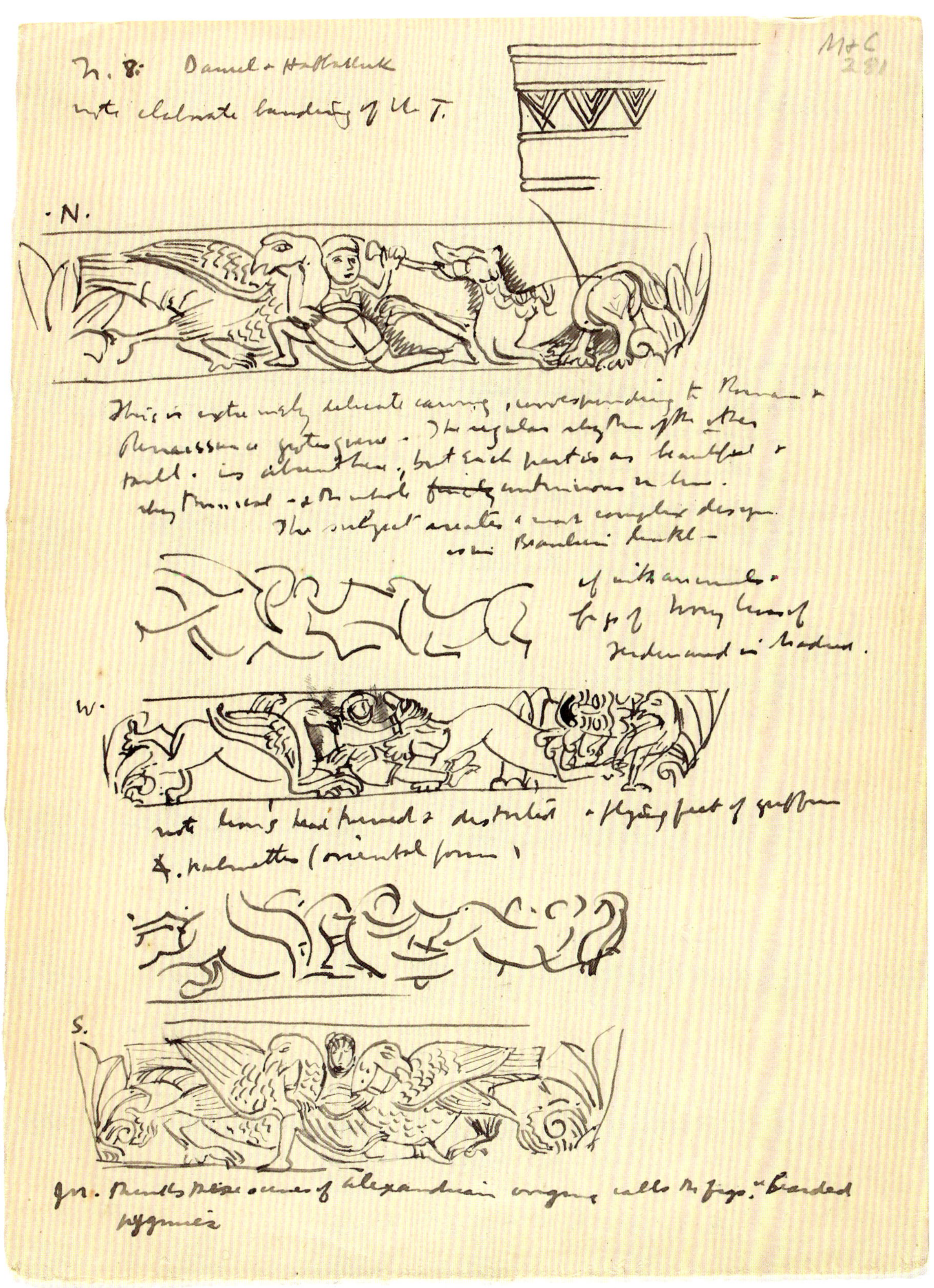

No. 71. Moissac, Abbaye de Saint-Pierre, 3–18 September 1927

Tailloirs of Capital 48, Daniel in the Lions' Den and Habbakuk

Black ink on paper

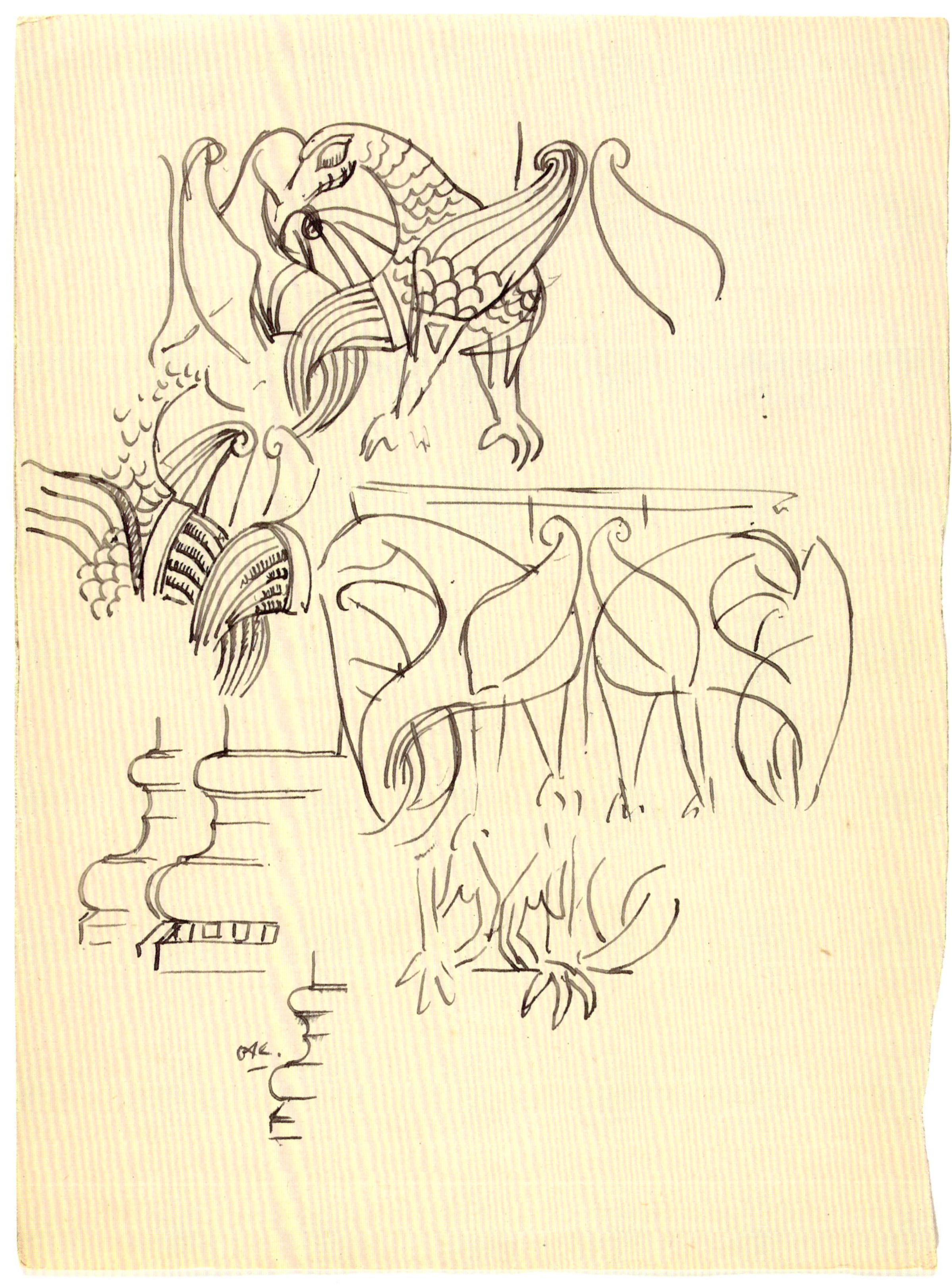

No. 72. Moissac, Abbaye de Saint-Pierre, 3–18 September 1927
Details of east or west face and column bases of Capital 43, Birds
Black ink on paper

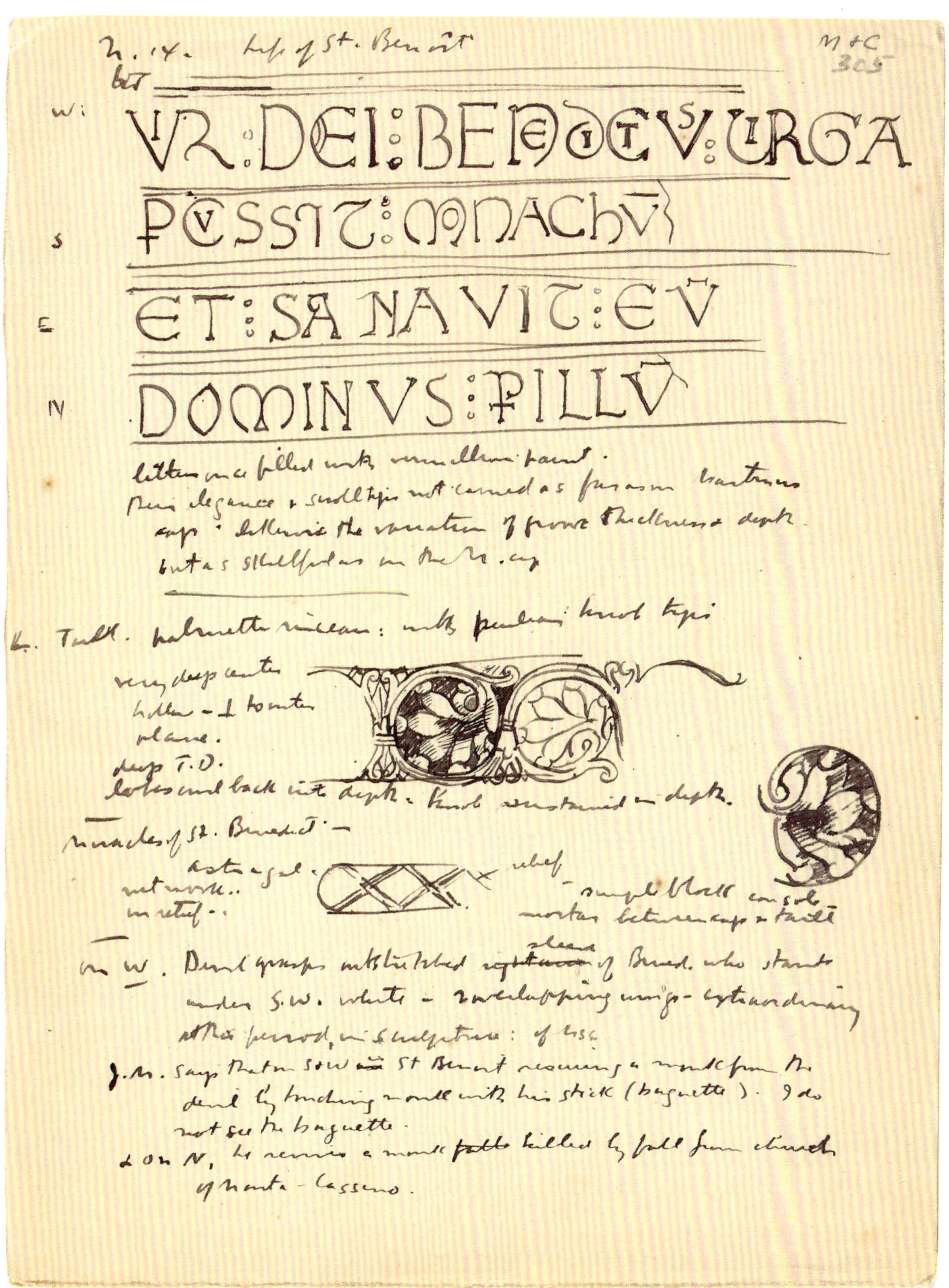

No. 73. Moissac, Abbaye de Saint-Pierre, 3–18 September 1927

Inscriptions and details of tailloirs of Capital 42, Miracle of Benedict

Black ink on paper

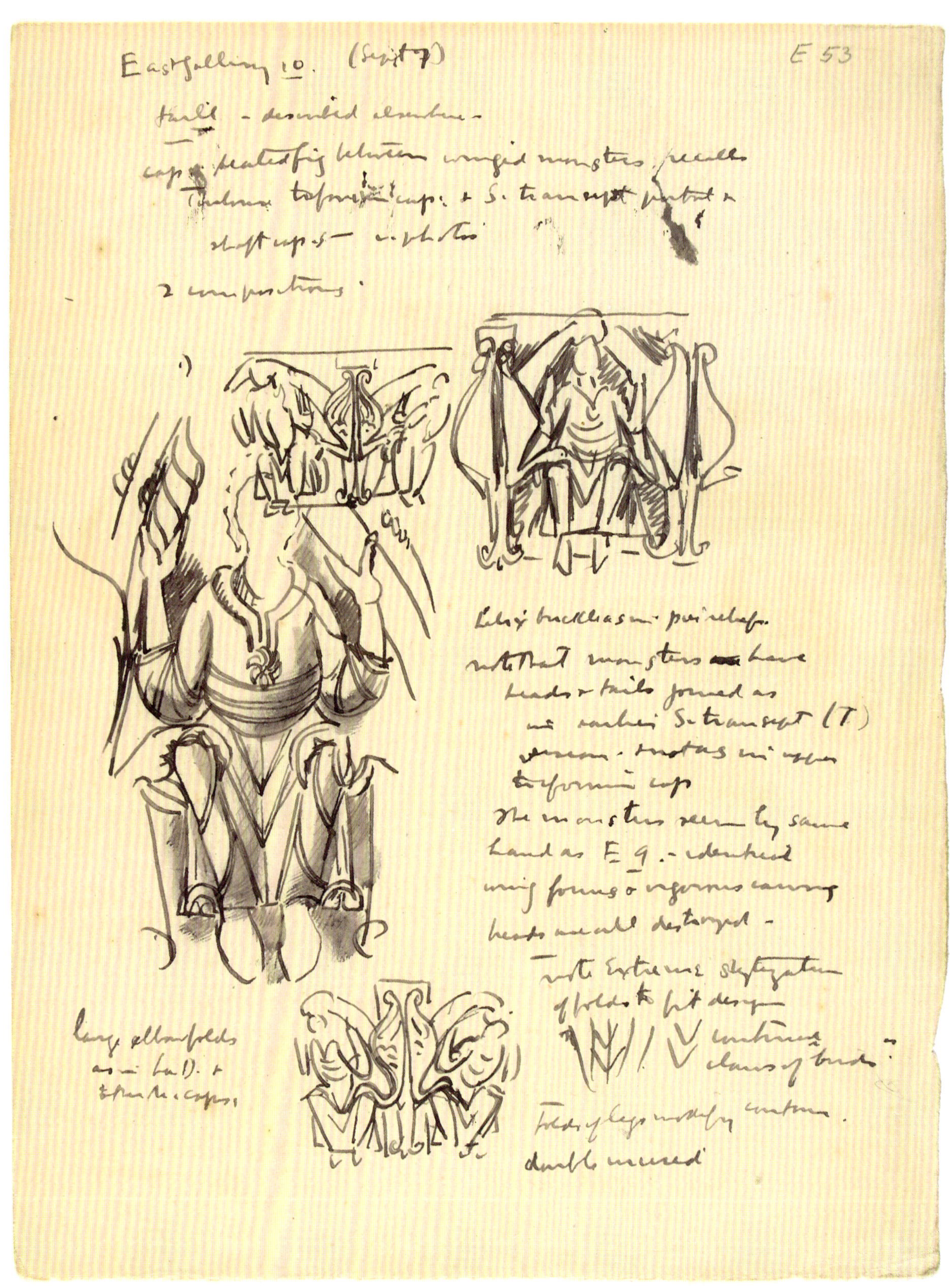

No. 74. Moissac, Abbaye de Saint-Pierre, 7 September 1927

Views from broad side and corner of Capital 29, Dragons and Figures

Black ink on paper

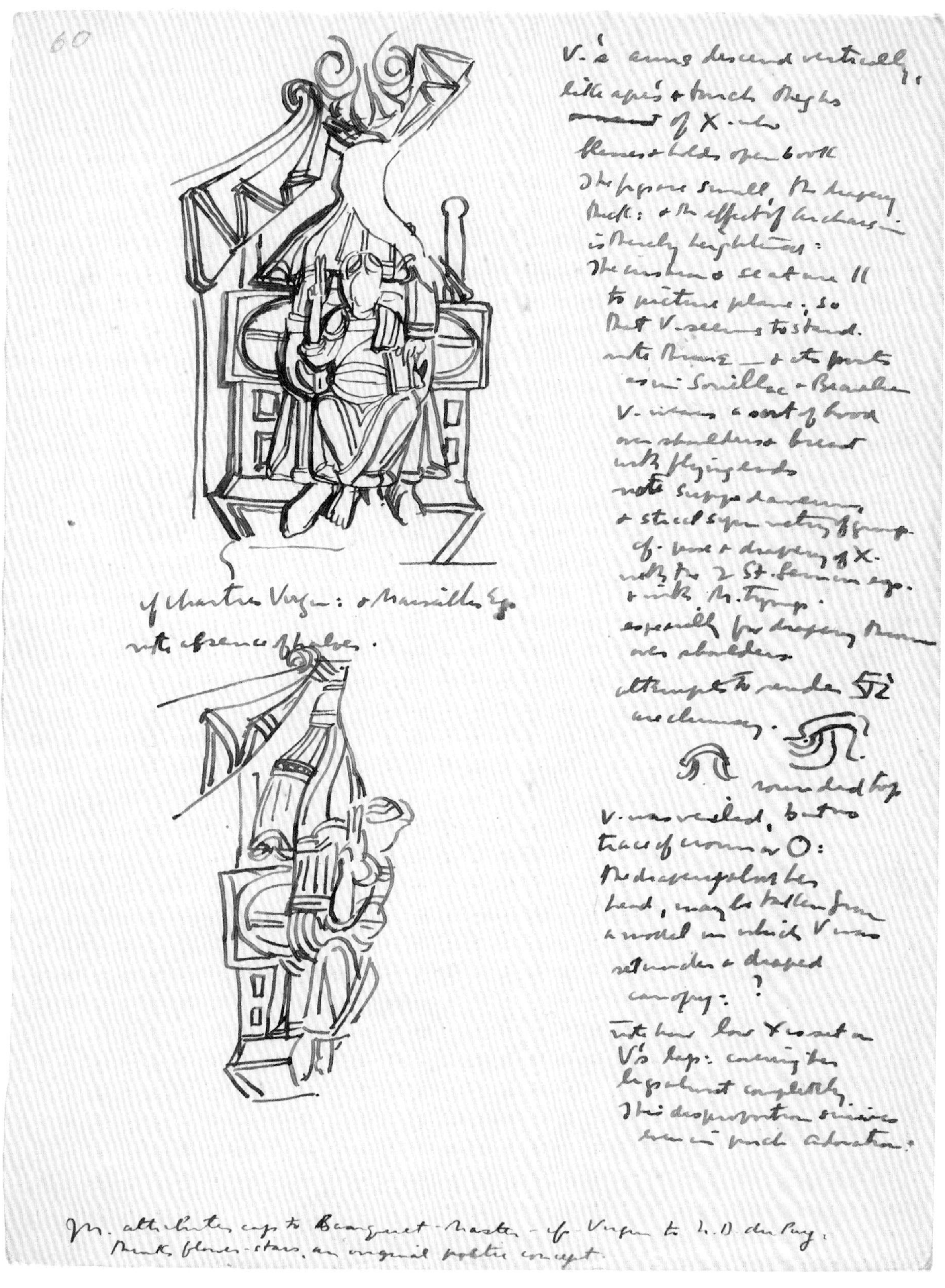

No. 75. Moissac, Abbaye de Saint-Pierre, 3–18 September 1927

Views of northeast corner of Capital 32, Adoration of the Magi

Black ink on paper

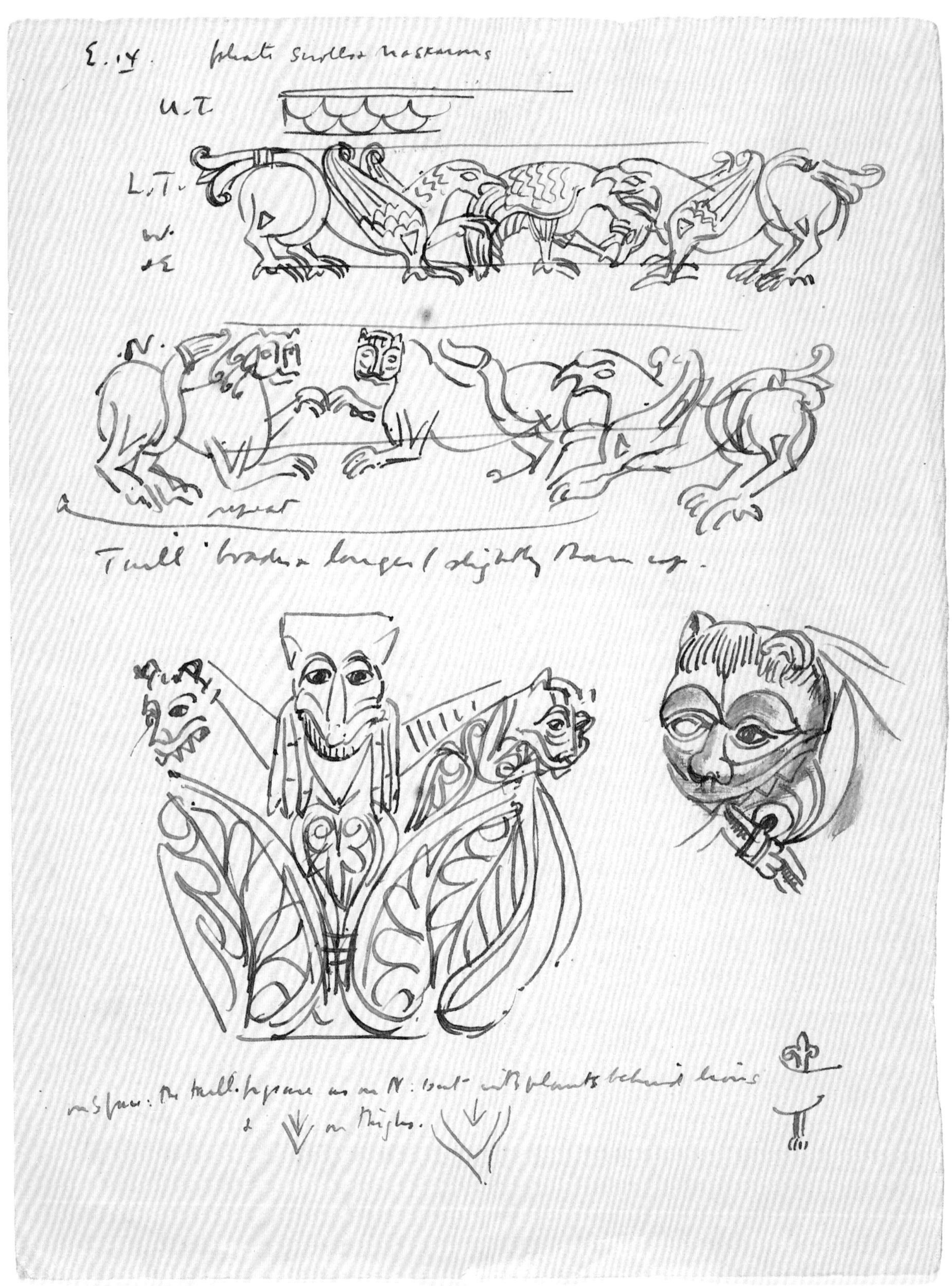

No. 76. Moissac, Abbaye de Saint-Pierre, 3–18 September 1927

Tailloirs and narrow side of Capital 33, Foliage

Black ink on paper

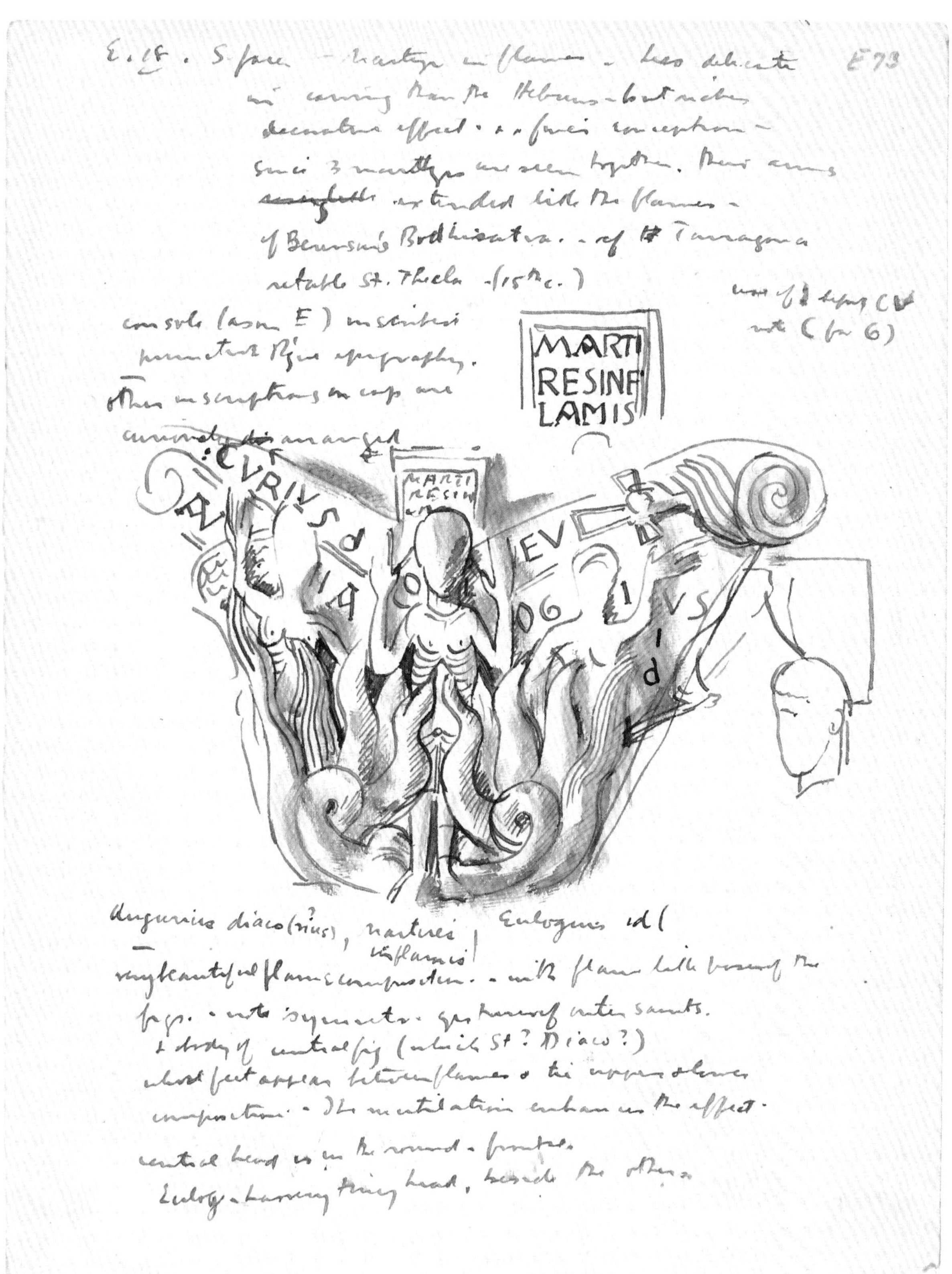

No. 77. Moissac, Abbaye de Saint-Pierre, 3–18 September 1927

South face of Capital 37, Martyrdom of Fructuosus, Eulogius, and Augurius

Black ink on paper

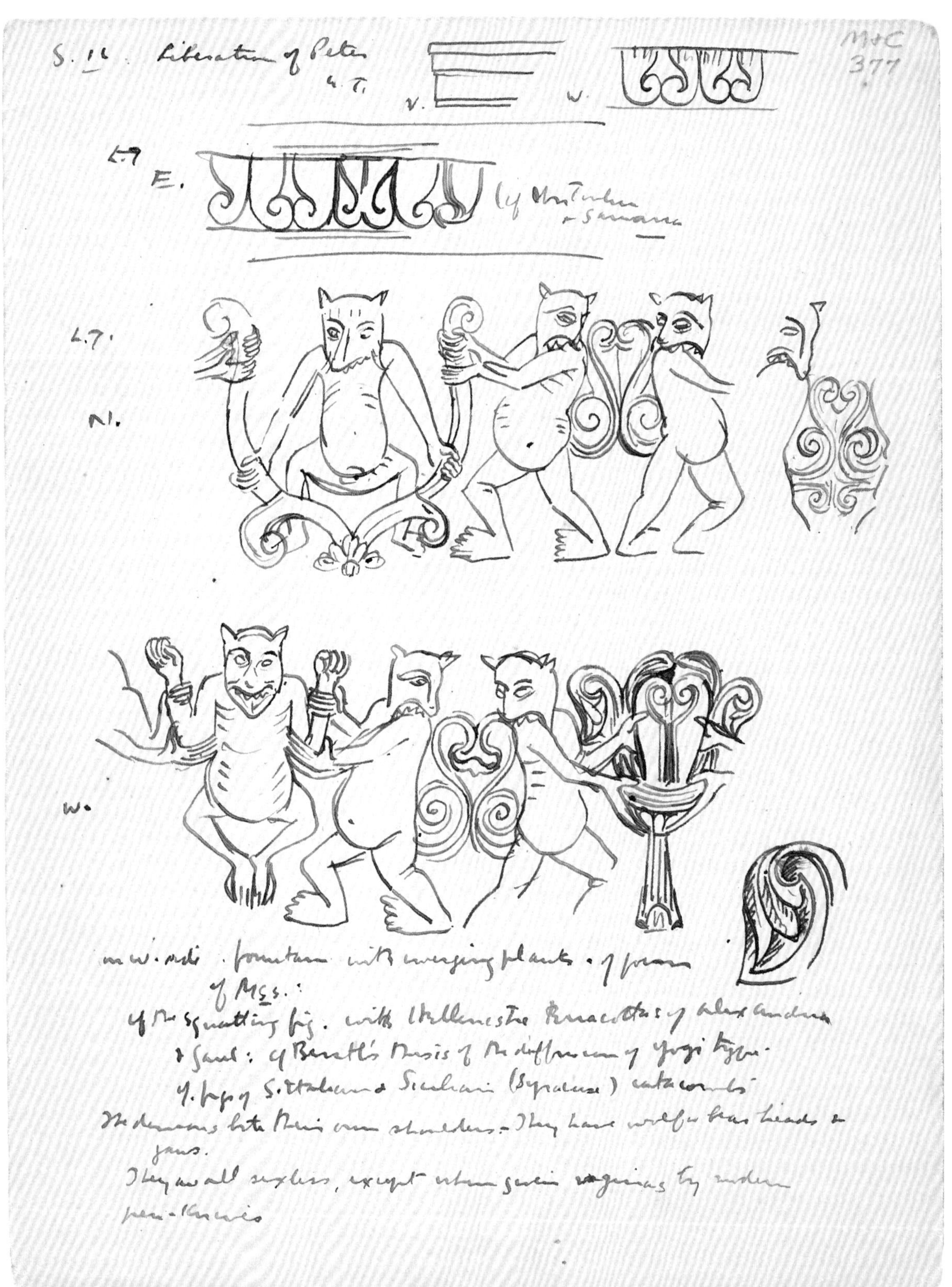

No. 78. Moissac, Abbaye de Saint-Pierre, 3–18 September 1927
Details of tailloirs of Capital 17, Deliverance of Peter
Black ink on paper

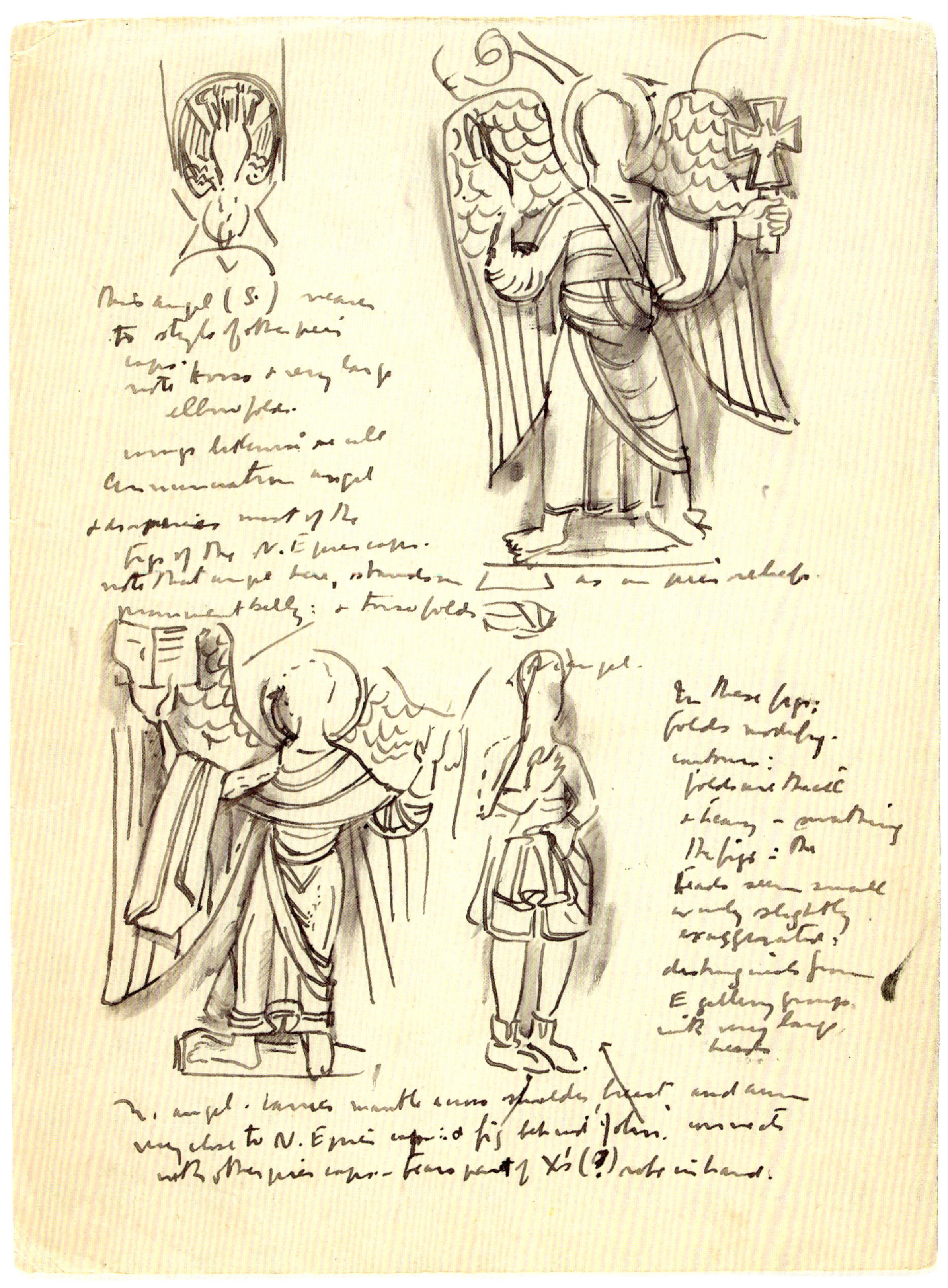

No. 79. Moissac, Abbaye de Saint-Pierre, 3–18 September 1927

Details of faces of Capital 18, Baptism of Christ

Black ink on paper

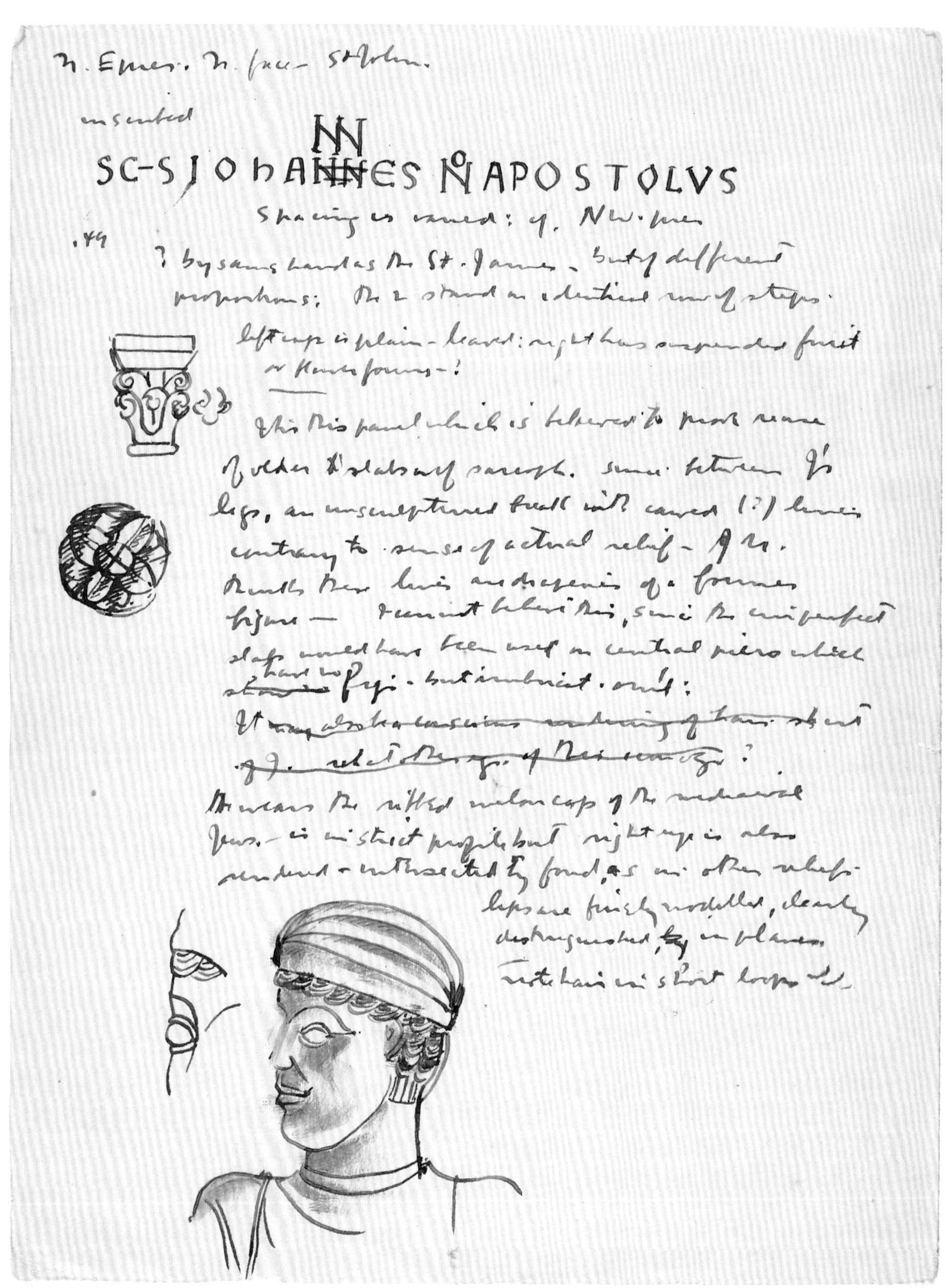

No. 80. Moissac, Abbaye de Saint-Pierre, 3–18 September 1927

Details of north face of northeast pier, John

Black ink on paper

Note on the Travel Notebook Transcriptions

The notebook pages have been transcribed in blocks, moving from left to right and top to bottom. Squares indicate new blocks, and vertical lines denote line breaks.

Emendations essential to the reader's understanding have been placed in square brackets. Editorial comments appear in italic in square brackets, noting, for example, illegible phrases or use of pencil. Where the reading of a word was uncertain, it is followed by an italic question mark in square brackets. Empty brackets indicate an editorial deletion, usually involving punctuation.

Underlining has not been noted.

Where it was possible to make out a crossed-out word, we have reproduced the word struck through.

Alphabetic drawings of initials and opening words found in manuscripts have been treated as drawings and thus not transcribed.

Throughout the notebooks, Schapiro used abbreviations and symbols. Instead of expanding his shorthand in the transcriptions, abbreviations and symbols have been transcribed as they appear on the page. His most common abbreviations and symbols include the following:

∠	angle, angles, angled
⊙	circle, circular
†	cross
‖	parallel
⊥	perpendicular
△	triangle, triangular
c.	century, circa
col	column, columns
f	folio
frag't	fragment
L. T.	Lower Tailloir
M.	Moissac
N. D.	Notre-Dame
no	number
orn't	ornament
r	recto
Romanq	Romanesque
Rque	Romanesque
Sa.	Santiago
S. D. S.	Santo Domingo de Silos
T.	Toulouse
T. D.	Tief Dunkel
tymp	tympanum
U. T.	Upper Tailloir
v	vault, verso, vide, voir
V	Virgin
X	Christ, Christian, or cross
X'd	crossed

No. 1. Cherbourg, Église de Sainte-Trinité, 10 July 1926

▪ Cherbourg: Eglise Catholique de S. Trinité | Place Napoleon Ste. Trinité ▪ nave—5 [*crossed out, text illegible*] bays—cylindrical | piers decorated with zig-zags & | scrolls between—painted | narrow cavetto caps | penetrating archivolt | mouldings—scroll painted | spandrels: shaft divides spandrels | but does not reach capital & is | itself separated from the vault | ribs by a horizontal triforium | parapet sculptured screen with | scenes from the Passion against a | diapered gold ground.—the sculpture | is painted blue red & flesh color. | The spandrel shaft terminates below on a triangular | corbelling which instead of being attached to the | wall produces a bud. | On the aisle sides the nave cols have their | shafts attached, about 10 ft high.— | (The nave cols. from base to cap are not more than ~~10~~ 15 ft— | & the vault crown c. 55 ft.) | The arches are low pointed segments | over-numerous mouldings. | The clerestory windows are small | The " system [*clerestory*] | wall ribs spring from | pilaster of rectangular | section—while the | diagonal & transverse spring without | caps by interpen-etrat. from the | shaft attached to the pilaster which | appears as rising above the [] nave | column ▪ longitudinal ridge rib with pendants—large at the diagonal | inter-section: & smaller at the transversals.

No. 2. Nantes, Musée Dobrée, 17 July 1926

▪ Nantes, Musée Dobrée [*later addition by Lillian Schapiro*]| Romanesque. ▪ from above front side ▪ central fig. has double set of eyes: 1 set on cheeks. | all pupils are drill holes.— | all hair & wings incised with || & herringbone | patterns. & spiral ending. | but left monsters hair is knobbed. | hollowed leaf lines [*drawing*] section of leaf

No. 3. Le Mans, Église de Notre-Dame-de-la-Couture, 23 July 1926

▪ arches have | smaller stones | than walls. | in Romanesque | parts[?] ▪ stilted | round | arches. ▪ 1st nave wall pier. ▪ pillar | column piers of many | stones in one course | at least 2. | cf. Gothic where | there is one) ▪ choir bay | Romanesque | much restored in | places. ▪ alternation of 1 stone & 2 or 3 | red brick courses in | ambulatory arches | & in transept. ▪ fine set of Romanesque | caps in ambulatory | & crypt: | foliate, interlace | & figures | monsters | & Biblical scenes | mss types ▪ note slanting | caps | on central | cluster ▪ tympanum | over N. Transept | w. doorway | has opus reticulatum | arch has 1 stone, 2 brick | alternation ▪ clere-story windows

No. 4. Paris, Musée du Louvre, August 1926

▪ care of the [*missing*] dressing, the curls [*line not visible in image*] | & regularity [*crossed out, text illegible*] enhance the effect of cruelty— | & remind me of the cruel Caesars, & the modern | conception of deliberate villains. | The goose (or "swan"—catalogue) bends[?] at the ends | of the bow are a fine conception: | —a piece of | assyrian introversion[?]. | The arrangement of arm, bow & sword, etc are interesting | as ∠ line design & could be studied | profitably by modern abstraction painters | note huge ear-~~ring~~pendant—"arrow head".—wrist & arm rings | sandals finely laced ▪ 31) details of heads as above | note double chin of beardless fig | ear pendants varied: | bearded fig has | ridged neck. | as in african figs | arm bracelets. ▪ both are sandaled as | on 32. & right foot | forward. | the body absolutely flat | under clothing— | even legs: cf above. ▪ swords ▪ upper border (diagonal) of stola has | 3 bands of squares. | (cf necks of triforium | monsters of St. Sernin) ▪ stola—rendering of | wool by || grooves or | long strips. ▪ fringes

No. 5. Auxerre, Musée d'Auxerre, 4 September 1926

▪ Gall Rom fragt ▪ LX. Arch fragments: | monolith ▪ cf. Esper[endieu] ▪ cornucopia ▪ rosettes | egg & dart ▪ 2½ ft × 5 ft | 20—sarcoph. lid | cf Nantes ▪ acanthus | stylized ▪ cable moulding under cap. | note 3 mouldings of arch. cf Romanesque | fine flat carving of spandrel fig. with | beautiful linear [*drawing*]. ▪ XLII: stele. 3+ ft: × 1 ft. | birds paired on top of tree | tree ||| & one bird on lower | left—the leaves are | acanthus in | profile or ½ palmettes ▪ XXXVI Gall. Rom. ▪ 91—Cast of Vezelay Ecclesia Key Stone. ▪ The standard is carried back to the wall & not | detached, note its margins | knee folds ▪ Crown: | developed modelling, torso & lap—but ~~feet~~ legs | far apart & their folds with one exception | do not modify leg contour. whole fig—quite flat | in pose ▪ incised breast lines:— | note how space is filled out— || incised folds, | but also in larger modeled draperies | drilled eyeholes ▪ profile ▪ note paleography—which seems more | archaic than Cluny caps—

No. 6. Auxerre, Cathédrale de Saint-Étienne, 4 September 1926

▪ Auxerre | Cathedral ▪ Square axis chapel (Virgin?) 2 bays on N & S, 3 bays on E. W. sides | note slender columns at entrance of chapel | cf St Serge Angers, choir & amb— ▪ note how | the wall | ribs are | detached from | the wall ▪ restored except for windows (or only 2 windows[ )] ▪ wall | passage | platform ▪ E N S. W ▪ plan | of corner ▪ This chapel gallery also usculates thru | the walls of the ambul—with same | arcatures on the lower wall beneath

No. 7. Vézelay, Basilique de Sainte-Madeleine, 5 or 6 September 1926

▪ Vezelay: interior | nave & aisles | 10 bays—each c. 18–20 ft wide ▪ wrong upper story | it terminates in | tribunes of narthex | wall. ▪ lower ▪ too narrow ▪ Vezelay | nave & aisles: inner west wall. | (last bay). ▪ 10 bays—each c. ▪ in narthex, the diagonal | ribs are differently | handled— | N. aisle wall. ▪ the arcs avoided | in narthex | nave ▪ diag ▪ but in aisle piers: diag. groin starts | lower than on wall, & in between the | other ribs ▪ in narthex | nave [*crossed out, text illegible*] (except | E. bay) the | groins spring | from yet lower | pt. than in | aisles, but still | above rib springs ▪ diags ▪ doubleau

No. 8. Tournus, Église de Saint-Philibert, 11 September 1926

▪ Tournus — St Philibert ▪ nave ▪ narthex | wall ▪ 3.70 m. | 5.45 m | level ▪ 1.27 | 5.45 m ▪ 5 bays. | square aisle bays — groin vaulted | transept barrel vaulted | crossing — cloister vault on corner tromps. ▪ narthex — 3 aisles: the bas | cotés narrower than those of | the church; — & with transverse | barrels; while the center | aisle has groin v. | — pillars & ½ | pill. as in church

No. 9. Autun, Cathédrale de Saint-Lazare, 11–12 September 1926

▪ Autun St Lazare (Beggar at the portal) ▪ nave has 7 bays | barrel vault pointed | on doubleaux ▪ doubleaux of nave ▪ aisles groin vaulted | doubleaux pointed ▪ col ▪ the pilast. arches | & moulds are | very flat ▪ cols. ▪ 2 flutes | blind | wall | niche | deep set | with | barrel | vault ▪ aisle doubleaux | The aisle groins spring from | higher than the doubleaux, | from the | pt. of tang- | ency of | doubleaux | & wall | ribs ▪ rosettes ▪ 5 flutes in | pilaster | partout ▪ pier base plan ▪ cf Vezelay ▪ nave bay ▪ nave arch | section | pier crown | mould. ▪ arcade of 7 (blind) | fluted | pil. ▪ termination of fluting ▪ base moulding | of nave pier ▪ in same[?] there is a modelled | pier at the end. ▪ note nave upper widening ▪ transept N. wall. | barrel vaulted — | transverse[?] to nave ▪ crossing cloister vault

No. 10. Autun, Bibliothèque municipale, MS Lat. 3, 11–12 September 1926

▪ f 13fr[?] Q of 3 fishes ▪ f 15fr[?] — A of fish & bar of interlace (— 3 continuous): | green, red, yellow, white ▪ 21^r P. | green ▪ f48^v ▪ 22^r N | green ▪ 32^v | 1 interlace as | bar f 47^r | 3 strands ▪ f.28^v I^N ills | white | green | & yellow ▪ similar bird but | with interlace band | instead of plumage | on 29^r. ▪ 33^r ▪ bird's head? | cf S. Russia | & fibula orn. ▪ — 3 band interlace | ~~red~~ yellow | green | white | on black gr ▪ 38^r | the crests | occur on bird | [*illegible*] 179^v. | also spiral wing ▪ 34^r — Bird & serpent as T. | also 56^r | (& with 2 birds as M f59^r) | note the great skill in | drawing birds — cf | provenance of birds in | barbarian metal | (Lombardy etc) — but in | quite different forms | prolong ▪ 36^r

No. 11. Nevers, Église de Saint-Étienne, 14 September 1926

▪ nave St Etienne, Nevers ▪ transept ▪ n. side ▪ apse. ▪ ~~banded shaft~~ a modern | hoop for strength. ▪ note stilting of height | of aisle pier shaft to | raise height of aisle | doubleaux. ▪ 6 nave bays — barrel v. ▪ caps are bases | with a few geometr. | & stylized except- | ions — ▪ aisles groin vaulted — | no wall archs — | note — spring of groins |& shape of doubleaux | Easternmost nave bay has inner | engaged shaft corbelled half way down ▪ S. aisle windows are more deeply | splayed & have smaller outer | openings than the N. ▪ triforium has wall arcade

| springing from floor | without base or cap ▪ tribune over west bay of church | gives fine [*crossed out, text illegible*] view of whole interior

No. 12. Moulins, Cathédrale de Notre-Dame, 15 September 1926

▪ X The west facade is exactly symmetrical—part for part—unusual in so large | a building & testifies to the basic | academicism of V. | le Duc's feeling for | Gothic ▪ ~~Boudins~~ archivolt ▪ order | triunate[?] | at head | likewise | below ▪ plan of | tower ▪ statue ▪ buttress | cantonned | on outer | corners ▪ side gallery: section | inner portals—similar mould'gs | & profiles, but side portals | have stilted arches & reach | same height as center—& have | same no of [*crossed out, text illegible*] jamb cols—10 | tymp are painted | (modern) ▪ bullet string | under cornice | cf Nevers | colored stone brown & | cream in rose window | & tower arches ▪ gateway of | cathedral ▪ dark | stone ▪ porch portal (center) has 10 full cols in jamb ∠s. | billet mould'g ~~under~~ in tailloir hollow | only 2 such cols on side portals. ▪ portal on S.(E) side | of nave: 2 stilted | arch-gables, 4 | jamb cols ▪ caps of leaves, with lobes hollow & convex ▪ archivolts ▪ The bottom piers ~~mould'g~~ | is [*illegible*] supported by | modillions ▪ jamb free edges are | cantonned ▪ billet | jamb | tailloir ▪ bases | note hollowing

No. 13. Moulins, Musée Anne de Beaujeu, 15 September 1926

▪ Museum, Moulins: | Fine coll of Gallo-Roman Kleinplastik & fragts. ▪ 342. Basalt Bust of Man—Gauloise:—fine pieces. ▪ 345. Terracotta: Apollo? —crocket spiral hairs: | 349: from Beaune (Allier) | River Goddess? | cf the Aachen ivories | & the Coptic || s | 543 traces of | wings behind | a Nike | on sphere ▪ 324— | Bronze lamp ▪ 306: Fig in niche, female—Primitive. ▪ Gallo R. axes, spears, ▪ 44. Incised bowl geometrical designs (bronze[ )] | Large Bronze Necklace with pendants. ▪ 47 | bronze

No. 14. Paray-le-Monial, Musée eucharistique du Hiéron, 16 September 1926

▪ Musée Hieron: Paray le Monial ▪ Portal of Anzy le Duc.—yellow stone, reddish-pinkish from | paint. cf Vezelay ▪ tymp. Christ in Majesty in Mandorla supported by | 2 angels: on lintel: Virgo Lactans & 8 Sts. | Jamb shaft caps (4) each with a single fig.— | The tymp is c. 7 ft wide at diameter; the Christ | is deep—arch has no key but ▪ Christ cross-nimbed, blesses | & book in lap. | Incised pupil | moustache—lock of | hair on shoulder ▪ archivolt | orn | one on each | voussure ▪ note horizontal | drapery across | lap—& also the |torso band (cf M.) | the piece falling | from the right | arm is not | clear. ▪ angels have backs | turned to Christ | note wings of left angel ▪ & neck fold. ▪ note | seat has | no foot rest ▪ folds are [*crossed out, text illegible*] later | Vezelay develop't ▪ cf Mss. ▪ The head seems more archaic | than the body folds. ▪ Lintel: Child plays with exposed breast: (cf Saqqara) | slit collar—fine network of || lines. (head of child restored) Madonna's veil in Byz. | fashion slung over 1 shoulder | ~~yellow~~ cf 2nd left fig with M. Peter | & Isaiah ▪ St Peter has X legs.— | several of the fig ▪ Note ∠ poses—¾ of | The caps voluted ▪ females at right have folds | note classic lines | & | cf attic relief | & & ▪ 2 caryatids with | scrolls—seated | & 2 others | against foliage | seated with a scroll | band horizontal ▪ knee folds as in M.

No. 15. Charlieu, ruins of the Abbaye Bénédictine, 19 September 1926

▪ Orn—The triple ~~W.~~ E. arcade is vertically orn—outer archivolt surrounds | all 3, & bends—has leaf orn: hollowed ▪ 2nd archivolt: (center) palmettes with varying no of | petals & form. 3) spiral fluting ▪ Caps & Tailloirs ▪ Corinthoid—1) acanthus with grapes pendant | from central lobe tip ▪ ~~Eagle~~ Bird with human | head ▪ incised pupil | eye well | modelled ▪ Bases. ▪ on ~~W.~~ E. arcade; the base tori are orn.

No. 16. Rodez, Musée de la Ville, 24 September 1926

▪ Rodez Musée de la Ville. ▪ 234 Cast of Roman medallion with portrait bust: profile—original in | marble—similar busts made in Renaiss—cf House of | Armagnac (Rodez) ▪ Moulds for terra cotta lamps—Gallo-R. ▪ Meroving. Fibulae from Louyri ▪ Bronze. | cloisons | cloisons | cloisons ▪ interlace—not clear—late, broken | down, but forms | with varied symmetry | traces of claws & | feet & perhaps eyes ▪ cloisons ▪ [*crossed out, text illegible*] nut ▪ holes joined | by incised | line. | note decay of | "absidioles" | vs cloisons ▪ cf Gundohinus ▪ former meplat & | relief patterns | merely incised ▪ ajouré ▪ Lion's heads in relief ▪ 4 to 5″ long

No. 17. Conques, Abbatiale de Sainte-Foy, 26–28 September 1926

▪ N. Trifor:—Inner trifor. arch (discharge falls on a corbel head. | 1. Twin nave shaft: ~~Col.~~ Taill. in 3 bands, not clear | 2. Cap & [*illegible*]—one beast with his head on the other—not clear | the jaws open, teeth show;—is this | love or strife—cf the opposite cap on | S. of the horses—note tails, ribs | ribbed legs à l'orient— ▪ W. trif. arc—twin caps—on S. side—Flat seated fig—head in higher | relief (as in animals)—plain Taill—head disproport. large. | flat overlapp. ∠ folds left arm not clear | note archaic style of westmost cap (highest) | position therefore no exact indication | of date of carving— ▪ Caryatid—(note sleeves)— | one on each cap. leaf & spiral between | grooved leaf ▪ shoe ▪ 3. Center cols: | Taill: thick ½ palm. rinceaux. ▪ note how spiral leaf changes into ▪ Cap. on S. face: St Michael—v. photo. | Framed by corner banana shaped pendants—beautif compos— | Flat grooved drapery in || lines—wings incised—ptd shield— | huge hand—but good gesture—from earlier classic | model(?)—note torso band—incised ▪ On each side a lion, adossed to lion of adjoining | cap—foliate tip tails interlacing grooved | features ▪ on the E. | face they | are griffons | birds heads. | [*crossed out, text illegible*] interlaced | tails— | wings divided | in 2 parts | bearded (?) | birds | beaks touch | wing tip ▪ cf lion's hair | with Nantes | cap. ▪ on n. face—2 birds ~~affronted~~ adossed | chalice between—high stand

No. 18. Toulouse, Basilique de Saint-Sernin, 2–26 October 1926
▪ St Sernin—transverse section ▪ note [*crossed out, text illegible*] the point of | abutment of the ½ triforium | arch—above the spring of the | nave vault: at its haunch. | likewise in transept (S.) ▪ too wide? | & too tall ▪ same width | as higher | aisle ▪ transverse section ▪ South side

No. 19. Toulouse, Basilique de Saint-Sernin, 2–26 October 1926
▪ St Sernin: South Portal. ▪ archivolts, practically identical | with those of W. portal ▪ bro[a]den a little. | in jamb corners are | engaged colonnettes | cantonnés—terminating | below in ▪ Cornice:—supported by 8 | modillions: of copeaux | type: but with grotesques, | grapes, animals & human | heads—modern restorations | not clear— | note rosettes in soffits | & in wall between modill's. | cf Lescure—some of the latter | are ancient. ▪ likewise in soubassement ▪ West | but note change of | motif on inner | tailloir | v. notes on | caps ▪ East

No. 20. Toulouse, Basilique de Saint-Sernin, 2–26 October 1926
▪ Ambul. figs: Christ ▪ inscribed init: ▪ border of robe ▪ profile of folds ▪ border of | glory ▪ zigzag folds with V section | at right behind | book ▪ flat nose | heavy chin | projecting lower lip ▪ bas ▪ left arm foreshortened.—no fore arm represented: | Matthew symbol head—like those of portal caps. & trifor. caps. | & the smaller seraphim—face almost identical with | seraph at right (Possidet etc)—likewise hair except for | horizontal band—note lap folds ▪ note that only the smaller reliefs are inscribed; only the larger | (3 of them) have bevelled arches

No. 21. Moissac, Abbaye de Saint-Pierre, 28 October–5 November 1926
▪ South ~~North South~~ Gallery—4th cap twin | upper taill inscribed ▪ Haec e(st) Babel in magna quam | ego haedificavi ▪ hidae ▪ Babel ▪ Ego haedificavi Tibi Dicitur ~~Rex~~ Nabuchodonosor ▪ te sedet ▪ super te—none haec ▪ L. T. palmettes with scroll stems.—v. photo. Same style as S. 2. | only the motif is varied: symmetrical leaf & scroll. | note binding of stems—drill hole in Kreisblatt [*drawing*] | The motif is really the S2. palmette doubled | There are 2 asymmetrical palmettes: 2 hollows—divided | by a central lobe—If in S2 the scroll was turned ~~back~~ ahead | once at each alternate ⊙ we would have an approach to this motif. ▪ In the ∠ ▪ base of cap has a moulding ▪ Cap. N. face | The lower arches are heavily archivolted | engaged jamb cols. represented | cf heads in 2nd story with Mss | &

ivories. ▪ Ridged volute | leaves ▪ On E face—triple arcade: under center arch—seated King with Xd legs | mantle buckled in center— ▪ note his boots: exactly like | boots of Magi on porch. | & of the Signs in Toulouse ▪ Note shape of | arch—is this an | imitation | of Persian | ovoid arches or domes?

No. 22. Moissac, Abbaye de Saint-Pierre, 28 October–5 November 1926

▪ [*crossed out, text illegible*] PETER cap (cont'd) on S. face ▪ at left: fig. seated in profile—legs crossed on a cushion— | huge ⊙ disk—orn'td with rosette center & beaded borders: | behind him, a col & ½ arch that ends with his head | The col is spiral fluted; with high base | & cap: of 2 rows of leaves—which are ribbed | & incised the arch ▪ The disk is very thick ▪ The seated fig (~~High Priest~~ Nero? [*in pencil*]) is obviously later than | those of the other caps: His proportions are new: very | tall—with small head—the feet are less archaic in | pose. one frontal, the other profile. | The body is strongly modelled; especially thigh & buttock | and a large series of overlapping planes: eg the | mantle falls behind the cushion & reappears under it | against the col which it encircles ▪ a long flying fold as on the portal | rear bas also carved: sleeve border orn'td | right foot on cap base; left on ⊙ foot rest | finely modelled left hand—detailed & | careful study: disproportionately long fingers | right arm undercut & detached from | ground: right sleeve deeply cut in hollow | He seems to be adjusting his left sleeve— | & adressing the saint at the right ▪ At the right 2 figs—headless—debout | one leads the saint away, holding his | left wrist & shoulder (right) | The st's draperies are free & curved. ▪ cf St. Benoit of | Porch costume

No. 23. Poitiers, Église de Saint-Porchaire, 9–14 November 1926

▪ Porch: (base of tower) interior barrel vault from | crown moulding, as above, but || to axis of church | broad doubleaux from pilaster at E. ▪ E ▪ E. ▪ W ▪ square ▪ the 4 portal cols bear 11th c. caps. ▪ S. ▪ N. ▪ rosette? in tail end? | lozenge ▪ left ▪ inner cap: | affronted lions | !* & combination of sacred tree | & vase base—trefoil leaf—each | lobe with 1 drill hole. | note the 2 E's in inscription | bodies in meplat—heads in higher relief | but really in 2 planes—formed by upper cap. | nose being the ∠ & sharp line: ▪ note teeth | as in Languedoc ▪ outer cap. on right side: 2 birds drinking from high-stemmed vase. | grotesque head above ~~cup~~ vase in cap ∠—palmette scrolls—grooved | issue from his jaw—From "tail" | left bird interlace bands which | perhaps issued from destroyed | left scroll— ▪ human[?] other side with hand in volute | corner: tail is forked—1 end in mouth— | other ▪ In center: opposed | lions, cf tree with | opposite cap: nt lozenge | on flank. cf Moissac. | at right another lion whose | head is common to the right | lion of the heraldic group ▪ Right: Inner—

No. 24. Poitiers, Église de Notre-Dame-la-Grande, 11 November 1926

▪ Poitiers — N. D. la Grande — Romanesque. | narrow, low — church: | nave: 7 bays & tribune: barrel vault on doubleaux | abutted by high-aisle X groin vaults, massive walls. | The barrel v. is surbaissé. ▪ curved ▪ the pier between | 1st & 2nd W. bays | is heavier than | the others — larger | core (longitud- | inally) ▪ S. | porch ▪ no bases ▪ nave section ▪ elevation of nave bay. ▪ aisle doubleaux carry wall up to stilted arch which raises vault arch | crowns to c. same level: — [*crossed out, text illegible*] the wall arch crown seems | higher the vault crown but this may be perspective | illusion — aisle bays are rectangular — [*crossed out, text illegible*] longer from E to W. | nave bays do not all seem to be of same span — 2nd (W) & 1st W. | are broader than the others — painted longitudinal — | barrel vault crown line, shows vault crown to be irregular | & deviating from bay to bay.

No. 25. Poitiers, Église de Notre-Dame-la-Grande, 11 November 1926

▪ West façade (N. D. la Grande, Poitiers) Nov 11: (Armistice Day) ▪ The façade is perfectly | symmetrical architecturally | except for a few details — | what enlivens this regularity | is the variety of ornament | & sculpture & the symmetry | from top to bottom; the | differences between the | central members of each | stage & the nice proportions | also the contrast of line | between the arches & the | roof contour — the richness | of detail tends to subordinate | the larger symmetrical | parts ▪ portal archivolt ▪ Architect. note enriching[?] of all lines & curves by orn't — dentil raking | cornice (or billets of large size) — curved outline of gables | note finial — upper pediment △ constructed of | reticulate stones — | note shape of △ — cf outline | of stone courses. ▪ pediment finial broken ▪ Base of △ decorated with continuous course of pine-cones ▪ pediment cornice of 2 sizes — upper — little billets — 2 rows? | — lower large billets or dentil & [*illegible*]

No. 26. Poitiers, Église de Notre-Dame-la-Grande, 11 November 1926

▪ The corner turrets — gables rest on ~~table~~ arched corbel table | with modillion heads: The corbel form is interesting, | not simply a deep arch, but niched in cul de four | or rather in a half cloister vault | since the plan is square or rectang. | cf Syria: this found in all | the corbel tables of the façade — ▪ On the arched surface — boutons, fleurons & balls. | one of these recalls Moissac narthex & porch. ▪ several are unornt'd | modillions — animal & human heads — several foliate ▪ The corbel crowns ~~an open arcade~~ a turret story — ⊙ in plan | ~~of~~ with 4 round arches on its W & N. W. ~~sides~~ arcs. (W & S. W. | on S. side) | falling, (in the N. turret) on clustered | colonnettes — short & thick — 3 groups of 4? each — may be 3 | & at the ends & open[?] — 2 sets of 2 each. | The arcade is in 2 orders & the outer décor with a | continuous string. ▪ The caps of each group form | a unit with a single tailloir of | foliate & geom. orn't (1 with billets) | tailloirs ▪ main orn't | double band | cf Perigueux & Ang[oulême] ▪ lower leaves have | more lobes than upper ▪ caps. | 2 opposed beasts with 1 head ▪ Bases of cols. not clear — seem to be | lower torus heavier

No. 27. Paris, Bibliothèque nationale de France, MS n.a.l. 1438, November 1926

▪ p 5 | Quoniam ▪ QVIT | MULTI CONATI S etc. ▪ note use of color as in p.1. & in later mss (the bright red yellow | reminds me of the Beatus group & cf Merovingian mss | the trefoils are curiously designed—in festoons.—a primitive | form (cf [*drawings*]: Celtic metals & pottery, etc.) ▪ The orn't is more regular than my drawing indicates: | The word is uncertain to me. Is it QM̄ (?) | Quoniam | In quit ▪ The fish (theriomorphic Ω) seems to be a specific form | rather than a generalized [*drawing*])—cf Merovingian [*in pencil, added after 1931*] | note rounding out of letters by [*drawing*] or [*drawing*] ▪ p 11: Capital F of Fuit inquit indiebus herodis etc. ▪ a crude purple nearer to | sepia ▪ 12 long ▪ The 1st 8 | lines of text | are in verm- | illion rustics | touched with | yellow. [*text from "a crude purple" through "yellow" added, probably in 1931*] ▪ yellow | purple. | interlace—white on black ▪ cf. interlace, animal head & leaf finial | with later types 1491 et alia | The pages seem to have been | resewn to the cores in such a way | that the inner margins are | partly lost & the initial ends | difficult to see— ▪ cf 1441, f62vo | sepia

No. 28. Paris, Bibliothèque nationale de France, MS n.a.l. 1491, November 1926

▪ note on P of 111—stalks intersect leaves & pass thru | them—Note that the trefoil leaf does not occur | in this large letter ▪ [*drawing*] p 111 note M d & c & b | [*drawing*] on p 110 ▪ Note rectangle on outer side of P ⊙—in | blue & yellow—blue is ultramarine | rather than cobalt of my crayon ▪ p 117 ▪ p 133 P—bird's head terminates ▪ p 135 ▪ 133 P ▪ 6 × 9 ▪ p 139 I, | note leaves curled around | stalks or bands of the letter ▪ red | centers | blue & | green | lobes | note leaf in center | of cloven stalk | of Q | also on Q of 158 | but in flying band | likewise Q | on Q of 171 ▪ p 145: bird at head | of [*drawing*]: but with | ears ▪ p 142: Q | end of Q ▪ p 183: note large | leaves & flourishing | scroll lines—veins | rendered by ||s & dots ▪ bl ▪ p 185 interlace on bar of | I—cf one continuous | band & 3 ⊙s or ◎ ▪ red, gr, bl

No. 29. Paris, Bibliothèque nationale de France, MS n.a.l. 1496, November–December 1926

▪ 1496: f 35 cf Montpellier Fa.M.30 ▪ on green fond. black | pen drawing with ~~gre~~ red | border & green inner line. | giving plastic effect in | places, but not partout. | cf the curling of stem & | leaves over outer ⊙ stem | with Winchester, Poitou, | & La Daurade tailloir— | Is this found in Burgundy? ▪ radial scroll scheme—symmetrical as a group— | but varied details—fine || lines for shading | & relief of central bird or | fruit. (?)— | note "eyes" between leaves: | as in Corinthian acanth- | us—develop't of 3rd | dimension in ~~use of~~ | enwrapping of one stem | by another. ▪ f35vo | red & yellow | black line | cf 11th & 10th c. mss | of Cluny

| esp. for ends: ▪ f41vo | black pen drawing. | details in red & | yellow & black | green fond. | yellow leaves: | rough application | of paint: ▪ f41vo — | cf. 11th c. mss

No. 30. Paris, Bibliothèque nationale de France, MS n.a.l. 1461, November – December 1926

▪ N.A. Latin 1461: — Commentary of Rabanus Maurus | on Ecclesiastes — Delisle p 110/11: | dates it "end of 10th, 1st ½ of 11th — & identifies | it with #343 of 12th c. Catal. "Volumen in | quo continetur (Rabani stilus) in librum | Jhesu filii Sirach" ▪ it is included in the Consuet[udines] Farf[enses] list. | Wilmart pp 103, 104 | who dates it | XI, 1 [*text from "it is included" through "XI, 1" in blue ink*] | see Mercier for reprod. [*in pencil, added after 1931*] ▪ f1. Domino ▪ interlace is white on black fond. | green added after pen line details — the whole | drawing is remarkably smooth & skillful. | end of N is torn: ▪ cf. central grotesque of M with sculptured forms | note collar around griffins' necks: cf lacertines & biting | figs with 1438, 1455, etc. ▪ f6. ▪ f6

No. 31. Paris, Bibliothèque nationale de France, MS Lat. 3779, November – December 1926

▪ f121vo P ▪ white [*in pencil*] ▪ outlines in thin sepia. vermill & yellow | (& green) fond — sepia applied | solid to fill smaller spaces | or "cracks": — use of dots & | short lines for veins, etc — | also || lines: spiraliform | lobes of leaves: (cf Kreisblätter) | spiral knobs — interlace (note | central line (nehistreifig[*?*]) — zigzag | use of [*drawing*] in lobes — ½ palmettes: | [*drawing*] [*drawing*] | tail of upper center & beast joins to head of | upper left. ▪ height of text:

No. 32. Paris, Bibliothèque nationale de France, MS Lat. 1631, December 1926

▪ Latin 1631 — Origenis in Leviticum Homiliae XVI: | quarto — ~~f 67vo - 2 cols.~~ | 1st ½ of 12th: orn't style as in Latin 52: | some initials probably by same hand. ▪ Colbert 889 | Regius 3956 | 1 · a · ▪ M f 68vo, 12th c hand. | [*drawing*] ▪ 68ff, 290 × 195, 2 cols of 37 lines, miniscule | of c. 1100 ff [*?*] | dry rulings | N.S. quater. marked | at end of gathering [*drawing*] [*text from "M f 68vo" through "gathering" added later*] ▪ f 1. (photo) whole page: 18 × 24 | .125 | × .93 [*text from "f 1." through "× .93" added later*] ▪ S in red, blue & green | fond: — with red border: | foliate interlace — | animal heads as | ends with scrolls | issuing from jaws ▪ blue | outer, | green & | red inner | fond ▪ bl blue [*in drawing*] ▪ vermill ▪ pen drawn | letter & ornt ▪ red [*in pencil*] | neutral [*in pencil*] ▪ intense blue as in Limoges [*text from "blue | outer" through "Limoges" added later*] | cf the spiral leaf outline | with Cluny Mss. (3779) ▪ The most interesting part of the | page is not the initial — but the | caps below, one line of which imitates | a Kufic inscription ▪ sepia ▪ reserved

| on | vermill [*text from "sepia" through "vermill" added later*] ▪ a much clearer eg of | Kufic inspiration is the | inscribed & foliate border | of Dijon 132 f2 (Jerome | on Daniel—Oursel pl XLV ▪ sepia ▪ sepia verbū dei ex Maria in red: localizes | r. col—as significant [*text from "sepia" through "significant" added later*]

No. 33. Paris, Bibliothèque nationale de France, MS Lat. 1631, December 1926

▪ f3vo: red lines & details on green inner, blue outer | fond—no frame: .060 × .043 | very skillful drawing: thickened contours | firm lines [*text from ".060" through "firm lines" added later*] | f 7. in sepia & red lines ▪ photo | 9-12 | adjoining | inscr. in | sepia |vermill | sepia ▪ f6—upper marginal note is crowned by ▪ animal biting his own | legs & completely | turned in ⊙—photo 9-12 [*text from "animal biting" through "photo 9-12" added later*] ▪ f12—S in red lines of varying thickness— | .060 × .045 ▪ photo [*text from ".060" through "photo" added later*] ▪ f28vo—in red | .07[?] high [*text from "f28vo" through "high" added later*] | cf lat 7. ▪ developt of everted | forms: illusory | forms [*text from "developt" through second "forms" added later*] | f16vo in red, pink | (with sepia black details of feet & wings | .056. × .056 ▪ f34vo ▪ vermill | sepia | sepia | vermill ▪ inscr in sepia & vermill | is integral part of the | design. | B at bottom of f16vo. ▪ f25 [*text from "inscr" through "f25" added later*]

No. 34. Paris, Bibliothèque nationale de France, MS Lat. 1656A, December 1926–January 1927 or June 1927

▪ f 9 vo. [*drawing*] scroll—leaves issuing from inner | turn of stem, are curled around | the broad outer turn of | stem ▪ .059 × .060 | yellow is | B588/589 | gr = 905 | red = inter (322) 329, 330 (307) [*text from ".059" through "(307)" added later*] ▪ central blossom. ▪ note sheath- | ing [*this line, along with drawing above and below, from 1931*] | f16: P: cf Latin 52:—from which is derived the | fig. at the base?—The letter is unfinished.—the red | outer fond has been outlined, but its painting has | not gone farther than a tiny bit in the upper | left ▪ .50 | .162 | gr = 902? 905?| yell as in beast | of 1822 ▪ Blue is 1151 | but possibly | nearer to 1143 | originally. [*text from ".50" through "originally" added later*] ▪ note fine shading of fig: parallel lines ▪ The common color scheme; the resemblance of other initials in this | book to 52: the fig & animal & foliate types—point to a relation between | the 2: but the fig may be derived from a common model: or if | copied from 52: then copied from memory & not the actual model.

No. 35. Paris, Bibliothèque nationale de France, MS Lat. 2138, December 1926–January 1927 or June 1927

▪ L. 2138 (cont'd) ▪ photo | 9-12 [*"photo 9-12" added later*] ▪ f66vo ▪ the blue is much darker: | sepia outline: dot & dash | leaf modelling & veins | hair | cf 1822 f1—for fig & | beast on head | X legs: (cf Avianus ms.) ▪ 95 × 62. ▪ darker blue. [*text from "95" through "blue" added later*] ▪ 143 × 050 | deep | soft blue | dull flesh color ▪ f75vo. blue outer fond—red | outline: red dots, ⊙s. | etc,—yellow | fond of fig: cf. L.52. | acrobat: opposed beasts | with 1 head.—plastic curled | leaves ▪ f83: C with birds whose necks are | interlaced as in f58. | 98 × 82 [*"98 × 82" added later*] | wings have foliate forms & ends. | heavy foliage: red yellow blue, | green & pink, white colors. ▪ palmettes—yellow on red

No. 36. Paris, Bibliothèque nationale de France, MS Lat. 1822, December 1926–January 1927 or June 1927

▪ Latin 1822: Jerome—Comment on Jeremiah | late 11th ~~early 12~~th? ▪ Colbert 888 | Regius 3990 ▪ Delisle puts a ? mark after 1822 in his | list of Moissac mss—but I can hardly | doubt the Moissac origin.—cf L. 52.— | & 1656A (which is undoubted Moissac) | for miniatures & initial style— | Of course, I would like to believe it Moissac.— | & I adopt it over-easily than otherwise. | But if not from M. it is at least | sufficiently close in style to be grouped | with its school of illumination. ▪ 2 + 152 ff, 285 × 180, 32 long lls. | long lines (208 × 117)—min- | uscule of 2nd ½ 11th c.—quaternions in | Roman numbers ▪ f1. photo (hair side) | .13 [*text from "2 + 152 ff" through "13" added later*] ▪ 6¼ lines of caps altern. | red & black.—uncial with | several squares—pointed | O. [*drawing*] etc—no foliate ends. | [*drawing*] etc. next to the initial | (P) is a line in black with | green "shad- ows" ▪ The following details relate to sculpture: | 1) The head in the animals' jaws (was this | suggested remotely by classic | figs. or coin types with lion head | as headdress? note that fig's face | is quite remote from the Languedoc types— | The break of the mouth [*drawing*] does not | develop in sculpture till the end of | the Romanq. period. 2) The rendering | of hair on the "lion" & the spiral or curved | ends of the body lines: 3. The tail ending | in a leaf: cf. L. 52—etc. | 4.) The collar of the fig 5) his torso | folds. 6.) proportions & crossed legs as | in M. cloister: narrow shoulders.

No. 37. Cairo, Mausoleum of Al-Sayeda Ruqquyah, 12–22? February 1927

▪ Mausol. of | at Ruqqayah ▪ omit ▪ open ▪ black lines are wood panelling ▪ note porch—3 keel arches— | on 2 sets of twin cols. | & outer walls—wood | tie rods— ▪ omit ▪ note 2 niches beside | portal: ▪ crests ▪ remains of stucco ornt | on N. side ▪ relief | [*drawing; Ks indicates Kufic*] ▪ Kufic | Kufic ▪ 7 "ampulla" | gaufrée: checker & | grooved polygons ▪ side chamber niches: | ~~Kell~~ Keel arched scallop conch ▪ buttress on E: with gachis—may | be recent?

No. 38. Cairo, Mausoleum of Atteca, 12–22? February 1927

▪ Atiká Mausoleum brick ▪ do not touch ▪ note gachis ▪ higher ▪ maybe a later addition—fresh | bricks ▪ ornt ▪ ornt | dome of East chamber has lost its | stucco interior — simple brick. | no ribbing. as in W: | note: slight setting back of dome | window form repeats contour | of squinch arches. ▪ guilloche ▪ Kufic

No. 39. Jerusalem, Church of the Holy Sepulchre, 11–17 March 1927
▪ Ornt: tailloir mouldg (v. photo ▪ detailed meplat: rinceaux. — cf St Trophime cloister | ornt | The stones are not perfectly fitted | & the rinceaux is interrupted | at each joint — likewise the | egg & dart | leaf edge is [*drawing*] — drill holes | in leaf. pomegranates | in ⊙ as in Syrian. | richly detailed kelch for | issue of each leaf. ▪ bead & reel ▪ marble ▪ compact — ornt: ▪ archivolt hood mouldg. — ¼ round. | rinceaux — broader treatment | than lower one: but flat — deeply | undercut for T. D. | rosette center: cf Syrian, Coptic egs. | lobes are flat: with deep, sharp, knife | line incision — spiky & long. | in concentric lines. | note helix rosette. | carving of line in relief to bind stems | before kelch: ▪ lower cornice — note ressaut on E. end. ▪ alternate acanthus & spiral | bead & reel below — | Hohl kable[?] | egg ~~& dart~~ crown of console & between consoles | no dart ▪ deep cut | spiky | V grooved. ▪ or ▪ & ▪ palmette | ornt also | used in place | of spiral ▪ dentil radial leaf in soffit | square between | consoles ▪ ~~Acanthus~~ Lesbian | Cymatium ▪ spiky acanthus on console ▪ incised cable string ▪ egg & dart ▪ Lesbian Cymatium

No. 40. Jerusalem, Museum of Antiquities, 11–17 March 1927
▪ Early Bronze Age c 2000 B.C. | unpainted ware | hand turned ware: red, white, | grey, pinks: transverse | lug-holes — pierced | no slip or glaze — | holes at shoulder: & at center ▪ 4″ | 4 to 8″ high. ▪ [*crossed out, text illegible*] pots with more developed handles & spouts | show only very slight if any technical | advance: same thickness & surface. ▪ Large Pots: c. 10 to 16″ high ▪ no trace of lug hole: | simple horizontal | shelf at sides | similar small egs. |in one eg: the shelf is | modelled ▪ one large ~~low~~ pot: ball shaped: c. 18–20″ in diameter | egs. cf. shelf with diag. handle ▪ also ▪ moulded mouth ~~& neck~~.

No. 41. Damascus, Umayyad Mosque, 23–27 March 1927
▪ Ommayad Mosque. Dome. ▪ slightly | ptd horseshoe ▪ ptd | horseshoe ▪ S–N.

No. 42. Baalbek, Temple of Venus, 28 March 1927
▪ Baalbek: Circular Temple of Venus(?) | grand ~~appareil~~ ashlar ▪ Cornice concave. ▪ 2 different types of | acanthus flank | the spiral palmette ▪ double fluted | consoles | close — dentils ▪ but same leaf lobe | form ▪ rosettes between | varied Lesbian on same wall. ▪ foliage, etc replaces | dart. | frieze: large torus | unfinished ▪ unfluted cols — | entasis: on | pentagonal base plinth | & on podium | that follows | ~~form of~~ plan | of entablature ▪ Entablature | en ressaut — concave | at ends — which | rest on free cols.

No. 43. Beaulieu, Église de Saint-Pierre, 4–6 July 1927

▪ jamb of doorway — below outer jamb cap level | by ~~distance of~~ height of | lintel. ▪ crown mould'g ▪ door jambs. ▪ very fine cap. best preserved on right (E) | large leaves with pomegranates in Zwickch[?] ▪ adjoining | slender col. cap. | pomegr. volutes. | the 2 caps | carved in | one block | & joined in | design ▪ bases rest on 2 animals) ▪ much worn: not clear, | probably were thus | cf beasts on Moissac | Narthex bases

No. 44. Beaulieu, Église de Saint-Pierre, 4–6 July 1927

▪ The pose of Christ very common from Early | X times — in Byz. ivories, Mss. etc & in | Caroling. but in Languedoc it has a | special history: it cf's very strikingly | with the Angoulême tymp — figs ▪ Christ ▪ Devil ▪ curved wing tips ▪ opened arch — deep ▪ what is lumpy | shapeless object | at foot of tower? | The treasures offered by | the devil? | cf Devil types with | Prudentius Mss? | note exaggeration of | all parts. female | belly & haunches. | animal details — | tail — private parts | are covered!! ▪ note fine | shadows | formed by contours | & modelling of | devil!

No. 45. Carennac, Église de Saint-Pierre, 7 July 1927

▪ Carennac: Inner Portal — no tymp. two orders, | moulded 4 caps: on engaged [*crossed out, text illegible*] cols. | crown of arch, about 12 to 13 ft high. ▪ left. ▪ meplat palmettes | alternatively up & | down: slight | spoon hollows ▪ left tailloir — upper band inscribed | Girbertus cementarius fecit istum portarium — | Benedicta sit anima eius. ▪ no uncial except O.: | This inscription is important for palaeography — | for it shows that the proportions of letters is affected | by spacing: thus the name Girbertus Cementarius | is of broad letters: the rest of the inscription of | long — narrow ones ▪ The actual form of the letter is more significant than | proportions — (contra Porter) ▪ The stone has a pinkish tint that reminds me of Vézelay — | perhaps this too was once painted

No. 46. Cuxa, Abbaye de Saint-Michel-de-Cuxa, 14 July 1927

▪ Cuxa: St Michel: old portal now serves as [*crossed out, text illegible*] portal | of adjoining monastery v. photo — ▪ doorway c. 8–9 ft wide. | jambs preceded by 2 pillars — on front | faces of which Peter & Paul: on | inner side faces: animals in | [*crossed out, text illegible*] wave & interlaced ⊙s ▪ These pillars of pink red marble | like the Prades caps: | but the jambs, arch & spandrels | seem to be of a yellowish stone. — more closely | examined they prove to be of same material | difference due to paint & exposure & polishing ▪ upper courses. ▪ incised flat | cable ornt ▪ flat palmettes | & rosettes | in interlace | strands. ▪ ½ palmette | filling in ∠s ▪ rosettes in | compact series ▪ dents d'engrenage ▪ ½ palmette | beaded rinceau | 6 modillions | & ½ palmette | rinceau ▪ ½ palmette | rinceau | above

No. 47. Codalet, Église paroissiale de Saint-Félix, 14 July 1927

▪ Codalet: (between Cuxa & Prades) | Fountain — v. 3 photos — in pinkish-orange | marble like | Prades fragts ▪ archivolt | spring ▪ boutons ▪ cf. Moissac | Collonges | etc | in archivolt ▪ broken in front | face: clearer | on inner side ▪ 1 head | for | 2 beasts ▪ spiral | fluting ▪ drill holes ▪ similar motif | of legs & lions | on Prades left cap | frag'ts ▪ cf striation of drum of | cap with Cuxa portal | figs of seraphs | & symbols ▪ right

No. 48. Ripoll, Monasterio de Santa Maria, 19 July 1927

▪ Caps ▪ billet | tailloir ▪ taill

No. 49. Saragossa, Museo Arqueológico, 24 July 1927

▪ marble cap — Corinthoid finely stylized | note styliz of volute | wrappings. | elongated proport. ▪ 103 ▪ cf 99 — very beautiful cap. | v. photo | volutes form interlacing | polylobe arches ▪ another cap with ▪ cap 84 with simplified acanthus filled with T. D. | palmettes

No. 50. Huesca, Iglesia de San Pedro el Viejo, 25 July 1927

▪ Huesca cloister: San Pedro | Iconog. very rich | Note Ascension cap | opened book ▪ 5 kneeling figs on left — 3 standing on right | 3 standing | Christ ▪ note that all the apostles have hand on breast | cf M. & T. figs (pier & ambul) | ribbed sleeves & wrists ▪ immense eyes | reaching to hair | crocket | curls ▪ hatching & spiral lines | suggest Mss prototype | desire to fill all areas | with [*drawing*] | on wing also ▪ cf caps from | St Germain | des Prés —

No. 51. Jaca, Catedral de Jaca, 28 July 1927

▪ Jaca Cathedral: July 28 | S. E. chapel — Rque ▪ cornice — billet string: 2 billets | modillions ▪ billet ▪ under cornice — on soffit | rosettes: as in Toulouse, Lescure, | & Languedoc—partout. | I am told this is exceptional in | Aragon. Not found in Santa | Cruz (except ~~under~~ above crown of arch | of portal). ▪ between modillions are metopes: with animals, rosettes, set in frame | engaged full col: flanks south side of window — | which has billet archivolt & springs from billet | string ▪ hollow palmette | also in cap — | as in nave of chevet | cf Toulouse ▪ palmette of | tailloir

No. 52. Jaca, Archivo de Catedral de Jaca, Leg. 1, Docs. Reales 10, E, 28 July 1927

▪ Jaca Cathedral: Archives — July 28 ▪ In the Consecration Doc't of 1063 (no 1) — Visigothic | characters: but in 1098 donation of Pedro | purely French with no (?) traces of Visigothic — | The miniature styles likewise vary. | note the calligraphic "official style" flourishes ▪ no 10 ▪ sepia drawn miniature — v Burlington 1924

| finer lines between thicker folds ▪ note throne ornt | cf South France | Mss. ▪ note misdrawing | of arm & shoulder ▪ note foliate | capitals | Pedro's signature in | Arabic important for history of Spanish | culture: ▪ fig of Bishop.—throne with birds heads | & claws ▪ folds: note broken line | of folds ▪ note torso lines

No. 53. Toledo, Mezquita del Cristo de la Luz, 3 August 1927

▪ Toledo. San Cristo de la Luz. brick construct | in front of choir & apse. | a 9 compartment chamber | of lower level—each domed on | purely decorative ribs ▪ have been | maybe reconstructed | in restorations ▪ cf with nearby brick | vault of Puerta ~~del Sol~~ (not del Sol) [*later addition in pencil*] ▪ crown | ▪ dents d'engr[enage] ▪ choir vault of brick | but domical ▪ W. ▪ domical | surface. | groin | makes no | break. ▪ also domical | & between 2 doubleaux | arches [*later addition in pencil*] ▪ E. side ▪ W.

No. 54. Ávila, Iglesia de San Vicente, 5 August 1927

▪ heavy torus on | trif. & clearst. | windows higher ▪ [*illegible*] plan | at spring of vault ▪ rib of

No. 55. Santiago de Compostela, Catedral de Santiago de Compostela, 9–11 August 1927

▪ E. shaft. great variety of col forms & ornt ▪ bases griffes— | finely detailed—but flatter | than S. D. S. eg. ▪ lower range—left | anaxial head | cf Cuxa ▪ This fig is remarkably like the | M. piers—but more developed. | plastically & in detail. | note the collar unknown | in M & T. but appears | once in Santiago interior | in cap of N. transept | opposite doorway—in fig | of X of pure Toulouse style— | likewise the treatment of | hair is here more plastic— | powerful spiral curls.— | deeper torso folds than at | M.—note the cap— | which appears in | early La Daurade. | broken wrist & short arm | as of M. apostles. | The torso folds are nearer to | Porte Miegeville tymp | cf Moissac—this center incision |or double incised ridge |appears in most of the | shaft figs.

No. 56. Santiago de Compostela, Catedral de Santiago de Compostela, 9–11 August 1927

▪ fig style: as on E.—absence of beards permits clearer | modelling of head—no hats—hair of freely | stylized curls—relate to T. ▪ heads turned at ∠ to body: & related in pose | to adjacent figs.— ▪ heads in high relief—practically in | round like T. angel ▪ very long schematized | hands ▪ cf heads | with nimbed | angels above | E. shaft ▪ very thick | necks ▪ note on lower angel—right—wrist folds | as in La Daurade caps | straight bas line ▪ use of ▪ figs tightly placed in arches—contour not defined but | lost against colennettes. ▪ slight smile of most of these angels—recalls the T. ambul. | fig—These have smooth eyes—the other hollow.

No. 57. León, Museo Arqueológico, 12–14 August 1927

▪ Leon—Museo Arqueologico ▪ Inscript 117. ▪ Incluso ▪ ? The celebrated horseshoe stelae do not seem horseshoe arches | to me—but damaged ⊙s & rectangles—or rather | a conventionalized ⊙ & rectangle | orn't | it is clear from the stone cutting | that the left ⊙ was continued | & perhaps the right. | This is evidenced by the absence of | tailloir, cap or mouldg as transition | & the 5/6 (circa) circumference| resting on the horizontal | good evidence of the | purely decorative & (non | (architectural character) | are the similar stelae | in which a ⊙ rests on a rectangle— | which is narrower than its diameter ▪ 1200 ▪ 1952; 136 ▪ note in 328 | cf Etruscan ▪ (over)

No. 58. León, Basílica de San Isidoro, 12–14 August 1927

▪ N. chapel N. E window has 2 fine caps ▪ [*crossed out, text illegible*] deep cut palmettes— | soft lobes—complete | concavity | & not ▪ similar figs | in S. chapel window | cap ▪ interlace (3 strand) | tailloir—pinecone | in ∠ ▪ cf S. portal | cap ▪ 3 lobed palmette | in tailloir | over buttress in ∠ | between chapel | & transept—N. ▪ claws ▪ hermaphrodite devil ▪ windows above E. portal of transept—tailloir continuous | across chapel wall to chapel | arch. ▪ left cap. ▪ interlace tailloir ▪ cf Pommevic | & Vezelay [*later addition in pencil*] ▪ over right cap ▪ billet base mouldg of windows.—tailloir—

No. 59. Santo Domingo de Silos, Monasterio de Santo Domingo de Silos, 16?–19? August 1927

▪ IV Taill ▪ as in cap ~~II~~ I. ▪ cap—heraldic lions affronted: adossed from whose | jaws issue coiled ends of bird monsters | who ~~pec~~ bite the lion's backs. ▪ wonderful line diagr. cf late Fatimid | arabesques & textiles—also the wood | carvings & stuccoes with spirals—volute detail. | leaf form of wings. fine spiral lions | hairs of section ▪ foliate tail | ends of lions ▪ tiny cuneiform notches on body of birds | on lion's thigh—cf textile | flat haunches as if in garment | with incised ||. ▪ console block is checkered | slightly | diamond form. | cf León

No. 60. Santo Domingo de Silos, Monasterio de Santo Domingo de Silos, 16?–19? August 1927

▪ 11. interlace taill. beaded border | birds—beautiful heraldic | contours— | (goats or) deer's heads—horned | & cloven hoofed ▪ both horns represented on | same plane—cf paleolithic art | likewise hoofs | legs emerge from sheathes | as on other caps. | serpent issues from jaws of | deer & winds around feet— | rather: the deer terminates in a coil which | winds around feet & issues from mouth of deer | fine accent of relief of rear of animals | & contrast with flat upright wings ▪ 12. purely foliate—interlacing scrolls issue | from small mascarons—cf French & English Mss. [*in pencil*] ▪ from stalks issue leaves | interlace in widest areas ▪ cf Lyon 12th c | textile

No. 61. Santo Domingo de Silos, Monasterio de Santo Domingo de Silos, 16?–19? August 1927

▪ 14 close serried design | of △ areas & diagonals ▪ upper curves are | beautiful & continuous | fine combination | of central superposed | groups of affronted | birds & lions. | birds pick at chins | of harpies in delicate | throat line repeated | in flying veil | tails of lions between legs ▪ cf Limoges ms of fig between 2 birds [*later addition in pencil*] ▪ E. 15—adossed to N. E. ∠ pier—affronted birds— | elongated graceful necks, cross, & bite each other's | thigh—plants between them—interlace | birds

No. 62. Moissac, Abbaye de Saint-Pierre, 31 August–3 September 1927

▪ E22 ▪ On W: narrow face—3 figs—& inscript ▪ 2 apostles on sides hold up garment—to volute | very fine scheme. Use of triple & 4ple incised | folds. & lines.—also of ends. | fig stuck between 2 others is very well | managed. fine pose of head & body of left fig | beautiful linear combinations—cf Leon figs. (Panteon | his right arm is enormous—because of desire | to show it on 2 faces of cap: N & W—(cf. | Assyrian animals with 5 legs at gateways. | note left sleeve of center fig—less exaggerated | than in other caps— ▪ J[ules] M[omméja] writes that "MANDATUM" signified in Moissac ("at least") | the "distribution of abundant alms"

No. 63. Moissac, Abbaye de Saint-Pierre, 31 August–3 September 1927

▪ W 4. ▪ plan ▪ & ▪ on cap. opposed lions grasp human head.—no volutes | or [*drawing*] ▪ note [*drawing*] of thighs | block console | or ▪ ∠ lions—heads tangent—(not one) bite their | intertwined tails with their common teeth | hold fig only on long sides of cap (N. S.) | note his pious gesture on S.— ▪ but on N. ▪ note Chinese Han pottery style | of this fig ▪ This cap rests on 2 cols. that are | broader than the other twin cols. | the ~~bas~~ necking of the caps—is | broader than of the others—or | usual type—all dimensions as | in other caps: except the necking | long axis—(.40) ▪ cols. are | instead of | base seems restored | upper torus—.40 | .40 ▪ note that this cap corresponds to the | Annunc. to Shepherds—W15.—4th from | N. end; as this one is 4th from S. end.

No. 64. Moissac, Abbaye de Saint-Pierre, 31 August–3 September 1927

▪ Punctuation is a | wedge notch | cf 1100 inscript: | & 1063. ▪ What is the history of the standing effigy type? cf Gothic incised | tombstone portraits: of which this is the earliest example | I know—(very fine inscription—sharp & skillful cutting | head is tonsured—hair in fine ||s falling over brow. | tied by fillet—ear, too high & very small. | covered in part by the hair.—beautifully arched | eyebrows—make a point of this. | this is conventional, not | realistic; it appears in many | of the caps & pier figs. | sharp clear cutting of planes of | brow &

eye.—eyes smooth | & only slightly convex: no bulge— | eyes are close together | (cf. description of 13th peasant | as having eyes a fist apart) | prominent cheeks, & long chin. | found in other caps. but mouth | ? seems peculiar to this relief | small, mouth large lipped. lower lip is not [*drawing*] as | usual but [*drawing*]: equally thick at ends as in | middle: wedge corners of mouth. [*drawing*]: | upper lip, & broad at corners also.—Beautiful | carving of ~~head~~ face surface—flow of plane & bone. on cheeks | & chin. head squared at cheek bone. head is | remarkably long: Simplicity of whole egg form | is admirable. The so-called []gaussant expression | comes from later mutilation of upper lip—or rather | is heightened by it—The break at the corner of the upper | lip: gives effect of [*drawing*]—ironic smile.

No. 65. Moissac, Abbaye de Saint-Pierre, 3 September 1927

▪ W11. (Sept 3) twin cap | U. T. ▪ palmettes—broad—with | [*crossed out, text illegible*] curled tips. ▪ cf St Sernin & Leon | ornt ▪ This may be the original | type: since we have | here, above the palmette, | the leaf—as in | Leon & Toulouse ▪ note the banding (double folds) | across the palm. & behind the | palmette | large leaves are grooved. ▪ The broad surface is especially interesting for the use of | 5 foliate forms in one [*crossed out, text illegible*] pattern of proportional design | & with various surface & relief plans.—not so clear in | my drawing—fine effect of ∠ curled leaf (replaces | volutes)—convex: & the inner lines & surface—note | play of straight & curve line of leaves. & of banding | & of upper leaf tips & palmette: fine variety of | zigzag forms.

No. 66. Moissac, Abbaye de Saint-Pierre, 3–18 September 1927

▪ on W. face—another shepherd, in orant pose—cf classic egs— | cf Auvergne, Toulouse | St. Etienne, etc ▪ The letters of this cap are |the most primitive in cloister ▪ note that shepherd's left foot | is above ground—higher than | right: note torso folds—as in | St Sernin transept portal | but animals are [*illegible*] ▪ note dots [*drawing*] instead of [*drawing*] as | elsewhere.—but also the | [*drawing*] which appears on | other caps of advanced | type(?) | study headgear | cf mitres & Jewish | priesthood. cap. | note absence | of | seat: but cushion | is rendered! | cf. St Stephen cap. | Deformations may | be conscious decoration | cf eyes with St Sernin— | very close ||. | note knobs on trees | in high relief | as in T. & Sa. & | S. D. S. | Inscript. on W & N. seem| diff. from those of S. | Lions & D[aniel] make fine | group. The frame | does not appear—a proof | of earlier date? ▪ N. face ▪ cf Daniel's | headgear |& hair. |with fig | on W.4 ▪ lions very | similar to | W 4. which | corresponds | to this cap | architecturally ▪ on E face: affronted goats before tree— | cf St. Sernin caps: & St Martin d'Aunay. ▪ for SILVA? | the reversal of Cabras | is purely decorative— | for symmetry. | of what romance tongue is "CAbRAS"? | note how even in a genre subject, the | artist reduces his fig poses to decor. groups | (note "silva" = horn[?]—may indicate that | these heraldic groups had a genuine meaning to artist.

No. 67. Moissac, Abbaye de Saint-Pierre, 3–18 September 1927

▪ W. 17. twin cap—foliate | central rosette has alternately, | a hollow, & a bulbous center. | in ∠. ▪ fruit or ~~pine cones~~ ⊙ has been | destroyed except for 1 on | N. side & fragt on S. | note on E. face—console | block the chrism type is | not the usual Languedoc | Pyrenees variety—but the | early X. form—~~Remem~~ survival of | early X cap type ▪ en creux [] ▪ is palmette | survival of volute ▪ polygonal plan of cap. | but surface is rounded | & simple: individual | leaves are plastic behind | outer uniform surface | en creux.—T. D.— ▪ Corinthian | sources ▪ leaves of upper now are larger | & with more plastic lobes | than of lower ▪ S. block ▪ on W. console— | early X ||s?

No. 68. Moissac, Abbaye de Saint-Pierre, 3–18 September 1927

▪ on E & W faces. an angel with outspread wings & | hands— ▪ cf design with N10. & W1. | & with musician of | S7. also bird of W7. | distortion of body is | purposeful.—fig does not | rest on necking: feet properly | drawn: tho in generalized | view. | note touch of contraposto. | beautiful play of wings & | folds.—head properly proportioned | note halo in part concealed by | volute band—big belly | jewelled band across breast | relates to line below of legs. | note turn of head | wavy hair (like Simon's.) | neck striations for muscles | in relief. ▪ on S. face | 2 angels bear †—Crux gemmata whose | back is shrouded: cf La Daurade cap | cable about central ⊙ with [*drawing*] | & on ½ ⊙s at ends of cross. ▪ † & figs also make beautiful line | design ▪ angels with | very large | heads. ▪ angels occupy | ∠s of the caps, heads | turned away from | †: legs advanced | towards it—so that the rear | legs do not share in the | design of this ~~fa~~ side of cap. | but of E & W. ▪ base ▪ note boutons | on scotia

No. 69. Moissac, Abbaye de Saint-Pierre, 5 September 1927

▪ N. side ▪ L. T. as on S.—note long tail ends of griffons | foliate ▪ Cap Standing X between 2 angels—I infer X from the cross | nimbus. He holds a robe between his hands—very beautifully | composed— ▪ fine overlapping || planes as in | modern sculpture—of Robe— | of X, of wings, of volutes— | note how right angel is fitted in | between X & horse | & beautiful surface & pose of left | fig—also of right! whose turn | of head is classic. ▪ The robe folds are pure decoration & impossible in nature | heads well proportioned—plastic contrast of round bodies— | & superposed flat planes—~~ad~~[*illegible*] aided by round lines—of | folds—& diagonals of volutes etc: note † effect of fig. console— | & robe. ▪ E side ▪ repeat

No. 70. Moissac, Abbaye de Saint-Pierre, 3–18 September 1927

▪ N.7. Entry of Crusaders in Jerusalem ▪ rosettes in knotted ⊙s. | varied forms as in | W cap ▪ T. D. technique. ▪ on N face center: (taill, L) a bird replaces | rosette—bites scroll ▪ astragal ▪ E. face. Holy Sepulchre. | the 2 doorways do not | prove Holy Sepulchre | attribution as | pretended by Momméja | why the angel if these are | Crusaders? Is there any | legend of Crusaders met by | angels? why the unmilitary | costume of the "Crusaders"? why | does one carry a book & a long handled | cross? May not these be pilgrims—Octagonal towers known in | Italian & French Rque—But this seems to be a great drum of | a dome? note how it crosses roof—are the slanting sides | designed to represent an octagonal plan building? ▪ The strong carving of the architectural planes is excellent. | note how † & angel fill the capital on this side. | cf. building in Martinus cap. N 2 (S. face)—also with double | portal, contrary to J[ules] M[omméja]'s remark.

No. 71. Moissac, Abbaye de Saint-Pierre, 3–18 September 1927

▪ N. 8: Daniel & Habbakuk | note elaborate banding of U. T. ▪ N. ▪ This is extremely delicate carving, corresponding to Roman & | Renaissance grotesquerie. The regular rhythm of the other | taill. is absent here; but each part is as beautiful & | rhythmical—& the whole ~~finely~~ continuous in line. | The subject creates a more complex design | as in Beaulieu lintel— | cf with animals & | figs of Ivory Cross of | Ferdinand in Madrid. ▪ W. ▪ note lion's head turned & distorted & flying feet of griffon | ∠ palmettes (oriental form) ▪ S. ▪ J[ules] M[omméja] thinks these scenes of Alexandrian origin, calls the figs. "bearded | pygmies["]

No. 72. Moissac, Abbaye de Saint-Pierre, 3–18 September 1927

[*No text*]

No. 73. Moissac, Abbaye de Saint-Pierre, 3–18 September 1927

▪ N. 14. Life of St. Benoît | U. T. ▪ W. ▪ S ▪ E ▪ N ▪ letters once filled with vermillion paint. | Their elegance & scroll tips not carried as far as on Martinus | cap—likewise the variation of groove thickness & depth. | but as skillful as on the M[artinus] cap ▪ L. Taill. palmette rinceau: with peculiar knob tips | very deep center | hollow—⊥ to outer | plane. | deep T. D. | lobes curl back into depth: knob sustained in depth. ▪ Miracles of St. Benedict— | Astragal | network. | in relief ▪ relief ▪ simple block console,| mortar between cap & taill ▪ on W. Devil grasps outstretched ~~right arm~~ sleeve of Bened[ict] who stands | under S. W. volute—2 overlapping wings—extraordinary | at this period, in sculpture: cf Mss ▪ J[ules] M[omméja] says that on S & W is St Benoit rescuing monk from the | devil by touching monk with his stick (baguette). I do | not see the baguette. ▪ & on N, he revives a monk ~~falle~~ killed by fall from church | of Monte Cassino.

No. 74. Moissac, Abbaye de Saint-Pierre, 7 September 1927

▪ East Gallery 10. (Sept 7) ▪ taill—described elsewhere— ▪ cap—seated fig between winged monsters recalls | Toulouse triforium cap: & S. transept portal & | shaft caps—v. photos ▪ 2 compositions. ▪ 1) ▪ helix buckle as in pier reliefs. | note that monsters ~~are~~ have | heads & tails joined as | in earlier S. transept (T.) | version—& not as in upper | triforium cap | The monsters seem by same | hand as E9.—identical | wing forms & vigorous carving | heads are all destroyed— | note extreme stylization | of folds to fit design | continue | claws of "birds." ▪ large elbow folds | as in La D[aurade] & | other M. caps. ▪ folds of legs modify contour. | double incised

No. 75. Moissac, Abbaye de Saint-Pierre, 3–18 September 1927

▪ V[irgin]'s arms descend vertically, | like ape's & touch thighs | ~~or waist~~ of X.-who | blesses & holds open book | The figs are small, the drapery | thick: & the effect of Archaism | is thereby heightened: | The cushion & seat are || | to picture plane; so | that V. seems to stand. | note throne—& its posts | as in Souillac & Beaulieu | V. wears a sort of hood | over shoulders & breast | with flying ends | note suppedaneum, | & strict symmetry of group. | cf. pose & drapery of X. | with the 2 St. Sernin egs. | & with M. tymp. | especially for drapery thrown | over shoulders | attempts to render | are clumsy. | rounded top ▪ cf Chartres Virgin: & Marseilles Eg. | note absence of haloes. ▪ V. was veiled, but no | trace of crown or [*drawing*]: | the drapery above her | head, may be taken from | a model in which V was | set under a draped | canopy:? ▪ note how low X is set on | V's lap: covering her | legs almost completely. | This disproportion survives | even in porch Adoration. ▪ J[ules] M[omméja] attributes cap to Banquet-Master—cfs Virgin to N. D. du Puy: | thinks flower-stars an original poetic concept.

No. 76. Moissac, Abbaye de Saint-Pierre, 3–18 September 1927

▪ E. 14. foliate scrolls & mascarons ▪ U. T. ▪ L. T. ▪ W. | & E ▪ N. ▪ repeat ▪ Taill broader & longer / slightly than cap. ▪ on S face: the taill. figs are as on N: but with plants behind lions | & on thighs.

No. 77. Moissac, Abbaye de Saint-Pierre, 3–18 September 1927

▪ E. 18. S. face—Martyr in flames—less delicate | in carving than the Hebrews—but richer | decorative effect & a finer conception— | since 3 martyrs are seen together. Their arms | ~~rising like~~ extended like the flames— | cf Berenson's Bodhisatva.—cf Tarragona | retable St. Thecla—(15th c.) ▪ console (as on E) inscribed | primitive Rque epigraphy. ▪ use of : before CV | note [*drawing*] for G [] ▪ other inscriptions on cap are | curiously ~~dis~~ arranged ▪ Augurius diaco(nus?), martires in flamis | Eulogius id (▪ very beautiful flame composition—with flame like poses of the | figs.—note symmetr. gestures of outer saints. | & body of central fig (which St? Diaco?) | whose feet appear between flames & tie upper & lower | composition.—The mutilation enhances the effect. | central head is in the round—frontal. | Eulog[ius] has very tiny head, beside the others.

No. 78. Moissac, Abbaye de Saint-Pierre, 3–18 September 1927

▪ S. 16 Liberation of Peter ▪ U. T. | N. | W. ▪ L. T. | E. | [] cf | Ibn Tulum | & Samarra ▪ L. T. ▪ N. ▪ W. ▪ on W. side: fountain with emerging plants—of form | cf Mss.: ▪ cf the squatting fig. with Hellenistic terracottas of Alexandria | & Gaul: cf Berstl's thesis of the diffusion of Yogi type— | cf. figs of S. Italian & Sicilian (Syracuse) catacombs— ▪ The demons bite their own shoulders—They have wolf or bear heads & | jaws. ▪ They are all sexless, except when given vaginas by modern pen-knives

No. 79. Moissac, Abbaye de Saint-Pierre, 3–18 September 1927

▪ This angel (S.) nearer | to the style of other pier | caps. | note torso & very large | elbow folds. | wings likewise recall | Annunciation angel | & draperies most of the | figs of the N. E pier caps. | note that angel here, stands on [*drawing*] as in pier reliefs. | prominent belly: & torso folds ▪ N. angel ▪ In these figs: | folds modify | contours: | folds are thick | & heavy—swathing | the figs: the | heads seem small | or only slightly | exaggerated: | distinguish from | E gallery group | with very large | heads ▪ N. angel carries mantle across shoulder, breast, and arm | very close to N. E pier cap: & fig behind 'John' connects | with other pier caps.—bears part of X's (?) robe in hand.

No. 80. Moissac, Abbaye de Saint-Pierre, 3–18 September 1927

▪ N. E pier: N. face—St John. | inscribed ▪ Spacing is varied: cf. NW. pier ▪ .49 ▪ ? by same hand as the St. James, but of different | proportions: the 2 stand on identical row of steps. | left cap is plain-leaved: right has suspended fruit | of flower forms—? ▪ Tho this panel which is believed to prove reuse | of older [*crossed out, text illegible*] slabs or of sarcoph. since between J[ohn]'s | legs, an unsculptured break with carved (?) lines | contrary to sense of actual relief—J[ules] M[omméja] | thinks these lines are draperies of a former | figure—I cannot believe this, since the imperfect | slabs would have been used on central piers which | ~~show no~~ have no figs.—but imbricat. orn't: ~~It may also be a conscious rendering of hair shirt | of J. what other egs. of this iconogr?~~ | He wears the ribbed melon cap of the mediaeval | Jews.—is in strict profile but right eye is also | rendered & intersected by fond, as in other reliefs. | lips are finely modelled, clearly | distinguished, ~~by~~ in planes. | note hair in short loops

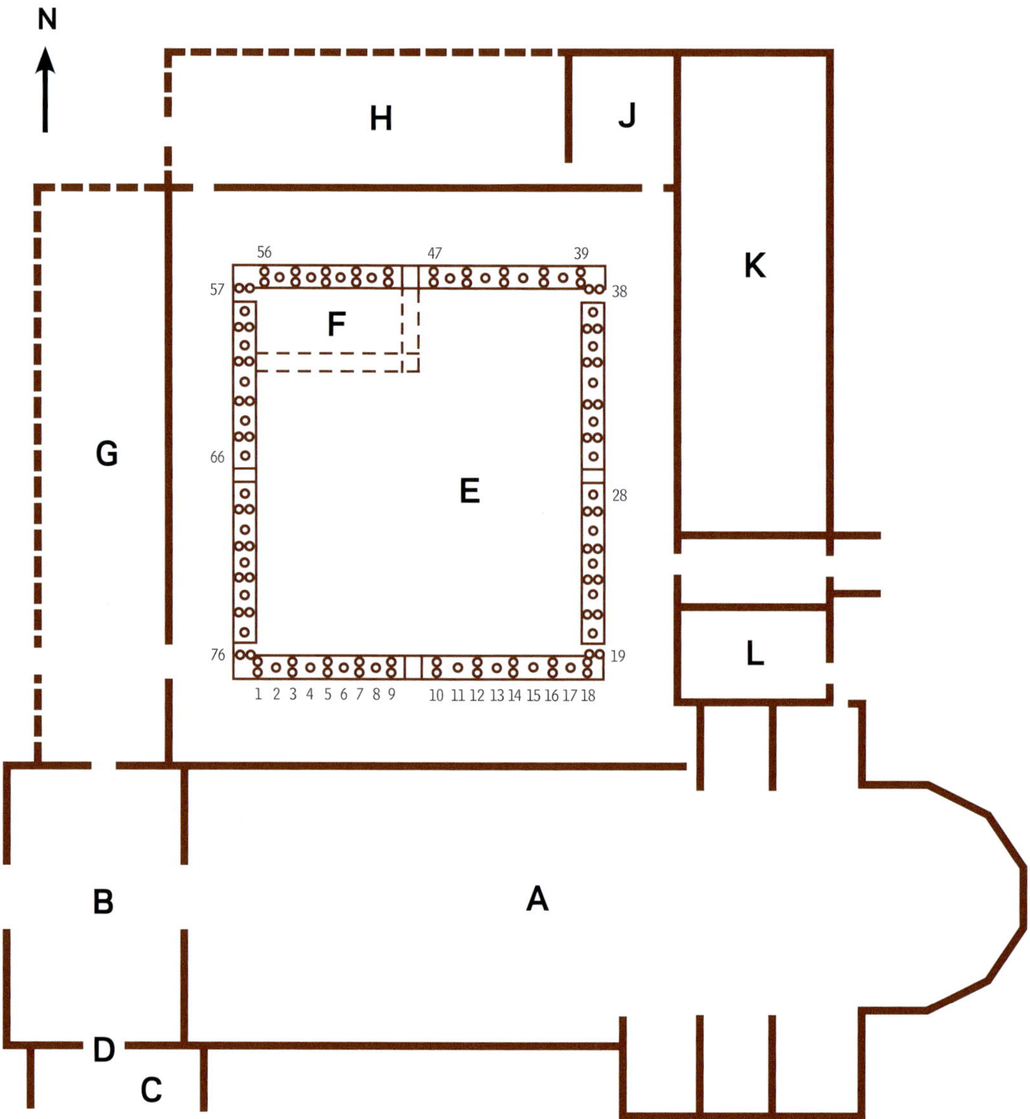

A. Gothic church of the 15th century with remains of Romanesque nave walls (ca. 1151–1130); **B.** narthex (ca. 1115); **C.** porch (ca. 1115–1130); **D.** tympanum (before 1115); **E.** cloister (completed in 1100); **F.** lavatorium (destroyed); **G.** chapel and dormitory (destroyed); **H.** refectory (destroyed); **J.** kitchen; **K.** Gothic chapterhouse; **L.** sacristy

Subjects of the Capitals and Pier Sculptures

South Gallery

1. Martyrdom of John the Baptist
2. Birds in Trees
3. Babylonia Magna
4. Birds
5. Nebuchadnezzar as a Beast
6. Martyrdom of Stephen
7. Foliage
8. David and His Musicians
9. Jerusalem Sancta

Unsculptured Pier

10. Chaining of the Devil; Og and Magog
11. Symbols of the Evangelists
12. Miracles of Christ; the Centurion of Capernaum and the Canaanite Woman
13. The Good Samaritan
14. Temptation of Christ
15. Vision of John the Evangelist
16. Transfiguration
17. Deliverance of Peter
18. Baptism

Southeast Pier: Paul; Peter

East Gallery

19. Samson and the Lion; Samson with the Jaw Bone
20. Martyrdom of Peter and Paul
21. Foliage
22. Adam and Eve; Temptation; Expulsion; Labors
23. Foliage
24. Martyrdom of Lawrence
25. Washing of Feet
26. Foliage
27. Lazarus and Dives
28. Dragons

Pier: Abbot Durand (1047–1072)

29. Dragons and Figures
30. Wedding at Cana
31. Foliage
32. Adoration of the Magi; Massacre of the Innocents
33. Foliage
34. Foliage
35. Martyrdom of Saturninus
36. Foliage
37. Martyrdom of Fructuosus; Eulogius; and Augurius
38. Annunciation and Visitation

Northeast Pier: James; John

North Gallery

39. Michael Slaying the Dragon
40. Birds
41. Foliage
42. Miracle of Benedict
43. Birds
44. Miracle of Peter
45. Foliage
46. Angels
47. Calling of the Apostles
48. Daniel in the Lions' Den; Habbakuk
49. Crusaders before Jerusalem
50. Foliage
51. Four Evangelists with Symbolic Beast Heads
52. Birds
53. Three Hebrews in the Fiery Furnace
54. Martin and the Beggar; Miracle of Martin
55. Foliage
56. Christ and the Samaritan Woman

Northwest Pier: Andrew; Philip

West Gallery

57. Sacrifice of Isaac
58. Angels with the Cross
59. Foliage
60. Birds
61. Daniel in the Lions' Den; Annunciation to the Shepherds
62. Foliage
63. Grotesque Bowmen
64. Raising of Lazarus
65. Foliage
66. Dragons and Figures

Pier: Inscription of 1100; Simon

67. Anointing of David
68. Foliage
69. Birds and Beasts
70. Foliage
71. Beatitudes
72. Lions and Figures
73. Cain and Abel
74. Foliage
75. Ascension of Alexander
76. David and Goliath

Southwest Pier: Bartholomew; Matthew

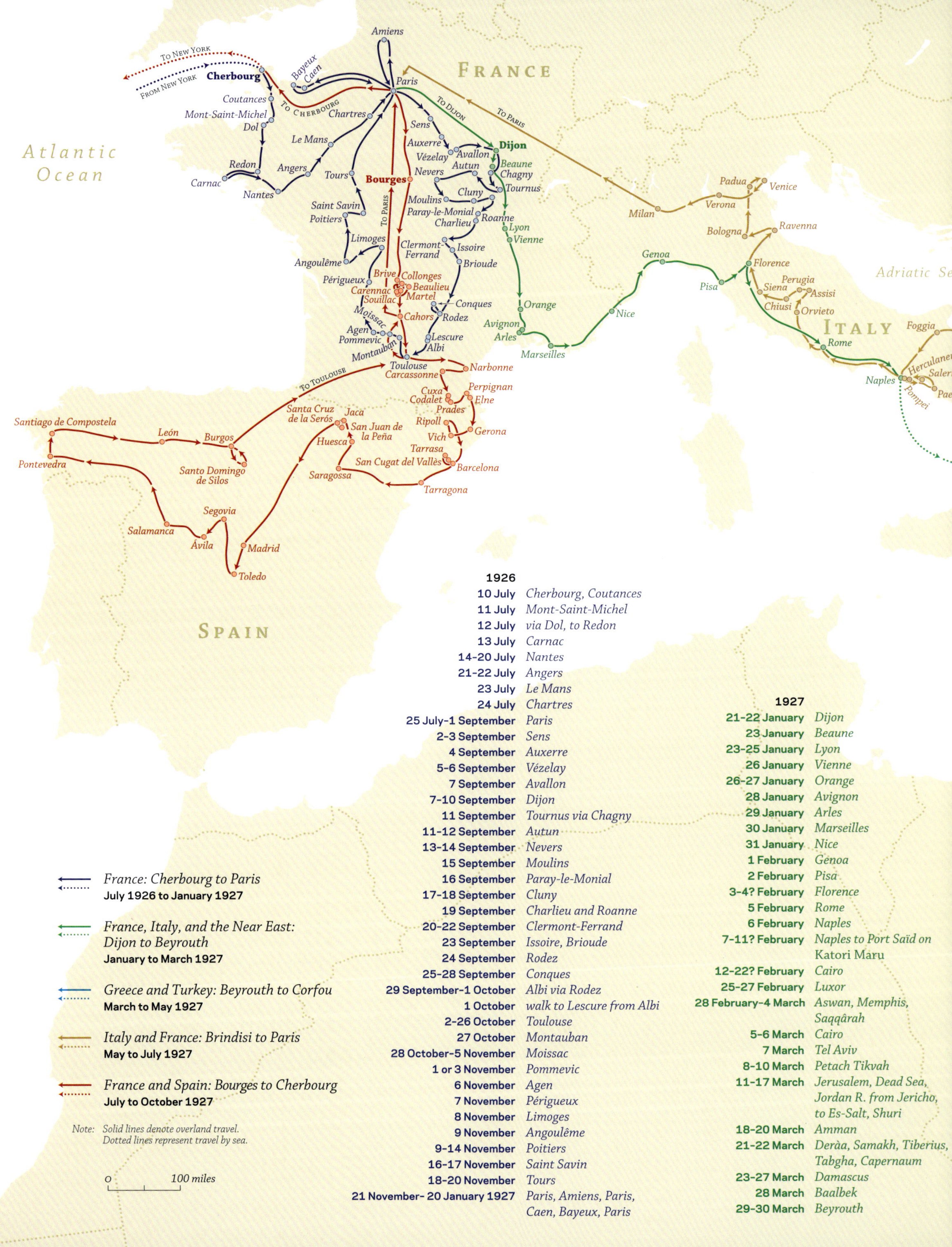

1926

10 July	Cherbourg, Coutances
11 July	Mont-Saint-Michel
12 July	via Dol, to Redon
13 July	Carnac
14–20 July	Nantes
21–22 July	Angers
23 July	Le Mans
24 July	Chartres
25 July–1 September	Paris
2–3 September	Sens
4 September	Auxerre
5–6 September	Vézelay
7 September	Avallon
7–10 September	Dijon
11 September	Tournus via Chagny
11–12 September	Autun
13–14 September	Nevers
15 September	Moulins
16 September	Paray-le-Monial
17–18 September	Cluny
19 September	Charlieu and Roanne
20–22 September	Clermont-Ferrand
23 September	Issoire, Brioude
24 September	Rodez
25–28 September	Conques
29 September–1 October	Albi via Rodez
1 October	walk to Lescure from Albi
2–26 October	Toulouse
27 October	Montauban
28 October–5 November	Moissac
1 or 3 November	Pommevic
6 November	Agen
7 November	Périgueux
8 November	Limoges
9 November	Angoulême
9–14 November	Poitiers
16–17 November	Saint Savin
18–20 November	Tours
21 November–20 January 1927	Paris, Amiens, Paris, Caen, Bayeux, Paris

1927

21–22 January	Dijon
23 January	Beaune
23–25 January	Lyon
26 January	Vienne
26–27 January	Orange
28 January	Avignon
29 January	Arles
30 January	Marseilles
31 January	Nice
1 February	Genoa
2 February	Pisa
3–4? February	Florence
5 February	Rome
6 February	Naples
7–11? February	Naples to Port Saïd on Katori Maru
12–22? February	Cairo
25–27 February	Luxor
28 February–4 March	Aswan, Memphis, Saqqârah
5–6 March	Cairo
7 March	Tel Aviv
8–10 March	Petach Tikvah
11–17 March	Jerusalem, Dead Sea, Jordan R. from Jericho, to Es-Salt, Shuri
18–20 March	Amman
21–22 March	Deràa, Samakh, Tiberius, Tabgha, Capernaum
23–27 March	Damascus
28 March	Baalbek
29–30 March	Beyrouth

France: Cherbourg to Paris
July 1926 to January 1927

France, Italy, and the Near East: Dijon to Beyrouth
January to March 1927

Greece and Turkey: Beyrouth to Corfou
March to May 1927

Italy and France: Brindisi to Paris
May to July 1927

France and Spain: Bourges to Cherbourg
July to October 1927

Note: *Solid lines denote overland travel. Dotted lines represent travel by sea.*

0 100 miles

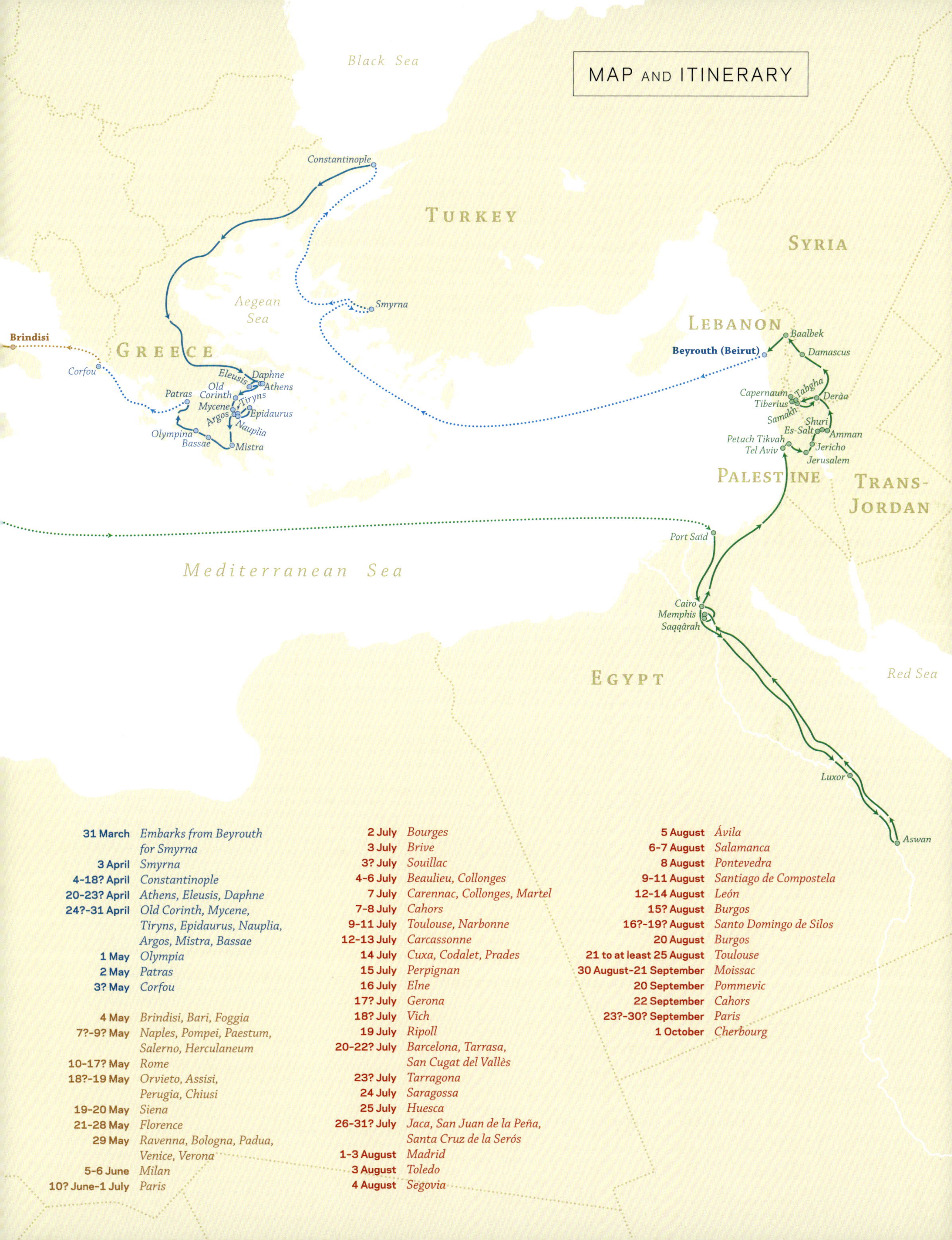

MAP AND ITINERARY
Black Sea
Constantinople
TURKEY
SYRIA
Aegean Sea
Smyrna
LEBANON
Baalbek
Beyrouth (Beirut)
Damascus
Brindisi
GREECE
Corfou
Eleusis
Daphne
Athens
Old Corinth
Patras
Mycene
Tiryns
Argos
Epidaurus
Nauplia
Olympina
Bassae
Mistra
Capernaum
Tabgha
Tiberius
Deràa
Samakh
Shuri
Es-Salt
Amman
Petach Tikvah
Tel Aviv
Jericho
Jerusalem
PALESTINE
TRANS-JORDAN
Port Saïd
Mediterranean Sea
Cairo
Memphis
Saqqârah
EGYPT
Red Sea
Luxor
Aswan
31 March Embarks from Beyrouth for Smyrna
3 April Smyrna
4-18? April Constantinople
20-23? April Athens, Eleusis, Daphne
24?-31 April Old Corinth, Mycene, Tiryns, Epidaurus, Nauplia, Argos, Mistra, Bassae
1 May Olympia
2 May Patras
3? May Corfou
4 May Brindisi, Bari, Foggia
7?-9? May Naples, Pompei, Paestum, Salerno, Herculaneum
10-17? May Rome
18?-19 May Orvieto, Assisi, Perugia, Chiusi
19-20 May Siena
21-28 May Florence
29 May Ravenna, Bologna, Padua, Venice, Verona
5-6 June Milan
10? June-1 July Paris
2 July Bourges
3 July Brive
3? July Souillac
4-6 July Beaulieu, Collonges
7 July Carennac, Collonges, Martel
7-8 July Cahors
9-11 July Toulouse, Narbonne
12-13 July Carcassonne
14 July Cuxa, Codalet, Prades
15 July Perpignan
16 July Elne
17? July Gerona
18? July Vich
19 July Ripoll
20-22? July Barcelona, Tarrasa, San Cugat del Vallès
23? July Tarragona
24 July Saragossa
25 July Huesca
26-31? July Jaca, San Juan de la Peña, Santa Cruz de la Serós
1-3 August Madrid
3 August Toledo
4 August Segovia
5 August Ávila
6-7 August Salamanca
8 August Pontevedra
9-11 August Santiago de Compostela
12-14 August León
15? August Burgos
16?-19? August Santo Domingo de Silos
20 August Burgos
21 to at least 25 August Toulouse
30 August-21 September Moissac
20 September Pommevic
22 September Cahors
23?-30? September Paris
1 October Cherbourg

ILLUSTRATION CREDITS

The personal letters of Meyer Schapiro are in the possession of Miriam Schapiro Grosof, the Schapiros' daughter. The travel notebooks are now housed at the Columbia University Rare Book and Manuscript Library along with the rest of Schapiro's professional papers. At the time of publication they had not been systematically catalogued and coded.

Portrait no. 1	Courtesy Miriam Schapiro Grosof
Portrait no. 2	Photo courtesy of the New York University School of Medicine, Ehrman Medical Library, Archives
Portrait no. 3	Courtesy Miriam Schapiro Grosof
Letters fig. 1	Courtesy Miriam Schapiro Grosof
Letters fig. 2	Courtesy Miriam Schapiro Grosof
Letters fig. 3	Courtesy Miriam Schapiro Grosof
Letters fig. 4	Courtesy Miriam Schapiro Grosof
Notebook fig. 1	Notebook 7, p. 3
Notebook fig. 2	Notebook 7, p. 125 (erased)
Notebook fig. 3	Notebook 7, p. 120 (erased)
Notebook fig. 4	Notebook 14, n.p.
Notebook fig. 5	Notebook 7, p. [119]
Notebook fig. 6	Notebook 7, p. [125]
Notebook fig. 7	Notebook 7, p. 88
Notebook fig. 8	Notebook 7, p. 287
Notebook fig. 9	Notebook 7, p. 295
Notebook fig. 10	"MSS Arles . . . Charleville" (folder in box), n.p.
Notebook fig. 11	Notebook 7, p. 315
Notebook fig. 12	Notebook 7, p. 319
Notebook fig. 13	Notebook 7, p. 327
Notebook fig. 14	Notebook 7, p. [334]
Notebook fig. 15	Notebook 7, p. [268]
Notebook fig. 16	Notebook 7, p. 203
Notebook fig. 17	Notebook 7, p. 185
Notebook fig. 18	Notebook 9, p. comp. 3
Notebook fig. 19	Notebook 9, p. comp. 13
Notebook fig. 20	Notebook 9, p. comp. [24]
Notebook fig. 21	Notebook 6, p. M & C 327
Notebook fig. 22	Notebook 6, p. M & C 379
Notebook fig. 23	Notebook 12, p. [46]
Notebook fig. 24	Notebook 12, p. 55
Notebook fig. 25	Notebook 12, p. 63
Notebook fig. 26	Notebook 12, p. [66]
Notebook fig. 27	Schapiro file II, 1, "Cluny manuscripts Xth century" (folder)
Notebook fig. 28	Schapiro file II, 1, "Cluny manuscripts in Bibliothèque nationale" (folder)

Notebook fig. 29	Schapiro file II, 1, "Cluny manuscripts in Bibliothèque nationale" (folder)
Notebook fig. 30	Schapiro file II, 1, "Cluny manuscripts Xth century" (folder)
Notebook fig. 31	Schapiro file II, 1, "Cluny manuscripts in Bibliothèque nationale" (folder)
Notebook fig. 32	Schapiro file II, 1, "Moissac manuscripts description" (folder), right envelope
Notebook fig. 33	Schapiro file II, 1, "Moissac manuscripts description" (folder), right envelope
Notebook fig. 34	Schapiro file II, 1, "Moissac manuscripts description" (folder), right envelope
Notebook fig. 35	Schapiro file II, 1, "Moissac and region manuscripts" (folder), right group
Notebook fig. 36	Schapiro file II, 1, "Moissac manuscripts description" (folder), left envelope
Notebook fig. 37	"Notebooks of Travels in Near East, 1927," p. 77
Notebook fig. 38	"Notebooks of Travels in Near East, 1927," p. 79
Notebook fig. 39	"Notebooks of Travels in Near East, 1927," p. 148
Notebook fig. 40	"Notebooks of Travels in Near East, 1927," p. 180
Notebook fig. 41	"Damascus Notes" (notebook), p. 23
Notebook fig. 42	"Damascus Notes" (notebook), p. 53
Notebook fig. 43	Notebook 10, n.p.
Notebook fig. 44	Notebook 10, n.p.
Notebook fig. 45	Notebook 8, n.p.
Notebook fig. 46	Notebook 7, p. 409
Notebook fig. 47	Notebook 7, p. 419
Notebook fig. 48	Notebook 13, n.p.
Notebook fig. 49	"Spain Romanesque, notes of travel Aragon 1927" (notebook), n.p.
Notebook fig. 50	"Spain Romanesque, notes of travel Aragon 1927" (notebook), n.p.
Notebook fig. 51	"Spain Romanesque, notes of travel Aragon 1927" (notebook), n.p.
Notebook fig. 52	"Spain Romanesque, notes of travel Aragon 1927" (notebook), n.p.
Notebook fig. 53	"August 1927, Spain" (notebook), n.p.
Notebook fig. 54	"Spain Romanesque, notes of travel Aragon 1927" (notebook), n.p.
Notebook fig. 55	"August 1927, Spain" (notebook), p. 57c
Notebook fig. 56	"August 1927, Spain" (notebook), p. 60
Notebook fig. 57	"August 1927, Spain" (notebook), p. 30
Notebook fig. 58	"August 1927, Spain" (notebook), p. 24
Notebook fig. 59	"Santo Domingo de Silos" (folder in box), n.p.
Notebook fig. 60	"Santo Domingo de Silos" (folder in box), n.p.
Notebook fig. 61	"Santo Domingo de Silos" (folder in box), n.p.
Notebook fig. 62	Matted in envelope from "Moissac, east gallery caps . . ." (folder), p. E22. The rest of this folder is in the box

Notebook fig. 63	"Moissac cloister west gallery caps" (folder in box), n.p.
Notebook fig. 64	"Moissac cloister pier reliefs" (folder in box), n.p.
Notebook fig. 65	"Moissac cloister ornament (2)" (folder in box), n.p.
Notebook fig. 66	"Moissac cloister west gallery caps" (folder in box), n.p.
Notebook fig. 67	"Moissac cloister ornament (2)" (folder in box), n.p.
Notebook fig. 68	"Moissac cloister west gallery caps" (folder in box), n.p.
Notebook fig. 69	Notebook 6, p. M & C 271
Notebook fig. 70	Notebook 6, p. M & C 279
Notebook fig. 71	Matted in envelope from notebook 6, p. M & C 281
Notebook fig. 72	Notebook 6, p. [M & C 304]
Notebook fig. 73	Notebook 6, p. M & C 325
Notebook fig. 74	"Moissac, east gallery caps..." (folder in box), p. E53
Notebook fig. 75	"Moissac, east gallery caps..." (folder in box), p. [E]60
Notebook fig. 76	"Moissac cloister ornament (2)" (folder in box), n.p.
Notebook fig. 77	Matted in envelope from "Moissac, east gallery caps..." (folder), p. E73. The rest of this folder is in the box.
Notebook fig. 78	Notebook 6, p. M & C 377
Notebook fig. 79	Notebook 6, n.p. [p. M & C 388?]
Notebook fig. 80	"Moissac cloiser pier reliefs" (folder in box), n.p.
Plan of Moissac	Based on the plan that appeared in Meyer Schapiro, "The Romanesque Sculpture of Moissac," *Art Bulletin* 13 (1931): 250
Map	Cartography by David L. Fuller, DLF Group

INDEX

Page references to illustrations are in italic.

MEYER SCHAPIRO ABROAD: LETTERS TO LILLIAN AND TRAVEL NOTEBOOKS

Daniel Esterman received his bachelor's degree from Columbia College and completed graduate coursework in art history at Harvard University, where he specialized in Romanesque art. At both institutions he was privileged to attend his uncle Meyer Schapiro's courses and lectures. In the years before Schapiro's death in 1996, Esterman spent many afternoons with his uncle cataloguing his drawings. He coedited with his aunt, Lillian Milgram Schapiro, *Meyer Schapiro: His Painting, Drawing, and Sculpture* (2000). After working as an animation cameraman, he retired in 2001. For the past six years, Esterman has been a part-time volunteer teacher's assistant in the third grade of a public school in East Harlem in New York City.

Hubert Damisch is a philosopher, an art historian, and a former director of studies at the École des hautes études en sciences sociales in Paris. There he founded the Centre d'histoire/théorie de l'art (CEHTA), which he headed for many years. Damisch was a close friend of Meyer Schapiro, to whom he dedicated one of his major works, *The Origin of Perspective* (1994). He is the author of numerous other books on art history and theory, including most recently *Waiting for High Water* (with Jana Sterbak, 2006), *Voyage à Laversine* (2004), *A Childhood Memory by Piero della Francesca* (2002), *Theory of the Cloud: Toward a History of Painting* (2002), *La dénivelée: À l'épreuve de la photographie* (2001), *Skyline: The Narcissistic City* (2001) and the *Judgment of Paris* (1996). He has also written exhibition catalogs, magazine articles, and forewords (including one for *Les mots et les images*, the 2002 French edition of Schapiro's *Words, Script, and Pictures*). As a curator, Damisch has presented landmark exhibitions such as *Traité du trait* (1995) at the Musée du Louvre in Paris and *Moves: Playing Chess and Cards with the Museum* (1997) at the Boymans Museum in Rotterdam.

BOOKS FEATURING THE HOLDINGS OF THE RESEARCH LIBRARY AT THE GETTY RESEARCH INSTITUTE

The Getty Murúa: Essays on the Making of Martín de Murúa's "Historia General del Piru," J. Paul Getty Museum Ms. Ludwig XIII 16
Edited by Thomas B. F. Cummins and Barbara Anderson
ISBN 978-0-89236-894-5 (hardcover)

Allan Kaprow—Art as Life
Edited by Eva Meyer-Hermann, Andrew Perchuk, and Stephanie Rosenthal
ISBN 978-0-89236-890-7 (hardcover)

China on Paper: European and Chinese Works from the Late Sixteenth to the Early Nineteenth Century
Edited by Marcia Reed and Paola Demattè
ISBN 978-0-89236-869-3 (hardcover)

Art, Anti-Art, Non-Art: Experimentations in the Public Sphere in Postwar Japan, 1950–1970
Edited by Charles Merewether with Rika Iezumi Hiro
ISBN 978-0-89236-866-2 (hardcover)

Lucien Hervé: Building Images
Olivier Beer
ISBN 978-0-89236-754-2 (hardcover)

Had gadya: The Only Kid: Facsimile of El Lissitzky's Edition of 1919
Edited by Arnold J. Band
ISBN 978-0-89236-744-3 (paper)

Aldo Rossi: I Quaderni azzurri
Aldo Rossi
ISBN 978-0-89236-589-0 (boxed set)

Devices of Wonder: From the World in a Box to Images on a Screen
Barbara Maria Stafford and Frances Terpak
ISBN 978-0-89236-590-6 (paper)

Making a Prince's Museum: Drawings for the Late-Eighteenth-Century Redecoration of the Villa Borghese
Carole Paul
ISBN 978-0-89236-539-5 (paper)

Maiolica in the Making: The Gentili/Barnabei Archive
Catherine Hess
ISBN 978-0-89236-500-5 (paper)

Russian Modernism
Compiled by David Woodruff and Ljiljana Grubišić
ISBN 978-0-89236-385-8 (paper)

Designed by Jim Drobka
Coordinated by Amita Molloy
Type composed by Diane Franco in Chaparral and Galaxie Polaris
Printed in China through Asia Pacific Offset, Inc.